Study Methods And Reading Techniques

Second Edition

Debbie Guice Longman
Southeastern Louisiana University

Rhonda Holt Atkinson
Louisiana State University

 Wadsworth Publishing Company

I(T)P® An International Thomson Publishing Company

Belmont, CA · Albany, NY · Boston · Cincinnati · Johannesburg · London · Madrid · Melbourne
Mexico City · New York · Pacific Grove, CA · Scottsdale, AZ · Singapore · Tokyo · Toronto

Publisher: Karen Allanson
Senior Editorial Assistant: Godwin Chu
Developmental Editor: Kim Johnson
Marketing Manager: Jennie Burger
Project Editor: Christal Niederer
Print Buyer: Barbara Britton
Permissions Manager: Robert Kauser
Production: Robin Gold, Forbes Mill Press
Cover Design: Bill Stanton
Cover Photo: Tony Stone Images
Compositor: Wolf Creek Press
Printer: Courier, Kendallville, Indiana

Printed in the United States of America
1 2 3 4 5 6 7 8 9 10

For more information, contact Wadsworth Publishing Company, 10 Davis Drive, Belmont, CA 94002, or
electronically at http://www.wadsworth.com

International Thomson Publishing Europe
Berkshire House
168-173 High Holborn
London, WC1V 7AA, United Kingdom

International Thomson Editores
Seneca, 53
Colonia Polanco
11560 México D.F. México

Nelson ITP, Australia
102 Dodds Street
South Melbourne
Victoria 3205 Australia

International Thomson Publishing Asia
60 Albert Street #15-01
Albert Complex
Singapore 189969

Nelson Canada
1120 Birchmount Road
Scarborough, Ontario
Canada M1K 5G4

International Thomson Publishing Japan
Hirakawa-cho Kyowa Building, 3F
2-2-1 Hirakawa-cho, Chiyoda-ku
Tokyo 102, Japan

International Thomson Publishing Southern Africa
Building 18, Constantia Square
138 Sixteenth Road, P.O. Box 2459
Halfway House, 1685 South Africa

Library of Congress Cataloging-in-Publication Data

Longman, Debbie Guice.
    Study methods and reading techniques / Debbie Guice Longman,
Rhonda Holt Atkinson. —2nd ed.
        p.   cm.
    Includes bibliographical references and index.
    ISBN 0-534-54981-0
    1. Study skills.   2. Reading (higher education) 3. Test-taking
skills.   I. Atkinson, Rhonda Holt.   II. Title.
LB2395.L59   1998
378.1'7'0281—dc21   98-52847

William Arthur Ward once said,
"The mediocre teacher tells. The good teacher explains.
The superior teacher demonstrates. The great teacher inspires."
My work on *SMART* is dedicated with familial love and scholarly appreciation
to Mrs. **Thelma Brooks** and **Mrs. Nan Brooks Guice,**
great teachers who taught the inspirational lessons
that makes each manuscript I write possible.

—Debbie Guice Longman

And, as Anthony Brandt once said,
"Other things may change us, but we start and end with the family."
My work on *SMART* is dedicated with love
to my extended family
—my **grandparents, aunts,** uncles, and cousins—
as well as to my **parents, husband, and daughter**—
who have shaped and continue to shape my life.

—Rhonda Holt Atkinson

In Memoriam
Mrs. Thelma Brooks
(1908–1995)

THE WADSWORTH COLLEGE SUCCESS SERIES

Santrock and Halonen, *Your Guide to College Success: Strategies for Achieving Your Goals* (1999). ISBN: 0-534-53354-X

Holkeboer and Walker, *Right from the Start: Taking Charge of Your College Success,* 3rd Ed. (1999). ISBN: 0-534-56412-7

Petrie and Denson, *A Student Athlete's Guide to College Success: Peak Performance in Class and Life* (1999). ISBN: 0-534-54792-3

Van Blerkom, *Orientation to College Learning,* 2nd Ed. (1999). ISBN: 0-534-52389-7

Wahlstrom and Williams, *Learning Success: Being Your Best at College & Life,* 2nd Ed. (1999). ISBN: 0-534-53424-4

Corey, *Living and Learning* (1997). ISBN: 0-534-50501-5

Campbell, *The Power to Learn: Helping Yourself to College Success,* 2nd Ed. (1997). ISBN: 0-534-26352-6

The Freshman Year Experience™ Series

Gardner and Jewler, *Your College Experience: Strategies for Success*, 3rd Ed. (1997). ISBN: 0-534-51895-8

Concise Third Edition (1998). ISBN: 0-534-53749-9

Expanded Reader Edition (1997). ISBN: 0-534-51898-2

Expanded Workbook Edition (1997). ISBN: 0-534-51897-4

Study Skills/Critical Thinking

Longman and Atkinson, *CLASS: College Learning and Study Skills*, 5th Ed. (1999). ISBN: 0-534-54972-1

Longman, Atkinson and Breeden, *Strategic Thinking and Reading* (1997).

Sotiriou, *Integrating College Study Skills: Reasoning in Reading, Listening, and Writing,* 5th Ed. (1999). ISBN: 0-534-54990-X

Smith, Knudsvig, and Walter, *Critical Thinking: Building the Basics* (1998). ISBN: 0-534-19284-X

Van Blerkom, *College Study Skills: Becoming a Strategic Learner*, 2nd Ed. (1997). ISBN: 0-534-51679-3

Kurland, *I Know What It Says . . . What Does It Mean? Critical Skills for Critical Reading* (1995). ISBN: 0-534-24486-6

Contents

Preface

The *SMART* Solution

Study Methods and Reading Techniques (SMART) began as an idea for a new reading and study skills class that would address a key problem: Students were often not able to apply what they learned in study skills class to their content classes. Because some students enroll in only English, math, and reading/study skills for their first semester, they do not have a content class in which to immediately apply their developing skills. Unfortunately, by the time these students take history, biology, or psychology courses, they have forgotten the reading and study strategies they learned the previous semester. Students frequently realize too late that they are having difficulty and their grades suffer. *SMART* solves this problem by

- Modeling the four basic processes of learning required for content course success: (1) listening and taking notes; (2) reading text chapters; (3) preparing for a test; (4) successfully taking a test.

- Providing structured, facilitated practice of the processes in additional content subjects.

- Including chapters from a variety of content areas to give students the additional practice they need to internalize the processes and adapt their strategies to fit different content areas.

Organization

SMART consists of two major sections:

Section One. The first section consists of five instructional chapters. Chapter 1 introduces the learning process and describes the concepts that underlie the learning processes—critical thinking, time management, and learning style. The next four chapters are each devoted to one of the four basic learning processes: reading, listening and notetaking, test preparation, and test taking.

Section Two. Once you complete these chapters, the rest of the term can be devoted to the second section: applying the processes to the other content chapters included in the texts. Videotapes of college professors teaching the content of each chapter enables course instructors to be, first, reading and study skills instructors, and then, second, facilitators—not deliverers—of content.

New to This Edition

Although the processes of learning remain the same, there have been many changes in the content of today's higher education classroom. New features and content in *SMART* 2nd edition reflect these important changes since the last edition: technology, student need for language and vocabulary development, and updated content areas. This new edition includes the following:

- *SMART* **Information and** *SMART* **Site exercises**. Today's students must not only learn what's in the book and in their notes, they must learn how to learn via electronic formats. Thus, each chapter of *SMART* 2nd edition contains exercises that engage students with the Internet and the Wadsworth InfoTrac College Edition, an online archive of articles.

- **Speaking Figuratively exercises**. Students have a greater need for language and vocabulary development, so each chapter now includes a special section on figurative language. These exercises meet the language and vocabulary development needs of today's college students.

- **Updated Content Chapters.** *SMART* 2nd edition includes the most recent editions of sample chapters on anthropology, economics, history, and fitness.

- **New Content Chapter Pedagogy.** Each content chapter now includes an introduction that describes how to apply *SMART* 2nd edition to that subject area. Each chapter also has a copy of the text's table of contents so the student can see how the application chapter fits into the scheme of the entire text.

Key Features

SMART 2nd edition contains many innovative features found in the first edition. These include

- Chapter maps and outlines that organize information in right and left brain formats
- Cooperative learning activities to foster group activities
- Critical thinking exercises to foster higher-level application

- Interim and summary review questions that contribute to the ability to synthesize learning
- Action plans to help students personalize and set goals for learning

SMART Supplements

A wide variety of supplements are available with this text to assist you in teaching this course and to promote student involvement and learning.

Print

- *Instructor's Manual* (0-534-54982-9). Revised for this new edition, the Instructor's Manual contains exercise answers, suggestions for instruction, and sample exams.
- *The Wadsworth College Success Course Guide* (0-534-22991-3). A wide-ranging guide to the issues and challenges of teaching the college success course.
- *Wadsworth College Success Internet at a Glance,* by Daniel J. Kurland (0-534-54370-7). A handy pocket guide containing URL sites related to topics such as health, financial management, career searching, and more. This trifold supplement can be bundled with any Wadsworth College Success text at a very small cost. Contact your Wadsworth representative for more information.
- *College Success Guide to the Internet,* by Daniel Kurland (0-534-54369-3). Lists sites and activities for topics of interest to students.
- *Franklin-Covey Day Planner Collegiate Edition* (0-534-53352-3). A daily planner to help students manage their college and professional careers.
- *Critical Thinking: Building the Basics,* by Smith, Knudsvig and Walter (0-534-19284-X). A simple, concise approach for improving one's method of learning through critical thinking.
- *The Keystone College Success Newsletter.* This newsletter of the Wadsworth College Success Series brings you ideas and information about events and resources from your colleagues around the country.
- *Custom Publishing Program.* You can combine your choice of chapters from specific Wadsworth titles with your own materials in a custom-bound book. To place your order, call the ITP Custom Order Center at 1-800-245-6724.

Videos

- *Wadsworth Study Skills Video Series*
  - *Volume 1: Improving Your Grades* (0-534-54983-7). Highlights study strategies for college students, such as goal setting, time management, learning styles, and SQ3R.

- *Volume 2: Lectures for Notetaking Practice* (0-534-54984-5). Provides academic lectures for notetaking practice on a variety of topics, including anthropology, psychology, economics, health, and history.

- *CNN College Success Video Companion* (0-534-53746-4). CNN reports on a variety of topics of student interest, including: The college experience, technology on campus, majors and career choice, values, student involvement and service learning, diversity, health issues, and money management.

- *The Wadsworth College Success Video Series.* These videos cover a wide variety of topics of interest to students, including managing stress, improving grades, maximizing mental performance, and more.

- *A World of Diversity,* by David Matsumoto (0-534-23229-9 and 0-534-23230-2). A powerful two-video program designed to help students learn basic skills for interacting effectively with students from different cultural backgrounds.

Technology

- **Success Online**. http://www.success.wadsworth.com. Wadsworth's College Success Web site has resources for instructors and students, including online discussions, training, tutorials, and financial aid information.

- **Wadsworth College Success Home Page.** http://csuccess.wadsworth.com. Provides updates to URLs in this text as well as a range of free services and information.

- **InfoTrac College Edition**. Designed to help your students make the best use of the Internet, Wadsworth's exclusive InfoTrac College Edition provides them with access to full-length articles from more than 600 scholarly and popular periodicals, updated daily, and dating as far back as four years. A four-month subscription available free for adopting instructors. Contact your local Wadsworth representative for more information.

- **Thomson World Class Course**. The easy and effective way to create your own dynamic web site. Post your own course information, office hours, lesson information, assignments, sample tests, and link to rich web content, including student review and enrichment material from Wadsworth. Updates are quick and easy and customer support is available 24 hours a day, seven days a week. More information is available at http://www.worldclasslearning.com.

- **AT&T World Net**. Get your students on the Internet with AT&T—one of the fastest growing Internet access service providers. Contact your local Wadsworth representative for more information.

Acknowledgments

SMART is one of our first texts published by our new publishing company—Wadsworth Publishing Company. We appreciate the support of our new editorial team, Karen Allanson, Kim Johnson, and Godwin Chu, as well as the members of the production team responsible for converting our manuscript into a finished product, Christal Niederer, Robin Gold, and Linda Weidemann. We thank our families and friends whose understanding supports us in all of our professional endeavors. Finally, we extend our heartfelt appreciation to our reviewers whose comments shaped both the first and second editions of this text:

Second edition reviewers: Maria Dolores Costa, California State University—Los Angeles; Martha S. French, Fairmont State College; Lynda E. Guevrement, Palm Beach Community College, Eissey Campus; Carolyn Hopper, Middle Tennessee State University; Judith Lynch, Kansas State University; Katherine Ploeger, California State University—Stanislaus and Modesto Junior College; Brian A. Richardson, Arizona State University; Donna M. Smith, University of Findlay; and Patricia Zdrowak, Palm Beach Community College, Eissey Campus.

First edition reviewers: Susan A. Anderson, Eastern Michigan University; Jackie Betts, Berea College; Lorene F. Brown, El Camino College; Patricia R. Eney, Goucher College; Martha S. French, Fairmont State College; Caroline Gilbert, University of Minnesota; Paul S. Hayes, Onondaga Community College; Carol Helton, Tennessee State University; Richard Kelder, State University of New York at New Paltz; Kay L. Lopate, University of Miami; Barbara Lyman, University of Southwest Texas at San Marcos; Bonnie Mercer, Rochester Community College; James R. Olson, Georgia State College; Faye Z. Ross, Philadelphia College of Textiles and Science; Merritt W. Stark, Jr., Henderson State University; Linda V. Thomas, University of the Virgin Islands; and Marolyn E. Whitley, Tennessee State University.

STUDY METHODS AND READING TECHNIQUES

Critical Thinking with SMART: One at a Time, All at Once

OBJECTIVES

After you finish this chapter, you will be able to do the following:

1. Identify and apply the levels of thinking in Bloom's taxonomy to learning situations.

2. Describe and assess background knowledge.

3. Create time-management schedules and apply methods for avoiding procrastination.

4. Identify ways to maximize study time through multisensory, multifaceted learning strategies.

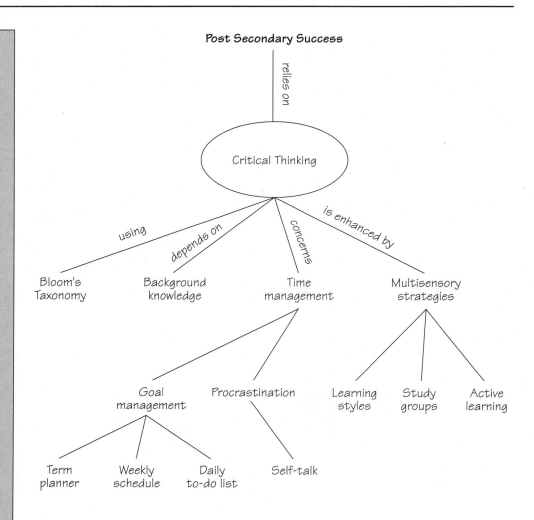

CHAPTER OUTLINE

I. Thinking about thinking
   A. Levels of thinking: Bloom's taxonomy
   B. Applying Bloom's taxonomy to learning
II. Thinking about what you know: Background knowledge
   A. Measuring background knowledge
   B. Increasing background knowledge
III. Thinking about time
   A. Goal management
      1. Establishing a term calendar
      2. Managing the week
      3. Managing the day
   B. Procrastination
      1. Self-talk
      2. Lack of closure
      3. Burnout
IV. Thinking about learning styles: Maximizing study time
   A. Assessing and capitalizing on learning styles
      1. Brain dominance
      2. Sensory variables
      3. Environmental factors
      4. Interpersonal variables
      5. Intrapersonal characteristics
   B. Forming and maintaining study groups
   C. Active learning

*"I knew the competition in class was going to be tough,
but competition for a parking space is tougher!"*

Welcome to higher education—whoever and wherever you are! Are you
new to postsecondary education, or do you have several courses under
your belt? Are you a continuing student or one who has been out of school
for a while? Are you in a small college, a large university, or a technical program? Whatever the case, you face the challenges and demands of postsecondary education.

What challenges and demands? First, many of the forces—both positive
and negative—that already affected your decision to attend college will continue to influence you (see Figure 1.1). And you're in a different academic
league. You must think at higher levels, face unknown competitors, and handle many tasks and stressors—often at the same time. You interact with demanding faculty and other students. By the time you get your degree (see
Figure 1.2), you will complete forty-five to sixty courses. In them, you will
read twenty-four thousand to forty thousand pages of text and take one hundred to two hundred tests and exams. You will complete library research and
written assignments, as well as laboratory and other class-related projects.

Postsecondary challenges and courses might lead you to think that what
you're getting from education are new *products*—solutions, experience, knowledge, credits, and ultimately, a degree. But, what you really get is a new *process*
of thinking. This process—**critical thinking**—involves consciously considering how you think about and how you think through information and situations. Critical thinking is not simply mastering a few isolated and specialized
techniques. Critical thinking goes beyond any one technique and becomes a

Figure 1.1   Force Field Analysis of College Persistence

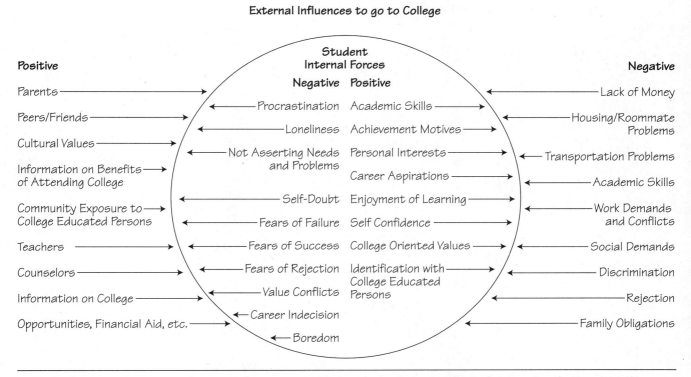

SOURCE: Reprinted with permission from L. Noel, R. Levitz, D. Saluri, and Associates. *Increasing Student Retention*. San Francisco: Jossey-Bass. 1987, p. 51.

way of life. Thus, critical thinking is not something you only read about in this text or apply to postsecondary courses. It involves thought processes that you continually practice, improve, and refine throughout your life.

Feel overwhelmed? Most students do. You face many classes in history, English, math, biology, or other fields. Academic success depends on your ability to read texts, attend lectures, take notes, study, and excel on tests. You must be able to shift between memorizing information (for example, a formula) and solving complex problems (for example, an algebra problem). Although you do each of these one at a time, your courses require you to complete everything all at once. Doing everything "one at a time, all at once" sounds impossible. And it is, if you aren't expert at every process or level of thinking.

Chapters 1 through 5 of this text provide you with the processes and kinds of thinking you need for academic success. You will apply these strategies one at a time to anthropology (Sample Chapter 6). In the additional sample chapters you will begin to do everything at once. You will read, listen to and take lecture notes, prepare for, and take tests in a variety of subjects in simulated course conditions. This allows you to refine your academic learning

Figure 1.2   College Requirements

College Requirements

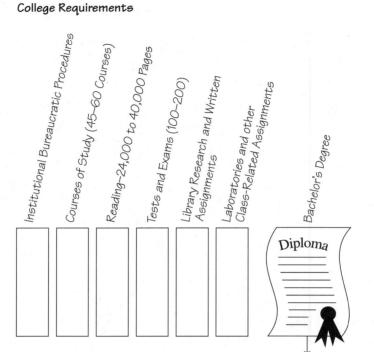

Institutional Bureaucratic Procedures

Courses of Study (45–60 Courses)

Reading–24,000 to 40,000 Pages

Tests and Exams (100–200)

Library Research and Written Assignments

Laboratories and other Class-Related Assignments

Bachelor's Degree

Diploma

Future Professional
Career Interests

SOURCE: Reprinted with permission from L. Noel, R. Levitz, D. Saluri, and Associates. *Increasing Student Retention.* San Francisco: Jossey-Bass. 1987, p. 51.

strategies without risking a grade in a "real" course. As a result, you will have greater confidence in your ability to think critically and to succeed in postsecondary coursework. You will master *Study Methods and Reading Techniques.*

THINKING ABOUT THINKING

At first glance, the information you learn in postsecondary courses appears to be more of what you learned in high school. Math, English, social studies, and science seem like courses you took before. However, most students describe college courses as somehow "not what they expected." The difference between their expectations and the realities of postsecondary courses lies in the degree of understanding. Most high school courses focus on lower levels of understanding. Often you need only recognize the correct answer or restate information. Postsecondary course work assumes you already know how to do that. It requires you to think at different and higher levels.

Levels of Thinking: Bloom's Taxonomy

Luckily, you know how to do the kinds of thinking required by postsecondary courses. You already know that the thinking you do when you stare into space differs from the thinking you do when solving a problem. The thinking you use when recalling a phone number differs from that which you use when making a decision. All you need to know now is how to identify the kinds of thinking you already do and when to use each kind. To think about thinking, then, you need a way to classify and organize your thought processes. Figure 1.3 shows levels of thinking according to a system called **Bloom's Taxonomy** of Educational Objectives (Bloom, 1956).

You make sense of the world based on what you already know. You learn by connecting new information with this information that you already have. You process information—make the connections—at many different levels, however. Table 1.1 provides examples of learning found at different levels of thought. Thinking at each level depends on and involves thinking at the levels beneath it.

Figure 1.3   Levels of Thinking According to Bloom's Taxonomy

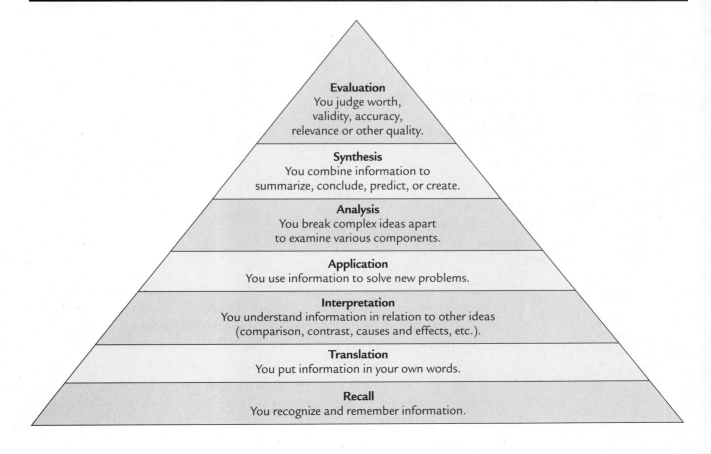

Evaluation
You judge worth, validity, accuracy, relevance or other quality.

Synthesis
You combine information to summarize, conclude, predict, or create.

Analysis
You break complex ideas apart to examine various components.

Application
You use information to solve new problems.

Interpretation
You understand information in relation to other ideas (comparison, contrast, causes and effects, etc.).

Translation
You put information in your own words.

Recall
You recognize and remember information.

Table 1.1   Examples of Learning Tasks by Level of Thinking

Level	Learning Task	Level	Learning Task
Recall	Foreign language vocabulary	*Analysis*	Identifying stated or inferred details that support a main idea or conclusion
	Lines of poetry		
	Musical phrases or melodies		Examining the form or style of music, poetry, literature, or art
	Mathematical facts (for example, multiplication tables)		Identifying a math or scientific problem by type
	Rules of grammar		
Translation	Paraphrasing information		Identifying information relevant to the solution of a problem
	Notetaking		Identifying statements of fact, opinion, or expert opinion
	Reducing equations to lowest terms		
	Creating a chart, diagram, or other visual device based on written information		Identifying figures of speech
			Identifying gaps in logical sequences of arguments
	Describing art, music, process, or other event		Determining how text format (headings, subheadings, and so on) affects the organization of information
Interpretation	Generalizing		
	Drawing analogies		
	Comparing and contrasting	*Synthesis*	Writing creatively
	Determining causes and effects		Composing music
	Identifying spatial relationships		Creating works of art
	Identifying denotations and connotations		Devising a solution for a complex problem
Application	Solving problems different from those previously seen		Solving a mystery
			Designing an experiment
	Using a theory or formula to solve problems		Writing a research paper
			Drawing conclusions to form a main idea
	Following directions to complete a task or project		Summarizing
	Grouping or classifying information according to a rule or principle		Predicting outcomes
			Identifying the main ideas of graphics
	Solving mathematical word problems	*Evaluation*	Checking internal consistency within a document
			Determining consistency across several texts
			Making decisions
			Judging worth

"I believe we've finally got this new trainer thinking on our level."

Applying Bloom's Taxonomy to Learning

Although the levels of Bloom's taxonomy are separate, few learning situations depend solely on one level or another. Instead, learning allows you to begin or end at any level in the taxonomy and requires making decisions as you move through the levels. For instance, consider the subfields of anthropology (physical anthropology, archaeology, anthropological linguistics, cultural anthropology and applied anthropology) as described in the first five pages of Sample Chapter 6. An exam on this information might ask the following question:

> You meet someone who tells you that although she enjoys history, she dislikes English and sociology. She is majoring in anthropology. What anthropological subfield most likely interests her?

How could you use the levels of Bloom's taxonomy in answering this question? First, you recall the names of the subfields. Then you translate what each subfield involves into your own words. Now you apply this information to a new situation. To do so, you analyze, compare (interpret), and evaluate each subfield. This allows you to compare and contrast the subfields, isolate components that might contribute to selecting a major, and judge which might be appropriate. Table 1.2 shows you the processes you used and the resulting decision.

THINKING CRITICALLY

Your goal is to buy a new car. On a separate sheet of paper or in your journal, give an example of a thinking task you might encounter for each level of Bloom's taxonomy.

Table 1.2   **Thought Processes and Actions for Determining Subfield of Anthropology According to Bloom's Taxonomy**

To answer the question, you must . . .

recall the names of the four subfields.	Physical anthropology Archaeology Anthropological linguistics Cultural anthropology
provide a **translation** of each field.	Physical anthropology—studies the biological and physical nature of humans Archaeology—study of ways of living in the past based on excavation and analysis of findings Anthropological linguistics—relates language, especially unwritten languages, to other aspects of behavior and thought Cultural anthropology—investigates social and cultural aspects of past and present societies

apply information to question.

	Involves History	Involves Writing	Involves Sociology
physical anthropology	X		
archaeology	X		
anthropological linguistics	X	X	
cultural anthropology	X	X	X

interpret results.	All subfields involve history. Anthropological linguistics and cultural anthropology involve writing. Cultural anthropology involves sociology.
analyze results.	Archaeology involves only history. All other subfields include topics that the individual in question dislikes.
evaluate results to make a decision.	The individual is most likely to be majoring in archaeology.

You make similar decisions when you study. Certainly, you have to know the essence—the recall and translation levels—of information. But you also make decisions about the content and ways you will study it. Again, consider the subfields of anthropology in Sample Chapter 6. What kinds of connections might you make in preparing to learn about the subfields? Organizing information lends itself to comparing and contrasting, rather than determining sequences, lists, or causes and effects. Thus, you might want to know how the subfields are similar or different. The preceding test question gives you an idea of how an instructor might ask a question to make students compare and contrast different subfields. In other words, you need to know all four subfields to distinguish among them and apply that information to obtain the answer.

What other kinds of questions might you pose? Perhaps you might think about where and how people interested in these different anthropological subfields work—in research, in the field, independently, and with others. To analyze such information, you think about the different components of each subfield or the kinds of course work that would prepare you for each one. To synthesize, you consider how the subfields fit together and complement one another. Finally, you evaluate which subfield(s) you prefer or judge the comparative difficulty of each one in terms of course work, professional preparation, or other factors. Exercises 1.1 and 1.2 provide practice with Bloom's Taxonomy.

Exercise 1.1   For each of the following levels in Bloom's taxonomy, list an occasion (other than the one given in the text) in which you already use that level of thinking.

Example

Recall
remembering the name of someone you just met

Translation
taking a telephone message

Interpretation
understanding abstract art

Application
repairing a flat tire

Analysis
reviewing a movie for a friend

Synthesis
writing a letter

Evaluation
choosing a friend

(continues)

Exercise 1.1   *Continued*

1. Recall
_____

2. Translation
_____

3. Interpretation
_____

4. Application
_____

5. Analysis
_____

6. Synthesis
_____

7. Evaluation
_____
_____

Exercise 1.2   List three of the classes in which you are now enrolled. Examine the course syllabus, text, notes, or any other course materials. Provide an example of how you might use each level of Bloom's taxonomy in learning the content of each course.

Example

CLASS	LEVEL	EXAMPLE
SMART (this class)	Recall	*Recalling the names of the seven levels of Bloom's taxonomy on page 7*
	Translation	*Understanding Figure 1.1 on page 5*
	Interpretation	*Understanding the introduction to "Background Knowledge" on page 14*
	Analysis	*Identifying if you are a right- or left-brained learner on page 34*
	Application	*Answering the chapter review questions on page 50*
	Synthesis	*Forming a study group, page 41*
	Evaluation	*Completing the action plan on page 52*

(continues)

Exercise 1.2   *Continued*

CLASS	**LEVEL**	**EXAMPLE**
1. _____	Recall	_____
	Translation	_____
	Interpretation	_____
	Application	_____
	Analysis	_____
	Synthesis	_____
	Evaluation	_____

CLASS	**LEVEL**	**EXAMPLE**
2. _____	Recall	_____
	Translation	_____
	Interpretation	_____
	Application	_____
	Analysis	_____
	Synthesis	_____
	Evaluation	_____

CLASS	**LEVEL**	**EXAMPLE**
3. _____	Recall	_____
	Translation	_____
	Interpretation	_____
	Application	_____
	Analysis	_____
	Synthesis	_____
	Evaluation	_____

THINKING CRITICALLY

Analyze your responses to Exercise 1.2. On a separate sheet of paper or in your journal, respond to the following: Other than the recall and translation levels, how are your examples for the other levels of thinking similar? How are they different? What do you think accounts for these similarities and differences? Why?

THINKING ABOUT WHAT YOU KNOW: BACKGROUND KNOWLEDGE

> The process of reading is reciprocal; the book is no more than a formula, to be furnished out with images out of the reader's mind.
>
> —Elizabeth Bowen
> *Twentieth century Irish author*

Consider the quotation by Elizabeth Bowen. Although Bowen refers to the process of reading, her comment also applies to other kinds of learning. As shown in Figure 1.4, learning occurs in a cycle (Lapp, Flood, & Farnan, 1989). In this view, learning is more than the accumulation of facts. Your **background knowledge** helps you set purposes for learning that, in turn, affect how you direct your attention. Connections between background knowledge and new information form understanding. Your prior knowledge is modified as a result of new information, and the cycle begins again. Thus, what you already know influences and controls future learning.

Measuring Background Knowledge

Measuring knowledge is unlike measuring most other things. No ruler or scale exactly determines how much you know. Depending on the situation and what you remember about them, concepts relate in different ways.

For example, what do the following words appear to have in common?

bowl	leash	cat	bones
litter	brush	tank	cage
goldfish	finnet	water	fleas
fur	fins	tails	paws
fidoism	kennel	veterinarian	pond

Figure 1.4   The Learning Cycle

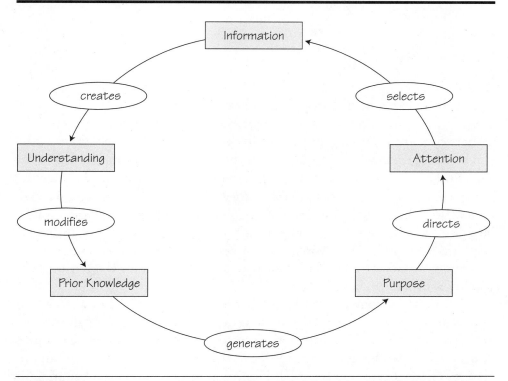

SOURCE: Reprinted from Lapp, D., Flood, J., and Farnan, N. (1989). *Content Area Reading and Learning: Instructional Strategies.* Englewood Cliffs, NJ: Prentice-Hall, p. 61.

You probably recognize that these words relate to animals and, specifically, pets. Look at the list again. How do the words relate to pets and to each other? Consider the following:

Kinds of Pets	*Pets and Their Natural Enemies*
cat	goldfish, cat
dog	cat, dog
goldfish	

Care of Dogs	*Habitat*	*Food*
fleas	bowl	bones
brush	tank	water
leash	water	bowl
veterinarian	cage	
fur	kennel	
	pond	

Care of Cats	Interior	Exterior
fleas	bones	fur
brush		fins
litter		claws
veterinarian		tails
fur		

Your background knowledge tells you how words fit together. Some words relate only to one kind of pet. For example, *litter* relates mostly to cats. Others concern each kind of pet but in different ways. For example, a *bowl* can be the place in which a goldfish lives or the dish from which a dog or cat eats. Still other words—*finnet* and *fidoism*—cannot be categorized under any factor concerning pets. That's because they are nonsense words and have no connection to pets. Your understanding, then, depends on what you know. If you don't know a word or know how it fits together with other words, you don't understand it. Thus, you need to assess information so you know what you know and what you don't know. You need a method for estimating what you know based.

Without a systematic way to estimate your background knowledge, you may be unpleasantly surprised at which courses prove to be difficult for you. Perhaps you correctly assume that a freshman-level Spanish course requires you to learn a whole new language. You enter the class prepared for an on-slaught of new terms. On the other hand, you misjudge the number and dif-ficulty of concepts in an introductory-level biology course because you think you can rely on information you recall from high school. Surprisingly, intro-ductory biology often requires you to learn as many new words, if not more, than an introductory-level foreign language course. Some of the words you encounter in biology are words you probably already know. Others are words that you thought you knew but which are used in new ways. Still other words are entirely new to you. But which are which?

According to a variation of Edgar Dale's theory of vocabulary (1958), your understanding of concepts develops in progressive stages. Understanding ranges from having no knowledge of the concept (stage 1) to the ability to use the concept to learn other information (stage 4). Thus, you don't just "know" a concept. You know you understand the concept because you can link it to other information. When you consciously analyze and rate your understanding, you are thinking critically about background knowledge. This helps you identify gaps in your understanding and makes your store of background knowledge more powerful and complete. Assessing what you know ensures your success. Table 1.3 summarizes the stages of concept development.

Concept development in stage 1 involves realizing that an idea is new to you—either completely new or new in the context in which it is found. At the second stage, you recognize a concept as one you've seen, but you have lim-ited knowledge of its meaning. In the third stage, you can relate an idea to its

Table 1.3	**Stages of Vocabulary (Concept) Development**
Stage 1 *No Knowledge*	You see or hear a word or phrase and recognize it as an entirely new concept or new in the context.
Stage 2 *Limited Knowledge*	You recognize a word or phrase as one you've seen or heard, but you are unsure of its meaning and have no associations for it.
Stage 3 *General Understanding*	You know you've seen or heard a word or phrase and can make general associations concerning its meaning.
Stage 4 *Specific Understanding*	You know you've seen or heard a concept, you can understand its meaning when reading or listening, and you can use it effectively in speaking or writing.

general category. For example, suppose you read or hear the word *dementia*. You recognize the word as connected with a mental state. Although you fail to exactly define the word, your association helps you derive a general meaning. Using stage 3 understanding, you build toward the exact understanding found in stage 4. In this final stage of understanding, your knowledge of the concept helps you make use of it in listening, reading, writing, and speaking.

The stages of concept development help you estimate background knowledge. To do so, you rank each chapter term and chapter heading and subheading. When you study, your objective is to ultimately reach stage 4 understanding. If you rank anything as stage 1, 2, or 3, you need to write its definition from the glossary or from **context** in your own words.

Your attempt to identify what you know about key terms and chapter headings and subheadings serves several purposes. First, consciously thinking about a concept increases your chances of knowing it the next time you encounter it. This happens because repetition strengthens your recall. Second, your attempts to refine and expand understanding increases the associations you form between a word and other concepts. Third, the more you relate ideas, the more you make future connections. Finally, defining unknown concepts increases your ability to link information and expands background knowledge.

Increasing Background Knowledge

"Comprehension is the use of prior knowledge to create new knowledge. Without prior knowledge, a complex object, such as a text, is not just difficult to interpret; strictly speaking, it is meaningless" (Adams & Bruce, 1980). Many college courses are difficult because they cover topics that are entirely new to you. As a result, you possess little or no background knowledge on which to build. Fortunately, you can increase background knowledge.

> **THINKING CRITICALLY**
>
> On a separate sheet of paper or in your journal, describe how background knowledge affects your relationships with friends, relatives, acquaintances, and strangers. In your opinion, which of these is most affected by background knowledge? Why?

Talking to others is a powerful way to build background knowledge. Making an appointment with your instructor to ask about complex concepts results in added background information. Asking your instructor for names of professionals in the field and interviewing them also yields additional data. Study groups and informal discussions with classmates are other ways to build background knowledge. As you discuss information with others, you gain access to different points of view about a topic.

In addition, you can consult other written sources about a topic to gain background knowledge. A high school text, written in simpler language, often gives you enough basic information to make sense of your postsecondary text or lectures. Encyclopedias or articles in popular magazines and journals serve the same purpose. Your instructor or campus librarian can help you find additional sources of written information.

The table of contents in your text also provides you with a way to increase background knowledge. It shows the context into which each chapter fits. In addition, in some texts, a chapter is part of a larger organized section of related topics. Thus, a chapter's placement often tells you something about its content. Introductory chapters often are more general in nature and broader in scope. Middle or ending chapters may provide an in-depth analysis of a topic or provide a look at the future directions.

A table of contents is qualitative in that it provides a description of contents. It uses different type styles, spacing, and design elements to indicate the relationships among major headings and subsections. A table of contents is also quantitative. You can count the number of sections in a text, the number of chapters in each section, the number of major headings or pages in a chapter, and so on. Quantitative information helps you determine the relative importance an author places on each topic.

Just as you can analyze chapter terms to determine your stages of concept development, you can also apply the scale to the concepts you find in the table of contents. This helps you assess your level of background knowledge and, thus, identify your strengths and weaknesses in a subject.

The table of contents provides you with an in-depth outline of a book's content. As such, it is your first, best source for determining the main ideas of a text. Main ideas, in turn, summarize the information you need to know. Exercises 1.3 and 1.4 provide practice with using content chapter information.

Exercise 1.3   Classify your knowledge of each of the following terms from Sample Chapter 6, "The Study of Humanity," according to the stages of vocabulary development in Table 1.3. Do not use a dictionary. Rate your own knowledge.

	STAGE 1 No Knowledge	STAGE 2 Limited Understanding	STAGE 3 General Understanding	STAGE 4 Specific Understanding
1. physical anthropology	_____	_____	_____	_____
2. paleoanthropologists	_____	_____	_____	_____
3. primatologists	_____	_____	_____	_____
4. archaeology	_____	_____	_____	_____
5. linguistics	_____	_____	_____	_____
6. cultural anthropology	_____	_____	_____	_____
7. ethnography	_____	_____	_____	_____
8. ethnology	_____	_____	_____	_____
9. holistic perspective	_____	_____	_____	_____
10. comparative perspective	_____	_____	_____	_____
11. cultural relativism	_____	_____	_____	_____
12. ethnocentrism	_____	_____	_____	_____
13. medical anthropology	_____	_____	_____	_____
14. contract archaeology	_____	_____	_____	_____
15. field work	_____	_____	_____	_____

Exercise 1.4   Use the table of contents for Sample Chapter 6, "The Study of Humanity," to answer the following questions.

1. Where does Sample Chapter 6 fit into the context of the textbook?

   _____

   _____

   _____

2. How many larger, organized sections does the text contain? How are these labeled?

   _____

   _____

   _____

(continues)

Exercise 1.4   *Continued*

3. List the titles of Parts I, II, III, and IV below. Identify the number of chapters for each part.

_____

_____

_____

_____

_____

4. Based on your answer to the preceding question, what can you determine about the relative significance of each part? List them in order of importance, according to this information.

_____

_____

_____

_____

5. List below the titles of each chapter in the anthropology textbook. Next, examine the headings and subheadings under each title. Based on Table 1.3 in this chapter, identify your level of knowledge about each chapter.

_____

_____

_____

_____

_____

_____

_____

_____

_____

6. Other than Chapter 1, in what chapter(s) would you find information related to anthropological linguistics (study of language)?

_____

_____

Exercise 1.4   *Continued*

7. Other than Chapter One, in what chapter(s) would you find information related to the study of cultural anthropology today?

_____

_____

_____

8. Other than Chapter 1, in what chapter(s) would you find information related to the history of anthropology?

_____

_____

_____

9. In what chapter(s) would you find information about religion?

_____

_____

_____

10. Based on your examination of the Table of Contents, identify five major concepts studied by anthropologists.

_____

_____

_____

_____

_____

_____

THINKING CRITICALLY

Examine your answers to Exercises 1.3 and 1.4. On a separate sheet of paper or in your journal, describe the factors that might contribute to the differences in understanding. How could you accommodate for any deficits in knowledge?

SMART Information 1.1

Using your password for this course, access InfoTrac College Edition on the World Wide Web. Search for one of these topics: *learning styles, critical thinking* or *time management.* Respond to the following questions:

1. Which topic did you choose?

   _____

2. Why did you choose that topic?

   _____

   _____

   _____

   _____

   _____

3. Choose any article and give the title and reference information in the space below.

   _____

   _____

   _____

   _____

4. Read the article and describe how it relates to the information in this chapter.

   _____

   _____

   _____

   _____

   _____

   _____

   _____

   _____

   _____

   _____

Smart Review 1.2

Check your understanding of the preceding section by answering the following questions on a separate sheet of paper:

1. Explain the cycle of learning. What role does background knowledge play in the cycle?

2. Compare and contrast measuring background knowledge with measuring age.

3. Use Dale's stages (Table 1.3) to rank your knowledge of the following concepts:

    a.   Greek architecture
    b.   William Shakespeare
    c.   Calculus
    d.   Amphibians
    e.   Bosnia

4. Identify ways in which you can increase background knowledge about a concept.

SOURCE: Calvin and Hobbes copyright 1993 Watterson. Reprinted with permission of Universal Press Syndicate. All rights reserved.

THINKING ABOUT TIME

Like Calvin, you might find yourself overwhelmed by the problem of academic assignments. And if, like Calvin, you don't have a plan for accomplishing the task at hand, you, too, may eventually ask yourself, "Do I even care?"

You need a plan to manage study time. This plan encourages you to schedule academic assignments by the term, the week, and the day. In addition, it helps you understand how procrastination leads to an attitude like Calvin's.

Goal Management

A business principle also applies to study. Successful business people set goals and then allocate time to accomplish them on schedule. Setting goals and allocating time form the basis of a management plan. Your management plan should give you an overall view of what you want to accomplish, a weekly plan of events, and a daily, prioritized list of tasks to accomplish.

Establishing a Term Calendar

Your course work dictates many of your long-term goals each term. Getting a grip on the scope and sequence of your activities is the basis of a time management plan. The plan helps you think ahead and budget your time accordingly. Thus, you become proactive in preparing to meet your commitments instead of forgetting about assignments and reacting in haste to prevent disaster.

The first thing to do to manage a term is to get a monthly calendar, tear out the pages, and post them in a location where you can refer to them easily. Posting all of the pages lets you see your entire term at a glance. Then, using your college's academic calendar and the syllabus or course outline for each of your courses, you identify your institution's important dates (for example, the last day to drop a course) and schedule assignments, tests, and so on for each course. Finally, you note any other commitments that you want to keep (work schedule, special events, or other occasions). Table 1.4 provides steps for constructing a **term calendar.** Exercise 1.5 helps you complete a term calendar.

Table 1.4   Steps in Completing a Term Calendar

1. Obtain a calendar with large spaces for each day of a month.
2. Remove the pages for the current term and post them in a visible place.
3. Obtain an academic calendar for the current term and use it to record the following dates:
   - Holidays, school vacations, or social commitments
   - Midterm and final exam periods
   - Dates for dropping and adding courses, resigning, and so on
4. Collect course outlines and assignments for each course in which you are enrolled and use them to record the following dates:
   - Exam dates
   - Due dates for papers or other projects
   - Intermediary deadlines you set to complete phases of a lengthy project
5. Record other social commitments or family obligations you need to keep.
6. Record work commitments.

Exercise 1.5 Using a calendar for this year and the process outlined in Table 1.4, construct a term calendar. Photocopy this calendar and provide a copy for your instructor.

Managing the Week

Sometimes, the sheer amount of work required in a term can be overwhelming. Breaking commitments into week-long spans often makes them seem more achievable. Your weekly plan consists of a weekly calendar of events and a daily "to do" list. Your weekly calendar shows your fixed commitments. It also helps you find the most important items to record on a daily "to do" lists. Reviewing your commitments on a weekly basis helps you construct weekly plans with short-term goals for successfully managing the term. Table 1.5 provides steps for setting up a weekly calendar.

Table 1.5   Steps in Constructing a Weekly Calendar

1. *List fixed commitments first.* This includes classes, meals, sleep, travel time to class, and so on. Allow a realistic amount of time for each activity. For example, daily travel times differ according to the time of day, amount of traffic, and route taken. The time it takes to get to campus during rush hour may be very different from the time it takes to get home in the middle of the afternoon. Or, if you live on campus, consider that the lines at the cafeteria are longer at noon than they are an hour later. Time spent eating increases as the lines grow longer.

2. *Set aside a few minutes before each class to review your notes and preview that day's topic.* This is time usually spent in purposeless staring. Leave a few minutes following each class to review, correct, and add to your notes. If this is not possible, do so as soon as you can within twelve hours. Frequent reviews facilitate transfer of information to long-term memory.

3. *Identify any blocks of free time.*

4. *Look for ways to group activities and schedule these in the blocks of free time.* For example, if you have two papers to write, you may be able to complete all your library work at once and avoid making two trips.

5. *Plan to complete activities before their due date to allow for unexpected delays.*

6. *Schedule recreational breaks.*

7. *Schedule time for studying.* Two hours of out-of-class study for every hour of in-class time is often advised. However, the time you need varies according to your expertise in the subject and course demands. Full-time employment and family commitments further complicate you ability to schedule this much study time. If you have these or other time-consuming commitments, you need to be careful not to overburden yourself. If you see you don't have enough time to realistically accomplish everything, you may need to drop one or more classes.

8. *Plan for flexibility in scheduling.* Although you need to plan your time, you can adjust your schedule as necessary. For instance, you might find that the two hours you allotted for working on a research paper was too short a time. If you still feel energetic and focused, you continue to work on the project, even though that block of time was reserved for an algebra assignment due next week. Time set aside for one assignment might be better spent in another way, as long as you remember to "repay" the time.

> I recommend you to take care of the minutes; for hours will take care of themselves.
>
> —Lord C. K. Chesterton
> *Twentieth century British author*

Managing the Day

Managing your minutes is best accomplished through a prioritized "to do" list. Although many people construct "to do" lists, they often do not follow them. Instead, they tend to do those activities that can be finished quickly or aren't difficult to complete. The really terrible, boring, or difficult tasks never seem to get done. Prioritizing your "to do" list helps you eliminate such problems. You accomplish what needs to be done first.

Your tasks on the "to do" list consist of (1) that day's commitments transferred from your weekly calendar and (2) any items left over from the previous day. You add other items as you think of them. Your next step is to rank the items on your "to do" list by numbering each item in the order of its importance. Next, you look for blocks of free time in your day and schedule tasks for specific times. Chances are you won't get to the end of your "to do" list by the end of the day. But if you placed your commitments in their order of importance, then you finished the most important goals first. Prioritizing does not necessarily eliminate flexibility, and what is a priority today might not be a priority tomorrow. Buying gas for the car today might be a top priority if the gauge has been on empty for three days. Buying gas for the car when you still have a quarter of a tank left is less important. To obtain closure, at the end of each day, update that day's "to do" list and construct a new list for the next day. Exercise 1.6 asks you to create a weekly plan and a "To Do" list.

Exercise 1.6   Develop a weekly plan for next week and a "TO DO" list for Monday.

Weekly Planner	Week Beginning _____						
	Sun	Mon	Tues	Wed	Thur	Fri	Sat
6:00–7:00 A.M.							
7:00–8:00 A.M.							
8:00–9:00 A.M.							
9:00–10:00 A.M.							
10:00–11:00 A.M.							
11:00 A.M. –12:00 P.M.							
12:00–1:00 p.m.							
1:00–2:00 P.M.							
2:00-3:00 P.M.							
3:00-4:00 P.M.							

Exercise 1.6   *Continued*

	Sun	Mon	Tues	Wed	Thur	Fri	Sat
4:00–5:00 P.M.							
5:00–6:00 P.M.							
6:00–7:00 P.M.							
7:00–8:00 P.M.							
8:00–9:00-P.M.							
9:00–10:00 P.M.							
10:00–11:00 P.M.							
11:00 P.M.–12:00 A.M.							
12:00–1:00 A.M.							
1:00–2:00 A.M.							
2:00–3:00 A.M.							
3:00–4:00 A.M.							
4:00-5:00 A.M.							
5:00-6:00 A.M.							

To Do

_____

_____

_____

_____

_____

Prioritized Order

_____

_____

_____

_____

_____

_____

Procrastination

Students—and others—procrastinate, or put things off, and fail to complete goals for many reasons. One of the most common misconceptions about **procrastination** is that it results from laziness or from being like Calvin and just not caring enough to do the work. Generally, if you've had enough drive and ambition to get to a postsecondary institution, laziness is not your problem. Negative self-talk, lack of closure, and burnout are far more common reasons for procrastination.

Self-Talk

Karen Coltharp of West Point Military Academy describes procrastination in terms of Eric Berne's (1966) concept of transactional analysis. Coltharp suggests that, as a time manager, you function in one of three modes: **child, critic,** or **adult.**

The child is the part of yourself that wants to have fun and have it now. When the child within you gains control, you avoid those tasks that seem dull, boring, or too difficult.

The voice of the critic causes you to doubt your abilities, goals, and self. The critic foretells failure at every turn. When a task seems difficult for you, this voice insists you don't have the right background, experience, or intelligence to get the job done. With such encouragement, you find yourself procrastinating instead of meeting challenges head on.

The adult in you provides the voice of reason and logic. This voice knows that some tasks are no fun but must be accomplished anyway. The adult satisfies the child by giving rewards upon completion of tasks. Rewards don't satisfy the critic. The adult must outtalk the critic: "Yes, this is difficult, but I've been successful before," "I lack experience in this particular area, but I have similar experiences upon which I can draw," "I don't have the right background, but I can learn it," and "Others have been successful and I can be, too."

The role in which you function affects the way you work and the ways in which you perceive problems. The child's primary activity is avoiding constructive, purposeful activity. Conversing with friends, partying, and other leisure activities prevent the child from ever getting to the business at hand. Worry is the critic's chief activity. Instead of studying, the critic worries about studying. This includes such self-talk as "Can I learn this? What if I don't? If I don't, I may fail . . . What if I fail? What will I do then? What will other people think?" Problem solving is the adult's strength. When the adult studies, the adult thinks, "What do I have to learn? What would be the best way to learn this? Am I learning it? If not, how can I rethink my understanding?"

What seems to be simple procrastination can actually an informed decision. The difference is in the reason for procrastinating. If your reason for postponing something is sound and appropriate, it may be the best plan of action. For example, you may be considering dropping a course after the first month of class. You've regularly attended class. Your grades are good. However, your financial status shows that you need to increase your work hours. Logically, you decide you cannot do justice to the course and work more hours. What appears to be procrastination (taking the class next semester) is actually a logical decision based on the reality of the situation.

Lack of Closure

Closure is the positive feeling you get when you finish a task. Lack of closure (not finishing the task) results in the panicked feeling that you still have a million things to do. And this stress may entice you to give up entirely.

Dividing a task into manageable goals, listing them, and checking them off your list as you complete them helps you obtain closure. For example, suppose your chemistry professor assigns three chapters of reading. If your goal is to read all three chapters, you may feel discouraged if you don't complete the reading at one time. A more effective way to complete the assignment involves dividing the assignment into smaller goals. Think of each chapter as a separate goal, or subdivide the chapters into sections. You experience more success by completing each section or chapter. Even if you fail to complete all three chapters in one sitting, your progress results in feelings of accomplishment.

Unfinished business also results in a lack of closure and procrastination. You may have several tasks with the same deadline. Although changing from one task to another serves as a break, changing tasks too often wastes time. Each time you switch, you lose momentum. You may be unable to change gears fast enough or find yourself out of the studying mood. You may find yourself thinking about the old project when you should be concentrating on the new one. In addition, when you return to the first task, you lose time. This happens because you have to review where you were and what steps are still left to be finished.

Often you solve this problem by determining how much time you have to work. If the time available is short (that is, an hour or less), you concentrate on one task. Alternate tasks when you have more time. Completing one task or a large portion of a task contributes to the feeling of closure.

Sometimes, when working on a long-term project, other, unrelated tasks often take precedence before you can complete it. If this occurs, take time to write a few notes before moving to the new task. The clarity of your thinking or the status of your progress may seem fresh at the time, but you'll forget what you were doing after awhile. Your notes could include the goal of the task, how far along you are toward its completion, and a list of questions to be answered or objectives to be reached. You need to store references, papers, and other materials for the task together. This provides important organization when you return to it.

Burnout

Sometimes you procrastinate and fail to get things done because you are burned out. **Burnout** often results when you work without breaks. Burnout is unusual in that its causes are the same as its symptoms. Fatigue, boredom, and stress are both signs and causes of burnout.

Cramming; difficult course loads; balancing work, family, and academic schedules; and overloaded social calendars often result in burnout. In addition, many students find burnout a problem around exam times, particularly midterms and finals. Some students burn out in December as the result of the long, unbroken stretch between Labor Day and Thanksgiving holidays. Other students experience burnout in the spring semester, at the end of the academic year.

Balancing break time and work time helps you avoid burnout. Therefore, you need to plan for breaks as well as study time. A break does not have to be recreational to be effective. It simply might be a change from one task to another, such as switching from working math problems to reading an assignment. Although you can sometimes lose momentum by switching tasks, doing so is better than burning out. Another way to avoid burnout is to leave flexibility in your daily schedule. If you schedule commitments too tightly, you won't complete your goals and achieve closure. This defeats you psychologically because you fail to do what you planned.

Smart Review 1.3

Check your understanding of the preceding section by answering the following questions on a separate sheet of paper or in your journal:

1. Create a chart that compares and contrasts ways to effectively manage a day, a week, and a term.
2. You face the difficult task of writing a term paper on the linguistics of South African natives. Relative to Coltharp's ideas about transactional analysis, what message would your inner child say to you? Your critic? Your adult?
3. How does achieving closure help you avoid procrastination?
4. What is burnout, and why does it occur?
5. Provide examples of breaks you can use to reduce stress while you are studying for a final exam.

SMART SITES   **Using the Web to Manage Learning Time**

A wealth of information related to the topics in this chapter is available on the World Wide Web. For this exercise, access the *Bootstraps* archives from http://www.selfhelp.com/bootarchv.html (for the most up-to-date URLs, go to http://csuccess.wadsworth.com). Examine the information on this Web page including the definition of *bootstrap*. Read any one of the articles and respond to the following:

1. How does Ellis's definitions of *bootstrap* relate to the content of this chapter?

_____

_____

_____

2. How does Ellis describe his goal-setting guide? Do you think you are one of the people to whom he refers? Why or why not?

_____

_____

_____

3. How do you think Ellis's issues relate to the content of his book?

_____

_____

_____

4. Why did you choose the article you read?

_____

_____

_____

5. Summarize the content of the article. How does the content of the article relate to the content of this chapter?

_____

_____

_____

_____

THINKING CRITICALLY

Consider the roles—adult, child, critic—you play in procrastinating or avoiding procrastination. On a separate sheet of paper or in your journal, describe how interest and background knowledge might affect those roles? Why?

Thinking about Learning Styles: Maximizing Study Time

> There's a certain
> Slant of light,
>
> Winter
> Afternoons—
>
> That oppresses,
> like the Heft
>
> Of Cathedral
> Tunes—
>
> —Emily Dickinson
> *Nineteenth century*
> *American poet*

Dickinson's poem evokes sensory impressions—the visual image of light through a window, the feeling of the coldness of a winter afternoon, a sense of physical pressure and exertion, the sensation of reverence you encounter when hearing the sounds of music in a cathedral. In short, Dickinson provides a **multisensory** (having many connections with the senses) description which uses your understanding of how things look, sound, and feel. Such descriptions are often easy to recall because they impact memory in more than one way. Similarly, issues and ideas are generally multifaceted—having more than one side or perspective. This, too, enhances recall. You have a variety of ways to think about and remember a concept. Multisensory, multifaceted learning, then, involves learning from many different sensory channels and through as many avenues as possible.

Brain Dominance

In 1981, psychobiologist Roger Sperry won a Nobel Prize for his work on brain dominance. He specialized in treating individuals with severe and almost constant epileptic seizures. To treat them, he surgically split their brains. As a result, each individual essentially possessed two distinctly separate brains. Sperry conducted a variety of experiments with these people to see how the surgery affected their thinking.

The results indicated that language was mostly a function of the left brain. The left brain also seems more involved in processing math and judging time, rhythm, speech, and writing. The left brain generally analyzes information by breaking it into parts. It tends to process information in sequential, linear, logical ways.

The right brain controls different reasoning processes. The right brain processes information in holistic, visual forms. Thus, it prefers to synthesize, rather than analyze. Recognition of patterns, faces, and melodies, as well as other kinds of perceptual understanding, are within the right brain's domain.

What does Sperry's work have to do with your learning? Although you combine the skills of both sides of the brain in most activities, the ways in which you study affect the two sides of your brain differently. Most information is presented and studied in ways that appeal to the operations of the left brain—linear, verbal, textual information. The kinds of formats that appeal to the right brain—visual, holistic, spatial information—are often lacking. Learning information in a variety of ways takes advantage of the multisensory and multifaceted ways in which the brain processes information. A summary of the functions attributed to left and

Table 1.6   Right and Left Brain Attributes

Left-Brain Processing	Application to Learning
Linear; sequential parts and segments	Ordered detail-by-detail understanding; notes and outlines; analysis of ideas
Symbolic	Formulas; acronyms and acrostics; algebraic and abstract math computation
Logical; serious; verifying; non-fiction; improving on the known; reality-based; replication	Factual, unemotional information; proofs of theorems; grammar; practical application of learning to known situations
Verbal; written	Notes; outlines; lectures; text information; auditory review
Temporal; controlled; planning	Structured management of time, ideas, or resources
Focal thinking	Concentration on a single issue or point of view
Objective; dislikes improvisation	Multiple-choice; true-or-false matching formats

Right-Brain Processing	Application to Learning
Holistic; general overviews	Synthesis of information; mapping; charting
Concrete; spatial	Geometry; math facts; mapping; diagrams
Intuitive; assumptions inventing the unknown; fantasy-based; fictitious	Creative writing; interpreting literature; understanding symbolism or figurative language; drawing conclusions about an issue or idea; use of metaphors and analogies; humor
Nonverbal; kinesthetic; visual	Experimentation; hands-on learning; graphics; photographs; feelings; visualizing notes or situations; drawing; mapping; charting; role playing
Random; nontemporal	Unstructured management of time, ideas, or resources
Diffused thinking	Concentration on a variety of views or issues
Subjective; likes improvising	Essays exams; short-answer questions; creative writing

right hemispheres of the brain appears in Table 1.6 with corresponding applications to learning.

Just as you have a dominant hand with which you prefer to write, you probably possess a dominant side of the brain with which you prefer to learn. The assessment in Exercise 1.7 helps you determine if you are left- or right-brain dominant.

Assessing and Capitalizing on Learning Styles

Learning styles describe the preferences you have for thinking, sensing, relating to the environment, relating to others, and relating to yourself. Grasha (1984) suggests that the way you think influences the ways in which you acquire, retain, and retrieve information.

Exercise 1.7   Respond to the following questions.

1. How do you prefer making decisions?
   a. intuitively
   b. logically

2. Which do you remember more easily?
   a. names
   b. faces

3. Do you prefer
   a. planning your activities in advance
   b. doing things spontaneously

4. In social situations, do you prefer being the
   a. listener
   b. speaker

5. When listening to a speaker, do you pay more attention to
   a. what the speaker is saying
   b. the speaker's body language

6. Do you consider yourself to be a goal-oriented person?
   a. yes
   b. no

7. Is your main study area
   a. messy
   b. neat and well organized

8. Are you usually aware of what time it is and how much time has passed?
   a. yes
   b. no

9. When you write papers, do you
   a. let ideas flow freely
   b. plan the sequence of ideas in advance

10. After you have heard music, are you more likely to remember the
    a. words
    b. tunes

11. Which do you prefer doing?
    a. watching a movie
    b. working a crossword puzzle

12. Do you frequently move your furniture around in your home?
    a. yes
    b. no

13. Are you a good memorizer?
    a. yes
    b. no

14. When you doodle, do you create
    a. shapes
    b. words

15. Clasp your hands together. Which thumb is on top?
    a. left
    b. right

16. Which subject do you prefer?
    a. algebra
    b. trigonometry

17. In planning your day, do you
    a. make a list of what you need to accomplish
    b. just let things happen

18. Are you good at expressing your feelings?
    a. yes
    b. no

19. If you are in an argument with someone else, do you
    a. listen and consider the point of view of the other person
    b. insist that you are right

20. When you use a tube of toothpaste, do you
    a. carefully roll it up from the bottom
    b. squeeze it in the middle

(continues)

Exercise 1.7 *Continued*

Transfer your responses to the diagram by shading your responses. The shape with the most shaded pieces indicates your preference.

Sensory Variables

Sensory variables concern the ways you prefer to acquire information: seeing (visual), hearing (auditory), touching (tactile), or physically manipulating (kinesthetic). Exercise 1.8 provides a test of sensory variables. Take this test, then analyze your responses using the following:

Count the number of *A, B,* and *C* responses. If you have three or more of any one letter, that is your dominant style. *A* responses generally describe visual learners who learn best by seeing information. You might use flash cards, visual outlines or maps, diagrams, charts, and graphics to help you assimilate information more easily. Adding meaningful symbols and graphics to notes also provides visual cues. When you participate in class discussions or study groups, focus on how people look when they speak. Visualize how information appears on a page. Consider perspective—how you "see" a concept.

B responses generally describe auditory learners who learn best by hearing. If you are an auditory learner, consider recording your written lecture notes for auditory review. To do so, first review and edit your notes to identify the main points and important details. Then read your notes aloud into a tape recorder, leaving brief amounts of time between ideas. For example, you

Exercise 1.8   Test of Sensory Variables

1. If you could choose any way to learn, you would choose
   a. to read information for yourself
   b. to attend a lecture
   c. to participate in a demonstration

2. Are you more likely to recall
   a. a person's face
   b. a person's name
   c. how you interacted with that person

3. Which would you prefer?
   a. seeing a movie
   b. talking to a friend
   c. drawing a picture or creating other artwork

4. Do you generally remember
   a. things you've seen
   b. things you've heard
   c. things you've done

5. When presented with a word that you have difficulty spelling, are you more likely to
   a. examine the word in written form
   b. spell the word aloud
   c. write the word

Count the number of a, b, and c responses. If you have three or more of any one letter, that is your dominant style.

THINKING CRITICALLY

On a separate sheet of paper or in your journal, respond to the following: Based on the assessment, are you right- or left-brain dominant? Now that you've identified your preferred learning type, how might you apply that knowledge to learning Sample Chapter 6? How might a right-brain dominant person learn the information? How would a left-brain dominant person approach the information? What strategies would a person who had a balanced style use?

---

might say, "What is the process of photosynthesis?" and wait fifteen to twenty seconds before providing the answer. When you listen to the tape, these spaces provide you with chances to respond with answers before getting the reinforcement of your original reply. Reciting aloud and explaining information to yourself provides a second way to learn auditorially. Participation in study groups and class discussions helps you see how information "sounds" from another person's perspective.

C responses generally describe tactile and kinesthetic learners. Tactile learning refers to the sense of touch. Kinesthetic learning involves muscular movement. Both involve physical, rather than mental, feeling. If you are a tactile/kinesthetic learner, you probably learn best by activity—by writing, drawing, or otherwise participating in learning situations. Highlighting, underlining, labeling information, writing, and rewriting notes are ways to physically learn. Creating maps, charts, or other graphics also involves your tactile and kinesthetic senses. Creating models, conducting experiments, tutoring others, and participating in study groups provide additional opportunities for physical learning. Finally, you should get others to "show" you what they mean.

Environmental Factors

Learning style also determines which environmental conditions facilitate learning (for example, well-lit versus dimly lit, background noise versus complete silence). Complete the checklist in Exercise 1.9 to determine your environmental preferences. Then analyze your responses as follows:

Exercise 1.9   Assessment of Environmental Conditions

LIGHTING

1. _____ I often turn on extra lamps for reading.
2. _____ People sometimes tell me I'm reading in the dark.
3. _____ I prefer to sit by windows at home or in class.
4. _____ I prefer to sit in the back or corner of a classroom.
5. _____ I often choose seats directly below overhead lights.
6. _____ I find I sometimes shade my eyes while reading or solving math problems.
7. _____ Low light makes me sleepy.

STRUCTURE

1. _____ I prefer to stand and walk around when studying.
2. _____ I prefer to study seated on the floor rather than at a desk.
3. _____ I find it more difficult to concentrate in lectures than in lab experiments.
4. _____ I find I twitch and fidget after sitting for a short length of time.
5. _____ I find myself tapping a foot or knee after sitting for a short period of time.

SOUND

1. _____ I prefer to study in silence.
2. _____ When I really concentrate, I don't hear a thing.
3. _____ I find myself distracted by noises in a class, even when I am interested in the topic under discussion.
4. _____ Background noises—conversation, soft music, TV—don't affect my ability to study.

(continues)

Exercise 1.9   *Continued*

5. _____ Sometimes I wish I could tell my classmates to be quiet.

6. _____ I often hum to myself or tap while working.

VISUAL STIMULATION

1. _____ I find myself distracted by classroom movement, even when I am interested in the topic under discussion.

2. _____ When I study, I have notes, papers, texts, and other materials spread around me.

3. _____ I find busy environments—crowded stores, a variety of items on a desk, similar images—confusing.

4. _____ I prefer highly colored, busy patterns.

5. _____ I am very organized; when I study, I only have the bare essentials of what I need at hand.

6. _____ I enjoy courses in which the lecturer is theatrical and moves freely around the classroom.

If you checked the odd-numbered statements in the section on lighting, you probably prefer to study in strong light. If you checked the even-numbered statements, you prefer more subdued lighting.

If you checked any three of the five statements about structure, you probably prefer less structure and more mobility in your learning environment. In other words, you like to study somewhere other than a traditional desk. You prefer moving around. Although you may not be able to change your classroom situations, you can modify and adapt your study surroundings to match your structural needs. Thus, you may choose to sit on the floor or pace as you review.

Do you learn better with more or less noise around you? If you checked the odd-numbered statements in this group, you probably prefer to learn in silence. If you checked the even-numbered statements, you learn best with some auditory background noise. Though you lack control over classroom conditions, you do control your study site. You can alter it accordingly.

You tolerate a high degree of visual stimulation if you checked more of the even-numbered statements in this category. If you checked more of the odd-numbered statements, you may be more easily distracted by what you see around you. In a classroom, moving closer to the front eliminates distractions caused by other students. In your study environment, removing clutter and organizing study materials eliminates distractions.

Interpersonal Variables

The way you relate to others—interpersonal variables—concerns your ability to function in a group, leadership skills, communication, and so on. Take the inventory in Exercise 1.10 to obtain clues about how you best learn and process information in relationship to others.

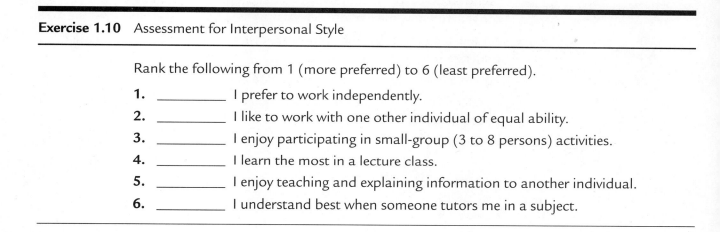

Exercise 1.10   Assessment for Interpersonal Style

Rank the following from 1 (more preferred) to 6 (least preferred).

1. _____ I prefer to work independently.
2. _____ I like to work with one other individual of equal ability.
3. _____ I enjoy participating in small-group (3 to 8 persons) activities.
4. _____ I learn the most in a lecture class.
5. _____ I enjoy teaching and explaining information to another individual.
6. _____ I understand best when someone tutors me in a subject.

What do your responses say about the interpersonal ways in which you learn? Do you prefer to learn alone (statement 1), in a small group (statement 3), or in a large group (statement 4)? Do you enjoy learning in pairs (statements 2, 5, and 6), and if so, do you prefer that relationship to be equal (statement 2), one in which you learn by helping another person (statement 5), or one in which you prefer to receive assistance (statement 6)? You need to structure learning situations so that they allow you to accommodate your interpersonal style.

Intrapersonal Characteristics

Intrapersonal style (the way you relate to yourself) determines the ways in which you set and achieve goals, your individual wants and needs, the way you live your life, and so on. Check the statements in Exercise 1.11 that apply to you.

What motivates you? Statements 1 (self-motivated, no matter what the situation), 2 (motivated by the attention of others), and 3 (motivated by external rewards) reflect differing motives for accomplishment. Statements 4 (high stress) and 5 (less stress) describe the amount of pressure you prefer in a course. Statements 6 (high level of personal freedom and choice) and 7 (structured learning situations) describe different levels of independent decision-making.

Exercise 1.11   Assessment of Intrapersonal Style

Check those that apply to you:

1. _____ If a topic is one I enjoy, I would learn as much in a class taken for pass/fail credit as one in which I would earn a letter grade.

2. _____ I tend to do better in courses with smaller enrollments in which the instructor gets to know me personally.

3. _____ An A in a course is the most important thing, even if I don't feel I really understand the course content.

4. _____ I prefer courses with all course work due at the end of the semester.

5. _____ I prefer a course with numerous scheduled quizzes instead of only a midterm and a final exam.

6. _____ I enjoy courses in which I have a choice concerning assignments and projects.

7. _____ I can learn anything, as long as I know exactly what a professor expects me to accomplish in a course.

THINKING CRITICALLY

Use the following chart to summarize your personal learning preferences. Then, on a separate sheet of paper or in your journal, explain how you should structure your learning to maximize your learning preferences.

Brain dominance   _____

Sensory variables   _____

Environmental conditions   _____

Interpersonal variables   _____

Intrapersonal characteristics _____

Forming and Maintaining Study Groups

Although assessing and targeting your own learning preferences provides you with a more effective learning style, multisensory and multifaceted methods maximize learning. Not only are you more likely to address the needs of your dominant style of learning, you also access a variety of other avenues by which you can learn.

Although multisensory, multifaceted techniques can be used alone, involvement in study groups maximizes such learning. Study groups provide opportunities for hearing information expressed in different ways and seeing the memory cues other students have devised. They afford the chance to experience and learn from others' learning styles, whether those styles are similar or dissimilar to your own.

Research indicates that study groups provide optimum learning opportunities. Students who participated regularly in a study group (Shanker, 1988) understood the material and scored better when tested on it than those who studied alone. When independent learners formed groups, their grades improved to the level of those already involved in group study. Work at Harvard University (Light, 1990; 1992) found that in every comparison, working in small groups was better than other formats. Small groups improved learning outcomes over large groups, independent study, or, in some cases, one-to-one tutoring from a faculty member. While changes in grades were modest, students' involvement in a course, enthusiasm for the course, and continued study of a topic increased. Students felt that working within groups taught them valuable strategies for working with others, strategies they had no other chance to learn.

What is a study group? A study group is two or more persons whose contact, proximity, and communication produce changes in each other. As part of a group, you interact with and influence other students. The purpose of your group is the active discussion of information. Therefore, your group needs to have communication skills, a common purpose, the ability to set tasks, and the skills to do those tasks. Creating and maintaining a group is often easier said than done. Guidelines for establishing and maintaining a study group appear in Table 1.7.

Table 1.7   Guidelines for Forming and Maintaining Study Groups

---

In forming a study group, you should:

1. **Select group members who have similar academic interests and dedication to the success of the group.** Friends do not always make the best study partners. Study group members need to be prepared to discuss the topic at hand, not what happened at last night's party. If you aren't sure which class members are interested in forming a study group, ask your instructor to announce the formation of a study group, or place a sign-up sheet on a nearby bulletin board or in the college's learning center.

2. **Seek group members with similar abilities and motivation.** The group functions best when each member contributes to the group's collectively learning and no one uses the group as a substitute for personally learning the information. You may need to dismiss members who fail to live up to their commitments.

(continues)

Table 1.7   *Continued*

3. **Limit group size to five or fewer students.** You need to feel comfortable with and actively participate in group processes. Too many people in a group often limits participation. In addition, scheduling meeting times for a large number of members may be impossible.

4. **Identify the purpose and lifetime of the group.** Some groups tend to continue without a real focus or way to conclude their service. What does the group want to accomplish, and how long will it take? Will you meet together until the next test, the completion of a project, or the end of the course? Will the group focus on problem solving, conceptual development, or a class project? Group goals require measurable outcomes and deadlines. Each session, as well as the group as a whole, needs a purpose. Feelings of accomplishment and closure at the end of each study session and at the conclusion of the group's life span contribute to your academic success.

5. **Schedule regular group meetings at the same time and place.** Meetings should begin and end promptly. Although needless interruptions should be discouraged, you should schedule breaks in study sessions as long as the group agrees to return to the task.

6. **Get acquainted.** As a group member, you invest much time and effort with the members of your group. Although you don't need to know their life histories, you do need to know something about their level of ability in a course (are they majoring in history, or is this their first course?), their current time commitments (do they have jobs, family, social, or other activities that affect when they can and cannot meet?), and their expectations for the group (is their goal to prepare for the next exam, to work on problems, or to share reading assignments?). At the very least, you need to exchange names and phone numbers so you can contact each other in case of an emergency.

What advantages do study groups have over independent study? When you study alone, you have only your own skills and strategies at your disposal. Group study allows you to see, hear, and practice a variety of problem-solving, communication, and learning skills. You learn more actively because you participate more fully than in individual study. Group study often helps focus attention and efforts. You have more chances to see, hear, verbalize, and otherwise come in contact with information. Group study also increases the ways in which you think about a subject. Other members of the group contribute their perspectives, learning styles, and insights. You have not only your own ideas but also the ideas of others.

Group study provides psychological as well as intellectual benefits. Your commitment to the group enhances your study. While you may be prone to break study dates with yourself, you'll be more likely to prepare if you know

"They're a great study group, but I don't think I want to party with them."

others depend on you. In addition, participation in a study group gives you support. Knowing that others are having difficulty or experiencing success lessens your anxiety and offers encouragement. Group members provide support for dealing with academic, personal, time, and financial problems.

Although group learning has many advantages, study groups have one potential disadvantage: Group study focuses on the verbal exchange of information. It sometimes fails to provide practice in generating the kinds of answers needed for essay exam questions. Although some students adequately explain information verbally, they fail to perform as well when asked to provide a written answer. If you have difficulty composing written responses to test items, you need to include writing in your study strategies.

Active Learning

Because *doing* results in understanding, you need to become an active learner—an involved participant in the learning of course content. Not a sea sponge that soaks up information, you need to become a shark that actively seeks, ingests, and digests information for growth and renewal. The hunt for knowledge begins long before you enter a classroom. It never ends. Active learning consists of collaborations among you, your instructor, your study group, your text, your notes, and so forth. These interactions, by very definition, must be actions which require you to use your senses—specifically, hearing, seeing, and touching—and to manipulate objects—specifically, notes, texts, and index cards—to maximize learning and recall. SMART teaches you a process for actively pursuing information and then provides you with opportunities to practice that process. Now that you've completed this introductory chapter, it's time to get moving.

In learning, it is said that "we hear and we forget; we see and we remember; we do and we understand."

—Anonymous

Smart Review 1.4

Check your understanding of the preceding section by answering the following on a separate sheet of paper:

1. What are the implications of Roger Sperry's work on learning?
2. List and define factors that contribute to learning style.
3. Explain the significance of study groups. List their pluses and minuses about them.
4. Describe active learning.

Speaking Figuratively, of Course . . .

In and Out of Context: Figurative Language

In the *Reader's Digest* "Campus Comedy" column, Stephen W. Balint (September, 1989) related a story about a physics professor who lectured about motion in a plane and then assigned several homework problems. One question gave information on the departure angle and velocity of a baseball hit during a game, as well as the field and wall dimensions of the field. Another asked: "Will the ball be a home run?" During the next class, the professor wanted to know if the class had had trouble with any of the homework problems. A foreign student inquired about the baseball question. The professor launched into a discussion about the relationship between velocity, departure angle, and distance. When the professor finished, the student said, "I understand that part." "Then what is your question?" the professor asked. "What is a home run?" replied the student.

The student's problem was that the words *home* and *run* were not in the context she expected. When combined, the words are **figurative language.** Their meaning is not literal.

Authors of poems, essays, short stories, novels, and other texts use figurative language to appeal to your imagination and to engage your senses. Through *figures of speech*, authors compare things or ideas that usually are considered totally dissimilar. Or, they may use figurative language to amuse, perplex, or inspire you. All figurative language requires you to relate what you already know about the world with what you are reading at a higher level of thinking. Even though understanding figurative language asks more of you as a reader, its vividness and variety, and its multisensory stimulation of recall, more than justifies its use.

Figurative Language 1.A

Read the following short story. Then answer the questions that follow.

A, B, and C—The Human Element in Mathematics
Stephen Leacock

The student of arithmetic who has mastered the first four rules of his art and successfully striven with money sums and fractions finds himself **confronted** by an unbroken **expanse** of questions known as problems. These are short stories of adventure and industry with the end omitted, and though betraying a strong family **resemblance,** are not without a certain element of romance.

The characters in the plot of the problem are three people called *A, B,* and *C;* the form of the question is generally of this sort:

"*A, B,* and *C* do a certain piece of work. *A* can do as much work in one hour as *B* in two, or *C* in four. Find how long they work at it."

Or thus: "*A, B,* and *C* are employed to dig a ditch. *A* can dig as much in one hour as *B* can dig in two, and *B* can dig twice as fast as *C.* Find how long, etc., etc."

Or after this was: "*A* lays a wager that he can walk faster than *B* or *C. A* can walk half as fast again as *B,* and *C* is only an indifferent walker. Find how far, and so forth."

The occupations of *A, B,* and *C* are many and varied. In the older arithmetics they contented themselves with doing a "certain piece of work." This statement of the case, however, was found too sly and mysterious, or possibly lacking in romantic charm. It became the fashion to define the job more clearly and to set them at walking matches, ditch-digging, regattas, and piling cordwood. At times, they became commercial and entered into partnership, having, with their old mystery, a "certain" capital. Above all they revel in motion. When they tire of walking matches, *A* rides on horseback, or borrows a bicycle and competes with his weaker-minded associates on foot. Now they race on locomotives; now they row; or again they become historical and engage stage-

coaches; or at times they are **aquatic** and swim. If their occupation is actual work, they prefer to pump water into cisterns, two of which leak through holes in the bottom and one of which is water-tight. *A,* of course, has the good one; he also takes the bicycle, and the best locomotive, and the right of swimming with the current. Whatever they do, they put money on it, being all three sports. *A* always wins.

In the early chapters of the arithmetic, their identity is concealed under the names of John, William, and Henry, and they **wrangle** over the division of marbles. In algebra they are often called *X, Y, Z.* But these are only their Christian names, and they are really the same people.

Now to one who has followed the history of these men through countless pages of problems, watched them in their leisure hours, dallying with cordwood, and seen their panting sides heave in the full frenzy of filling a cistern with a leak in it, they become something more than mere symbols. They appear as creatures of flesh and blood, living men with their own passions, ambitions, and aspirations like the rest of us.

A is full-blooded, hot-headed and strong-willed. It is he who proposes everything, challenges *B* to work, makes the bets, and bends the others to his will. He is a man of great physical strength and **phenomenal** endurance. He has been known to walk forty-eight hours at a stretch, and to pump ninety-six. His life is **arduous** and full of **peril.** A mistake in the working of a sum may keep him digging a fortnight without sleep. A repeated decimal in the answer might kill him.

B is a quiet, easy-going fellow, afraid of *A* and bullied by him, but very gentle and brotherly to little *C,* the weakling. He is quite in *A*'s power, having lost all his money in bets.

Poor *C* is an undersized, frail man, with a **plaintive** face. Constant walking, digging, and pumping have broken his health and ruined his nervous system. His joyless life has driven him to drink and smoke more than is good for him, and his hand often shakes as he digs ditches. He has not the strength to work as the others do, in fact, as Hamlin Smith has said, "*A* can do more work in one hour than *C* in four."

The first time that ever I saw these men was one evening after a regatta. They had all been rowing in it, and it had **transpired** that *A* could row as much in one hour as *B* in two, or *C* in four. *B* and *C* had come in dead fagged and *C* was coughing badly. "Never mind, old fellow," I heard *B* say, "I'll fix you up on the sofa and get you some hot tea." Just then *A* came blustering in and shouted, "I say, you fellows, Hamlin Smith has shown me three cisterns in his garden and he says we can pump them until tomorrow night. I bet I can beat you both. Come on. You can pump in your rowing things, you know. Your cistern leaks a little, I think, *C*." I heard *B* growl that it was a dirty shame and that *C* was used up now, but they went and presently I could tell from the sound of the water that *A* was pumping four times as fast as *C*.

For years after that I used to see them constantly about the town and always busy. I never head of any of them eating or sleeping. After that, owing to a long absence from home, I lost sight of them. On my return I was surprised to find *A*, *B*, and *C* no longer at their old tasks; on inquiry I heard that work in this line was now done by *N*, *M*, and *O*, and that some people were employing for algebraical jobs four foreigners called Alpha, Beta, Gamma, and Delta.

Now it chanced one day that I stumbled upon old *D*, in the little garden in front of his cottage, hoeing in the sun. *D* is an aged laboring man who used occasionally to be called in to help *A*, *B*, and *C*. "Did I know 'em, sir?" he answered. "Why I knowed 'em ever since they was little fellows in brackets. Master *A*, he were a fine-hearted lad, sir, though I always said, give me Master *B* for kind-heartedness-

like. Many's the job as we've been on together, sir, though I never did no racing nor aught of that, but just the plain labor, as you might say. I'm getting a bit too old and stiff for it nowadays, sir—just scratch about in the garden here and grow a bit of a logarithm, or raise a common denominator or two. But Mr. Euclid he uses me still for propositions, he do."

From the **garrulous** old man I learned the **melancholy** end of my former acquaintances. Soon after I left town, he told me, *C* had been ill. It seems that *A* and *B* had been rowing on the river for a wager, and *C* had been running on the bank and then sat in a **draught.** Of course the bank had refused the draught and *C* had taken ill. *A* and *B* came home and found *C* lying helpless in bed. *A* shook him roughly and said, "Get up, *C*, we're going to pile wood." *C* looked so worn and pitiful that *B* said, "Look here, *A*, I won't stand this, he isn't fit to pile wood tonight." *C* smiled feebly and said, "Perhaps I might pile a little if I sat up in bed." Then *B*, thoroughly alarmed, said, "See here, *A*, I'm going to fetch a doctor, he's dying." *A* flared up and answered, "You've got no money to fetch a doctor." "I'll reduce him to his lowest terms, " *B* said firmly, "that'll fetch him." *C*'s life might even then have been saved but they made a mistake about the medicine. It stood at the head of the bed on a bracket, and the nurse accidentally removed it from the bracket without changing the sign. After the fatal **blunder,** *C* seems to have sunk rapidly. On the evening of the next day, it was clear, as the shadows deepened, that the end was near. I think that even *A* was affected at the last as he stood with bowed head, aimlessly offering to bet with the doctor on *C*'s labored breathing. "*A*," whispered *C*, "I think I'm going fast." "How fast do you think you'll go, old man?" murmured *A*. "I don't know," said *C*, "but I'm going at any rate." The end came soon after that. *C* rallied for a moment and asked for a certain piece of work that he had left downstairs. *A* put it in his arms and he expired. As his soul sped heavenward, *A* watched its flight with melancholy admiration. *B* burst into a passionate flood of tears and sobbed, "Put away his little cistern and the rowing clothes he used to wear; I feel as if I could hardly ever dig again."—The funeral was plain and **unostentatious.** It differed in nothing from the ordinary, except that out of **deference** to sporting men, and mathematicians, *A* engaged two hearses. Both vehicles started at the same time, *B* driving the one which bore the sable parallelepipeds containing the last remains of his ill-fated friend. *A* on the box of the empty hearse generously consented to a handicap of a hundred years, but arrived first at the cemetery by driving four times as fast as *B*. (Find the distance to the cemetery.) As the sarcophagus was lowered, the grave was surrounded by the broken figures of the first book of Euclid.

It was noticed that after the death of *C*, *A* became a changed man. He lost interest in racing with *B*, and dug but languidly. He finally gave up his work and settled down to live on the interest of his bets. *B* never recovered from the shock of *C*'s death; his grief preyed upon his intellect and it became deranged. He grew moody and spoke only in monosyllables. His disease became rapidly aggravated, and he presently spoke in words whose spelling was regular and which presented no difficulty to the beginner. Realizing his **precarious** condition, he voluntarily submitted to be incarcerated in an asylum, where he **abjured** mathematics and devoted himself to writing the history of the Swiss Family Robinson in words of one syllable.

Answer the following questions about the essay:

1. What do you think are the first four rules of the student's art?

   _____

   _____

2. Why are *A, B,* and *C* called *John, William,* and *Henry* in the early chapters of arithmetic? _____

   _____

3. Why are *Alpha, Beta, Gamma,* and *Delta* considered foreigners?

   _____

   _____

4. Identify two meanings of *draught* used in this essay. How does this confusion contribute to the humor of the story? _____

   _____

   _____

5. Explain the literal and figurative meaning of each of the following:

   a. I'll reduce him to his lowest terms._____

   _____

   _____

   b. It stood at the head of the bed on a bracket, and the nurse accidentally removed it from the bracket without changing the sign._____

   _____

   _____

Figurative Language 1.B

Locate a recent news report of an athletic event. On a separate sheet of paper or in your journal, identify five figures of speech by the sportswriter. Then rewrite the article, creating your own figures of speech.

SMART Information 1.2

Using your password for this course, access InfoTrac College Edition on the World Wide Web. Search by subject for *anthropology* and respond to the following questions:

1. Analyze the subjects containing the word *anthropology*. How many subject areas are listed? How are they organized?

2. Review the outline of contents on the first page of Sample Chapter 6, "The Study of Humanity." Which InfoTrac subjects appear to be reflected in the content of Sample Chapter 6?

3. Read either the encyclopedia or reference book excerpt. Identify the excerpt you chose and describe how the information it contains helps you build background knowledge for the subject.

4. Search using *anthropology* as a keyword (rather than as a subject). How do the results differ? Which do you prefer? Why?

COOPERATIVE LEARNING ACTIVITY   YOUR ROLES AS A GROUP MEMBER

Some groups never seem to accomplish their goals. No one seems to know what to do, or someone takes the lead and tells everyone else what to do. Such endeavors fail to qualify as true study groups. Although they may be meeting regularly, their contact and communication fail to produce any lasting changes. Sometimes knowing what roles a group member should play helps a group function more smoothly. Group members can choose roles or rotate responsibilities. Acquiring, developing, and incorporating different roles leads to better thinking by each member of the group. Responsibilities and actions for different roles appear in the following table.

To practice thinking in different roles, group members need to select and study a limited amount of text information. Limit the information to two or three pages. Each member reads the text and then assumes a role. For example, the *goal-setter* might ask questions or establish learning tasks. The *informant* reviews the text and provides the information. The *processor* identifies other connections within the text or links the information to topics that the group has already discussed. The *evaluator* monitors the accuracy of the information as well as the appropriateness of the connections made by the processor. Finally, the *facilitator* ensures that the group stays on track and persists in responding to the goal-setter. The group then selects another passage to read and repeats the process. Members switch roles until each member plays all the roles. Finally, group members assess their strengths and weaknesses in terms of the roles and responsibilities they assumed. This allows the group to identify members to serve as role models.

Application

Use a text from one of the courses a group member is currently taking. Assign roles for studying a text section and follow the preceding instructions.

Table 1	Roles, Responsibilities, and Examples of Actions for Study Group Members	
Role	**Responsibilities**	**Examples of Actions**
Goal-Setter	Establishes purposes; poses questions; asks for information	"What is the best way to approach this problem?" "What information do we have?" "How did you know that?" "What's the best way to explain . . . ?"
Informant	Provides information; suggests new ideas, perspectives or opinions; translates information	"According to page 112, the three causes are. . . ." "This problem is like. . . ." "What that means is. . . ."
Processor	Probes for meanings; clarifies information; elaborates; interprets, applies and analyzes information	"How does the text support what we have in our notes?" "How could we use that principle in a problem?" "How does this idea compare with that one?"
Evaluator	Defines and monitors progress; checks to see if the group is ready to decide or come to a conclusion; summarizes and synthesizes results; resolves conflicts; judges results and outcomes	"So, the best response is to. . . ." "That is our answer?" "To summarize the process, we. . . ." "This solution is better because. . . ."
Facilitator	Stimulates group members; provides support and encouragement	"Let's look at the facts again." "How else might we solve this problem?" "What do you think about . . . ?"

SUMMARY

Postsecondary study poses a variety of challenges and encourages the development of critical thinking. This chapter applies Bloom's taxonomy to thinking about how you think and learn. Bloom's taxonomy consists of seven increasingly difficult levels of thinking: recall, translation, interpretation, application, analysis, synthesis, and evaluation. Thinking about thinking requires you to assess what you already know in terms of background knowledge. It also applies to time and goal management. The way you manage each term, week, and day affects your ability to attain goals. Whether you accomplish your goals or delay them depends on your self-talk, achievement of closure, and the balance you maintain between work and relaxation. Multisensory, multifaceted study techniques that affect both sides of the brain and match your preferred learning styles result in optimal learning conditions. This chapter provided assessments of learning styles and suggestions for developing and maintaining study groups.

CHAPTER REVIEW

1. Consider Bloom's taxonomy. Recall the levels of thinking and define each one in your own words. What are some other ways that you could interpret the stages in Bloom's taxonomy? Other than learning, what are some activities to which the taxonomy might be applied?

   _____

   _____

   _____

   _____

2. Think about the ways in which you studied last semester. How would you analyze your old study strategies in terms of Bloom's taxonomy?

   _____

   _____

   _____

   _____

3. Describe the relationship, if any, between Bloom's taxonomy and your background knowledge in terms of the courses in which you are enrolled.

   _____

   _____

   _____

4. Observe the kinds of self-talk you employ in the courses in which you are enrolled. How would you categorize these according to Coltharp's three modes of self-talk?

_____

_____

_____

_____

5. What do you see as your greatest obstacles to constructing, maintaining, and following a term calendar, weekly calendar, and daily "to do" list? Why?

_____

_____

_____

_____

6. At what times in the term are you least likely to achieve closure? Why? At what times in the term are you most susceptible to burnout? Why? How can your term calendar, weekly schedule, and daily "to do" list assist you in minimizing such problems?

_____

_____

_____

_____

7. Identify your learning style. Which of your current study techniques reinforce your learning style? Which study techniques do you need to modify to accommodate your learning style?

_____

_____

_____

_____

8. How does your learning style affect each course in which you are now enrolled? How might you adjust your learning strategies to accommodate your style?

_____

_____

_____

_____

9. Describe a situation in which you feel a study group would be most effective in helping you learn information. Describe a situation in which you feel a study group would NOT be effective in helping you learn. What accounts for the differences?

_____

_____

_____

_____

10. List the benefits of group study as identified by the chapter. What might be some disadvantages or problems that might develop? How could these be alleviated?

 MOVING ON

_____

Now you have the tools you need to address any course—time management, critical thinking, and self-understanding in terms of interest, background knowledge and learning style. You're ready for the next step—reading text chapters.

How satisfied are you with the textbook reading strategies you use? Circle the response that best describes your reading.

EXCELLENT   GOOD   AVERAGE   FAIR   POOR

Course readings form the nucleus of the class content. Such readings prepare you for courses that are new to you or complex in nature. They provide a guide to what the lectures cover. Readings define terms, provide graphics, and use other features to help you understand information. They are valuable resources when read. They are worthless when left sitting on the shelf. How valuable course readings are depends on what you make of them. All you need are the right reading strategies and the time to use them. The next chapter discusses the strategies you need. The time you acquire through effective time management. Check the strategies you need to improve.

☐ Knowing how to mark and label course readings

☐ Setting goals for reading

☐ Evaluating your understanding as you read

☐ Knowing what to do if you don't understand what you've read

☐ Finding important information in course readings

☐ Previewing information to help you understand

☐ Defining words used in course readings

☐ Outlining

☐ Getting organized to read

☐ Recalling meanings of new words

☐ Identifying an author's organizational plan

☐ Mapping

☐ Relating supplemental readings to course content

☐ Reading literary text

Chapter 2 provides you with the strategies you need for reading text chapters, so move on to learn more about understanding college texts.

ACTION PLAN

Review the information this chapter contains and respond to the following:

Action Plan

⭐ Ideas I already use:

⭐ Ideas new to me:

⭐ Ideas I'd like to try:

Understanding the Texts You Read

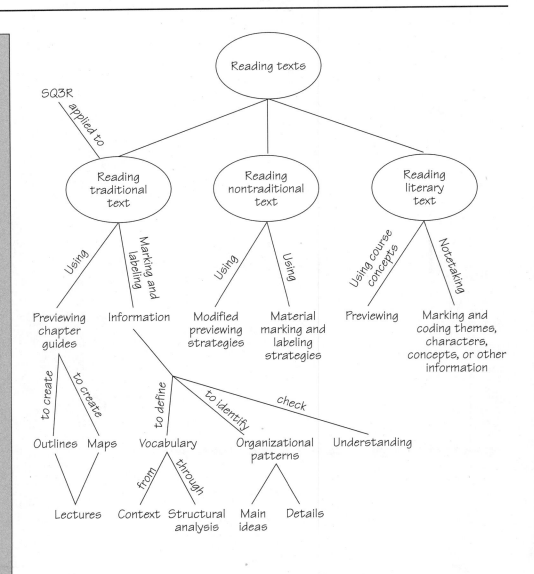

CHAPTER OUTLINE

"This semester I'm organizing my reading lists in a new way."

> **The traveler was active; he went strenuously in search of people, of adventure, of experience. The tourist is passive; he expects interesting things to happen to him. He goes "sight-seeing."**
>
> —Daniel J. Boorstin
> *Twentieth century American historian*

PREVIEWING TEXTS TO SET READING GOALS

Like the passive tourist, you might be doing more sight-seeing than anything else when you prepare to read. You passively take what the text offers. Examining key terms and concepts before reading helps you leave your role as tourist and become a traveler, an active participant in the adventure of learning.

Examining the Author's Organizational Plan

Your goal in previewing, or surveying, is to get your bearings. Texts provide special surroundings to help you cope with their content. These surroundings form a context that helps you organize information and find what you need. Authors of collegiate texts use various signs and signals to help you know what to expect (see Figure 2.1). Some guides occur at the beginning and the end of chapters. Others are found throughout the chapter (see Table 2.1). No matter their placement, they help you connect what you already know about a topic with the new information in the chapter.

Figure 2.1   Illustrations of Prechapter, Intrachapter, and Postchapter Guides

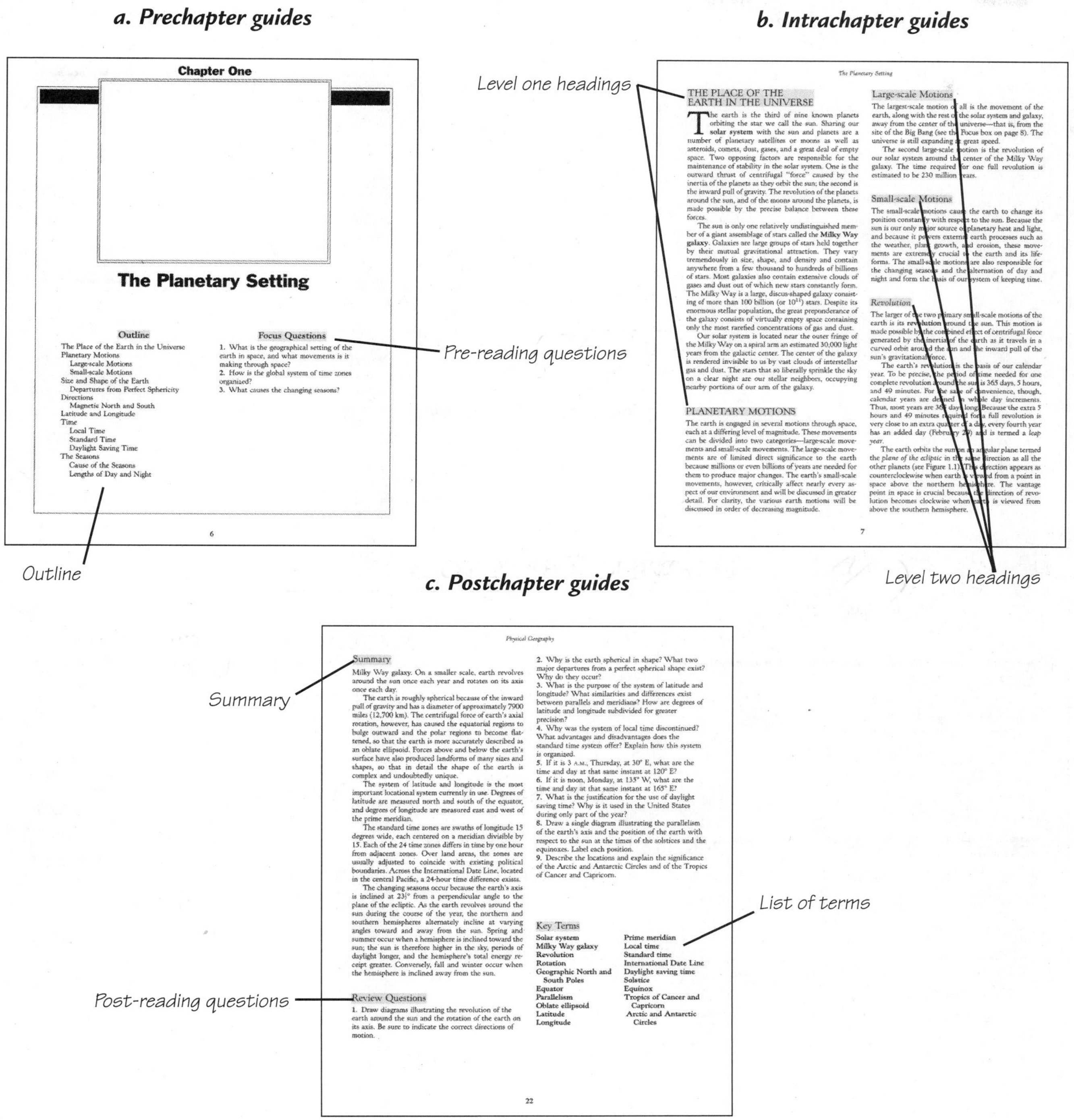

a. Prechapter guides

b. Intrachapter guides

Level one headings

Pre-reading questions

Outline

Level two headings

c. Postchapter guides

Summary

List of terms

Post-reading questions

(continues)

Figure 2.1   *Continued*

a. Prechapter guides

b. Intrachapter guides

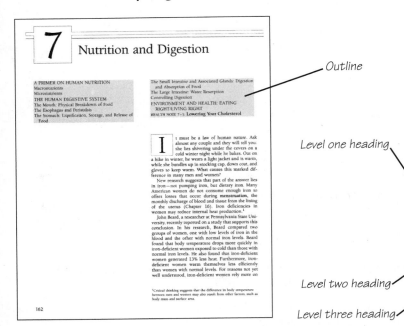

Outline

Level one heading

Level two heading

Level three heading

c. Postchapter guides

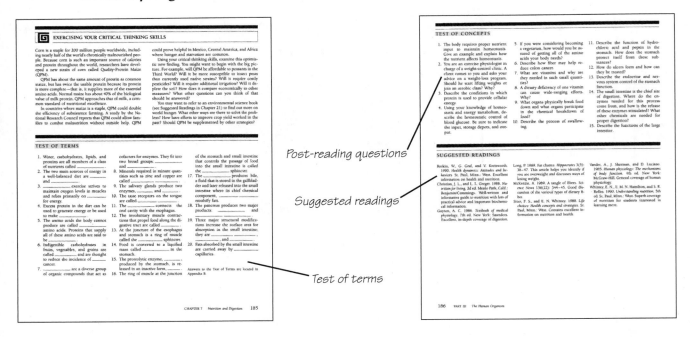

Post-reading questions

Suggested readings

Test of terms

Table 2.1   List of Prechapter, Intrachapter, and Postchapter Guides

Prechapter Guides	Interchapter Guides	Postchapter Guides
Title	Headings	Summary
Introduction	Subheadings	Review questions
Prereading questions	Terms in context	Terms
Terms	Boxed Information	Suggested readings
Outlines or concept maps	Graphics	
Objectives	Marginal notes	

Prechapter Guides

Information at the beginning of a chapter, or prechapter guides, sets the stage for what follows. Questions, quotations, case studies, and, often, the title of the chapter help you access background knowledge, focus your thoughts, and become interested. Some introductions state the subject directly in the first sentence or paragraph. Others tell a story, give an illustration, or use statements that excite, surprise, or arouse curiosity. Introductory lists of terms and outlines also focus your thoughts but in different ways. They identify the concepts the author deems most important. Introductions can also begin with challenging questions, facts that show the importance of the subject, or a quotation or idea from an expert or authority. Some introductions start with a case study—a specific and real example of the topic discussed in the chapter. Other introductions present a thought-provoking picture. Whatever the case, introductions convey the nature of the subject and the author's opinions about it.

Intrachapter Guides

Text signals within a chapter, or intrachapter guides, provide direction as you read. They focus your attention on what is important and establish the order of the information. Highlighted words (boldfaced, italicized, or both) indicate key terms in the chapter. Major headings and subheadings trace relationships among pieces of information. Headings and subheadings may show two, three, or four levels of information. Publishers use capital letters, boldface and italic type, color, and other design features to indicate the relative importance of headings, with major headings displayed most prominently. Subheadings also receive special treatment but are less conspicuous. Determining this hierarchy helps you recognize the author's organizational plan for the chapter.

Postchapter Guides

Information found at the end of a chapter summarizes important concepts and focuses your attention on the chapter's contents. Chapter reviews help you check your understanding, while lists of terms reinforce learning. Suggested readings provide sources of information to clarify or expand on what you've read.

So, with all these signs and signals to assist you, what makes reading a college text so difficult? Chesterton's observation also applies to a text's print format and organization—its external surroundings. While each text provides an organizational context (in the form of guides) to help you, the appearance of the guides often differs. That's because authors choose various ways to organize information. For instance, some authors select boldface to show terms (as in this text), while others use italics. Some use capital letters to indicate major headings. Others show major headings in capital and lowercase letters. Which signals an author decides to use depends on personal preference, text level or design, and subject matter. In addition, authors differ in writing style. Some authors write in a style that is clear, well-organized, and easily understandable. Other styles are more formal and less conversational, which can make them more difficult to understand. Making sense of your texts, then, is not so much a matter of finding or not finding what you need but not finding what you need in the places you expect it to be. Previewing text chapters before reading provides a solution to this dilemma.

Previewing helps you recall what you know about a subject. It provides you with basic information on which to build deeper understanding. In previewing, you accomplish two objectives. First, you assess what you already know about the topic. Second, you create an outline or map to guide your understanding of the chapter and set goals for reading. Exercise 2.1 provides practice in identifying text guides.

> ❝❞
> **What affects men sharply about a foreign nation is not so much finding or not finding familiar things; it is rather not finding them in familiar places.**
>
> —Lord G. K. Chesterton
> *Twentieth century English author*

Exercise 2.1   For two of the chapters you are currently studying, identify the text guides that the author provides. The first question has been done as an example using Sample Chapter 6, "The Study of Humanity."

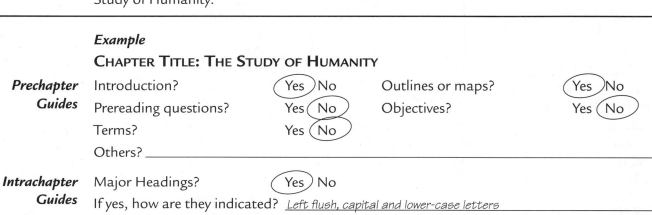

Example

CHAPTER TITLE: THE STUDY OF HUMANITY

Prechapter Guides

Introduction?	(Yes) No	Outlines or maps?	(Yes) No
Prereading questions?	Yes (No)	Objectives?	Yes (No)
Terms?	Yes (No)		

Others? _____

Intrachapter Guides

Major Headings?   (Yes) No

If yes, how are they indicated? *Left flush, capital and lower-case letters*

_____

(continues)

Exercise 2.1   *Continued*

List headings on the following lines:

Scope of Anthropology

Cultural Anthropology Today

Anthropological Perspectives

The Value of Anthropology

Subheadings?   (Yes) No

If yes, how many levels are shown in the text?   (2)   3   4

How are they indicated? Second: *Left flush, capital and lower-case letters; italicized; graphic*

Third: _____

Fourth: _____

List one of each level on the lines below:

Physical anthropology

Relativism

Terms in context?   (Yes) No

If yes, how are they indicated? _____

List the first 5 terms on the lines below:

physical (biological) anthropology

paleoanthropologists

primatologists

archeology

prehistoric archeology

Boxed information?   (Yes) No

If yes, what kind? *supplemental information*

Graphics?   (Yes) No

If yes, what kind? *photographs*

Marginal notes?   Yes (No)

If yes, what kind? _____

Others _____

(continues)

Exercise 2.1   *Continued*

Post Chapter Guides

Summary?	(Yes) No	Terms?	(Yes) No
Review questions?	Yes (No)	Suggested readings?	(Yes) No

Others? _____

_____

1. CHAPTER TITLE _____

Prechapter Guides

Introduction?	Yes No	Outlines or maps?	Yes No
Prereading questions?	Yes No	Objectives?	Yes No
Terms?	Yes No		

Others? _____

Intrachapter Guides

Major Headings?   Yes No

If yes, how are they indicated? _____

_____

List headings on the following lines:

_____

_____

_____

_____

Subheadings?   Yes No

If yes, how many levels are shown in the text?   2   3   4

How are they indicated? Second: _____

                Third: _____

                Fourth: _____

List one of each level on the lines below:

_____

_____

Terms in context?   Yes No

If yes, how are they indicated? _____

_____

List the first 5 terms on the lines below:

_____

_____

_____

_____

(continues)

Exercise 2.1   *Continued*

_____

_____

Boxed information?   Yes   No

If yes, what kind? _____

_____

Graphics?   Yes   No

If yes, what kind? _____

_____

Marginal notes?   Yes   No

If yes, what kind? _____

_____

Others? _____

_____

Post Chapter Guides	Summary?	Yes No	Terms?	Yes No
	Review questions?	Yes No	Suggested readings?	Yes No
	Others? _____			

_____

2. CHAPTER TITLE _____

Prechapter Guides	Introduction?	Yes No	Outlines or maps?	Yes No
	Prereading questions?	Yes No	Objectives?	Yes No
	Terms?	Yes No		
	Others? _____			
Intrachapter Guides	Major Headings?	Yes No		
	If yes, how are they indicated? _____			

List headings on the following lines:

_____

_____

_____

_____

(continues)

Exercise 2.1   *Continued*

Subheadings?   Yes   No

If yes, how many levels are shown in the text?   2   3   4

How are they indicated? Second: _____

Third: _____

Fourth: _____

List one of each level on the lines below:

_____

_____

Terms in context?   Yes   No

If yes, how are they indicated? _____

_____

List the first 5 terms on the lines below:

_____

_____

_____

_____

_____

Boxed information?   Yes   No

If yes, what kind? _____

_____

Graphics?   Yes   No

If yes, what kind? _____

_____

Marginal notes?   Yes   No

If yes, what kind? _____

_____

Others? _____

_____

Post Chapter Summary?   Yes   No   Terms?   Yes   No

Guides Review questions?   Yes   No   Suggested readings?   Yes   No

Others? _____

_____

Organizing Course Content to Set Reading Goals

Outlines and **maps** help you predict and organize information while survey-ing. This is particularly true if you rephrase headings and subheadings into questions or connect chapter titles with headings and subheadings to ques-tions. Questions require you to look for answers and, thus, make reading more active. You read to answer *what, how, when, who, which, where, and why* (see Table 2.2). When previewing, you will often be looking for **main ideas.** Thus, *why, how,* and *what* questions will form the basis of your previewing outline. Question outlines and maps make previewing concrete. They help set goals for reading.

Organizing Through Outlining

An outline consists of a written collection of ideas ranked according to im-portance. Every idea is subordinate to or summarized by another idea, except for the main idea. Thus, an outline forms an ordered picture of information. You determine importance based on the ways in which ideas fit together.

The subject of the chapter serves as the subject of your outline. The ques-tion you created from each major heading in the chapter is a major heading in your outline. Each question you formed from a subheading becomes a minor heading. Information found under subheadings becomes questions about supporting details.

Table 2.2   Questioning Words

Questioning Words for Main Ideas

IF YOU WANT TO KNOW . . .	THEN ASK . . .
a reason	Why?
a way	How?
a purpose or definition	What?
a fact	What?

Questioning Words for Details

IF YOU WANT TO KNOW . . .	THEN ASK . . .
a person	Who?
a number or amount	How many?/How much?
a choice	Which?
a time	When?
a place	Where?

Table 2.3   Formal and Informal Outline Formats

Formal Outline	Informal Outline with Dashes	Informal Outline with Symbol or Print Differences
I. EXAMPLES OF STRESSORS	EXAMPLES OF STRESSORS	EXAMPLES OF STRESSORS
A. Physical	Physical	Physical
1. Injury	—Injury	• Injury
2. Exertion	—Exertion	• Exertion
3. Bacteria	—Bacteria	• Bacteria
4. Heat/cold	—Heat/cold	• Heat/cold
5. Sound	—Sound	• Sound
B. Psychosocial	Psychosocial	Psychosocial
1. Spouse's death	—Spouse's death	• Spouse's death
2. Job change	—Job change	• Job change
3. Divorce	—Divorce	• Divorce
4. Financial change	—Financial change	• Financial Change

Outlines can be in formal or informal formats (see Table 2.3). The formal format uses Roman numerals (I, II, III) placed on the left side of the page or margin to note major concepts. You indent ideas that support the major concepts. You indicate these secondary points by capital letters. You show lesser ideas, or supporting details with indented Arabic numerals (1, 2, 3). You note details that refer to these third-level facts with lowercase letters (a, b, c).

Informal outlines look much like formal outlines. The key difference is that they don't follow the Roman and Arabic alphanumeric format. Instead, you indent lines or use other symbols to identify major and minor points. The purpose of the outline is to organize ideas, and the formality of the outline adds little to understanding. Informal outlines are just as useful as formal outlines.

Organizing Through Mapping

Maps provide a quick means for determining the plan of a chapter. They form pictures that show relationships among concepts. In addition, they express patterns of thought. You sketch a map by using headings and subheadings in a combination boxed-branching format (see Table 2.4 and Figure 2.2). You place each question you created from major headings in separate boxes horizontally (from left to right) in the order in which they appear in the chapter. You then arrange questions about subheadings in a branching formation within the box.

Table 2.4   Steps in Constructing a Chapter Map

---

1. Turn a sheet of paper horizontally.
2. Change the first major heading into a question and write it in the top left corner.
3. Change the second-level headings into questions and write them underneath the major heading with lines showing their relationship to the major heading.
4. Change the third-level headings, if any, into questions and write them underneath the appropriate second-level heading.
5. Continue the pattern until you come to the next major heading.
6. Repeat the process until the end of the chapter.

Figure 2.2   Example of a Question Chapter Map

Step 1

Step 2

Understanding the texts you read

Step 3

Understanding the texts you read
Previewing texts to set reading goals

Step 4

Understanding the texts you read
Previewing texts to set reading goals

Examining the authors'   Organizing   Previewing
organizational plan   course content   process
                              to set reading goals

Steps 5–6

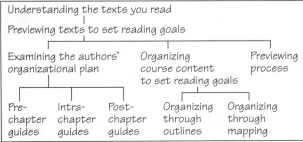

Understanding the texts you read
Previewing texts to set reading goals

Examining the authors'   Organizing   Previewing
organizational plan   course content   process
                              to set reading goals

Pre-   Intra-   Post-   Organizing   Organizing
chapter   chapter   chapter   through   through
guides   guides   guides   outlines   mapping

COOPERATIVE LEARNING ACTIVITY   READING STRATEGIES FOR GROUPS

An important phase of reading and learning information is monitoring. This stage helps you determine when you know information or when you need to reflect and review. However, many students lack the self-awareness to differentiate between when they know information and when they don't know it. The following cooperative learning strategy helps you learn to monitor yourself as well as practice summarization and memory skills. This strategy incorporates visual, verbal, and aural components to help you master text information. It provides group members with opportunities to see how others identify, organize, and learn important information.

The following steps, based on cooperative learning instructions (Larson and Dansereau, 1986), can be used in your in-class study group:

1. Select and study a limited amount of text information. Initially, or when reading complex or unfamiliar information, this might be as little as a section introduced by a minor subheading. It never should be more than two or three pages.

2. Each group member should practice appropriate marking and labeling strategies in reading the information.

3. Members continue to study and reflect on the information until everyone has completed the task.

4. Select one person to recall and summarize the information *without looking at the text*. That person should include important terms and ideas in the summary, describing mnemonic devices, analogies, charts, drawings, or other visual aids that reinforce and clarify information.

5. As the recaller summarizes information, group members *using their texts* check the accuracy and completeness of the summary. Group members correct errors and supply or elaborate on information following the summary, again using mnemonic devices (see Chapter 5), analogies, charts, drawings, or other visual aids to reinforce and clarify information.

6. The group then discusses the information, continues to clarify information, and suggests ways to consider and remember concepts.

7. During discussion, each person should note important information, terms, visuals, or other information for later individual study.

8. Repeat the process with another member of the group serving as the recaller until all the information has been studied or all the members have had the opportunity to serve as recallers. To be most effective, group members need to actively facilitate everyone's understanding through questioning, elaborating, and otherwise amplifying information.

Application

Using the same text material, compare notes with other groups in the class, focusing on how others identify important information and facilitate learning.

The Previewing Process

Previewing begins the process of actively learning the information in a text chapter. Your map or outline provides you with the basics for understanding a chapter's content. The previewing process provides the additional details.

Much like a trip to a new place, your trip through new information can be difficult. Consider the role of a travel agent. He or she guides your travel by suggesting places you might like to visit, stay, and eat. You receive an itinerary—a plan of action so that you do not forget where you're going or what you're supposed to do when you get there. The previewing process forms (see Table 2.5) your itinerary for learning.

By learning this process, you become a more expert reader—one who approaches a variety of texts with a plan for learning their information. Like other processes, previewing requires conscious effort and practice before you fully absorb it. Once you do so, you'll find you can do many of its steps in your head. Until then, you need to write your responses. Writing focuses your attention on the process and ensures that you become an active and conscious reader. Exercises 2.2 and 2.3 provide practice constructing chapter outlines.

Table 2.5   A Plan for Previewing Texts

1. Read the title. What is the chapter about? What do you already know about this topic? Write this title on the top of a blank sheet of paper.

2. Read the introduction or first paragraph. It often contains the main idea. Summarize the main idea in a sentence and write it under the title. Leave space for an additional sentence to follow.

3. Read the objectives or other prechapter guides.

4. As you read the major headings, change each one into a goal-setting question. Write each major heading question as a major heading of a chapter outline or map. Write each subheading question as a minor heading or detail of a chapter outline or map.

5. Note all typographical aids (boldface, italics, underlining, color, type size or style). In the body of the text, highlight these important terms. When found in margins, typographical aids may outline important facts. List these facts under the corresponding headings and subheadings on your outline or map.

6. Examine accompanying charts and pictures. Visual aids usually summarize or emphasize information.

7. Read the summary or last paragraph to confirm your understanding of the main points or conclusions. Create a sentence that summarizes the main idea of the summary and write it under your sentence that summarized the introductory paragraph.

Exercise 2.2   Using Sample Chapter 6, "The Study of Humanity," construct a chapter question outline or map.

Exercise 2.3   Construct a chapter question outline or map for one of the two chapters you used in Exercise 2.1.

Smart Review 2.1

Check your understanding of the preceding section by answering the following on a separate sheet of paper or in your journal:

1. Explain how prechapter, intrachapter, and postchapter guides help you identify an author's organizational plan.
2. How does organizing text content help you set reading goals?
3. What's the difference between outlining and mapping information?
4. Using Sample Chapter 6, "The Study of Humanity," identify the items you would examine in previewing.

READING YOUR TEXT

> *IS FORBIDDEN TO STEAL TOWELS,*
> *PLEASE IF YOU ARE NOT PERSON*
> *TO DO SUCH IS PLEASE TO NOT*
> *READ NOTICE*

—found in a Tokyo hotel
John-Roger and Peter McWilliams (1991)

The complexity of the English language often results in translation errors like the one shown in the sign above. Even you, as a regular user of English, may have difficulty when you face a new and unfamiliar subject. You suddenly realize that reading a text and translating its meaning requires more than you might expect. This forces you to examine the vocabulary of the text and to use a plan for remembering what you read.

Vocabulary

> Knowing that language was the key to acceptance, they pored over their English books, struggling with new sounds, new words, and new rules of grammar. It was difficult. Many English words wouldn't translate into Hungarian, because Hungarian was a derivative language, one in which various ideas and nuances were expressed by complicated root-word modifications. English had prepositions, which in Hungarian were simply suffixes. In English, accent varied according to each word. In Hungarian, the first syllable always received the greatest stress. Hungarian had diacritical marks to aid pronunciation. English did not. English had silent letters. Hungarian did not.

SOURCE: Mortman, D. (1991). *The Wild Rose.* New York: Bantam Books, page 159

Learning a new language is almost always a struggle, whether it's English, French, or the vocabulary in a new course. Such words might be part of your text's **general vocabulary** (common words); on the other hand, both **technical vocabulary** (terms specific to a particular subject) and **specialized vocabulary** (common terms that possess a specific meaning in a particular subject) comprise words whose meanings need to be deciphered. Typographical aids often identify specialized or technical terms that authors consider difficult. Examples of the different kinds of vocabulary, and of typographical aids (from Sample Chapter 6, "The Study of Humanity") appear in Table 2.6.

Using Context Clues

Consider the word *set.* In *The Mother Tongue: The English Language and How It Got That Way,* Bill Bryson (1990) says that it takes 60,000 words in the *Oxford English Dictionary* to provide all the meanings of *set.* It has 58 different meanings as a noun, 126 as a verb, and ten as a participle adjective. Without context clues (or the surroundings of a word), you cannot know which meaning you need. *Set* might refer to a tennis match, a group of numbers, a collection, or an established price. Consider the word *set* again, this time in context: "After I bought a new racquet and took lessons, I improved both my serve

Table 2.6	Examples of Vocabulary from Sample Chapter 6, "The Study of Humanity"
General Vocabulary	reverently, contemporary, ecology, espoused
Technical Vocabulary	paleoanthropology, primatologists, ethnology, ethnocentrism
Specialized Vocabulary	discipline, scope, origins, diversity, fieldwork, relativity, applied, culture
Typographical Aids	boldface, italics

and my backhand; as a result, I won two of three *sets* in the last game." You know *set* refers to a tennis game because of the words that surround it. Now consider the word *set* again in context: *"God Is an Englishman* is the first of a *set* (the first of three volumes in the group)." While you may not have known this meaning of *set,* the context clues in the sentence provide the meaning for you. *Set* in the context of different content areas appears in Table 2.7.

Even if English isn't your best subject, your knowledge of the English language helps you figure out context clues. You understand sentence structure and punctuation. This knowledge provides some information about the word's meaning. It also helps you search through your vocabulary and identify words that might be similar in meaning to the unknown word.

Using context involves using clues in a sentence or paragraph to predict the meaning of an unknown word. Thus, context comes in two forms. One, a **background-based context,** depends on what you know about language and the world to detect meaning. When you use background-based context, you infer meanings for unknown words. The second, **text-based context,**

Table 2.7   *Set* **in Content Area Contexts**

Content areas	Definition
Agriculture	To sit on eggs to hatch them
Art	To make a color fast
Botany	To form fruit in the blossom
Business	To record on paper
Criminal justice	To establish a law or penalty
Geography	To fix boundaries
Health	To fix into normal position
Home economics	To put aside dough to rise
	To place tableware for dining
	To allow gelatin to harden
Industrial technology	To put a moveable part of a machine in place
Journalism	To compose type
	To put a manuscript into type
Literature	A collection of literary works
Math	A group of things
Music	To write (or fit) words to music
Physical education	To prepare to begin a game or other activity
	A group of six or more tennis games
Psychology	A tendency or inclination
Theater	The constructed scenery for a play
	A place in a given locale

uses punctuation and other clues in a sentence to signal meanings of unknown words.

To use background-based context, use your understanding of the world and of language to examine key words surrounding the unknown term. Thus, when meanings of unknown words are not directly stated, you derive their meanings by drawing conclusions. For example, consider the term *just desert* in the paragraph below:

> **A more current version of retribution theory exists in the concept of *just desert*. Whereas the two positions seems almost identical, desert appears to be a less threatening term than retribution, which often has been closely linked with revenge,**

Although the text fails to define *just desert* or provide other stated clues, the words *retribution* and *revenge* let you know *just desert* refers to some sort of punishment. The words *less threatening* suggest that this punishment will not be spiteful or unjust. Thus, you determine that the definition of *just desert* is deserved punishment.

How did you know *desert* concerned punishment and not sunparched land? You determine this by **connotation,** a specialized environment for background-based context that is highly related to world knowledge and emotion. It indirectly affects your definition of a new word because your connotations of surrounding words color your perception. For example, consider the sentence "The speech coach helped actors perfect standard speech, specializing in southern *elisions.*" From the sentence, you know that *elisions* concerns southern speech patterns. Deciding whether this is a pattern to keep or to avoid depends on your attitudes and experiences. Connotation, then, is your interpretation of what a word means.

Other types of background-based context (see Table 2.8) require you to use background knowledge to infer meaning. Such clues indicate both synonymous (comparison and example context clues) and anonymous (contrast context clues) relationships among ideas. To find the meanings of words from comparisons or examples, you first identify the definition of the word(s) you know. Then you infer that the unknown word is similar to that of the known word(s). Contrast clues also require you to recognize the definition of one word in the sentence. You then infer that this meaning is dissimilar to or opposite of the word you do not know. Thus, almost by default, you have the definition you need.

Example clues offer an unusual challenge in that they require you to identify what the word has in common with the other examples. For instance, suppose you are determining the meaning of *unguent* in the sentence that follows: "Doctors often suggest *unguents,* such as Ben Gay and Deep Heat, to the

---

Table 2.8   **Examples of Background-Based Context Clues**

Type	Stated Clues	Example(s)
Comparison	similarly, both, as well as, likewise, in addition	1
Contrast	however, on the other hand, on the contrary, while, but, instead of, although, whereas, nevertheless, yet	2
Example	such as, like, e.g., for example, other, that is	3

1. If they are not eligible for some sort of community supervision program because of the seriousness of their crimes, felons usually are *incarcerated* in state or federal prisons. *Misdemeanants* are housed in county jails or reformatories. In addition, there exists a wide variety of community-based correctional institutions and half-way houses.

   Both *shock probation* and *split sentences* systems operate under the belief that the shock of a prison stay will jolt the offender into conventional behavior.

2. Some defense attorneys offer *private counsel,* but the majority are appointed and paid for by the state.

   Cerebral allergies cause an excessive reaction of the brain, whereas *neuro-allergies* affect the nervous system.

3. For one thing, members often manifest *short-run hedonism.* That is, they live for today and let tomorrow take care of itself.

   The culture of poverty is marked by apathy, cynicism, helplessness, and mistrust of *social institutions,* such as schools, government agencies, and the police.

SOURCE: Reprinted with permission from *Criminology,* 3E by Siegel, L. J.; © 1989 by West Publishing Company. All rights reserved.

elderly because they lessen the pain of arthritis." What do *Ben Gay* and *Deep Heat* have in common? They are both medicated creams. You infer, then, that *unguent* means medicated cream.

Text-based context clues (punctuation and key words) signal the meanings of unknown words through stated clues (see Table 2.9). For example, punctuation clues usually identify **appositives** (words that define the words they follow). Definition clues link terms with other words which describe or rename the terms. Thus, in text-based context, you find the definitions of difficult terms directly stated. You often see examples of text-based context clues in textbooks, because authors realize certain technical and specialized terms are new to you.

The stated, literal meaning of a term, derived through text-based context clues, is its denotation. Although a specialized term has a specific denotation within a subject area, its connotations may vary. For example, consider the following sentence: "Because the suspect was a *minor* (under legal age), he

Table 2.9   Types of Text-Based Context Clues

Type	Stated Clues	Example(s)
Punctuation	Commas . . . Parentheses () Dashes — Brackets [ ]	1
Definition	is, was, were, are, refers to, involves, seems, is called, i.e., which means, resembles, means	2

1. Disposition usually involves either a fine, a term of community supervision *(probation),* a period of incarceration in a penal institution, or some combination of the above.

   According to Akers, people learn social behavior by *operant conditioning,* behavior controlled by stimuli that follow the behavior.

   The content of the law, therefore, may create a clash between conventional, middle-class rules and splinter groups such as ethnic and racial minorities, who maintain their own set of *conduct norms*—rules governing the day-to-day living conditions within these subcultures.

2. *Voluntary manslaughter* refers to a killing committed in the heat of passion or during a sudden quarrel considered to have provided sufficient provocation to produce violence; while intent may be present, malice is not.

   Subcultures are groups of like-minded individuals who share similar ideas and values and who bond together for support, defense, and mutual need.

   Containment involves segregation of deviants into isolated geographic areas so that they can easily be controlled—for example by creating a ghetto.

was not arrested as an adult." The denotation of *minor* is "under legal age"; its connotations vary, however, with personal, governmental, or legal perceptions of physical maturity.

Using Structural Analysis

Latin and Greek word parts (**affixes** and roots) form the basis of more than 70 percent of all English words. Using knowledge of these parts to define unknown terms helps you in a number of ways. First, it gives you confidence. When faced with an overwhelming number of new terms in a class, you find you at least recognize parts of them. This helps you approximate meaning. As a result, you can view a list of terms knowing that you have some information on which to build learning. Because you relate new words with those you already know, you recall meanings more easily. Finally, knowing word parts often helps you spell new terms correctly.

Structural analysis involves splitting words into parts to discover meaning. Parts of words provide essential meaning—these are called bases, or **roots.** Some bases, used alone, are words. Others must be combined with other bases and/or affixes **(prefixes** and **suffixes).** Prefixes, suffixes, and bases can be used in different combinations. Prefixes precede a base and affect meaning. Suffixes follow a base and determine part of speech as well as contribute to meaning. For example, consider the word *immobilized* in the following sentence: "During civil rights demonstrations, the police often *immobilized* rowdy participants." What does *immobilized* mean? By examining its parts, you determine its meaning—the prefix *im* means *not,* the base *mobil* means *moveable,* and the suffix *ize* means *to make.* The meaning of *immobilized,* then, is "made not moveable."

You can learn word parts in various ways. Memorizing is less effective than relating the bases and affixes to words or subjects you know. Tables 2.10, 2.11, 2.12, and 2.13 list word parts, their meanings, and examples organized by content areas. Exercises 2.4 and 2.5 provide practice with word parts.

Table 2.10   List of Humanities Word Parts and Their Meanings

Word Part and Meaning	Example	Personal Example
Art		
1. tact, tang—touch	tactile	_____
2. form—feel by touching	transform	_____
3. arc—bow or curve	arch	_____
4. art—skill	artisan	_____
5. struct—build or arrange	construct	_____
6. tex—weave	texture	_____
Music		
1. son, sono, sona—sound	resonant	_____
2. phon—sound	phonograph	_____
3. aud, audit—hear	audible	_____
English		
1. voc, vok—call or voice	vocal	_____
2. nounce, nunci—voice, declare	pronounce	_____
3. dict—speak or tell	diction	_____
4. locu, loqu—speak or talk	eloquence	_____
5. nym—name	synonym	_____
6. leg, lect—read, spoken	lecture	_____
7. log—work, speech	monologue	_____
8. scrib, script—write	postscript	_____

Table 2.11   List of Mathematical Word Parts and Their Meanings

Word Part and Meaning	Example	Personal Example
1. angle, angul—corner	triangle	_____
2. gon—angle	octagon	_____
3. lateral—side	equilateral	_____
4. quadr, quartus, quarter, quatr—four	quarter	_____
5. kilo—one thousand	kilogram	_____
6. multi—many	multiply	_____
7. numer—number	numeral	_____
8. cent—one hundred	percentage	_____
9. uni—one	unilinear	_____
10. bi—two	bilateral	_____
11. di, du—two	disect	_____
12. dec—ten	decade	_____
13. tri—three	triangle	_____
14. milli—one thousandth	millimeter	_____
15. ord—row or tank	ordinal	_____
16. equ—equal	equilateral	_____
17. struct—build or arrange	construct	_____

Table 2.12   List of Science Word Parts and Their Meanings

Word Part and Meaning	Example	Personal Example
General Science		
1. ology—study of	biology	_____
2. scope—see	telescope	_____
3. meter—measure	barometer	_____
Astronomy		
1. stella-star	constellation	_____
2. astro, aster—star	astronomy	_____
3. aer, aero—air	aerobic	_____
Chemistry		
1. solv, solu—loose	dissolve	_____
2. lysis—dissolving	analysis	_____

(continues)

Table 2.12   *Continued*

Word Part and Meaning	Example	Personal Example
3. hydr, hydro—water	hydrogen	_____
4. flag, flam—blaze or burn	conflagration	_____

Geology

Word Part and Meaning	Example	Personal Example
1. aqua, aqui—water	aquatic	_____
2. cav—hallow	excavate	_____
3. lith—stone	monolith	_____

Physics

Word Part and Meaning	Example	Personal Example
1. tele—far	telegraph	_____
2. ject—throw	projectile	_____
3. lev—raise	leverage	_____
4. mot, mov—move	motion	_____
5. flect, flex—bend or turn	reflex	_____
6. grad, gress—move by steps	gradient	_____
7. therm—heat	thermal	_____
8. vers, vert—turn	convert	_____
9. cand—glow, light	incandescent	_____
10. photo—light	photosynthesis	_____
11. micro—small	microscope	_____
12. macro—large or long	macrocosm	_____
13. rad, ray—ray	radiant	_____
14. vac, vacu—empty	vacuum	_____
15. cycl—circle or wheel	kilocycle	_____
16. tract—pull or drag	traction	_____
17. pel, pul—push	repel	_____
18. flu, flux—flow	fluid	_____

Biology, Zoology, Botany

Word Part and Meaning	Example	Personal Example
1. carn—flesh	carnivore	_____
2. bio—living	biology	_____
3. viv, vit—life	vitamin	_____
4. ped, pod—foot	anthropod	_____
5. ocu, opt—eye	optic	_____
6. corp—body	corpuscle	_____
7. spir, spire—breathe	respiration	_____
8. derm—skin	epidermis	_____
9. hema, hemo, emia, hemia—blood	anemic	_____
10. ov—egg	ovulate	_____

Table 2.13   List of Social Science Word Parts and Their Meanings

Word Part and Meaning	Example	Personal Example
1. neo—new	neolithic	_____
2. ann, enn—year	biennial	_____
3. temp—time	contemporary	_____
4. post—after	postwar	_____
5. pre—before	prehistoric	_____
6. chrono—time	chronological	_____
7. jus, jud, jur—law or right	judicial	_____
8. demo—people	democracy	_____
9. domin—master	dominion	_____
10. reg—royal, rule	regiment	_____
11. vice—second in command, in place of	vice-general	_____
12. popul—people	populate	_____

Geography

1. terra—earth	territory	_____
2. geo—earth	geography	_____
3. port—carry	export	_____
4. loc—place	locality	_____

Psychology, Sociology, Anthropology

1. nat—born	natural	_____
2. greg—gather, group	segregate	_____
3. phil—love	philosophy	_____
4. phob—fear	phobia	_____
5. fid—faithful	confidence	_____
6. sens, sent—feelings	sentiment	_____
7. mania—(literally, mad or crazy) mental illness	kleptomania	_____
8. path—suffering, feeling	sympathy	_____
9. psych—soul or mind	psychology	_____
10. mnem, memor, mem—memory	amnesia	_____
11. cogn—know	cognition	_____
12. homa, homo, homi—man, human	Homo sapiens	_____

(continues)

Table 2.13   *Continued*

Word Part and Meaning	Example	Personal Example
13. anthro—man, human	anthropology	_____
14. hib, hab—live	habitat	_____
15. auto—self	autonomy	_____
16. hetero—different	heterosexual	_____
17. homo—same	homosexual	_____
18. ben, bene—good	benign	_____
19. mal—bad	malignant	_____

Exercise 2.4   Examine Tables 2.10 through 2.13. Provide your own example of another word for each of the word parts on the blank lines in the tables.

Exercise 2.5   On a separate sheet of paper or in your journal, define the following boldfaced terms (from Sample Chapter 6, "The Study of Humanity") from context. Words appear in the exercise in the same order as in the chapter. Circle **T** if you derived the meaning from text-based context. Circle **B** if you used background-based context.

1.	physical (biological) anthropology	T	B
2.	paleoanthropologists	T	B
3.	primatologists	T	B
4.	archaeology	T	B
5.	prehistoric archaeology	T	B
6.	cultural anthropology	T	B
7.	anthropological linguistics	T	B
8.	cultural resource management	T	B
9.	contract anthropology	T	B
10.	medical anthropology	T	B
11.	developmental anthropology	T	B
12.	educational anthropology	T	B
13.	holistic perspective	T	B
14.	comparative perspective	T	B
15.	ethnocentrism	T	B

THINKING CRITICALLY
Consider general, specialized, and technical vocabularies. How are they alike? How are they different? How does each relate to the others? On a separate sheet of paper or in your journal, create a drawing that shows the relationships among general, specialized, and technical vocabularies.

Common Organizational Patterns in Texts

Authors either consciously or unconsciously organize information into a pattern before presenting it. Often, how well you understand depends on how well they organize. For example, if authors present information in a random or confusing way, comprehension falters. On the other hand, authors facilitate comprehension by making a piece's structure very clear. Your goal, then, is to identify the organizational pattern used in a piece of text. Recognizing this pattern helps locate main ideas, identify supporting details and make connections among sections of the text. One caution: authors sometimes mix patterns to present information. Patterns are not always found in their truest forms.

Tables 2.14, 2.15, and 2.16 contain common organizational patterns listed by content areas in which they are most often found. Notice that some patterns are found in more than one subject area.

Marking and Labeling Your Text

When you study, you certainly don't want to have to slow down and reread an entire chapter or set of chapters to remember the material in them. What you want to do is quickly recall what you read the first time. Text marking and labeling provides ways for you to trigger your memory.

Table 2.14   Text Patterns in Math

---

1. **Concept development:** Concept is identified by color, type style, boldface, or italics and usually followed by a sample problem that illustrates it.

2. **Principle development:** Concept is identified by color, type style, boldface, or italics and usually followed by a set of problems that indicate how a basic law, postulate, or theorem is derived.

3. **Problem-solving:** Standard pattern for word problems, presents a problem and asks for a solution.

SOURCE: Adapted from Devine, T. G. (1987). *Teaching Study Skills.* Boston: Allyn & Bacon.

Text Marking: What's Important?

Text marking sounds simple. You find important information and mark it. However, nothing is that simple. Text marking requires a systematic approach.

First, if you previewed and asked goal-setting questions, what you mark should answer your questions. Thus, you mark the information that highlights terms and main ideas.

Table 2.15   Text Patterns in Science

---

1. **Enumeration:** The topic is provided and explained through a list of traits, features, or descriptions.
2. **Classification:** The topic is divided into two or more parts with each part containing its own subsections.
3. **Generalization:** A principle, hypothesis, or conclusion is stated and supported with examples and details.
4. **Problem-solution:** This takes one of four forms: (1) problem and solution are clearly stated; (2) problem is clearly stated with clearly stated hypothetical solutions; (3) problem is clearly stated with no solutions; (4) neither problem nor solution is given. The pattern must be inferred.
5. **Sequence:** Steps in a process or an experiment are explained.
6. **Cause and effect:** A description of an event follows or precedes reasons or causes.

SOURCE: Adapted from Devine, T. G. (1987). *Teaching Study Skills,* Boston: Allyn & Bacon.

Table 2.16   Text Patterns in Social Sciences and Humanities

---

1. **Enumeration:** The topic is provided and explained through a list of traits, features, or descriptions.
2. **Generalization:** A principle, hypothesis, or conclusion is stated and supported with examples and details.
3. **Time:** A list of related events or items is organized in the order the events or items occurred. Sometimes authors begin with one time period and then move either forward or backward in time to discuss related events.
4. **Climax:** Items or events are arranged in a specific way (that is, from least to most important, poorest to best, back to front, smallest to largest, and so on) but are presented in another order.
5. **Comparison and contrast:** Author describes similarities or dissimilarities among two or more people, ideas, or objects.
6. **Cause and effect:** A description of an event follows or precedes its reasons or causes.

SOURCE: Adapted from Devine, T. G. (1987). *Teaching Study Skills,* Boston: Allyn & Bacon.

*"If you buy the jumbo page highlighter,
you can mark a whole page at a time!"*

Second, you might include other details that support your response. These could be the steps in a sequence or other kinds of lists, reasons, conclusions, and so on. To know which and what kind of details to mark, examine returned tests. For example, suppose many test questions ask about sequences of events or causes and effects. When studying future chapters, you mark such points. Critical evaluation of lecture content also provides this information. For example, class discussions of major composers might compare and contrast their works. In reading future chapters, you highlight such information.

Third, what you mark depends on how much you already know about the topic. Consider what might happen if you were studying about oceans. If you're from Florida, you'd probably mark less. This is because you might already know some of the information. In contrast, if you're from Nebraska, you may know less about oceans and need to mark more. Generally, the less you know about a subject, the more information you mark. The more you know about a subject, the less information you mark.

Fourth, you need to be sure that marking text is done with thought. For example, consider the first example in Example 2.1. Here, the student marked too much information for study. Remember that the purpose of text marking is to set important information apart from the unimportant. If you habitually mark every word you read, you accomplish nothing. Even if you know nothing about a subject, marking more than one-half of the information defeats your purpose.

Example 2.1   Overmarking Text

Organizing Course Content to Set Reading Goals

Think again about how you best learn information (see Chapter 1). Outlines and maps help you predict and organize information while surveying. This is particularly true if you rephrase headings and subheadings into questions or connect chapter titles with headings and subheadings to questions. Questions require you to look for answers and, thus, make reading more active. You read to answer *what, how, when, who, which, where,* and *why* (see Table 2.3). When previewing, you will normally be looking for main ideas. Thus, *why, how,* and *what* questions will form the basis of your previewing outline. Question outlines and maps make previewing less covert and more concrete. They help set goals for reading.

Example 2.2   Undermarking Text

Organizing Course Content to Set Reading Goals

Think again about how you best learn information (see Chapter 1). Outlines and maps help you predict and organize information while surveying. This is particularly true if you rephrase headings and subheadings into questions or connect chapter titles with headings and subheadings to questions. Questions require you to look for answers and, thus, make reading more active. You read to answer *what, how, when, who, which, where,* and *why* (see Table 2.3). When previewing, you will normally be looking for main ideas. Thus, *why, how,* and *what* questions will form the basis of your previewing outline. Question outlines and maps make previewing less covert and more concrete. They help set goals for reading.

Now consider the text in Example 2.2. Here, the student marked too little information. Perhaps the student already feels confident about the information. Undermarking sometimes signals a lack of attention, poor understanding, or not knowing what sort of information to mark. Example 2.3 shows a better example of text marking.

Labeling Main Ideas and Details

Imagine you visit a city for the first time. You lose your way and stop to ask directions to your hotel. A friendly person gets a map for you and highlights the route you should take. You start once more. However, when you look at the map, you find no names for streets, buildings, or other locations. You may finally arrive at your hotel, but it will involve much effort.

Example 2.3   Appropriately Marking Text

Organizing Course Content to Set Reading Goals

Think again about how you best learn information (see Chapter 1). Outlines and maps help you predict and organize information while surveying. This is particularly true if you rephrase headings and subheadings into questions or connect chapter titles with headings and subheadings to questions. Questions require you to look for answers and, thus, make reading more active. You read to answer *what, how, when, who, which, where,* and *why* (see Table 2.3). When previewing, you will normally be looking for main ideas. Thus, *why, how,* and *what* questions will form the basis of your previewing outline. Question outlines and maps make previewing less covert and more concrete. They help set goals for reading.

Example 2.4   Text Marking and Labeling

Organizing Course Content to Set Reading Goals

Stated Information:
  Outlines/Maps = ways to organize info

Translation:
  Main Ideas = why, how, what

Application:
  maps/outlines also used for test preparation??

Think again about how you best learn information (see Chapter 1). Outlines and maps help you predict and organize information while surveying. This is particularly true if you rephrase headings and subheadings into questions or connect chapter titles with headings and subheadings to questions. Questions require you to look for answers and, thus, make reading more active. You read to answer *what, how, when, who, which, where,* and *why* (see Table 2.3). When previewing, you will normally be looking for main ideas. Thus, *why, how,* and *what* questions will form the basis of your previewing outline. Question outlines and maps make previewing less covert and more concrete. They help set goals for reading.

Much the same problem occurs in text marking. Many students read and mark information only to find themselves somewhat lost when they have to study. They then have to reconstruct the **main ideas** of their texts, and that takes effort.

Consider again the text marked in Example 2.3. Most students would agree that it appears to be appropriately marked. The answers to the purpose-setting question "How can I organize course content to set reading goals?" ranges across the section. Reviewing for a test several weeks later, however, you find you have forgotten how the information relates. You would need to reread most of what you marked to find the main ideas. Text

SMART SITES   **Using the Web to Create Outlines and Maps**

A wealth of information related to the topics in this chapter is available on the World Wide Web. For this exercise, access the Inspiration Web site at http://www.inspiration.com (for the most up-to-date URLs, go to http://csuccess.wadsworth.com) and download a demo copy of the program. Type in the outline from Sample Chapter 1 and convert to a map. Explore ways in which you can modify or rearrange the pieces of the map. On a separate sheet of paper or in your journal, describe which version you prefer—outline or map. Explain how the version you chose supports the results of your learning style preferences.

labeling—in conjunction with text marking—helps you identify the main ideas you need to study (see Example 2.4).

Text labeling involves several steps. First, you read and mark a section of your text. Second, you look for patterns and key concepts. Third, you think of an appropriate word or brief phrase that describes what you found. This is the main idea of the section. Fourth, you write this word or phrase in the margin. You also include notes about how or what to study. Finally, you create a summary sentence that answers the section's purpose-setting question. You write it in the margin next to the appropriate heading or subheading or on your map or outline under the appropriate question.

Text labels serve a variety of purposes. They highlight information directly stated in the text. Labels force you to restate, or translate, information into your words. You also use them to comment on information within the text. Through text labels, you draw conclusions and make generalizations. You can also use them to show how information could be applied in different situations. Finally, text labels help you analyze information and synthesize it for effective learning. Table 2.17 shows various purposes for and examples of text labels. A list of additional simple shorthand symbols and their meanings appears in Table 2.18.

Text labels aid your memory of text information in several ways. First, rereading and locating key points reinforces your preview and first reading of the chapter. Second, creating the labels helps you put information into your own words. Third, the process of creating labels and physically writing them aids memory. The thought and action involved in these processes lock the content in your mind.

Most important, text labels help you prepare for exams. For example, how would you use the labels to study? First, you examine the information in the label. Then you cover it and try to recall the differences. If you have difficulty, you uncover the label and practice recalling the details it condenses. If the information remains unclear, you reread marked information. Exercise 2.6 provides practice marking and labeling text.

Table 2.17   Types, Purposes, and Examples of Text Labels

Purpose	Type	Example
directly stated information	list or sequence quotation date person place accomplishment/event	Outlines/Maps (ways to organize) information Mapping process
translation (restated information)	restate problem explanation description	Main Ideas (why, how, what)
comment	agree/disagree unclear possible test question bias/propaganda	Good idea
conclude or generalize	group or classify information generalize from details to main idea summarize	Heading questions (focus attention)
apply	identify other uses, situations, and so on, based on background knowledge	Maps/outlines also used for test preparation
analysis	relationships (for example, cause/effect) comparisons/contrasts	Comparison/contrast of outline formats
synthesis	combine or condense information	Maps (for right-brain learning) Outlines (for left-brain learning)

THINKING CRITICALLY

On a separate sheet of paper or in your journal, respond to the following: The more guides and cues an author includes in a text, the more considerate that author is of the reader. How do considerate and inconsiderate texts affect your ability to mark and label information?

Table 2.18   Examples of Shorthand Symbols for Text Labeling

Symbol	Meaning
Ex	example or experiment
FOR	formula
Conc	conclusion
MI	main idea
! or *	important information
→	results, leads to, steps in a sequence
(1), (2), (3)	number and label points
circled words	summarizes process
?	disagree or unclear
TERM	important concept
SUM	summary
{ }	indicates certain pieces of information relate
OPIN	author's opinion, rather than fact

Exercise 2.6   Read, mark, and label Sample Chapter 6, "The Study of Humanity."

Smart Review 2.2

Check your understanding of the preceding section by answering the following on a separate sheet of paper or in your journal:

1. How can context and structural analysis improve your understanding and recall of new terms in a course?

2. How do text patterns facilitate understanding? Provide an example from Sample Chapter 6, "The Study of Humanity."

3. Create a chart that compares and contrasts marking a text, labeling a text, marking and labeling a text, and reading without marking or labeling.

CHECKING YOUR UNDERSTANDING

Grades form the most telling result of your ability to understand your text. Unfortunately, by the time you get your grades, it's too late to improve them. Checking your understanding as you read allows you to make adjustments while there's still time. Constant and active watchfulness helps you determine when you know information or when you need to reflect and review. This requires sufficient self-awareness to judge your grasp of information in terms of Bloom's taxonomy (see Chapter 1). For example, can you merely recall the information? Can you restate it? Do you know how it relates to other ideas? Can you apply it? How would you analyze the information? Could you use it to synthesize a new concept? What judgments can you make about it? Text labeling increases critical thinking because you interact with the text at different levels.

Some readers think the goal of studying is to complete a chapter, whether they know anything after they finish reading it or not. Answering purpose-setting questions helps you avoid this unproductive habit. If, at the end of reading a section of text, you can answer the question you posed, continue reading. If you cannot answer your question, your inability to do so may be traced to two general problems. Either you failed to ask the right question, or you failed to understand the author's words. You decide where the problem lies by looking at your question in light of the information. Does the content answer your question? If not, you formed the wrong question.

Your skill in developing purpose-setting questions improves with practice. Questioning becomes easier when you study with someone. This helps you see how others develop questions and find answers. You can also practice questioning by using a tape recorder. First, you record your questions. Then you read and record your answers. When you play your tape, see if your questions were appropriate and if your responses answered the questions correctly. Another way to practice involves writing your questions on index cards. Again, after reading, determine if your questions were appropriate. Then, write your answers on the back of the cards.

If you find your questions are inappropriate, you form new questions and reread. If your questions appear to be correct but you cannot answer them, you failed to understand the text. If so, reread carefully, paragraph by paragraph. Look for the main idea in each paragraph. Use context and/or a dictionary or glossary to make sure you understand the words and terms. Noting text patterns also helps you see relationships that were unclear in the first reading. What if you find you still don't understand? Sometimes, you need outside help. You might make an appointment with your instructor to discuss the information. Or you could form a study group to consider course content. Finally, consulting other written materials that present the same ideas in different and/or easier formats often gives you new insights. These materials include articles in popular magazines, encyclopedias, or high school texts. Table 2.19 provides a list of other common comprehension failures as well as the solutions for remedying them.

Table 2.19   Comprehension Monitoring Failures and Solutions

Problems	Solutions
Lack of experience in questioning	Practice with index cards by putting a question on one side and the answer on the other.
	Practice with a tape recorder.
	Practice with a study partner.
	Review types of questioning words.
Lack of concentration	Avoid external distractions.
	Study in short blocks of time over a longer period.
	Use a study system.
	Set learning goals.
Unfamiliar terms	Use context and structural analysis to decode unknown terms.
	Use the text's glossary.
	Find the word in a dictionary or thesaurus.
	Actively consider new terms in context.
Lack of understanding	Reread or skim for main ideas.
	Scan for specific information.
	Verbalize confusing points.
	Paraphrase, summarize, or outline main ideas.
	Consult an alternate source.
	Reset learning goals.
Speed	Adjust speed to purpose.
	Take a speed-reading course.
	Practice with a variety of materials.
	Read recreationally.
Failure to identify text structure	Examine transition words as you reread.
	Outline the paragraph or passage.
Failure to locate main idea	Label the main idea of each paragraph.
	Identify text structure.
	Outline details.
	Summarize the main idea in your own words.
Insufficient background knowledge for understanding	Find alternative source of information.
	Obtain tutoring.
Inability to set appropriate purpose-setting questions	Practice with a tape recorder.
	Practice with a friend.

Evaluating text marking also helps you check understanding. First, if you marked too much, you may fail to separate important from unimportant information. If this often happens, you need to use a pencil to lightly mark information. This allows you the freedom to rethink and erase your notes. If you overmark only on occasion, you can remark text with contrasting ink or highlighter. Second, if you marked too little, you may fail to get enough information to comprehend fully. Thus, you need to reexamine the text and mark more completely. Be sure you label all text markings. This lets you find important information at a glance. Third, if your labels are vague, then reread and relabel your text. Labels should concisely, yet completely, summarize what you've marked. You could identify any two of these three possible errors by monitoring your comprehension.

Smart Review 2.3

Check your understanding of the preceding section by answering the following on a separate sheet of paper or in your journal:

1. What is the value of checking your understanding as you read?
2. Give three examples of ways you monitor comprehension.

COURSE READINGS IN NONTRADITIONAL TEXT FORMATS

Not every course uses a textbook with traditional chapter formats. Some course texts consist of a collection of readings or essays. Students often find such texts confusing because they contain a variety of writing styles and text signals. However, authors usually organize the readings in some systematic way. Previewing helps you determine how the readings and the lecture will fit together.

Collections of articles, portions of chapters from books, examples, study guides, or other nontraditional course readings serve three important purposes. If used in addition to a traditional text, some reinforce information in a text chapter. These may provide extra information about topics briefly discussed in the chapter. They might simplify complex concepts. Others, such as study guides, help you learn text information more easily. Such materials often present more current information. This information may provide new or conflicting points of view on the topic; for example, such materials in a political science

THINKING CRITICALLY

On a separate sheet of paper or in your journal, explain why certain text patterns are found in certain content materials.

course might focus on recent elections. Finally, nontraditional text materials often provide background information. For instance, a psychology chapter about personality generally focuses on major personality theories. Additional readings might also include biographies of the theorists or case studies.

Previewing Nontraditional Text Formats

The format of some nontraditional text readings sometimes parallels that of text chapters. That is, these readings contain headings, subheadings, and summaries. You preview these just as you would preview text chapters (see Table 2.6). On the other hand, often these materials contain no text features to help you locate main points. Here, you use the title and any introductory or summary statements to survey the content. Reading the first sentence of each paragraph also gives you an overview of the material. You may find both patterns in any one collection or set of materials.

Previewing such materials helps you decide how this information relates to a chapter or lecture topic. Putting this connection in writing ensures that you surveyed the reading. Further, it makes reading interactive and provides a record for later study. Then, after reading, you confirm your prediction and revise your statement. When studying, this revision serves as a written summary of what you read.

Marking and Labeling Nontraditional Text Readings

Nontraditional text readings validate, expand, refute, or provide expert insight into text chapter readings. Your judgment of how the nontraditional text reading complements a text is critical to your understanding.

After previewing, you read, mark, and label nontraditional text readings just as you would a text chapter. You use headings and subheadings, if present, to set goals and focus attention. If the reading has no headings to guide you, you use the first sentence of each paragraph or section to identify main ideas and mark accordingly.

Nontraditional text readings require you to read analytically and critically. While you judged chapter information in terms of the text, you judge nontraditional readings in terms of the course as well. You seek the instructor's motive—the reason for including the reading. As you make these judgments, substantiate them by adding notes in the margins. Table 2.20 provides some questions to help you make such determinations.

Table 2.20   Criteria for Evaluating Nontraditional Text Readings

1. Does the reading provide information to help me understand the text or course more easily?

2. Does the reading restate text or lecture information in simpler language? If so, after I have read the nontraditional text reading, can I understand the text or lecture information more easily?

3. Does the reading provide details not included in the text? If so, how do those details relate to the text or lecture?

4. Does the reading provide related information that expands the scope of the text chapter or lecture? If so, can I describe the way in which the text or lecture information has been enhanced?

5. Does the reading provide new or technical information? If so, what is that information, and what is its importance?

6. Does the reading provide points of view different from those supported in the text or the lecture? If so, what are those points of view, and how do they differ?

7. Is the purpose of this material to intrigue, excite, or motivate me? or increase interest in the topic? If so, did it succeed? How well did it succeed?

8. Was this material included to change my point of view? If so, was it successful? Why or why not?

9. Does the reading present research information? If so, what is its purpose and significance?

10. Does the reading contain graphics or analogies that help me understand and remember the text or lecture information more easily? If so, how was this accomplished?

SMART Information 2.1

Using your password for this course, access InfoTrac College Edition on the World Wide Web, and respond to the following questions:

1. Review your response to Question 2 of **SMART Information 1.2** (page 48). Choose one subject from the list related to the content of Sample Chapter 6, "The Study of Humanity." Locate and print any two articles within that subject. Read, mark, and label the articles.

2. Complete the following chart using Table 2.20 to identify pertinent criteria:

Article Title		
Author		
Source		
Purpose (relationship between article and chapter content)		
Pertinent Criteria		

Course Readings in Literary Text

Reading narrative text or poetry in a literature class demands a specialized notetaking process. This process allows you to go beyond simple recall of details to a more complex level of understanding. You will compare, contrast, synthesize, and evaluate text in terms of word choice, figurative language, theme, plot, character, tone, setting, and literary type.

When an instructor assigns literary selections as part of course requirements, they usually outline the purpose for your reading. Such tasks might include summarizing the reading, analyzing character development, or identifying plot. On the other hand, sometimes instructors make assignments without providing needed instructions. When this happens, you may not know which goals to set. After all, narrative text contains no special features to guide your reading. The strategies you use for creating reading goals, marking, and labeling for nontraditional text work equally well for narrative text. Furthermore, Table 2.21 provides guidelines for previewing, reading, and evaluating narrative text.

Tomlinson (1997) created a six-step process for taking notes from literature. Step one suggests that you assign a code letter to each theme, character, and/or concept you need to follow throughout the text. Your second step is to create a directory of your codes either in the front of your book or in your notebook. Consistently using a code to denote a particular concept makes the process simpler and easier. Step three involves your listing the code letters in your notebook, leaving space between letters. In step four, you read your text, placing the appropriate code letter beside relevant information. Your fifth step is to list the page number next to the code number you have already written in your notebook. In step six, the final one, keep a notebook page for each major theme, character, or concept and write a brief summary or make notes about important details. You should also note text page numbers. Example 2.5 contains an example of a notetaking system.

Table 2.21   Questions for Previewing, Reading, and Evaluating Narrative Text

Before Previewing

1. What kind of literature is this? How is it representative of the time period in which it is written? How is it representative of its genre?

2. What can I determine from the title, size of print, illustrations, chapter headings, and opening pages?

3. For what age range is this literary selection appropriate?

4. What interests are reflected in this literary selection?

During Reading

Plot

5. Does the selection tell a good story?

6. Is the plot original and fresh?

7. It is plausible and credible? Is there preparation for the events? Is there a logical series of happenings? Do the happenings have causes and effects?

8. Is there an identifiable climax?

9. How do events build to a climax?

10. Is the plot well constructed?

Setting

11. Where does the action take place?

12. How does the author indicate time period?

13. How does the setting affect the action, characters, or theme?

14. Does the action transcend the setting and have universal implications?

Theme

15. Does the selection have a theme?

16. Is the theme a worthy one?

17. Does the theme emerge naturally from the action or is it stated too obviously?

18. Does the theme overpower the action?

19. Does it avoid moralizing?

(continues)

Table 2.21   *Continued*

Characterization

20. How does the author reveal characters? Through narration? In conversation? By thoughts of others? By thoughts of the character? Through action?

21. Are the characters convincing and credible?

22. Are their strengths and their weaknesses shown?

23. Does the author avoid stereotyping?

24. Is the behavior of the characters consistent with their ages and backgrounds?

25. Has the author shown the causes of character behavior or development?

Style

26. Is the style of writing appropriate to the subject?

27. Is the style straightforward or figurative?

28. Is the dialogue natural and suited to the characters?

29. Does the author balance narration and dialogue?

30. What are the main characteristics of the sentence patterns?

31. How did the author create a mood? Is the overall impression one of mystery, gloom, evil, joy, security?

32. What symbols has the author used to communicate meaning?

33. Is the point of view from which the action is told appropriate to the purposes of the selection?

Format

34. Does the selection contain illustrations? If so, do they enhance the action? Are they consistent with the action?

35. How is the format of the selection related to the text?

Evaluating

36. How does the selection compare with others on the same subject?

37. How does the selection compare with other selections by the same author?

38. How have other reviewers evaluated this selection?

Example 2.5   Example of a Notetaking System Applied to Characters in "After the First Death"

Code Directory Inside Front Cover

I – innocence

B – bravery

L – love

P – physical

I – intellectual

E – emotional

S – social

Code Directory Inside Back Cover

I   129, 144, 183
B   146, 211,
L   145,

Kate
P – 68, 144
I – 68, 69
E – 68, 69, 99, 105, 123,
S – 69, 129–130

Miro
. . .
Ben
. . .

Page 68 Coded

    . . . She was blond, fair skinned, slender, no
P   weight problems, had managed to avoid
    adolescent acne. A healthy body with one
P   exception: the weak bladder. . . . cheer-
    leader, prom queen, captain of the girls'
P   swimming team, budding actress in the
    Drama Club. . . . But there were other Kate
    Forresters, and she wondered about them
    sometimes. The Kate Forrester who awoke
E   suddenly at four in the morning and for no
    reason at all couldn't fall back to sleep. The
    Kate Forrester who couldn't stand the sight
    of blood. . . .

Page 69 Coded

She wanted to find somebody to love, to love
forever . . . That question brought up another   E
Kate Forrester disguise. Kate the manipulator
. . . Getting straight A's from Mr. Kelliher in   E
math and barely lifting a finger to do so but
knowing how to smile at him, feign interest . . .
She'd always been an excellent student in math.   I
She didn't know why she'd gone out of her
way to charm Mr. Kelliher. Just as she didn't
know why she used the same charm to win the
role of Emily in the Drama Club's presentation of *Our Town*. She knew she could play the
part, she was certain of her talent. . . . Gene
Sherman. Kate had been enthralled by him . . .   S
until they sat together during a lunch break

Smart Review 2.4

Check your understanding of the preceding section by answering the following on a separate sheet of paper or in your journal:

1. How do nontraditional text formats differ from traditional texts?
2. How does previewing nontraditional readings differ from previewing traditional texts?
3. How do marking and labeling nontraditional readings differ from marking and labeling traditional texts?
4. How do you mark and label literary texts? Describe the process.

SQ3R: A Plan for Understanding Texts

To paraphrase Homer, life doesn't always turn out the way you plan. This is true in reading, as well. To insure that your reading goes the way you plan, you need just that, a plan.

Developed by Frances Robinson during World War II as response to the needs of newly-inducted soldiers, the SQ3R study system is a plan for processing information from textbooks. Countless students of all ages use it to help them read and recall information. SQ3R involves five steps: *survey, question, read, recite,* and *review.*

These steps identify information presented in chapters one, two, and four in this text. Table 2.22 defines all steps of the SQ3R process and provides a quick index of where information about each step is found.

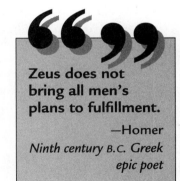

Zeus does not bring all men's plans to fulfillment.

—Homer
Ninth century B.C. Greek epic poet

Table 2.22   Steps in SQ3R and corresponding SMART information

SQ3R	Definition	Process used and location of information
Survey	Skimming to find main ideas or get the gist of a chapter.	Previewing. See Table 2.5.
Question	Predicting chapter content or setting purposes for reading.	Making predictions about content. See Table 2.2.
Read	Checking your predictions through literal and inferential comprehension.	Critical reading or processing of text. See Tables 1.1, 2.6–2.9, and 2.14–2.18.
Recite	Checking your understanding of the text.	Monitoring understanding. See Example 2.3.
Review	Transferring information from short-term to long-term memory.	Rehearsal through various memory strategies and mnemonic techniques. See Chapter 4.

Smart Review 2.5

Check your understanding of the preceding section by answering the following on a separate sheet of paper or in your journal:

1. How can having a plan like SQ3R increase your ability to read information more effectively?

2. List and define the steps in SQ3R.

3. Define the word *predict*. How does this word and its definition relate to the word *question,* step two of SQ3R?

4. Suppose the letter *T* indicated a sixth step in this process. What might it stand for? Which chapter of this book would it concern?

Speaking Figuratively, of Course...

Recognizing Irony

More than any other clue, context determines irony. **Irony** involves saying one thing and meaning the opposite. Ironic situations, when things work out to be completely different from what is expected, also occur. Irony often shows humor or sarcasm. **Sarcasm** is irony used to hurt the feelings of others. Sarcasm occurs when the opposite of literal words or phrases is intended.

It's often difficult to determine how irony is being used. The writer's or speaker's tone or manner can help you decide. If the rest of the passage or speech is basically humorous, then the phrase is meant to be humorous. If the writer or speaker wants to hurt the reader or listener or show anger, then sarcasm is being used.

Irony comes in several forms. The first is **understatement.** This occurs when the size, degree, or seriousness of something is shown as less than it really is. The second form of irony is **hyperbole.** Hyperbole is the opposite of understatement. It happens when something's description is exaggerated. **Structural irony** implies a discrepancy between what a character expects to get and gets, between what a character thinks and the reader knows, and between what a character deserves and gets. All types of irony occur in everyday life.

How can you tell if an author is being ironic? First, the context of the phrase helps. Second, the **tone** of the passage aids your decision. If the figure of speech has generally the same tone as the rest of the passage, the author does not intend irony. For example, if the rest of the passage is basically humorous, then the figure of speech is meant to be humorous.

Figurative Language 2.A

Read the following passage. Then answer the questions that follow.

The Cells of Henrietta Lacks

Biologists have learned much about cell structure and function by studying cells and fragments of tissue removed from multicellular organisms. They nurture and maintain these cells and tissues in special culture chambers under carefully controlled conditions. The first truly successful cell cultures were established in 1912 from heart muscle and fibroblast cells taken from chicken embryos. They grew and reproduced for thirty-four years before they were allowed to die. Today many human cell lines have been cultured continuously through thousands of cell generations.

The most famous of the human cell lines is that of HeLa cells, established in 1951 after a young black woman had been admitted to Baltimore's Johns Hopkins Hospital with suspected cervical cancer. As an essential part of the diagnosis, a small sample of living tissue was removed from her cervix. Some of this tissue was given to Dr. George Gey, a researcher at the hospital who was trying to culture various kinds of cancer cells. Until then, no one had been successful in culturing cells from human malignancies, but this time the cells flourished. They reproduced a new generation of cells as often as once a day. Because of this great breakthrough, research on these and similar cells began in earnest. HeLa cells were eventually sent to laboratories throughout the world, where they became the basic cell line for many kinds of cellular research.

What happened to the young woman whose cells were distributed to laboratories all over the world? Unfortunately, she died shortly after the diagnosis of cervical cancer was made, and she was soon forgotten. For many years even her name was a mystery. Many thought it was Helen Lane, others Helen Larson. HeLa is an acronym of her name. Today we know that her name was Henrietta Lacks, and although she is dead, her cells provide her with a unique type of immortality.

When carefully cultured, HeLa cells cling tenaciously to life. They have served as culture systems for numerous types of viruses, including the polio virus. If not for HeLa cells cultures, the development of the polio vaccine might have been long delayed. HeLa cells have been subjected to detailed chemical analyses and careful studies of nutritional requirements. They have been used to test the potential effects of radiation on human cells. They have been recipients of foreign nuclei, such as mouse nuclei, in studies of nuclear control of cell function. (In the latter instance, HeLa cells synthesized mouse proteins.) Recently, biologists around the world have found many human cell cultures contaminated and taken over by the highly competitive HeLa cells.

The use of HeLa cells for experimental purposes continues to increase, and special facilities have been established to grow them in large numbers. The National Science Foundation supports two such major centers, one at the University of Alabama in Birmingham, the other at the Massachusetts Institute of Technology in Cambridge. Both institutions have received unbelievable numbers of requests for HeLa cells.

The University of Alabama Center has received and filled single orders for as many as a trillion HeLa cells (approximately 1.5 kilograms). The Massachusetts Institute of Technology receives weekly orders for 2 billion cells from one scientist alone.

As cellular research continues to expand, during the next decade, additional culture centers may need to be established, and the cells of the young black woman will continue to be used in research on cancer, viral infections, developmental biology, and genetics. Few, if any, scientists expect to ever clone humans. But if they do succeed, maybe the first clone will be Henrietta Lacks.

---

1. How does Henrietta's last name reflect irony?

_____

_____

_____

_____

2. How is the sentence "When carefully cultured, HeLa cells cling tenaciously to life" ironic in light of what happened to Henrietta?

_____

_____

_____

_____

3. Consider the following sentence: " Recently, biologists around the world have found many human cell cultures contaminated and taken over by the highly competitive HeLa cells." What is ironic about this statement?

_____

_____

_____

_____

4. Reread the last paragraph of the excerpt. What is ironic about Henrietta's being used in cancer research?

_____

_____

_____

_____

Figurative Language 2.B

Consider the following quote from Roger Bacon, the greatest scientist of the 1200s: "There are four chief obstacles in grasping truth, which hinder every man … namely, submission to faulty and unworthy authority, influence of custom, popular prejudice, and concealment of ignorance accompanied by … a display of our knowledge." On a separate sheet of paper or in your journal, answer the following: Considering the time period and the quote, how did the use of Henrietta's cells show irony?

Figurative Language 2.C

Read the following poem. Then, on a separate sheet of paper or in your journal, complete the directions that follow the poem.

OH, YEAH! SAYS WHO?

What is truth? the philosophers cry.
What you believe may not be the same as I.
Scientists question, predict, theorize.
How do we know what are and aren't lies?

1. What is truth?

2. How can truth vary from one person to another?

3. What roles do philosophers and sicentists play in finding truth?

4. Describe a situation you have experienced in which your truth was different from that of someone else?

SUMMARY

Course readings, whether primary or nontraditional, form the nucleus of the class content. They prepare you for courses that are unfamiliar or complex in nature and serve as a guide to the lectures. To help you understand the information they contain, readings define terms, provide graphics, and rely on a variety of text features. To facilitate your understanding and recall, you need to preview before reading, outline or map information to discover the author's plan, set reading goals, and mark and label text. Once you've read the material, it's important that you check your understanding and fix any problems in comprehension. This chapter discussed all of these reading tasks.

CHAPTER REVIEW

1. Preview the next chapter in this text. What pre-, intra-, and postchapter guides does this text contain?

   _____

   _____

   _____

   _____

2. In your course notebooks, construct a map or outline in question form for each of the text chapters you are currently reading. How do these aid your study and recall?

   _____

   _____

   _____

   _____

3. Compare and contrast chapter outlines and maps. Which do you prefer? How do you account for this preference?

    _____

    _____

    _____

    _____

4. Mark and label each chapter you are currently reading in your courses. Summarize the main ideas in your labels and define the terms in context.

5. Identify the comprehension problem you most often encounter. How do you think this problem developed? How can you resolve it?

    _____

    _____

    _____

    _____

6. As you read the next chapter you are assigned in any one of your courses, identify three words that are new to you. Write down the sentences in which these words were used. Define these words from context, and then use a dictionary to check your definitions. What, if any, are the differences between the two meanings? What accounts for this difference?

    _____

    _____

    _____

    _____

7. Examine a list of terms from any course you are currently taking. List any of the terms you can define through structural analysis (taking apart the word). Define them. Then check their meanings with your glossary or a dictionary.

    _____

    _____

    _____

    _____

8. Which method of vocabulary decoding do you prefer—context or structural analysis? Which do you see as being the most versatile? Are there courses in which one seems to be more useful than the other? If so, why do you think this is so?

    _____

    _____

    _____

    _____

9. Compare and contrast previewing and reading nontraditional course readings with previewing and reading text chapters.

_____

_____

_____

_____

10. Compare and contrast reading traditional course texts with reading literary texts.

_____

_____

_____

_____

 MOVING ON

_____

Now you know when, how, and why reading text chapters and nontraditional text information work to improve your recall and understanding of course information. The next step in the postsecondary learning cycle is listening and notetaking.

How would you judge your ability to listen and take notes in lectures? Circle the response that best describes your notetaking strategies.

EXCELLENT   GOOD   AVERAGE   FAIR   POOR

Most students describe college courses in terms of their instructors and the way in which information is presented in lectures. How well you understand this material often determines the quality and quantity of information you get from the course. Maximizing your listening and notetaking skills increases your chances of academic success. The skills discussed in the next chapter are listed here. Check the ones you need to improve.

☐ Classroom listening strategies
☐ Relating lecture content to text information
☐ Knowing how to compensate for conflicting teaching and learning styles
☐ Determining what's important in the lecture
☐ Daydreaming during class
☐ Following the flow of ideas in the lecture
☐ Following the flow of information from class to class
☐ Taking notes in an organized manner

Reading course information prepares you for what comes next—it's time to move on to a discussion of listening and notetaking.

ACTION PLAN

Review the information this chapter contains and respond to the following:

Action Plan

⭐ **Ideas I already use:**

⭐ **Ideas new to me:**

⭐ **Ideas I'd like to try:**

Active Listening
and Notetaking Strategies

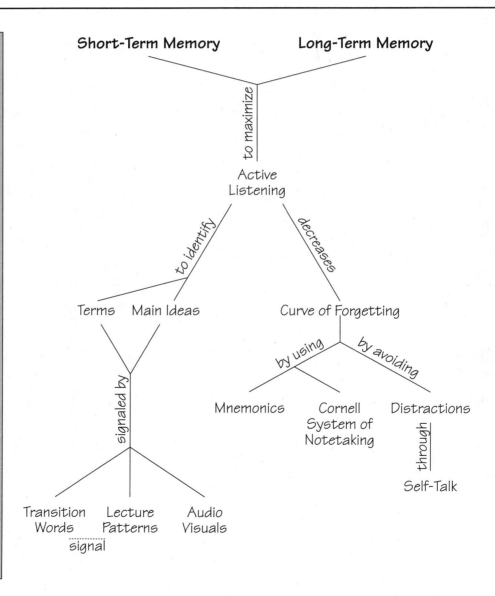

CHAPTER OUTLINE

I. Listening: An interaction
   A. Lecture processing
      1. Lectures dependent on the text
      2. Lectures independent on the text
      3. Postlecture reading
   B. Teaching styles and listening responsibilities
   C. Strategies for listening
      1. Identifying main ideas
      2. Identifying important information
      3. Focusing concentration
      4. Increasing recall
II. Notetaking: The act in active listening
   A. Personalizing your notes
   B. Cornell system of notetaking
   C. Getting the business: Borrowed notes

Easy listening exists only on the radio.

—David Barken
Twentieth century American lecturer

Hearing information is both the easiest and the most difficult way to learn. It's easy because it's something you've done all your life. It requires only the equipment you have with you. And, you can do it in all your classes and at any time. It's difficult because few students are trained to be good listeners. Elementary and secondary school teachers tend to explain clearly the facts, concepts, and relationships they want students to know. At those levels, a good memory for details often leads to good grades. In post-secondary settings, however, instructors cover a wide range of information. They expect you to think at higher levels as you apply information in various ways (see Chapter 1). Instructors take for granted that you know how to learn from lectures. Finally, hearing—contrary to what you may think—is not always the same as listening. **Active listening** is hearing with thoughtful attention. It is an alert process, not a state of being. Because many factors can adversely affect your understanding, you need a strategy for active listening.

How can you learn to listen better? Bob Bohlken of Northwest Missouri State University uses the listening inventory (see Exercise 3.1 for an adaptation of this inventory) to help his students become more aware of the importance of listening skills in lectures. Although there are no right or wrong answers to the questions, your answers can help you identify listening problems. Table 3.1 provides you with suggestions for becoming a more active listener.

Exercise 3.1   Choose the best answer for each of the following:

---

1. What classroom characteristic interferes most with your listening to a classroom lecture?
   a. temperature
   b. chalkboard and wall colors
   c. outside noise
   d. noise created by other students in class
   e. other

2. What instructor characteristics interfere most with your listening to classroom lectures?
   a. voice, speech rate, and/or accent
   b. thought organization
   c. appearance
   d. movement and behavior
   e. vocabulary

3. In the classroom where you listen best, where do you usually sit?
   a. front left
   b. front center
   c. front right
   d. middle
   e. back

(continues)

Exercise 3.1   *Continued*

4. In the classroom where you listen best, how often does the instructor look at you?
    a. very often
    b. often
    c. sometimes
    d. seldom
    e. very seldom

5. How often does the instructor look at you while lecturing?
    a. very often
    b. often
    c. sometimes
    d. seldom
    e. very seldom

6. What personal characteristic of the instructor interferes most with your listening to class lectures?
    a. tired
    b. hungry
    c. daydreaming
    d. preoccupied
    e. not interested in subject
    f. other

7. In the classroom where you listen best, how do you respond to the course?
    a. eye contact with instructor
    b. nod and acknowledge the instructor's comments with facial expressions
    c. take notes
    d. ask questions
    e. anticipate what will be said
    f. other

8. How do you respond to the instructor when he or she is lecturing?
    a. make eye contact
    b. nod and acknowledge instructor comments with facial expressions
    c. take notes
    d. ask questions
    e. anticipate what the instructor will say next
    f. other

9. At what time of the day do you listen best to classroom lectures?
    a. early morning
    b. mid-morning
    c. around noon
    d. mid-afternoon
    e. evening

(continues)

Exercise 3.1 *Continued*

10. How do you choose times for the courses you take?
   a. only one available
   b. fit my schedule
   c. considered my best time to listen
   d. instructor
   e. other

11. What is the nature of the lecture content to which you listen best?
   a. personally relevant
   b. dynamic
   c. familiar vocabulary and organization
   d. visually aided
   e. well supported with examples and comparisons

12. For what purpose do you listen in the class in which you listen best?
   a. to pass a test
   b. to relate to the instructor
   c. to satisfy an interest in the subject
   d. to learn new knowledge
   e. to apply information to self-improvement

13. For what purpose do you listen in a classroom?
   a. to pass a test
   b. to relate to instructor
   c. to satisfy an interest in subject
   d. to learn new knowledge
   e. to apply information to self-improvement

14. When you take notes, do you
   a. write down terms
   b. use a sentence outline
   c. paraphrase
   d. use topic outline
   e. other

15. What single factor influences your listening behavior most in a lecture?
   a. the room
   b. the instructor
   c. your purpose/attitude
   d. your physical and mental states
   e. other students

SOURCE: *The Teaching Professor,* Magna Publishing Company. January, 1993, pp. 3–4.

Table 3.1	Suggestions for Active Listening

1. Have a purpose for listening.

2. Pay careful attention to the instructor's introductory and summary statements. These usually emphasize main points.

3. Take notes.

4. Sit comfortably erect. Slouching makes you sleepy and indicates your disinterest to your instructor.

5. Look attentive. Show your interest by keeping your eyes on your instructor.

6. Concentrate on what the instructor says. Try to ignore external distractions. Try to eliminate internal distractions.

7. Think of questions you need to ask or comments you want to make.

8. Listen for transition words that signal main points.

9. Note words or references you don't understand. Do not try to figure them out at the time. Look them up later or ask about them in class.

10. Be flexible. Adjust your listening and notetaking pace to the lecture.

11. If the instructor speaks too quickly or unclearly, then (a) ask the instructor to speak more slowly or to repeat information; (b) leave plenty of white space and fill in missing details immediately after class; (c) exchange copies of notes with classmates; (d) ask the instructor for clarification after class; and (e) preview lecture topics before class.

12. Avoid being a distraction. (Keep your hands still, wait your turn in discussions, avoid whispering and fidgeting, etc.) This is particularly hard to do when you perceive a class to be boring. To combat classroom boredom, you (a) take detailed notes to prevent daydreaming; (b) move to the front of the class so that you are less likely to doze; (c) generate interest by holding a mental conversation with the lecturer (for example, saying: "I wonder why that is true?" "I disagree." "What if . . . ?").

LISTENING: AN INTERACTION

Listening involves an interaction between the content of the course, your instructor, and you. Your role is to hear and understand the content presented by the instructor. If you think your role is the easiest of the three, you're partly right and partly wrong.

Lecture Processing

Lectures follow two general formats. In the first, lecture content corresponds closely to assigned textbook chapters. In the second type, the lecture content is not necessarily contained in the text. Rather, the text complements lecture information.

Lectures Dependent on the Text

When lectures are text-based, the way you use your text during the lecture depends on your preclass preparation. Many instructors begin text-based lectures by identifying the sections that they will cover and the ones they will omit. As your instructor speaks, you highlight or otherwise identify important sections in the text and make any additional notes in the margins. You cross out information your instructor tells you to omit.

The outline or map you constructed during your preview of the chapter (see Chapter 2) provides the basis for your lecture notes. It helps you tell, at a glance, where the instructor is in the lecture. You note instructions and clarifying examples directly on your outline or map. Here, too, you highlight important sections and cross out the parts your instructor tells you to omit. When the instructor refers to specific graphics, quotations, or page numbers, you include them in your notes.

Lectures Independent of the Text

When instructors lecture on information not contained in the text, your responsibility for taking notes increases. Because you do not have the text to use as a reference, you need to be an especially active listener (see Table 3.1). In text-dependent lectures, the outline or map you developed in previewing gives you an overview of the lecture content. This helps you see how the lecture's details fit together. The process reverses for text-independent lectures. The lecture still provides you with the details. But you use these details *after* the lecture to discover the overall plan of the course content. Your class notes and syllabus aid you in this. The syllabus provides you with the lecture's topic. You examine your notes to find main ideas and general themes. You also examine them to determine how details support those main ideas. Then, you construct a map or outline to show the relationships you found.

Sometimes, the difficulty of a topic or gaps in your background knowledge lead you to question whether you fully grasped a lecture's content. A second, more thorough reading of text materials often satisfies this concern. Discussing course content with a classmate or reading supplementary information (see Chapter 2) also helps confirm your understanding. Finally, because text-independent lectures focus on what your instructor feels is most important, the instructor is the best source for clarifying confusing points. Feel free to ask him or her questions. Exercise 3.2 lets you practice differentiating between text-dependent and text-independent lectures.

Exercise 3.2   Compare the text with the notes that follow. Underline information in the notes that comes from the text readings. Determine if the lecture is text-dependent or text-independent. If text-dependent, place a *D* on the line beside the number. If text-independent, place an *I* on the line beside the number.

1. _____   TEXT CONTENT

Data processing is the collecting, manipulating, and distributing of data in order to achieve certain goals and make intelligent decisions. It is nothing new. People have processed data ever since they have had things to count. Shepherds have found ways to keep track of their sheep, merchants have kept records of their transactions, and physicians have monitored their patients. Schools have collected and processed data about students, grades, athletic events, books, and equipment for years. The only thing new about today's data processing is that computers do the routine work. They receive data, process it, and spit it out. They handle a lot of data all at once, or they let the user change data a piece at a time. And they do the work fast.

SOURCE: Reprinted with permission from Mandell, C. J., & Mandell, S. L. *Computers in education today.* St. Paul, MN: West, 24–25.

STUDENT'S LECTURE NOTES

DATA PROCESSING—collecting, manipulating, and distributing data
—not a new idea
—ADP (Automatic data processing). Done by early electromechanical machines
—EDP (Electronic data processing). Done by today's computers
—what data processing really is today!!!
OBJECTIVE OF DATA PROCESSING: convert raw data into information that can be used to make decisions
RAW DATA   —comes from many sources
—not organized in any way
—when organized and processed becomes INFORMATION
—INFORMATION used to make decisions
GOOD INFORMATION:
Accurate
Timely
Complete
Concise
Relevant
—if not then useless

(continues)

Exercise 3.2   *Continued*

---

2. _____   **TEXT CONTENT**

Processing. Once the data have been entered, they are processed. Processing occurs in the part of the computer called the central processing unit (CPU), examined later in this chapter. The CPU includes the circuitry needed for performing arithmetic and logical operations and providing primary memory—the internal storage that holds programs and data used during immediate processing. During processing, data can be categorized, sorted, calculated, summarized, stored, and otherwise manipulated. When I prepare the transparency, the CPU accepts and stores the text in primary memory. If I need to change something, the CPU recalls the relevant text and processes the change.

Source: Reprinted with permission from Mandell, C. J., & Mandell, S. L. *Computers in education today*. St. Paul, MN: West, 26.

STUDENT'S LECTURE NOTES

Processing
—happens after data is entered
—happens in part of the computer called the central processing unit (CPU)
CPU: (1) circuitry needed for performing arithmetic and logical operations
(2) primary memory—the internal storage that holds programs and data used during
immediate processing
During processing, data is
categorized
sorted
calculated
summarized
stored
manipulated
WHAT HAPPENS: 1. CPU accepts and stores the text in primary memory
2. If changes necessary, the CPU recalls text and processes the change

Postlecture Reading

If you read or preview chapters before class, the lecture forms your second exposure to the content. After the lecture, however, you read with a different purpose. Prelecture previews or readings give you a general sense of the material. The kind of postlecture reading you do depends on the focus of the lecture. Some lectures provide an in-depth analysis of a few topics, leaving the rest of the information for you to consider. Others cover all main points but in less depth. Case studies, problems, class discussions, and other formats are also parts of many courses, and can provide a focus for course readings. Postlecture reading, then, fleshes out your understanding depending on the information you still need. If you read the chapter in its entirety before the lecture, you now concentrate on topics that confused you or that were emphasized in class. If you previewed, this postlecture reading provides details, explanations, and examples that support the lecture. In both cases, postlecture reading completes the lecture process by filling in the gaps in your information.

Teaching Styles and Listening Responsibilities

Have you ever felt like your instructor gave lectures in stereo but you only had one speaker? Or that the instructor seemed to be broadcasting in FM while you only had an AM radio? Some of your difficulty in listening probably resulted from a lack of a match between your learning style and your instructor's teaching style. Just as your learning style determines your preferences in obtaining information (see Chapter 1), your instructor's teaching style determines, in part, how he or she delivers information. For example, perhaps you are an auditory learner, but your instructor uses pictures, transparencies, and other graphics to teach main ideas. Or perhaps you prefer a left-brained (detailed, linear, and straight-forward) approach, while your instructor uses a distinctly right-brain (holistic, visual, intuitive) format (see Table 3.2).

If your instructor's teaching style matches your learning style, you need only attend to the information that's presented. If, however, your instructor's teaching style differs from your preferred way of learning, your responsibilities increase. Your instructor can't possibly teach in a way that suits the needs of every student in every class. The responsibility for accommodating differences in teaching and learning styles falls on you. You cope with differing teaching and learning styles by using the suggestions in Table 3.3.

THINKING CRITICALLY

On a separate sheet of paper or in your journal, respond to the following: Contrast lectures in your high school with postsecondary lectures in terms of their text-dependence or text-independence. How do the differences, if any, affect your current level of performance in your postsecondary courses?

Table 3.2   Comparison of Teaching Styles and Student Responsibilities

Teaching Style	Preferred Teaching Method	Questioning Words Used	Elicits	Student Responsibilities

Left-brain
  Formal
 	
  Traditional
  Independent
	Lectures
	Calls on students
	  to answer questions
		Define
		Diagram
		Label
		List
		Outline
		Summarize
			Details
			Facts
				(1) Be specific
				(2) Provide facts
				(3) Analyze information
				(4) Synthesize information

Right-brain
  Informal
 	
  Intuitive
	Uses groups
	Asks for volunteer
	  students to answer
	  questions
		Describe
		Compare
		Contrast
		Criticize
		Discuss
		Evaluate
		Interpret
		Justify
		Relate
			Concepts
			Ideas
			Theories
				(1) Relate information
				(2) Evaluate information
				(3) Apply information
				(4) Interpret information

Table 3.3   Suggestions for Coping with Different Lecture Styles

If your instructor fails to . . .	Then you . . .
1. Explain goals of the lecture	Use your text and syllabus to set objectives
2. Review previous lecture material before beginning a new lecture	Set aside time before each class to review notes
3. State main ideas in introduction and summary of lecture	Write short summaries of the day's lecture immediately after class
4. Provide an outline on the lecture	Preview assigned readings before class or outline notes after class
5. Provide "wait time" for writing notes	Politely ask instructor to repeat information or speak more slowly
6. Speak clearly and at an appropriate volume	Politely ask instructor to repeat information or speak more loudly
7. Answer questions without sarcasm	Refrain from taking comments personally
8. Stay on topic and if tells what seem to be unrelated anecdotes	Discover how the anecdote relates to the topic or use the anecdote as a memory cue
9. Refrain from reading directly from the text	Mark passages in text that the instructor reads or summarize or outline these passages in the text margin
10. Emphasize main points	Supplement lectures through text previews and reading
11. Use transition words	Supplement lectures through text previews and reading

(continues)

Table 3.3   *Continued*

12. Give examples to illustrate difficult ideas	Ask instructor for clarifying examples, discuss ideas with other students, create examples for yourself
13. Write important words, dates, and concepts on the board	Supplement notes with terms, dates, and concepts listed in the text
14. Define important terms	Use text glossary or a dictionary
15. Use audiovisual aids to reinforce ideas	Relate information to what you know about the topic or create a clarifying example for yourself

Strategies for Listening

How many times have you gone to a movie and had someone taller sit in the seat in front of you? How much did you enjoy the movie? Probably your pleasure was directly proportional to the amount of screen you saw. For all you saw, you might as well have stayed home and saved your entertainment dollars. If your vision is blocked, your understanding, and thus your enjoyment, lessens.

Most students come to class as if someone tall sits in front of them. They fail to anticipate lecture content by completing assigned reading. They lack knowledge of course vocabulary. Thus, they depend on other students or the instructor to signal what's important to know and what's not. As a result, their understanding is diminished and the effectiveness of their class time decreased. To get the most from your educational dollar, you need to avoid these obstacles to listening.

Identifying Main Ideas

Understanding the main idea is hard to do when you have a passage in front of you. When listening, this task becomes even more difficult. Every lecture, though, follows a plan—a structure that indicates the purpose of the talk. These plans vary as the instructor's purposes change in the course of a lecture. Recognizing these plans helps you distinguish between main ideas and details. It also helps you recognize examples and understand the reasons for anecdotes. Lectures follow five plans, or patterns. Instructors either (1) briefly highlight main points in introductions or summaries; (2) develop topics through descriptive or explanatory examples, illustrations, and details or definition of terms; (3) list or sequence details; (4) present two (or more) sides of an issue; or (5) identify cause(s) and effect(s) or problem(s) and solution(s). Instructors usually mix these patterns in their lectures. That's because lectures are more informal and less structured than textbooks.

Identifying your instructor's mix and match of patterns helps you predict the direction of the lecture. Thus, you might find a list of problems and solutions, a comparison of steps in two sequences, a contrast of differing viewpoints, and so on. Identifying the patterns within a lecture also serves as the scaffolding for thinking about and later recalling information. Now, instead of thinking that information relates in an infinite number of ways, you analyze how information fits together and categorize it. Thus, when you review your notes, you see that the lecture as a whole discussed three solutions to an environmental problem, contrasted political policies, or compared characters in short stories.

You predict a lecture's direction by identifying the transition words your instructor uses. These words also mark the end of a lecture. The lecture's conclusion is important because instructors often restate main ideas in their summaries. Becoming familiar with transition words helps you organize lecture notes and listen more actively. Table 3.4 compares transition words with lecture patterns. Exercise 3.3 provides practice in identifying lecture types.

Table 3.4   Lecture Patterns and Corresponding Signals

Pattern	Description	Signal Words
Introduction/Summary	Identifies main points	Identified by location, either the beginning or end of a discussion of a topic, or by such signal words as *Today's lecture covers . . . ; The points I intend to discuss . . . ; Turn your attention to the topic of . . . ; in summary; in conclusion; as a review; to sum; to summarize;*
Subject Development	Provides details that relate to the subject but that have no relationship to each other	No specific signal words
Enumeration/Sequence	Lists or orders main points or presents a problem and steps for its solution	*First, second, third . . . ; first, next, then, finally, in addition, last, and then, most important, least important*
Comparison/Contrast	Describes ways in which concepts are alike or different or presents two or more sides of an issue	Comparison: *similarly, both, as well as, likewise, in like manner* Contrast: *however, on the other hand, but, yet, on the contrary, instead of, although, nevertheless*
Cause/Effect	Shows the result of action(s) or explains a problem and its solution	*Therefore, thus, as a result, because, in turn, then, hence, for this reason, results in, causes, effects*

Exercise 3.3   Underline the transition words found in each lecture excerpt. Use the following key and circle the lecture type that best describes the excerpt. The first one is done for you.

KEY:

I/S   Introductory/Summary
SD   Subject Development
E/S   Enumeration/Sequence
C/C   Comparison/Contrast
C/E   Cause/Effect

EXAMPLE

1. In many ways, hypnosis is similar to other altered states of consciousness, or ASCs. Like meditation and intoxication, it involves deliberate attempts to change our normal consciousness. Its history dates back to the mid-1700s in Europe. Anton Mesmer, a Viennese doctor, fascinated audiences by putting patients into trances. This led to the term *mesmerize,* which described the phenomenon. *Hypnosis,* a more recent and preferred term, comes from Hypnos, the Greek god of sleep. Initially, Mesmer's work was discredited by a French commission led by Benjamin Franklin. Later, researchers reexamined its uses and revived interest in it as a medical treatment. Even today, there is some disagreement about what hypnosis means and whether it is a valid ASC.

    I/S   SD   E/S   (C/C)   C/E

2. In theory, a star dies in one of two ways. A body can explode its mass outward at such a speed that all its atoms escape from one another and combine with interstellar matter. Or another body could evolve without losing matter into space. Ultimately, its nuclear and gravitational energy are entirely used. Because it no longer radiates, it becomes a dense black sphere. It is no longer, then, a star. In reality, a star's death falls between these two extremes. Many heavy stars lose mass into space. Many white dwarfs and undermassive red dwarfs evolve slowly toward their deaths. Both processes, then, are probably involved.

    I/S   SD   E/S   C/C   C/E

3. The caste system of India apparently originated around 1500 B.C. At that time, the Aryans invaded and conquered India. The Aryans were divided into four groups. The top group consisted of the priests and administrators of India. They were the Brahmans, considered to be the elite of India. The second level in the caste were the Kshatriya—the warriors. The Vaishya—the merchants—formed the third caste. Both the Kshatriya and Vaishya were relatively privileged. The fourth caste of people consisted of agricultural workers and artisans. They were not given same status as the other three castes. Finally, below the caste system existed the untouchables. These people were the outcasts—slaves to the other four groups. This was particularly ironic in that this last group were the descendants of the Indianic people first subjugated by those early Aryan invaders.

    I/S   SD   E/S   C/C   C/E

(continues)

Exercise 3.3   *Continued*

4. Americans consume more caffeine than any other national group. Coffee, tea, soft drinks, and chocolate—many of the staples of the American diet—all contain caffeine in varying degrees. Even so-called decaffeinated products contain some caffeine. Caffeine is a powerful central nervous system stimulant. As such, it can cause serious side effects. These include high blood pressure and increased heart rate. Caffeine use has been linked to cancer. Some researchers even suggest that links exist between caffeine usage and smoking.

   I/S   SD   E/S   C/C   C/E

5. Thus far in our discussion of galactic rotation, we've thought of stars as moving in circular paths in a flat plane. You might think of them as runners on a race track circling in an orderly manner. Actually, this fails to capture the realities of galactic movement. Today, we will see that stars near the sun follow eccentric paths.

   I/S   SD   E/S   C/C   C/E

6. As we have seen, behavior that works against the good of society as a whole is termed antisocial behavior. Like other forms of behavior we discussed, it occurs on a continuum. This continuum ranges from irresponsible acts to crime. Comments from social workers, psychologists, and juvenile officers often lead us to believe that these kinds of behavior are found in children whose parents could be termed antisocial. Challenges to this view form our next topic.

   I/S   SD   E/S   C/C   C/E

7. Archaeological discoveries indicate that religion has existed in some form in all known societies. Religion, then, fulfills a need of human existence. What are the functions of religion? First, religion legitimates some relationships. It explains why some people are strong and others weak or why some people are rich and others poor. Second, religion promotes social unity to provide group order. Without this, there would be chaos. Third, religion fosters a sense of meaning—a sense of personal worth or cosmic significance. Fourth, religion promotes a sense of belonging. It provides a group identity and a means of affiliation. Finally, religion impacts social change. It can be used to maintain the status quo or to promote change.

   I/S   SD   E/S   C/C   C/E

8. In our study of maladaptive behavior, the key to understanding the continuum is in the context, degree, severity, and duration of unusual behavior. Each of us—at one time or another—manifests symptoms that would be diagnosed as a mental illness in another context. In other words, you may begin to recognize yourself in some of these case studies. Unwary students may find themselves victims of "student's disease." This is the tendency to convince yourself that you have whatever behavior you are currently studying.

   I/S   SD   E/S   C/C   C/E

(continues)

Exercise 3.3   *Continued*

---

9. What is a group? Several factors must exist for a people to be described as a group. First, they must interact more than one time. Second, the group must have some kind of expectations and roles and must follow some set of societal rules. Next, members must identify with the group and feel a sense of belonging to it. Finally, group members must share something. This could be goals, expectations, territory, or any other thing that sets them apart from others.

I/S   SD   E/S   C/C   C/E

Identifying Important Information

Inability to identify important information also results in ineffective listening. This happens because all instructors emphasize and cue main points differently. There are, however, some common ways they let you know what's important. Careful observation helps you know when and how your instructor stresses main ideas.

First, some instructors write information on the chalkboard. They often place lecture outlines on the board before class begins. Instructors also write terms or key points on the board as they lecture. Copying this outline or list of terms aids learning in three ways. Initially, you learn as you write. Next, copying the information gives you an idea of the lecture's topic. Finally, the information serves as a guide for study. Some students think that copying what's on the board is all there is to notetaking. Although what an instructor writes is important, such information usually provides key points. You glean the rest of your notes from what the instructor says and does.

Instructors also cue important information by providing "wait time." When an instructor speaks more slowly or pauses, you get time to write what is being said. You also receive "wait time" when your instructor repeats information.

Third, instructors often change their tone of voice when stressing an important point. They may also change their voice volume or intensity. Listening for these changes helps you identify important information.

Fourth, instructors cue main points through body language. If your instructor pounds on the desk, moves closer to the class, or makes some other gesture to stress a point, that point is probably one essential to your understanding.

Audiovisuals are another way instructors convey main ideas. Films, overhead transparencies, videotapes, interactive videos, computer software, or other materials signal important topics but in different ways. Charts or graphs summarize information or classify data, while photographs or videotapes arouse emotion. Interactive videos and computer software allow you to apply learning, solve problems, or practice in other ways. Case studies provide realistic opportunities to analyze information. The creation of a graphic

---

Exercise 3.4   View the videotape (Lectures for Notetaking Practice) provided by your instructor. On a separate sheet of paper or in your journal, write down the points the instructor on the tape stresses. Following each point, list the cue used to emphasize the information.

---

or use of other audiovisual material often requires more effort on the instructor's part. Thus, their use always signals some important main idea or application of learning. Once you discover that idea, you record it in your notes for future consideration and study.

Sixth, some instructors refer to specific text pages. Information an instructor knows by page number is worth noting and remembering.

Finally, instructors stress information by referring to it as a possible test question. Your instructor might say, "You may see this again" or "This would make a good test question." Video-taped lectures and movies can provide practice for taking notes (see Exercise 3.4).

Focusing Concentration

Inactive listening results from **distractions.** These draw your attention from the subject being discussed. Some of these distractions are beyond your control; others are not.

Distractions beyond your control include traffic noises or other environmental sounds; sounds within the classroom, such as whispering, papers rattling, people moving, or hall noises; and other environmental interruptions. Your instructor's mannerisms pose another distraction you cannot control. Often an instructor's dialect, speech rate, and body language affect your concentration. Since you have no control over these distractions, you must learn to cope with them.

Increasing your interest in the subject is one way to cope. Interest in what is being said helps you ignore how it is said. Moving to a different seat may reduce environmental distractions. If you are in a large lecture class, moving closer to the instructor helps you hear better and focuses your attention. Moving away from a window or door helps you focus on what's inside instead of what's outside.

THINKING CRITICALLY

Consider your preferred learning style (see Chapter 1). On a separate sheet of paper or in your journal, identify which of the ways that instructors cue information would be most effective for you. Why?

"A cow just isn't a cow at this time of the day!"

Sometimes distractions are within you. These also affect concentration. Hunger, fatigue, or illness interfere with thinking. Proper nutrition, rest, and exercise can rid you of these physical distractions. Personal concerns, no matter how large or small, can never be solved during a class. If your problem is a large one, consulting a counselor or talking with a friend before or after class helps reduce anxiety. You solve minor problems (getting your laundry done, meeting a friend, running errands) by listing them on a separate page in your notebook. This allows you to forget them until the end of class. When class ends, you check the page, and your "to do" list is ready. Daydreaming forms another common internal distraction. You use self-talk to force yourself back to attention. Self-talk involves your interrupting your daydream with a strong internal command such as: "Stop! Pay attention now! Think about this later!" Finally, information overload often causes concentration loss. Excessive, unfamiliar, or complex materials tend to overwhelm you. Scheduling breaks between lecture classes helps you avoid mental exhaustion. Anticipating course content and completing assigned readings provide you with the background you need to understand new or difficult material. This, in turn, increases your self-confidence.

Figure 3.1   Curve of Forgetting

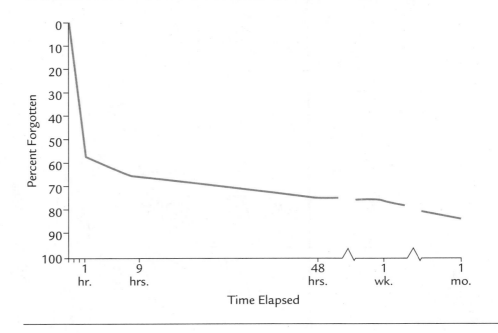

Increasing Recall

Sometimes a lecture is like a television movie that's continued over several nights. Often an instructor doesn't finish covering a topic during one class and continues discussing it for several classes. You need a review, similar to the "scenes from last night's exciting episode." Without this review, you forget what happened in the notes just as you might forget what happened in the movie. In either case, you lose continuity, interest, and understanding.

Frequent reviews aid recall by transferring information from short-term memory to long-term memory. The more you hear or read something, the easier it is to remember. The Ebbinghaus curve, or curve of forgetting (see Figure 3.1), shows the relationship between recall of information without review and time since presentation. The numbers along the left of the graph indicate amount of material remembered. Along the bottom you find the time that has passed since the material was presented. This curve explains why notes that seemed clear when you took them make no sense later. On the basis of one exposure, most information fades within the first twenty-four hours. Reviewing your notes immediately after class or at least within twenty-four hours after taking them reduces your curve of forgetting.

Reviewing your notes is your responsibility. After each day's class, reread your notes to refresh recall and look for gaps in information. Before the next class, review your notes again. This provides the context for that day's class.

Smart Review 3.1

Check your understanding of the preceding section by answering the following on a separate sheet of paper or in your journal:

1. Contrast active listening with hearing information.

2. Do you think it is easier to listen actively in a text-dependent lecture or in a text-independent lecture? Why?

3. How does lecture format (text-dependent or text-independent) impact postlecture reading?

4. How can teaching style enhance or hinder learning style?

5. Identify, describe, and provide three examples of signal words for each of the four lecture patterns described in this section. How do these patterns help you identify main ideas?

6. This section describes a variety of ways in which instructors emphasize important information. How might this relate to teaching and learning styles?

7. How are internal and external distractions alike? How are they different?

8. What do you think is the effect of previewing, lecture notetaking, and postlecture reading on the Ebbinghaus curve?

As you review, try to anticipate which topics the instructor might cover next. Think of questions you want answered and listen for that information during the lecture. These questions help you generate interest in the subject, relate new information to old knowledge, and remember information in a more coherent form.

NOTETAKING: THE ACT IN ACTIVE LISTENING

When you attend class, your role is to be an active listener, not a passive receiver of the instructor's voice. This means you selectively seek and note information about content and performance. Such active listening requires you to recognize important concepts and supporting details. Action—in this case, notetaking—enhances what you hear and remember (see Table 3.5).

Table 3.5   Guidelines for Taking Lecture Notes

1. Date each day's notes. This helps if you need to compare notes with someone, ask the instructor for clarification, or identify missing notes.

2. Use a notetaking system (see the following section).

3. Keep all your notes together. Use either a single spiral notebook or three-ring binder for each subject or two multisubject notebooks or loose-leaf binders, one for Monday-Wednesday-Friday classes and one for Tuesday-Thursday classes. Notebooks or binders with pockets are especially helpful.

4. Bring all necessary materials to each class.

5. Develop a key for your symbols and abbreviations and record it in your notebook.

6. Try to group and label information for recall.

7. Copy any information your instructor writes on the board.

8. Leave blank spaces. Skip lines to separate important groups of ideas.

9. Write only on the front of your paper.

10. Write legibly.

11. Mark in your text and record in your notes any page numbers mentioned by your instructor.

12. Highlight important information with colored pen or marker.

13. Compress your notes as you study. Create and record **mnemonic** strategies (see Chapter 4).

14. Read notes as soon after class as possible. Make corrections and additions.

15. Review notes before your next class to aid understanding.

Notetaking aids active listening in several important ways. First, some information in the lecture may not be found in the text or other course materials. Thus, the lecture is the only source for those ideas. Second, the information emphasized in a lecture often signals what will be found on exams. Next, class notes serve as a means of external storage. As a busy student, you cannot remember everything you hear. Thus, notes provide a form of memory.

Review is an important part of notetaking. In general, students who review notes achieve more than those who do not (Kiewra, 1985). Researchers found that if information was contained in notes, it had a 34 percent chance of being remembered (Howe, 1970). It had only a 5 percent chance of being remembered if it was not in notes.

Personalizing Your Notes

As a knowledgeable notetaker, you know you need to selectively record only important information. The information you record is your decision. You make this decision based on what you know about the lecture topic, the subject of the course, and the facts about the subject that your instructor emphasizes. When you are familiar with a topic, your notes need not be as detailed as when you are less familiar with a subject. Your notes are your personal record of what you need to learn.

Notes are not like a theme you submit for a grade. They need not be grammatically correct. They don't even have to contain complete words. In fact, as a good notetaker, you need to develop your own system of shorthand to record your notes. In creating your system, you need to limit the number of symbols you use. After you thoroughly learn a few symbols, you can add others. Table 3.6 shows you some rules for developing your own shorthand system. Exercise 3.5 provides information on which you can practice your shorthand system.

Table 3.6   Rules for Developing a Shorthand System

1. Limit the number of symbols you create.
2. Use the beginning letters of words.
   Examples

Abbreviation	Meaning
assoc	associated
w/	with
geog	geography
hist	history
info	information
intro	introduction

3. Use standard symbols.
   Examples

Abbreviation	Meaning
&	and
#	number
%	percent
$	money, dollars
?	question
+	in addition, plus
!	a major point
x	times, multiply
<	less than
>	greater than

4. Use traditional abbreviations but omit periods.
   Examples

Abbreviation	Meaning
lb	pound
ft	foot
wt	weight
mi	mile
Dec	December
US	United States

5. Omit vowels and keep only enough consonants to make the word recognizable.
   Examples

Abbreviation	Meaning
bkgrd	background
mxtr	mixture
dvlp	develop

6. Drop endings that do not contribute to word meaning.
   Examples
   ed
   ing
   ment
   er

(continues)

Table 3.6   *Continued*

7. Add "s" to show plurals.

8. Omit *a, an, the,* and unimportant verbs and adjectives.

    Example

    A cause of the Civil War was the issue of slavery.

    Cause of CW = slavery

9. Write out terms and proper names the first time. Show your abbreviation in parentheses after the term or name. Then, use the abbreviation throughout the rest of your notes.

10. Indicate dates numerically.

    Example

Abbreviation	Meaning
12/7/41	December 7, 1941

11. Use common misspellings of words.

    Examples

Abbreviation	Meaning
thru	through
nite	night
rite	right

12. Express numbers numerically.

    Examples

Word	Number
one	1
two	2
first	1st
second	2nd

Exercise 3.5   Use your personal shorthand to transcribe the first five paragraphs in Exercise 3.3.

1. _____
   _____
   _____
   _____
   _____
   _____
   _____
   _____

2. _____
   _____
   _____
   _____
   _____
   _____
   _____
   _____
   _____

(continues)

Exercise 3.5   *Continued*

3. _____

_____

_____

_____

_____

_____

_____

4. _____

_____

_____

_____

_____

_____

_____

5. _____

_____

_____

_____

_____

_____

_____

_____

Cornell System of Notetaking

Even good notetakers need a plan for taking notes during lectures. One plan, the Cornell system developed by Walter Pauk at Cornell University, involves a five-stage approach and results in notes that probably look different from and are more effective than those you normally take (see Figure 3.2).

Record forms Stage 1 in the Cornell system. You prepare for this stage by drawing a vertical line about two and a half inches from the left edge of your paper. You may find paper ruled in this format available at campus bookstores. You use the narrower, left-hand column as your recall column. You leave it blank until Stage 2. During the lecture, you listen actively. You

Figure 3.2   Notes Written Using the Cornell Notetaking System

	Shelters topic
	Shelters are more efficient made of natural (raw) materials
Tropical shelters list types and quantities	Tropical Dwellers 1) Frequent rainfall 2) Bamboo—made of 3) Roof sloped for run off 4) Floor raised for dryness
Grassland dwellers Types of weather cond. materials	Grassland Dwellers 1) Winds, cold nights, and severe winters 2) Use animal hides stretched over wood 3) These tents are portable
Desert Dwellers Types and quantities of materials	Desert Dwellers 1) Use mud masonry 2) Mud added to wood dries like brick 3) Mud insulates from severe climate changes (Hot day—cool nights) 4) Most are farmers or nomadic 5) Some dried brick shelters have lasted 1000 years
Summary	Shelters are more efficient made of raw materials. There are 3 main types or areas where shelters are built. Tropical, Grassland, and Desert Regions.

SOURCE: Courtesy of Greg Jones, Metropolitan State College, Denver, Colorado.

write as much information as you think is important in paragraph or outline form in the larger right-hand column.

Reduce is the key word in Stage 2. You reduce, or condense, notes by using a text-labeling approach (see Chapter 2) and record those labels in the recall (left) column. To condense notes, you omit most adjectives and adverbs and leave nouns and verbs intact to identify main ideas and key details. It's important to use as few words as possible. If you wish, you can transfer these cues to index cards and carry them with you for quick review. Reducing notes as soon as possible after class, at least within twenty-four hours, helps you increase recall.

Recite is Stage 3. During this stage, you cover your notes and say them in your own words. You use the recall column to cue memory. Then, you reveal your notes and check your accuracy. This review also decreases forgetting.

Reflect forms the action in Stage 4. After reciting your notes, you wait for some period of time. Then, you reread your notes and think about them. Next, you read your text to supplement and clarify your notes. You use your text and notes to discover the causes and effects of issues, define terms, and relate concepts. You make generalizations and draw conclusions. This helps you become a more active and critical thinker (see Chapter 1).

Review is the goal of Stage 5. Briefly reviewing your notes several times a week helps you retain what you have learned. This spaced study keeps information fresh, provides repetition, and decreases forgetting.

Getting the Business: Borrowed Notes

If you buy or borrow notes, you act as a silent partner with the notetaker. Unfortunately—unlike two business people planning together for mutual financial success—buying and borrowing notes forms a partnership in which the person who takes the notes becomes the only one who profits. The notetaker gets personalized notes, notes that reflect his or her background information and learning style. The notetaker also receives your money. You get notes that required no labor or action on your part. While this sounds like a great business deal, it's not. It's an empty effort, a passive one. Such notes are not a part of active listening. The most effective notes are those you take for yourself.

*"You guys have to show proof of age to get a copy of the study notes for
Advanced Human Sexuality."*

Similarly, using a tape recorder to take notes seems like a good solution. After all, a recorder copies every word the instructor says. A recorder doesn't become bored, daydream, or doodle. It appears to be the perfect notetaking solution. But using a tape recorder has drawbacks. First, replaying each tape in its entirety is too time-consuming. Transcribing a tape contributes little to your understanding of the lecture's main ideas. Like underlining too much on a text page, writing each word the lecturer says decreases your ability to highlight and later recall important information. Second, because a tape recorder only records auditory information, your notes lack diagrams, terms, and other information that the instructor might have written on the board. Third, technical difficulties sometimes arise. Problems such as dead batteries sometimes prevent you from getting the notes you need. Fourth, the use of tape recorders often offends or intimidates some instructors. If you decide to record notes, you need to get your instructor's permission before recording any lecture. Fifth, relying on recorders keeps you from learning good note-taking skills. The final and most important drawback is that, as with using borrowed notes, you remain a passive listener.

There is a place for borrowed or taped notes, however. When you are ill, unable to take notes for yourself, or absent from class, having someone else take or tape notes for you is better than not having any notes at all, as long as you take steps to process the information for yourself. Another acceptable use of taped notes is to record the lecture while you take notes. Taped notes allow you to fill in gaps during review. This method is especially helpful if your instructor speaks too rapidly. Whenever you use taped notes, you should listen to them before your next class. If you wait too long, you lose continuity, and understanding is impaired.

Exercise 3.6   Take notes from the videotaped lecture on psychology on a separate sheet of paper or in your journal. Compare your notes with the notes taken by your instructor or study group. What information is missing or inaccurate? Correct your notes.

Smart Review 3.2

Check your understanding of the preceding section by answering the following on a separate sheet of paper or in your journal:

1. Examine the guidelines for taking lecture notes in Table 3.5. Identify the rationale for each one.
2. What are some ways in which you might personalize your notes?
3. Take notes on the section on the Cornell system of notetaking. Record notes using the Cornell format.
4. What might be the effect of using the Cornell system of notetaking on the Ebbinghaus curve?
5. What are the disadvantages of taped or borrowed notes? What are the advantages?

SMART Information 3.1

Using your password for this course, access InfoTrac College Edition on the World Wide Web. Review the notes you took from the videotape lecture on Sample Chapter 6, "The Study of Humanity," for Exercise 3.6.

1. The lecturer discussed various types of anthropologists. Choose one type from your notes and use it for a keyword and for a subject search. Analyze the information you find. How do the results from the two searches compare?

   _____

   _____

   _____

2. The lecturer briefly discussed four major concepts. Choose one of these concepts from your notes and search by either keyword or subject. Review the abstracts of the sources. Write the citation of the article or other reference that you believe provides the best general discussion for that concept. How did you make your choice?

   _____

   _____

   _____

   _____

(continues

SMART Information 3.1   *Continued*

3. The lecturer used a circular graphic on the board which showed five different factors in anthropological study. Conduct a keyword or subject search of all five factors. Use the results to compete the following table. What do the results tell you about using these terms as search terms?

Term	Type of Search: Keyword/Subject	Results

SMART SITES

Using the Web to Improve Listening and Notetaking

A wealth of information related to the topics in this chapter is available on the World Wide Web. For this exercise access one of the following sites (for the most up-to-date URLs, go to http://csuccess.wadsworth.com):
http://www.uminet.net/~jackp/survive.html,
http://uhs.bsd.uchicago.edu/scrs/vpc/virtulets.html,
http://www.csbsju.edu/advising/helplist.html, http://www.ucc.vt.edu/stdy/skhlp.html,
http://www.utexas.edu/student/lsc/handouts/stutips.html,
http://www.dartmouth.adu/admin/acskills/index.html#study,
http://128.32.89.153/CalRENHP.html. Click on any link under the topic *Study Skills.*
Choose a topic that relates to listening and notetaking. Use the information to respond to the following questions on a separate sheet of paper or in your journal:

1. What topic did you choose?
2. Why did you choose that topic?
3. In what ways does the topic support the content of this chapter? What new information does it provide?
4. What do you think is the most important point of this source?? Why?
5. How can you apply the content to your classroom situations?

COOPERATIVE LEARNING ACTIVITY   EFFECTIVE NOTETAKING—GOOD STUDENTS, TAKE NOTE!

Effective notetaking requires active listening. Active listeners know how to control their attention to avoid classroom daydreaming. Here's a listening and notetaking plan that works for many students. The important steps are summarized by the letters LISAN, pronounced like the word *listen*.

L = *Lead. Don't follow.* Try to anticipate what the instructor is going to say. Try to set up questions as guides. Questions can come from the instructor's study guides or the reading assignments.

I = *Ideas.* Every lecture is based on a core of important ideas. Usually, an idea is introduced and examples or explanations are given. Ask yourself often, "What is the main idea now? What ideas support it?"

S = *Signal words.* Listen for words that tell you the direction the instructor is taking. For instance, here are some groups of signal words: *There are three reasons why* . . . Here come ideas, *Most important is* . . . Main idea, *On the contrary* . . . Opposite idea, *As an example* . . . Support for main idea, *Therefore* . . . Conclusion.

A = *Actively listen.* Sit where you can hear and where you can be seen if you need to ask a question. Look at the instructor while he or she talks. Bring questions you want answered from the last lecture or from your reading. Raise your hand at the beginning of class or approach your instructor before the lecture begins. Do anything that helps you to be active.

N = *Notetaking.* As you listen, write down only key points. Listen to everything, but be selective and don't try to write everything down. If you are too busy writing, you may not grasp what is being said. Any gaps in your notes can be filled in immediately after class.

Here is something more you should know: A revealing study found that most students take reasonably good notes—and then don't use them! Most students wait until just before exams to review their notes. By then, the notes have lost much of their meaning. This practice may help explain why students do poorly on test items based on lectures. If you don't want your notes to seem like hieroglyphics or "chicken scratches," it pays to review them on *a regular basis.* And remember, whenever it is important to listen effectively, the letters LISAN are a good guide.

Application

Use LISAN in the next lecture for this class or ask your instructor to give a brief sample lecture. In your study group, compare answers to the following questions:

1. What did you do to lead? What questions did you have? Where did you get your questions?

2. What was the core of the lecture's content? What details supported that idea?

3. What signal words were used in the lecture?

4. What did you do to actively participate in the lecture? Did other group members take note of your active participation?

5. Are you satisfied with your notes? What, gaps, if any, occurred? What caused these gaps? What could you do differently?

SOURCE: Coon, D, (1998). *Introduction to Psychology, Exploration and Application.* Pacific Grove, CA: Brooks/Cole.

Speaking Figuratively, of Course...

Recognizing Similes and Metaphors

Sometimes a writer who wants to compare something unfamiliar with something familiar uses a simile or metaphor. At first glance, the two ideas seem totally different. They appear to have nothing in common. However, a closer look reveals a basic relationship between them.

The words *like* or *as* signal that a **simile** is being used. In a **metaphor**, one idea is described as if it were another, without the use of *like* or *as*. Sometimes it is difficult to remember that similes, not metaphors, are cued by *like* or *as*. Remember this trick:

A
SimiLe
I
K
E

Some similes and metaphors are used so often they lose their freshness. When this happens, they no longer add vividness to language. They become ineffective. Such similes and metaphors are called **clichés.** Phrases like *pretty as a picture, hard as a rock,* and *slept like a baby* lost their effectiveness through overuse.

Figurative Language 3.A

Answer the following:

1. "Life with Mary was like being in a phone booth with an open umbrella. No matter which way you turned, you got it in the eye."—Barry Nelson in *Mary, Mary*
    a. Type: _____ Compares _____ and _____
    b. What kind of person was Mary?
    c. What kind of person was the speaker? Justify your response.

2. "A golf course is nothing but a poolroom moved outdoors."—Barry Fitzgerald in *Going My Way*
    a. Type: _____ Compares _____ and _____
    b. Identify three ways in which a poolroom is like a golf course.
    c. What is Fitzgerald's opinion of both golf and pool?

3. "I think you must have an adding machine for a heart."—Bette Davis in *Bordertown*

    a. Type: _____   Compares _____ and _____

    b. What kind of person has "an adding machine for a heart"?

    c. Describe a situation that would indicate a person has "an adding machine for a heart."

4. "You're the most beautiful plank in your husband's platform."—Adolphe Menjou in *State of the Union*

    a. Type: _____   Compares _____ and _____

    b. What was the husband's profession?

    c. What does plank mean in this context?

5. "Champagne's funny stuff. I'm used to whiskey. Whiskey is a slap on the back, and champagne's heavy mist before my eyes."—James Stewart in *The Philadelphia Story*

    a. Type: _____   Compares _____ and _____

    b. What does funny mean in this context?

    c. How is whiskey like a slap on the back?

Figurative Language 3.B

On a separate sheet of paper or in your journal, create and explain two metaphors and two similes.

Figurative Language 3.C

Read the following poem using the steps identified in Chapter 2 for reading literary text. Code for similes, metaphors, and characters' actions. Then answer the questions that accompany it on a separate sheet of paper or in your journal.

FOUR GLIMPSES OF NIGHT

I

Eagerly
Like a woman hurrying to her lover
Night comes to the room of the world
And lies, yielding and content
Against the cool round face
Of the moon.

II

Night is a curious child, wandering
Between earth and sky, creeping
In windows and doors, daubing
The entire neighborhood

With purple paint.
Day
Is an apologetic mother
Cloth in hand
Following after.

III

Peddling
From door to door
Night sells
Black bags of peppermint stars
Heaping cones of vanilla moon
Until
His wares are gone
Then shuffles homeward
Jingling the gray coins
Of daybreak.

IV

Night's brittle song, silver-thin,
Shatters into a billion fragments
Of quiet shadows
At the blaring jazz
Of a morning sun.

—Frank Marshall Davis

1. Identify three comparisons used in the first stanza of the poem. Indicate whether the comparisons are similes or metaphors and what two items are being compared.

2. Examine the comparisons you identified in the preceding question. Do the comparisons work? Why did Davis use them?

3. Identify two comparisons used in the second stanza of the poem. Indicate whether the comparisons are similes or metaphors and what two items are being compared.

4. What action does Davis attribute to each of the comparisons? Is this an accurate portrayal? Defend your answer.

5. Identify three comparisons used in the third stanza of the poem. Indicate whether the comparisons are similes or metaphors and what two items are being compared.

6. Examine the comparisons you identified in the preceding question. Do the comparisons work? Why did Davis use them?

7. List Davis's comparisons for night and his comparisons for day. What does each set of words have in common?

8. Which do you prefer—night or day? Considering this preference, how do you evaluate Davis's poem?

SUMMARY

Effective and active listening involves an interaction between the instructor, the lecture content, and you. Your responsibilities lessen when the lecture is text-dependent; they increase when the lecture is text-independent. Similarly, your responsibilities change when your learning style does not match your instructor's teaching style. Your effectiveness as a listener also affects your notetaking responsibilities. Active listening and notetaking strategies promote identification of main ideas or important information, concentration during class, and later recall of course content. Effective notetaking involves taking notes in a systematic manner such as the Cornell system. Taking your own notes is a responsibility that results in personal records of class content. These records then facilitate recall. The only time you should use borrowed or taped notes is when you have been ill, unable to take notes for yourself, or absent from class or for comparison to your own notes.

CHAPTER REVIEW

1. List below the courses in which you are enrolled. Identify the lectures in each as text-dependent or text-independent. Then explain how your notes in each course indicate lecture type and compensate for the differences in lecture types.

   _____

   _____

   _____

   _____

   _____

   _____

2. Examine the courses you listed in the preceding question. In which of these courses do you have the most difficulty taking notes? What accounts for these problems? How might you solve them?

   _____

   _____

   _____

   _____

   _____

   _____

3. List again the courses in which you are enrolled. Do you reread chapters after the lecture on that information? Why or why not? In which classes does (or might) postlecture reading benefit you? Why?

_____

_____

_____

_____

_____

4. List below the instructors you have now. Do their teaching styles match your learning style? If they differ, how do you compensate?

_____

_____

_____

_____

_____

5. Identify the reason(s) you sometimes fail to listen actively. Then describe methods for overcoming this failure.

_____

_____

_____

_____

_____

6. Explain "wait time." Describe a scenario (other than the one given in the text) when "wait time" might be used outside of class.

_____

_____

_____

_____

_____

7. Explain the curve of forgetting in Figure 3.1. What does this curve imply about the need for review?

_____

_____

_____

_____

_____

_____

8. Identify three shorthand symbols you use that are not included in this text. List three shorthand symbols listed in this text that you don't use but could incorporate into your notetaking. If possible, use these symbols in the next set of notes you take.

_____

_____

_____

_____

_____

_____

9. Compare and contrast the Cornell system of taking notes with the way you currently take notes.

_____

_____

_____

_____

_____

10. Use the Cornell system to take notes in any one of the classes you are taking this term. Bring these with you the next time this class meets and show them to your instructor.

ACTION PLAN

Review the information this chapter contains and respond to the following:

Action Plan

⭐ *Ideas I already use:*

⭐ *Ideas new to me:*

⭐ *Ideas I'd like to try:*

MOVING ON

You now possess a massive amount of information, acquired through both reading and listening. It's time to master this content. To do so, you need to organize it and develop techniques for remembering and applying it on tests. You need to think about preparing for exams.

Does the way you prepare for tests result in the grades you want? Circle the response that best indicates how you describe your preparation.

EXCELLENT   GOOD   AVERAGE   FAIR   POOR

Grades—you've got to get good ones to stay in school. You might find that you study harder and harder but your grades don't accurately reflect your efforts. More of the same old strategies you used in the past aren't going to help. You need new techniques to increase your effectiveness and efficiency in test preparation. The topics discussed in Chapter 4 are listed here. Check the ones you need to improve.

- ☐ Protecting prime study time
- ☐ Selecting a study site conducive to learning
- ☐ Organizing ideas with a concept map
- ☐ Organizing ideas with a chart
- ☐ Using mental and physical imagery to associate information
- ☐ Developing acronyms and acrostics to cue memory
- ☐ Using location or word games as memory aids
- ☐ Possessing a range of strategies for vocabulary development
- ☐ Possessing a variety of strategies for rehearsing information
- ☐ Having a plan for preparing for objective tests
- ☐ Having a plan for preparing for subjective tests

Listening and notetaking, along with your text materials, provide you with the information you need. Now you must show that you understand that information. It's time to move on to Chapter 4, "Test Preparation: Synthesizing and Reviewing Course Content.")

CHAPTER 4

Test Preparation: Synthesizing and Reviewing Course Content

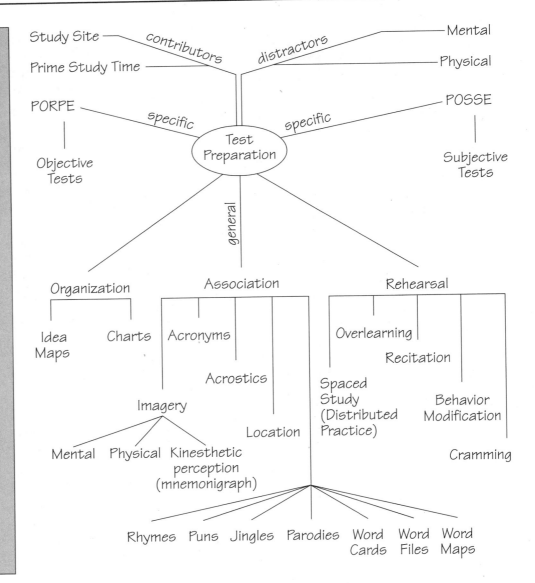

CHAPTER OUTLINE

I. General study strategies
   A. Prime study time
      1. Protecting prime study time
      2. Selecting a study site
   B. Organizing ideas: Analysis and synthesis
      1. Idea maps
      2. Charts
   C. Association
      1. Mental and physical imagery
      2. Acronyms and acrostics
      3. Location
      4. Word Games
      5. Vocabulary Strategies
   D. Rehearsal
      1. Spaced study versus cramming
      2. Recitation
      3. Overlearning
      4. Honest cheating
II. Using specific study plans to prepare for exams
   A. POSSE: A study plan for objective exams
   B. PORPE: A study plan for subjective exams

Tests give you chances to show how well you think and use your mind; however, tests are not games of chance. You improve your odds when you prepare yourself to think well.

If tests measure understanding of a subject, test preparation provides exercises in thinking critically about that subject. Effective test preparation requires constant evaluation of yourself and constant choices about which information you need to learn. Thus, you need a range of strategies from which to choose. Although general study strategies apply to any test, other, more specific strategies help you prepare for special exams.

GENERAL STUDY STRATEGIES

Some people seem to have all the luck. They appear to get breaks. They're always in the right place at the right time. However, such occurrences more often result from planning than chance. Being in the right place at the right time also facilitates learning. You improve your chances for learning by identifying your prime study site and time and planning to maximize your use of them. Being in the right place at the right time also facilitates learning.

Once you know where and when you best learn, you consider what and how to learn. The information you gain from texts and lectures forms merely the tip of the intellectual iceberg. Learning at all levels of Bloom's Taxonomy (see Chapter 1) occurs when you relate the textbook and the lecture and incorporate the new information into your own thinking. You must be able to analyze information; only then can you synthesize and evaluate it. Once you know what you want to learn, you use association and rehearsal strategies to reinforce thinking and transfer learning into long-term memory.

Prime Study Time

Deciding when to study is almost as important as deciding what to study. Your best learning occurs during your own **prime study time**—the time of day when you think and learn best. Prime study time varies from person to person. Your best time may be early morning, or you may be able to recall more when you study in the afternoon or at night. You determine your prime study time by observing when you get the most accomplished, when your studying results in higher grades, or when you feel most alert and able to concentrate. Your best time of the day needs to be spent studying your most difficult subjects or working on the assignments that are most important or that require the most effort. Tackling the most difficult or urgent task first allows you to work on that problem when you are most alert and fresh.

When is your best time of day? Exercise 4.1, adapted from a self-assessment questionnaire published in the *International Journal of Chronobiology,* helps you decide if you are a lark (a morning person) or an owl (a night person).

"Ms. Hill, has it ever dawned on you that 7:00 in the morning isn't the best time of the day for you to take classes?"

Protecting Prime Study Time

Once you know your prime study time, what keeps you from using that time wisely? Chances are that the threats to your prime study time are physical (those that affect your body), mental (those that affect your thinking), or external (those people or things that distract you).

Physical concerns often overshadow your ability to concentrate during prime study time. Being too hungry, too full, or cold, tired, or uncomfortable in any other way distracts you from your studies. You control most of these physical distractions by altering your sleeping or eating schedule, or by adjusting the temperature or other conditions.

Mental distractions often seem more difficult to discipline. You may find yourself thinking of other assignments or jobs you need to do instead of the task at hand. If so, keep a pad and pencil nearby and make a list of your concerns as you think of them. By doing so, you literally put your problems aside until you are free to work on them.

Worry often poses the greatest mental distraction; however, most worry focuses on past mistakes ("I really did poorly on that last test") or future problems ("What if I don't pass this test?"). Self-talk (see Chapter 1), from the vantage point of your adult role, helps you focus on your present task and gives you confidence in your abilities to prepare yourself for the test.

Exercise 4.1   For each of the following questions, circle the response that best describes you.

1. If you could choose, at what time do you prefer to wake up?
   a. 11:00 a.m. or later
   b. 10:00–11:00 A.M.
   c. 8:00–10:00 A.M.
   d. 6:30–8:00 A.M.
   e. 5:00–6:30 A.M.

2. How easy is it for you to get up in the morning?
   a. very difficult
   b. not very easy
   c. fairly easy
   d. very easy

3. How tired do you feel for the first thirty minutes you are awake?
   a. exhausted
   b. fairly tired
   c. fairly refreshed
   d. very refreshed and wide awake

4. You have a major exam tomorrow. You may choose the time at which you feel you will be at your best. You choose:
   a. evening (7:00–9:00 P.M.)
   b. afternoon (1:00–5:00 P.M.)
   c. later morning (11:00 A.M.–1:00 P.M.)
   d. early morning (8:00–10:00 A.M.)

5. One night you must remain awake to perform a night watch. You need to be awake between 4 and 6 A.M. You have no commitments the next day. How would you handle this situation?
   a. Stay awake all night until the watch ends.
   b. Catch a nap before and after the watch.
   c. Go to sleep early, do the watch, and take a nap after.
   d. Go to sleep early, do the watch, and remain awake for the rest of the day.

6. A friend invited you to go exercise tomorrow morning between 7 and 8 A.M. How do you think you will do?
   a. poorly
   b. experience difficulty
   c. OK
   d. very well

7. You have a class at the same time every morning. How dependent are you on an alarm clock to wake you?
   a. very dependent
   b. fairly dependent
   c. occasionally dependent
   d. never need an alarm clock

8. At what time of night do you feel tired and in need of sleep?
   a. 2:00–3:00 A.M.
   b. 1:00–2:00 A.M.
   c. 10:00 P.M.–1:00 A.M.
   d. 9:00–10:00 P.M.
   e. 8:00–9:00 P.M.

SCORING

Total your score using the following rating system:

A= 1

B= 2

C= 3

D= 4

E = 5

The lower your score, the more likely you are to be an owl. The higher your score, the more likely you are to be a lark. A score of 17 places you midway between being a lark and an owl.

SOURCE: Reprinted by permission of Gordon and Breach Science Publishers, 1976.

External distractions also threaten prime study time. All too often, invitations to go out with the gang come at prime study time. If you succumb to such requests, you may regret it later. One solution, while simple, is hard to implement. It involves saying no in an assertive way that makes your point clear without offending anyone. Alternatively, you can delay interruptions by arranging to meet friends after your prime study time. Then, you not only complete your study goals, but you enjoy yourself without guilt. Some friends won't take no for an answer or don't want to wait. At these times just being unavailable is easier than facing temptation. Unplugging the phone, hanging a "Do not disturb" sign outside your door, closing the door, or going somewhere else to study limits your availability. Noise is another external distraction. Loud next-door neighbors, unsympathetic family members, or inconsiderate roommates all threaten prime study time. Sometimes, they don't realize that their noise distracts you. Letting them know your needs in a polite yet assertive manner often solves your problem. (Examples of assertive language appear in Table 4.1.) Listening to soft music with headphones, using soft static (white noise) from a TV or radio, or studying somewhere else also allows you to overcome external distractions. Although you will probably never rid yourself of all interruptions during prime study time, you can minimize them.

Selecting a Study Site

Managing prime study time involves more than knowing the time of the day when you are at your best. You must also be able to manage your surroundings to maximize study time.

Where you choose to study—your **study site**—is as important as when you study. Your work place should be free of distractions and conducive to work, not relaxation or fun. For example, you may think the student center, a recreation room, or your living room is a good place to review. However, if learning information—not meeting friends or watching TV—is your goal, you may feel disappointed with the amount you accomplish in such a place. In addition, the place you study should not hinder your alertness. Some locations hold psychological attachments. When you go to the kitchen, you look for something to eat instead of thinking about what to study. Similarly, studying in bed often makes you sleepy. Your place of study needs to psychologically motivate you to learn.

Organizing Ideas: Analysis and Synthesis

The outline or map you made during your initial preview (see Chapter 2), your marked and labeled text (see Chapter 2), class handouts, your lecture notes (see Chapter 3), and other course materials comprise a vast quantity of information. You need to analyze each piece independently. Then you must organize and synthesize to determine how the information fits together. In a

Table 4.1   Types and Examples of Assertive Language

Type	Example
Broken Record (repeating the same message over and over in a calm voice)	*Friend:* Come with us! *You:* I'm getting ready for a test, and I'm busy studying. *Friend:* Everyone's going *You:* Yes, but I'm getting ready for a test, and I'm busy studying. *Friend:* Oh, you know that stuff. You always make good grades. *You:* Well, sometimes, but I'm getting ready for a test, and I'm busy studying.
Fogging (agreeing with the truth or principle)	*Friend:* Come with us! *You:* I'd love to come, but I need to read for history class. *Friend:* History! That's boring. You don't want to do that. *You:* History is boring sometimes, but I need to read the chapter now. *Friend:* Not now . . . read it tomorrow. *You:* You're right. I could read it tomorrow, but I want to read it now.
Compromise (agreeing but on your terms)	*Friend:* Come with us! *You:* I need to solve some problems for tomorrow's calculus class. *Friend:* You can do that later. Go with us now. *You:* I could, but I want to work them while the formula is fresh on my mind. I should be finished in an hour. Could I meet you then?
Understanding Assertion (encourages others to understand your point of view without offending them)	*Friend:* Come with us! *You:* I know you don't mean anything by it, but when you see me studying and ask me to go out, I am just too tempted because we have such a good time. Don't tempt me! I'm trying to be strong."

SOURCE: Adapted from Smith, M. J. (1975). *When I say no, I feel guilty.* New York: Dial.

sense, Machiavelli's political maxim, "divide and rule," applies to learning. You must isolate and analyze each bit of information before you can organize, synthesize, and rule it.

To divide and rule course information, you need two things. First, you require more than mere familiarity with information. In terms of Bloom's taxonomy of thinking (see Chapter 1), you need to recognize information and put it into your own words, relate it in different ways, and apply it to different situations before you can analyze, synthesize, and organize it. Thus, you cannot analyze and synthesize based on a single reading of course materials or a cursory glance at your class notes. Instead, you need time to absorb the information. This time provides you with the insight to make the connections you need. Second, your organizational system for coursework aids your analysis and facilitates synthesis. It allows you to arrange and rearrange information according to the relationships you find. The system that best

SMART SITES   **Using the Web to Assess Study Sites**

A wealth of information related to the topics in this chapter is available on the World Wide Web. For this exercise, access the *Study Distractions Analysis* Web page from the following URL http://www.vt.edu:10021/studentinfo/ucc.studydis.html (for the most up-to-date URLs, go to http://csuccess.wadsworth.com). Print the form or complete it on a separate sheet of paper or in your journal. Review your response to the *Thinking Critically* Activity on page 40. How did the results of your study distractions analysis relate to your learning preferences?

suits you depends on your learning style and goals as well as course emphasis and content. Sometimes instructors suggest organizational formats by identifying the structure of information to learn (theories, causes and effects, processes, problems and solutions, and so on) or by providing the general categories of information you need to know. More often, you'll identify your own organizational formats. Like many other learning aids, the organizational structures you create usually prove to be the most effective.

"One picture is worth a thousand words" expresses the rationale for using **idea maps** (ideas arranged spatially) and **charts** (ideas arranged by rows and columns) as aids in analyzing and synthesizing ideas. These provide visual representations of relationships among bits of information. Such graphics facilitate memory and recall as well as higher levels of thinking. Adding meaningful doodles, colors, or symbols (circles, squares, stars, and so on) also helps you remember what you learn, particularly if you are a right-brain learner (see Chapter 1). Because you take an active part in organizing information, you recall more with less effort.

Creating a chart or idea map of the content of an entire course often seems overwhelming. Creating graphics of single chapters or lectures is a good first step. Some graphic systems are more appropriate for certain content areas than others. Choosing the graphic you need depends on your learning style, the nature of the subject, and the organization of the lecturer or author. Once you analyze each lecture or chapter and other course materials, you can more easily see how the components of the course fit together as a whole.

Idea Maps

Idea maps are pictures that show relationships among concepts. They express patterns of thought. You use them to analyze, organize, and synthesize text chapters, lecture notes, and other course materials.

You might think of an idea map as being similar to a city map. If you are new to a city, you need more details. If the city is familiar to you, you require less direction. You also use a map differently when you look for a specific place than when you use it to understand the city's overall layout. Similarly, if a subject is familiar to you, you require fewer details than if the material is new. Looking at the entire range of a course differs from looking at one specific part in detail. Thus, the way you organize information depends on your background knowledge and purpose.

Idea maps represent your thoughts about a topic. Creating them requires higher levels of thinking. You not only recall information, you express it in your own words. You interpret information and find relationships. You might need to apply rules and principles to classify information appropriately. You analyze individual concepts and synthesize them to create the ultimate meaning of the whole map. Finally, you judge the relevance and importance of information as well as assess your own understanding of concepts.

Although idea maps relate information to a central topic, they indicate relationships among details in different ways. For example, elements that flow from one to another (for example, chronological order, steps in a process, causes and effects) differ from details that do not share a causal link (literary genres, biographical details, geological formations). In Figure 4.1, different informational structures are characterized by different elements, different content area applications, and different visual structures. Figures 4.2, 4.3, and 4.4 show how these might apply to various aspects of literature.

Figure 4.1   Visual Formats for Structuring Idea Maps

Type	Example of Elements	Content Area Applications	Visual Structure
Introductory/ Summary	main ideas supporting details	applicable to any content area	
Subject Development/ Definition	definitions supporting details examples characteristics types or kinds	scientific concepts psychological, medical educational, or other case studies genres of literature styles of music political philosophy	
Enumeration/ sequence	main points details steps elements procedures	mathematical process historical chronology literary plot scientific method computer science programs	

(continues)

Figure 4.1   *Continued*

Type	Example of Elements	Content Area Applications	Visual Structure
Comparison/ Contrast	similarities pros cons opinions time periods	authors composers case studies political philosophies psychological treatments educational principles scientific theories	
Cause/Effect	problems solutions	historical events scientific discovery mathematical principles scientific principles health and nutrition sociological conditions psychological problems	

Figure 4.2   **Example of a Web Map**

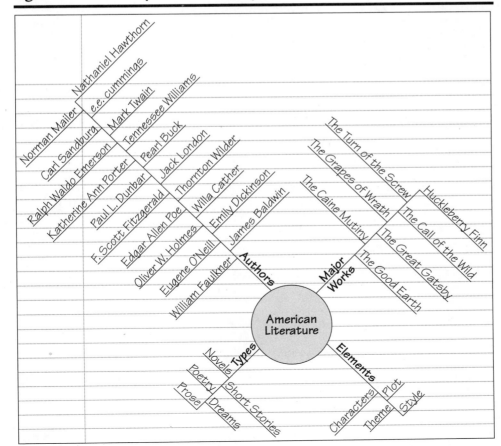

Figure 4.3   Example of a Flow-Chart Map

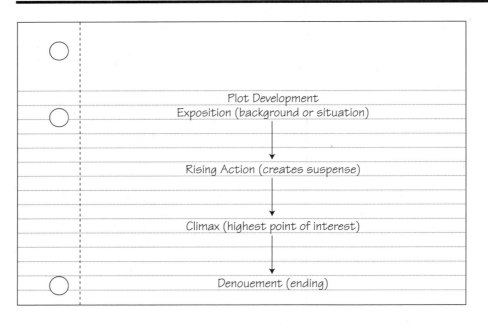

Figure 4.4   Example of a Branching Idea Map

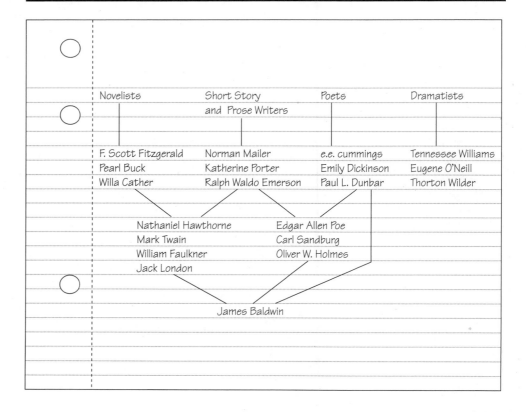

With the exception of chapter preview maps, which show an author's organization of ideas, maps depend on your own processing and interpretation of information. Thus, creation of a map requires regular class attendance, frequent review of class notes, completion of course readings, and familiarity with all other course materials. In other words, the ability to create maps depends on your preparation, background knowledge, and ability to think critically about the topic. Table 4.2 provides the steps in creating idea maps.

You remember map-related information more clearly than information that has only been processed through one of your senses (see Chapter 1). Notes and texts tend to be linear. As a result, you may tend to think about the information in only one way. Maps are more versatile because you can view them from many perspectives. Because you create them yourself, they accurately reflect the ways in which you processed and organized information.

There is, then, no wrong way to create a map; however, there are especially good ways to construct one. Look at Figure 4.5. Which map appears to be more effective? Fitzpatrick (1986) suggests that although both maps cover the same information, Map B is superior. Its main topic, support lines, and details are more exact. Map B contains more abbreviations, yet the meaning is clearer. Finally, Map B can be read without turning the paper. In Exercise 4.2, practice creating a concept map of terms from Sample Chapter 6, "The Study of Humanity."

Charts

Your understanding of the relationships among ideas can also be indicated by charting. Creating charts helps you analyze and categorize information. It allows you to compare, contrast, and identify relationships across and between different factors. Synthesis occurs when you summarize the content of the chart, draw conclusions about the information, or predict trends in information. Table 4.3 summarizes the steps in charting information.

Exercise 4.2   Based on your reading (see Chapter 2) of Sample Chapter 6 ("The Study of Humanity") and lecture notes (see Chapter 3), create a concept map on a separate piece of paper or in your journal using the following terms and concepts from Sample Chapter 6: *holism, ethnocentrism, cultural anthropology, physical anthropology, anthropological linguistics, ethnography, sociocultural anthropology, relativism, fieldwork, linguistics, comparativism, social anthropology, ethnocentrism, primatologists.* You can add additional words to your map to connect or expand these concepts.

Table 4.2   Steps in Constructing Idea Maps

1. Complete text reading. Review lecture notes, text information, and other course materials.

2. If you feel confident about either your ability to create a map or your general understanding of the information, create your map directly on a single sheet of paper. If you feel unsure about yourself or the information, use index cards to help you arrange and rearrange ideas into a workable organizational pattern.

3. Choose a word or phrase that represents the topic you wish to cover. The word or phrase could be a chapter title, purpose-setting question, heading, objective, term, or major classification.

4. Write this word or phrase at the top of a page or on an index card.

5. Identify and list information about the topic by reviewing lecture notes, text readings, course materials, and your own background knowledge. Information can be listed on a single page or on separate cards. Such information might include descriptive details, terms, steps in a process, causes, effects, functions, or reasons.

6. Examine the elements of your map to determine how they relate to one another. Identify any associations between elements (least to most, causes and effects, problems and solutions, nonequivalent elements, equivalent elements).

7. Arrange and rearrange the cards until you find an appropriate organizational pattern that appears to represent the kind of relationships you've identified.

8. If you find a word or phrase that you cannot fit into the organizational structure, keep reviewing and reading until you discern its relationship to the rest of the concepts in the map.

9. Sketch the map. Draw lines or arrows to indicate relationships among map elements and between the topic and details.

10. Write a summary statement that explains the map.

Table 4.3   Steps in Charting Information

1. Make a vertical list of the items you wish to compare.

2. Write out horizontally the factors you wish to examine about each item.

3. Draw a grid by sketching columns for each factor, and rows for each item. Be sure column and row runs for the full length of the vertical and horizontal lists.

4. Locate and record the information that fills each box of the grid.

Figure 4.5   Comparison of Good and Better Maps

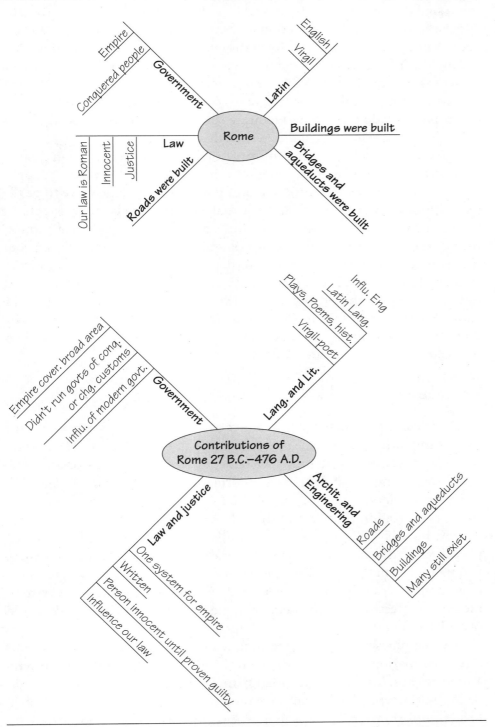

SOURCE: Permission granted from Elaine Fitzpatrick, *hm News,* hm Study Skills/NASSP. Newton, MA.

Charts have several advantages. First, charting information is probably a more familiar way to organize ideas. Because of its familiarity, you may feel more confident in your ability to create charts. Second, like idea maps, charts concisely summarize large amounts of information onto one page. Often, such summary sheets make information more manageable for study. Processing the information gleaned from your text and lecture notes becomes a more realistic goal. Third, like idea maps, charts graphically organize all sorts of information. Finally, while idea maps concisely organize information on one topic, they do not always facilitate comparisons across topics. Charts help you compare features of different topics.

To analyze and synthesize information by creating a chart, you create a column for each available source of information (text, lecture notes, supplementary readings, and so on). Beginning with what you perceive to be the most detailed and complete source—usually the text or class notes—you list the points you feel are most important. This analysis of your main source usually includes terms, major concepts, and supporting details. Using your next source, you identify information that matches what you already identified or, alternatively, is not found in your main source and add it to your chart. You repeat the procedure until you exhaust all sources. Figure 4.6 shows how you might analyze part of Sample Chapter 6, "The Study of Humanity" and accompanying lecture notes. In Exercise 4.3, you create a chart of the four subfields of anthropology.

Association

Association is a familiar process that you use daily. Perhaps you associate a certain song with a particular time, event, or person in your life. Hearing the song cues that memory. In much the same way, you can form associations between something you know and the information you need to recall. The most effective associations result from personal and meaningful experience rather than memorization. Once established, the links become automatic.

Although thinking about the familiar item automatically cues recall, your level of understanding can vary. For example, chemistry often requires you to apply what you know to solve problems. To do so, however, you need to accurately recall the formula you need. While association allows you to remember it effectively, what you do with the formula demonstrates your level of understanding.

Mnemonics consist of any technique for improving your ability to associate information. These include **mental** and **physical imagery, acronyms** and **acrostics, location,** and **word games**. The mnemonic you choose depends on the type of information you need to learn and your learning style. Lists of information or steps in a process might be most appropriate for acronyms or acrostics. A mental or physical image might help you recall a single process or concept. Right-brain learners might find mental imagery,

Figure 4.6   **Charting Primary and Secondary Sources of Course Information: Text, Notes, and Supplementary Reading: Anthropological Linguistics**

TYPE	DEFINITIONS	FOCUS OF RESEARCH	KEY NAMES	CONCLUSIONS
Text Notes	Linguistics—scientific study of language Anthropological linguistics —also unwritten languages and social contexts	1. Historical relationships 2. Universal values 3. Innate language abilities (??) 4. Similarities between structure of language and culture	None	Language—a form of shared knowledge. Similarities within differences
Lecture Notes	Historical = diachronic linguistics; changes over time Geographical linguistics— variations in linguistics in geographical areas	Since first millennium (India and Greece)	1. de Saussure (Swiss) father of modern linguistics— interdependence; language an interlocking structure 2. Sir Walter Jones (British)—many languages had a common source which probably no longer exists	Language always a topic of speculation —emphasis on connections of time and place

Exercise 4.3   On a separate piece of paper or in your journal, construct a chart of the four subfields of anthropology in Sample Chapter 6, "The Study of Humanity."

Exercise 4.4   On a separate sheet of paper or in your journal, create a chart that lists, defines, and provides an example of each of the mnemonics discussed in this chapter. Then, use each type of mnemonic to develop memory clues for Sample Chapter 6, "The Study of Humanity."

Table 4.4   Questions for Selecting an Association Technique

1. Does the concept remind you of anything?
2. Does the concept sound like or rhyme with a familiar word?
3. Can you visualize anything when you think of the concept?
4. Can you rearrange any letters to form a word or sentence that cues your memory?
5. Do you know any gimmicks to associate with the concept?
6. Can you draw a picture to associate with the concept?
7. Can you associate the concept with a familiar location?

---

physical imagery, or location to be most effective. Left-brain learners often prefer acronyms, acrostics, or word games. You can also combine various association techniques. Table 4.4 provides you with questions to aid you in selecting the most appropriate type of association technique. In Exercise 4.4, you create a chart that compares and contrasts mnemonic strategies.

Mental and Physical Imagery

When you picture something in your mind, you experience mental imagery. Mental imagery occurs naturally since you often think in pictures rather than in words. For example, suppose you think of a car. Do you think c-a-r, or do you picture what a car looks like and how it feels to drive or ride in one? This use of your visual and other senses aids your recall of both the familiar and the unfamiliar. Table 4.5 lists suggestions for creating effective mental images.

Many mental associations link concrete objects with their images (for example, a picture of an apple with the word *apple)* or abstract concepts with their symbols (a picture of a heart with the word *love).* Mental imagery also links unrelated objects, concepts, and ideas through visualization. For example, suppose you want to recall that the "holistic perspective," as discussed in Sample Chapter 6, describes a viewpoint in which no single aspect of a population makes sense without examining its relationship to other aspects of that system. You might visualize a hole with a variety of cultural aspects—languages, beliefs, customs and so on—in it. Similarly, you may need to know that the "comparative perspective" in anthropological theories considers diversity in terms of cultures and times. Here, you might visualize clothing

---

Table 4.5   Suggestions for Maximizing Mental Imagery

1. **Use common symbols whenever possible.** Suppose you want to remember that 1783 was the date of the treaty that declared peace between the American colonies and England and, thus, ended the Revolutionary War. To do so, you might picture a dove (the symbol of peace) carrying a red, white, and blue (symbolic of the United States) sign with the date 1783 on it.

2. **Use the clearest and closest image.** Suppose you want to remember the name Fischer. Rather than visualizing a dish because it rhymes with the name, think of a fish or a person fishing.

3. **Think of outrageous or humorous images.** For example, to recall four of the basic food groups (breads and cereals, dairy products, fish and meat, fruits and vegetables), you might think of a huge *cow* (dairy products and meat) eating a *banana* (fruit) *sandwich* (bread). Outrageous or humorous images are more memorable because they represent departures from the norm. A cow eating hay is not very memorable because hay is what a cow usually eats. A cow eating a banana sandwich would be a sight that would leave a more lasting impression.

4. **Make sexual connotations.** Perhaps you need to learn all of the planets in the solar system: Mercury, Earth, Venus, Mars, Jupiter, Saturn, Uranus, Neptune, and Pluto. You might picture a naked person with the names of the planets in strategic places.

5. **Create action-filled images.** Rather than picturing a fish to remember Fischer, visualize a person reeling in a big catch or a fish swimming in the water.

---

from different time periods or cultures—Victorian dresses, miniskirts, American Indian tribal dress, Roman togas—to remember that people's feelings, beliefs, and actions differ across time.

If you draw your mental image on paper, you make use of another of your senses, your **kinesthetic perception**. This type of memory aid is called a **mnemonigraph**. By actually making your mental image a concrete one, you provide yourself with a form of repetition that reinforces memory. Drawing or diagramming information also assists you in another way. A diagram often provides a comprehensive, concise way to master a large amount of information. Rather than learning a list of details, then, you might sketch a picture that includes the details you need to learn.

Acronyms and Acrostics

Many courses require you to learn lists of information, such as the bones in the body or the parts of a cell. Acronyms and acrostics provide you with the cues you need for recalling this kind of information.

THINKING CRITICALLY
Examine Table 4.5. On a separate sheet of paper or in your journal, explain why *common, clearest* and *closest, humorous, sexual,* or *action-filled* associations are best for cueing recall.

Acronyms consist of words created from the first letter or first few letters of the items on the list. *ROY G. BIV,* one of the most commonly used acronyms, aids you in recalling the colors of the rainbow in order (red, orange, yellow, green, blue, indigo, and violet). *HOMES,* another common acronym, cues your memory for the names of the Great Lakes (Huron, Ontario, Michigan, Erie, and Superior). Another acronym that aids your recall of the Great Lakes might be *SHO ME.* Acronyms, need not be real words. Whatever the case, they work best when you create them for yourself. For example, you might create *APACA* to recall the subfields of anthropology as described in Sample Chapter 6 (*a*pplied anthropology, *p*hysical anthropology, *a*rchaeology, *c*ultural anthropology, and *a*nthropological linguistics).

Acrostics consist of phrases or sentences created from the first letter or first few letters of the items on the list you need to remember. For example, "George eat old gray rat at Paul's house yesterday" helps you spell *geography* correctly. To be used as an acrostic, sentences need not be grammatically correct; they only need to make sense to you. Like *APACA,* an acrostic of "Able people always count anyway" also cues your memory for the names of the subfields of anthropology.

Location

The location method of memory dates back to a grisly story set in ancient Greece. According to Cicero (Bower, 1970), the Greek poet Simonides had just recited a poem when a messenger asked him to step outside the building. As he left the banquet hall, the roof collapsed, killing everyone inside. The guests were so mangled that family members could not recognize them. Simonides, recalling where each guest sat, came forward to help identify the corpses. Similarly, you use location memory when you remember an important concept by recalling where you were when you heard it, how it looked in your notes, which graphics were on the page containing the information, and so on.

You create location memory artificially by devising a memory map. To do so, you think of a familiar place or route and link the information you wish to recall to specific features you might see there. Then you visualize yourself walking around and looking at each feature as you go. As you mentally "see" each place, you recall the topic you've associated with it. Suppose you want to learn a list of chemical elements. You select a familiar location or route, such

COOPERATIVE LEARNING ACTIVITY
LOOKING AT ALL THE ANGLES: CUBING YOUR UNDERSTANDING

Sometimes it's easy to get into a mental rut. You begin to learn information at the same level of understanding instead of moving up and down Bloom's taxonomy. Cubing (Cowan and Cowan, 1980) is one way to track your understanding as you prepare for a test. Originally designed as a writing exercise, cubing invites you to imagine a topic, question, or issue as a six-sided block. As you mentally turn the block over, you work through the problem from different perspectives. Each side of the cube corresponds to one of the following levels in Bloom's taxonomy: recall, translation, interpretation, application, analysis, and synthesis. Evaluation—the final level in Bloom's taxonomy— forms the culmination of your cubing. Using the different levels of thinking encourages you to view the same information in different ways.

Choose a subject, issue, or problem and look at it from all angles! The following table provides sample questions for you to answer as you visualize each side of the cube. You will think of others as you use cubing with other topics.

Application

As a group, choose a topic from Sample Chapter 6 and apply the cubing strategy.

Table: Cubing Steps

1. Side 1, Recall: How did the text, lecture, notes, and so on identify the problem, issue, or subject?

2. Side 2, Translation: How would you describe the problem, issue, or subject?

3. Side 3, Interpretation: How does the problem, issue, or subject connect to other problems, issues, or subjects? What questions can you ask about these connections?

4. Side 4, Application: How can you use this information to solve other problems or understand other issues or subjects? What questions does this raise?

5. Side 5, Analysis: How can you break the problem, issue, or subject into smaller parts?

6. Side 6, Synthesis: What is the essence of the problem, issue, or subject?

7. After considering all sides of an issue, use the evaluation level of Bloom's taxonomy to judge the results, Which view of the problem, issue, or subject was your best? Why? Which view was your worst? Why? How can you improve your thinking on each side?

---

as the route you take to chemistry class. As you pass each building, you mentally assign it a chemical element. Later, in your chemistry class, you visualize your route; as you "pass" each building, you recall the element it represents.

Word Games

Some memory aids involve what amounts to playing games with information. Such techniques aid recall because they require you to think actively about the information in order to create the game. They provide clues that entertain you and stimulate your memory. Diverse in nature, word games can be both easy and difficult to devise.

Advertisers realize the value of **rhymes** and **jingles** in making their products memorable. The same principles that help you recall "Have you had your break today?" also help you recall academic information. An example of a common rhyme or jingle that aids recall of a spelling rule is "I before e except after c or when sounded like a as in *neighbor* or *weigh.*"

Puns and **parodies** consist of taking common words or poems, stories, songs, and so on and humorously imitating them. Puns involve using words or phrases to suggest more than one meaning, while parodies imitate serious works or phrases through satire or burlesque. The humor of puns and parodies brings cognitive benefits in that it, like other memory tricks, makes studying more imaginative and entertaining. Suppose you find you can't recall the meaning of *numismatist* (a coin collector). You might parody the children's nursery rhyme "Four and Twenty Blackbirds." Instead of the king being in his counting house, counting all his money, you change the rhyme to "The numismatist was in his counting house, counting all his money." Or you might develop a pun to help you recall the definition, such as "Two numismatists getting together for old 'dime's' sake."

Vocabulary Strategies

Adding new words to your vocabulary involves forming personal associations with words. Using the words in your conversation and writing also helps them become part of you through the formation of new associations. As you write a word, you need to be sure you pronounce it correctly to combine the word's visual and verbal components. After this step, repetition forms the key to remembering the word. **Word files, word cards,** and **word maps** help you practice new words.

A word file contains concepts you want to learn. To create a word file, you use word cards and a small card file box with alphabetical or subject tabs. Word cards often consist of the word on the front and its meaning on the back. This traditional format provides learning at the recognition and recall level of Bloom's taxonomy (see Chapter 1). You can create more effective word cards that help you connect personal associations with the concept. These increase your ability to think about the word at higher levels. As a result, they improve your ability to use and recall the word.

One way to do this (Carr, 1985) is to write the word on the card with two sets of connecting lines below it (see Figure 4.7). On the first set of lines, you write the word's meaning and synonym. On the second set, you write associations with the word. You study by covering the original word and using the other words as cues. A second way to make word cards more personal (Eeds and Cockrum, 1985) involves dividing each card into four equal spaces (see Figure 4.8). In one space, you write the word and a sentence using it.

"First aid kits are available to treat information retrieval injuries."

Figure 4.7   Association/Synonym Word Card

---

pariah

Charles Manson
rejected by society
outcast

Figure 4.8   **Four-Dimensional Word Card**

unscrupulous	Charles Manson
The unscrupulous candidate	criminals
Abraham Lincoln George Washington	Somebody who is dishonest

In the second, you list your associations with the word. The third space contains the word's definition. The fourth space contains antonyms of the word. Covering different parts of the card helps you think about the meaning in different ways. Figure 4.9 shows a word card that combines right-brain thinking (see Chapter 1) with a traditional word card approach in that the word appears on the front with the definition on the back. However, this card also includes a mnemonigraph that visually cues meaning. No matter what kind of word cards you devise, carrying them in your bookbag and reviewing them between classes, at the bus stop, or whenever you have a few free minutes helps lock words into your vocabulary. You might devise a system to separate the words that you know well from those that still need review. For example, you might rate your understanding in terms of the stages of your concept development (see Table 1.3 in Chapter 1). To do so, you would continue to include the card in your review until you reached level 4 understanding. Or you might put a small check mark on the card each time you successfully recall the meaning and delete the card from your review when you get three checks. In addition, you can vary the way you use your cards. Each side or part of the card cues a different kind of thinking. For example, you recall specific terms when cued by the sides or parts of the card that show the definitions, synonyms, and so on. By using the other side or parts of the card, you use the term to translate the meaning into your own words, associate the term with

Figure 4.9   Right-Brain Word Card

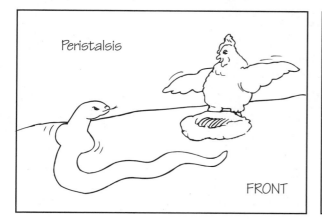

Peristalsis

FRONT

Involuntary contraction of the muscular wall of the esophagus to force food to the stomach and propel waste through the rest of the digestive tract.

BACK

Exercise 4.5   Create word cards for each of the terms in Sample Chapter 6, "The Study of Humanity." You may use a format discussed in this chapter or another one you devise for yourself.

Exercise 4.6   On a separate sheet of paper or in your journal, create a word map for each of the terms in Sample Chapter 6, "The Study of Humanity."

other words, or think about it in a variety of other ways. Exercise 4.5 allows you to create word cards for terms from Sample Chapter 6.

Creating a word map of the terms in a particular chapter is another way to aid recall and develop associations among terms. To do so, you identify general headings under which terms might fall. Then you draw a map showing these headings. Under each one, you list the appropriate terms. Then you draw two lines under each term, similar to those shown in Figure 4.10. On the first line, you draw a picture that you associate with the term and/or its meaning. On the second line, you write the term's meaning in your own words. To use this word map to study, you cover everything except the term. Then, you try to recall the concept's meaning. If unsuccessful, you uncover just the picture. Seeing your drawing often cues recall. If not, you can uncover the definition. Your final step in using this strategy is to spend a few seconds studying the term and recalling why you drew the picture you did. In Exercise 4.6, you create a word map of the terms from Sample Chapter 6.

Figure 4.10   Word Map

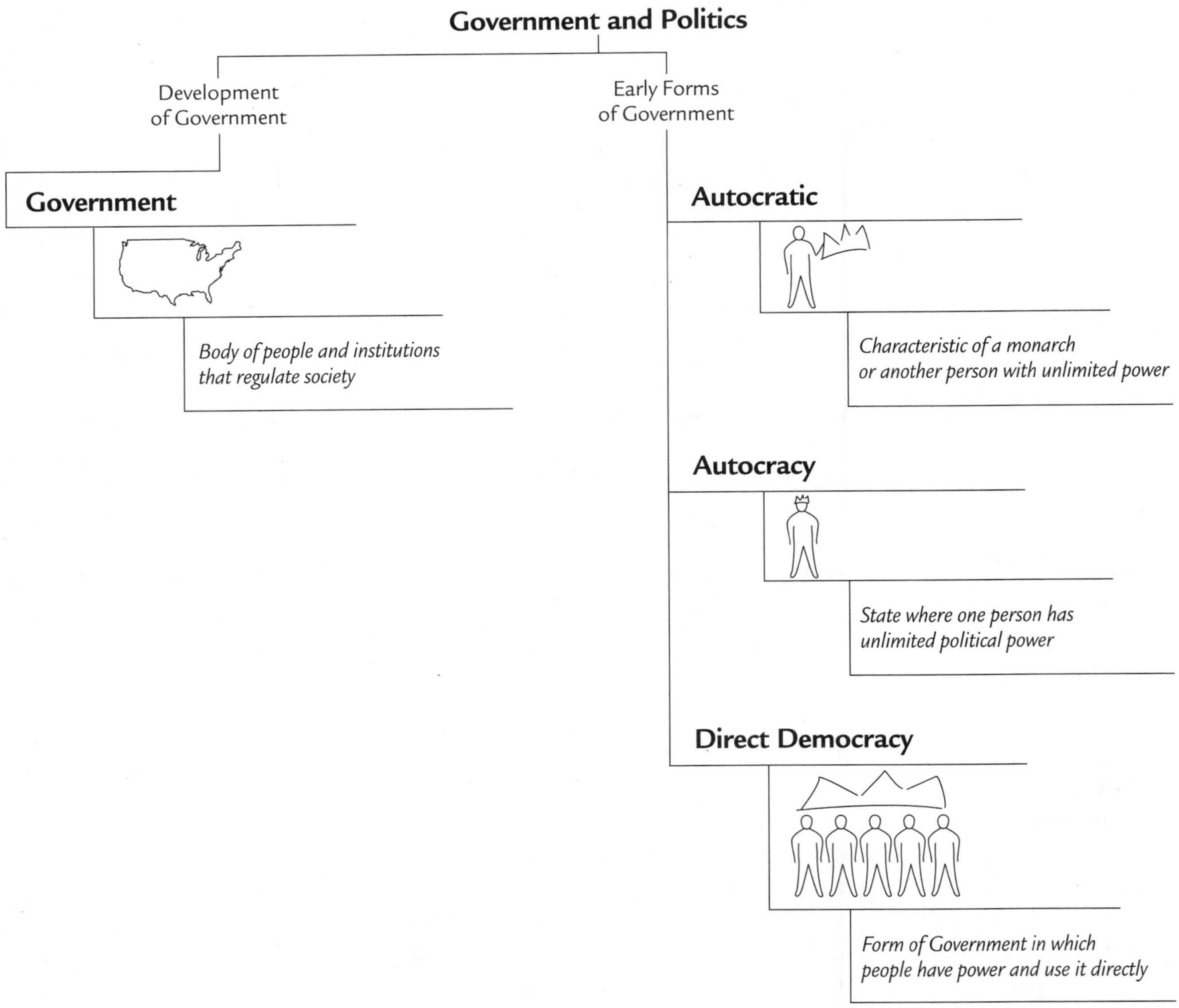

Government and Politics

Development of Government

Early Forms of Government

Government

Body of people and institutions that regulate society

Autocratic

Characteristic of a monarch or another person with unlimited power

Autocracy

State where one person has unlimited political power

Direct Democracy

Form of Government in which people have power and use it directly

---

THINKING CRITICALLY

On a separate sheet of paper or in your journal, design a new format for a word card. Label the components of your card and explain how they help you form personal associations with a word's meaning.

Rehearsal

In learning, rather than practice making perfect, it makes information more permanent and recall more automatic. Practice assumes many forms, some of which are used in combination. These forms vary in the amount of time each requires, the depth to which learning occurs, and the manner in which information is learned. Your purposes for learning and your learning style (see Chapter 1) affect your choice of practice activities. Whatever practice method(s) you select, each involves repetition of information in some way.

Spaced Study Versus Cramming

Spaced study, also known as **distributed practice,** consists of alternating short study sessions with breaks. You set study goals through time (for example, fifteen minutes) or task limits (such as, reading three pages of information). After accomplishing a goal or several goals, you allow yourself small rewards, such as a snack or free time to call friends, relax, or take a walk. This method helps you to gradually and more thoroughly process information into long-term memory.

As described in Bloom's taxonomy (see Chapter 1), learning occurs in stages and requires time and repetition to develop fully. As a result, time management (see Chapter 1) forms the basis of spaced study. You use your term calendar to plot your course of study over the entire term or between exams. Completing a weekly calendar helps you identify free time in your

"Calories were the only thing I ever retained from a night of cramming!"

schedule. Your daily, prioritized "to do" list helps you structure and maintain time for regular study.

Spaced study works for a number of reasons. First, spaced study builds a system of rewards for hard work. This form of study involves **behavior modification,** a type of learning based on work by B. F. Skinner, an American psychological researcher. In his studies with animals, Skinner found that they learned to respond when rewarded with food. The breaks in spaced study serve as your reward for completing a set amount or time of study. Second, because you work under a time deadline or task limit, you complete quality work. Knowing you have only a certain amount of time or information to study motivates you. Third, because working memory has limited capacity, study breaks provide opportunities for you to absorb information into long-term memory. Fourth, when studying complex, related information, study breaks prevent you from confusing similar details.

The opposite of spaced study—**cramming**—involves frantic, last-minute (and sometimes all-night) memorization of information. In cramming, you often "rent" information at the recall level until a test is over, rather than "owning" it at higher levels for longer periods of time. Probably the least effective means of practice, cramming often results in information being quickly forgotten because it was superficially processed.

Recitation

Recitation involves silent, oral, or written repetition of information in answer to study questions from either the text, the instructor, or yourself. Oral and written recitation facilitate recall because they involve more senses. The first step of recitation consists of locating or creating study questions. Next, you read or study information to answer these questions. Third, you recite the answers you find. Checking the accuracy of your answers by referring to your text or notes is the fourth step in recitation. Finally, the recitation of questions and answers keeps information in working memory. Repeated recitation transfers information to long-term memory.

Overlearning

Overlearning, which is most appropriate for specific facts or details (information you must memorize exactly, such as a poem or a formula), consists of overlapping study (Tenney, 1986). This form of practice continues to reinforce information following initial learning. For example, suppose you need to learn the botanical names of plants for a landscape course. You overlearn the list in one of two ways outlined in Table 4.6.

Table 4.6   Methods of Overlearning

Method 1

1. List each item separately on a note card.
2. Learn the first three cards.
3. Add one card.
4. Review and practice with all four cards.
5. Add one card.
6. Review and practice with all five cards.
7. Delete the card that you know the best from the original set and add one new card.
8. Review and practice with all five cards.
9. Repeat steps 7 and 8 until you know all the items.

Method 2

1. Divide the list into manageable units (three to five items per unit, depending on the difficulty of the material).
2. Learn one set.
3. Add other set.
4. Practice all sets.
5. Repeat steps 3 and 4 until you know all the items.

Smart Review 4.1

Check your understanding of the preceding section by answering the following on a separate sheet of paper or in your journal:

1. What factors contribute to identification of prime study time?
2. How do idea maps and charts facilitate analysis and synthesis in preparing for tests?
3. Consider the following association techniques: mental imagery, mnemonigraphs, acronyms, acrostics, location, word games, and vocabulary strategies. Define each one and provide an example of each using the content of this chapter. Do not repeat the examples you were given in the preceding section.
4. Describe how you could combine any three of the rehearsal techniques into a single practice system.

Honest Cheating

Students from the beginning of time have searched for ways to beat the system. They want good grades without studying. Some cram. Others borrow notes. A few resort to dishonest techniques. Cheat sheets are one of the techniques used most often.

Cheat sheets generally consist of small slips of paper inscribed with bits of information. The papers are hidden in clothing, books, or other papers. Some cheat sheets aren't even on paper. Some students use arms, ankles, and other bits of skin to record information for future use. Cheat sheets serve as ready, but dishonest, references for forgetful students.

What students fail to realize is that the benefit of cheat sheets is generally not in their use but in their construction. The activity of creating the cheat sheet is an exercise in critical thinking. You must read carefully to separate truly relevant from irrelevant information. You must recite to determine it. You must understand what you read. You must make decisions. You must think actively. These processes aid understanding and recall.

Such understanding results from various sources. Thinking of the perfect key words to trigger memory increases understanding. Writing the information provides motor learning. The effort made to synthesize information into as small an amount as possible serves as an active learning tool. If most students gave themselves the chance, they would find they could remember what they need from the cheat sheet without actually using it. Thus, the harm is not in creating a cheat sheet. Its creation actually aids learning as you read and recite what you need to know. The harm comes in using it on a test. Table 4.7 help you create honest cheat sheets you can use with a clear conscience.

Table 4.7   Steps in Creating Honest Cheat Sheets

1. Decide what information you need to know.
2. Determine what you already know.
3. Synthesize the remaining information as completely as possible.
4. Summarize and reduce the information using key words and acronyms.
5. Record your final product on a single sheet of paper.
6. Review frequently.
7. LEAVE YOUR CHEAT SHEET AT HOME!
8. Refer mentally to your cheat sheet during the test.

USING SPECIFIC STUDY PLANS
TO PREPARE FOR EXAMS

Preparation is based on expectation. To prepare for a test, you need to know what to expect from it. **Objective tests** (see Table 4.8) and **subjective tests** (see Table 4.9) require different kinds of thinking from you. Objective tests require that you recognize or reason information from the options you're given. Subjective exams require you to recall, recreate, and use information you've learned. Because objective and subjective exams differ in format, you need different plans for preparing for each.

Table 4.8   **Objective Test Formats**

Example of a true-false question:

T F Demographic transition theory interprets the modern population growth as the result of a temporary disequilibrium between birth rates and death rates.

Example of a multiple-choice question:
Which of the following is NOT a problem of the industrialized world?
A. Pollution
B. Inefficient animal-protein diets
C. Underdevelopment
D. Excessive government bureaucracy
E. Loss of farmland to competing uses

Example of matching questions:

1. Budget constraint   A. occurs when government expenditures outrun tax receipts

2. Budget deficit   B. occurs when tax receipts outstrip government expenditures

3. Budget surplus   C. graphic representation of all combinations a person can purchase given a certain money income and prices for the goods

Example of fill-in-the-blank questions:
induction   kinesis   heterotroph

1. A _____ is an example of an organism which cannot use nonorganic energy sources to synthesize all of its high-energy organic molecules.

2. The innate process by which an organism achieves an orientation to a stimulus by altering its speed of movement in response to the stimulus is called _____.

3. In embryos, _____ is the process by which a particular group of cells causes other cells to differentiate into a specific tissue type.

Table 4.9   Subjective Test Formats

Example of an essay question:
Compare and contrast Robert Frost's "Departmental" with W. H. Auden's "The Unknown Citizen" in terms of content, context, tone, and rhyme. Which, in your opinion, is the better poem and why?

Example of a short-answer question:
What would be an example of a question that would support *Boolean expression*?

Example of a fill-in-the-blank question:
A line is a(n) _____ for a curve if the distance between the line and the curve approaches zero as we move farther and farther along the line.

Test preparation requires different kinds of critical thinking tasks. You identify your expectations about a course to determine what you need to know. More important, you determine the level to which you must know information. The information emphasized in class, assigned readings, and the course syllabus leads you to draw conclusions concerning the content of the test. Analysis of the materials helps you identify effective ways to prepare for the test. Table 4.10 identifies ways to apply critical thinking as described in Bloom's Taxonomy to preparing for a test on this chapter.

POSSE: A Study Plan for Objective Exams

POSSE (*p*lan, *o*rganize, *s*chedule, *s*tudy, and *e*valuate) is an acronym for a system that helps you identify your study goals and make plans for achieving them. To follow the stages of **POSSE,** you answer a series of questions (see Table 4.11). Writing answers to the questions, instead of verbally answering them, forces you to concentrate more fully on each question. This also keeps you from inadvertently omitting questions. Moreover, it provides a means of reviewing your responses. Answers to many questions will come from either your syllabus, your instructor, your text, or your experiences in the class. Other questions, however, will force you to examine your study strengths and weaknesses. Your success depends on your honesty in dealing with such issues. It is also important that you begin the POSSE process at least a week before the test is scheduled to allow time for predicting test questions (see Exercise 4.7). By working through POSSE with care and determination, you make the best use of your study time and efforts.

**Table 4.10   Thinking Critically with Bloom's Taxonomy: Preparing
for a Test on Chapter 4**

Recall/Translation

WHAT TOPICS WERE COVERED IN THIS CHAPTER?

1. General study strategies: prime study time; using idea maps and charts to analyze and synthesize; association techniques, including mental and physical imagery, acronyms and acrostics, location, word games, and vocabulary strategies; and rehearsal strategies, including spaced study, cramming, recitation, and overlearning.

2. Using POSSE (objective) and PORPE (subjective) to prepare for exams.

Interpretation

WHAT CONCLUSIONS CAN I DRAW?

1. Two main topics in the chapter

2. Seem to be application-based

3. Evaluation required to determine which technique works best for which subject

4. Development of a personal study system results from synthesis

Application

HOW MIGHT I BE ASKED TO USE THIS INFORMATION?

1. Question describes a student in terms of course, learning style, and material to be learned and asks to devise a study plan.

2. Question describes a scenario where a student's prime time is threatened and asks how to solve the problem.

3. Question asks for a comparison and contrast of association techniques.

4. Question asks for a comparison and contrast of recitation techniques.

5. Question asks for a comparison and contrast of general and specific study plans.

6. Question asks for a comparison and contrast of POSSE and PORPE.

Analysis

1. Question asks to analyze components of POSSE.

2. Question asks to analyze components of PORPE.

Synthesis

1. Question asks to create a study schedule or plan for a specific situation.

Evaluation

1. Question describes a study situation and asks to determine what problems might arise and how to solve them.

2. Question asks to determine which association is most appropriate for a given situation.

3. Question asks to determine which parts of POSSE or PORPE are most critical.

Table 4.11   Stages of POSSE

To complete the stages of POSSE, consult your instructor, text, course syllabus, lecture notes, or other materials.

Plan

ANSWER THESE QUESTIONS:

What does the test cover?

Is the test comprehensive or noncomprehensive?

How many questions will the test contain?

Will the test require me to apply information?

How much does this test count in my final course grade?

When is the test?

Where will the test be given?

What special material(s) will I need to take the test?

Organize

ANSWER THESE QUESTIONS:

What materials do I need to study:

textbook?

handouts?

lecture notes?

supplemental readings?

old exams?

What study and memory methods will work best with this material?

Can I find a study partner or group to prepare for this test?

Can I predict test questions by:

answering chapter review questions?

examining old exams?

questioning former students or the instructor to obtain clues about test item construction?

creating a practice test of key points?

completing a practice test and go over the responses with my instructor?

Gather all study materials together. Construct study and memory aids.

Schedule

ANSWER THESE QUESTIONS:

How much time do I have before the exam?

How much time will I need to study for this test?

(continues)

Table 4.11   *Continued*

How much time each day will I study?

How will I distribute my study time?

Where will I study?

When will I meet with my study group or partner?

What obligations do I have that might interfere with this study time?

Study

AT THE END OF EACH STUDY SESSION, ANSWER THESE QUESTIONS:

Am I studying actively, that is, through writing or speaking?

Am I distributing my study time to avoid memory interference and physical fatigue?

Am I following my study schedule? Why or why not?

What adjustments do I need to make?

Am I learning efficiently? Why or why not? What adjustments do I need to make?

Evaluate

AFTER THE TEST IS RETURNED, COMPLETE THE WORKSHEET IN FIGURE 5.5
   (SEE CHAPTER 5, PAGE 224). ANSWER THESE QUESTIONS:

What pattern(s) emerge(s) from the worksheet?

What type of questions did I miss most often?

What changes can I make to my study plan to avoid such trends in the future?

File your POSSE plan, course materials, study aids, exam, after-exam worksheet, and evaluation for future reference.

Exercise 4.7   Consider the following: You are enrolled in Anthropology 101. You have a test next week on Sample Chapter 6. The test will be in an objective format. You will have 10 multiple choice questions and 10 matching questions. Predict the content of this test and construct a sample test using the *organize, schedule,* and *study* steps of POSSE. Use separate sheets of paper or your journal.

PORPE: A Study Plan for Subjective Exams

Studying for essay exams requires more of you than studying for other kinds of tests. These tests require you to understand major concepts and discuss them in a coherent written form. Essays require you to recall and translate information as well as use it to interpret, apply, analyze, synthesize, and/or evaluate what you know. Your essay needs to state main points and contain facts to support the ideas you express.

Often students fear subjective exams because they lack confidence in their ability to prepare for and write essay responses. A study plan exists to help you become a better writer. This plan, **PORPE**, consists of five stages: *predict, organize, rehearse, practice,* and *evaluate* (Simpson, 1986). When put into motion at least three days before an exam, PORPE helps you predict possible essay questions (see Exercise 4.8), organize your thoughts, and devise strategies for recalling information.

Even if you fail to predict the exact questions you find on your exam, PORPE will not be a waste of time for several reasons. First, your predicted questions probably reflect much of the information you will encounter. Thus, the information you rehearsed will be used, in part, to answer the questions you're given. Finally, the practice you get in writing not only increases your self-confidence, it also improves your writing ability.

To follow the stages in PORPE, you answer a series of questions and complete the steps at each stage. Table 4.12 identifies the steps, timeline, and questions in the PORPE process.

Exercise 4.8   Consider the following: You are enrolled in Anthropology 101. You have a test next week on Sample Chapter 6. The test will be subjective. You will have three essay questions and five short-answer questions. Using the *predict* step of PORPE, predict the content of this test and construct a sample test on a separate sheet of paper or in your journal. Remember, you need to predict three times as many questions as you will actually have.

Table 4.12   Stages of PORPE

Three days before the exam:

Predict

PREDICT INFORMATION ABOUT THE TEST BY ANSWERING THESE QUESTIONS:

　　What does the test cover?

　　Is the test comprehensive or noncomprehensive?

　　How many questions will the test contain?

　　What levels of thinking will most likely be required?

(continues)

Table 4.12   *Continued*

How much does this test count in my final course grade?

When is the test?

Where will the test be given?

What special material(s) will I need to take the test?

PREDICT ESSAY QUESTIONS BY ANSWERING THESE QUESTIONS:

What are the pros and cons of important issues?

How can I compare and contrast concepts?

How can I define basic terms? What are some examples or applications of the terms?

What information did the instructor stress during lectures?

PREDICT AT LEAST THREE TIMES AS MANY QUESTIONS AS YOUR INSTRUCTOR HAS INDICATED WILL BE ON THE EXAM.

Two days before the exam:

Organize

ORGANIZE INFORMATION BY ANSWERING THE FOLLOWING QUESTIONS:

What type of text structure will best answer each of these questions (cause and effect, subject development, enumeration or sequence, or comparison and contrast)?

What is the best way to organize this information (outline, map, chart, note cards, etc.)?

What information is essential for answering this question?

What information adds relevant, supporting details or examples?

What is the source of this information:

textbook?

lecture notes?

supplemental readings?

class materials or handouts?

other?

Construct sample written responses to your predicted essay questions.

Rehearse

LOCK INFORMATION INTO MEMORY BY ANSWERING THESE QUESTIONS:

What mnemonic techniques (acronyms, acrostics, word games, etc.) can I use to practice this information?

How much time each day will I study?

When will I study?

How will I distribute my study time?

(continues)

Table 4.12   *Continued*

Where will I study?

If necessary, when will I meet with my study group or partner?

What obligations do I have that might interfere with this study time?

CONSTRUCT MNEMONIC AIDS.

INCORPORATE ACTIVE METHODS (SPEAKING AND WRITING) INTO STUDY.

One day before the exam:

Practice

PRACTICE WRITING YOUR RESPONSES FROM MEMORY.

Evaluate

JUDGE THE QUALITY OF YOUR PRACTICE RESPONSES AS OBJECTIVELY AS POSSIBLE BY ANSWERING THE FOLLOWING QUESTIONS:

Did I answer the question that was asked?

Did my response begin with an introduction?

Did my answer end with a conclusion?

Was my answer well-organized?

Did I include all essential information?

Did I include any relevant details or examples?

Did I use transition words?

Is my writing neat and easily read?

Did I check spelling and grammar?

IF POSSIBLE, TALK WITH YOUR INSTRUCTOR OR OTHER STUDENTS AND ASK THEM TO CRITIQUE YOUR WORK.

IF YOU ANSWERED ANY OF THESE QUESTIONS NEGATIVELY, YOU NEED TO CONTINUE PRACTICING YOUR ANSWERS.

REPEAT THE FINAL FOUR STAGES OF PORPE UNTIL YOU CAN ANSWER YES TO EACH QUESTION.

AFTER THE EXAM HAS BEEN RETURNED, READ YOUR INSTRUCTOR'S COMMENTS AND COMPARE THEM WITH THE LAST EVALUATION YOU MADE DURING YOUR STUDY SESSIONS.

LOOK FOR NEGATIVE TRENDS YOU CAN AVOID OR POSITIVE TRENDS YOU CAN REINFORCE WHEN YOU STUDY FOR YOUR NEXT EXAM.

File your PORPE plan, course materials, study aids, and evaluation data for future reference.

SMART Information 4.1

Using your password for this course, access InfoTrac College Edition on the World Wide Web.

1. Your instructor tells the class that at least one test question will focus exclusively on the specific type of anthropologist that you used for your search in Question 1 of **SMART Information 3.1.** Using the type of search you found most effective, repeat the search. This time, locate and print one article that you think provides the most helpful discussion for that topic. Read, mark, and label the article. Create notecards, an outline, or a map that reflects the information within the article.

2. Your instructor also tells you that you must be prepared to discuss one of the major concepts described in the videotape lecture. Luckily, you recall that you wrote the citation for a good article in Question 2 of **SMART Information 3.1.** Using the citation information, locate and print the article. Read, mark, and label the article. Use the information from the article and integrate it into a map or outline of related information from Sample Chapter 6, "The Study of Humanity."

3. Your instructor tell the class that the factors of anthropological study (religion, politics, society, technology, and economy) will be used as perspectives for an essay question. Review your response to Question 3 of **SMART Information 3.1.** Choose one of the topics and describe how you could narrow your search to create a more manageable list of citations.

   _____

   _____

   _____

   _____

   _____

   _____

4. The articles you used in questions 1 and 2 will be on your next test. Create three objective questions and one essay question for each article.

   _____

   _____

   _____

   _____

   _____

   _____

   _____

   _____

   _____

   _____

Smart Review 4.2

Check your understanding of the preceding section by answering the following on a separate sheet of paper or in your journal:

1. How is preparing for an objective test different from preparing for a subjective test? How is it similar?
2. Using this chapter, create an example of each type of objective test question and each type of subjective test question identified in Tables 4.8 and 4.9.
3. Identify the five stages of POSSE. Which one would be most difficult for you to implement? Why?
4. Identify the five stages of PORPE. Which one would be most difficult for you to implement? Why?

Speaking Figuratively, of Course...

Identifying Symbols

Symbols are based on your own background knowledge and experiences. In general, symbols are universally understood. This is due to years of association between a symbol and the object it represents.

Some symbols mean different things in different cultures. For example, in Western countries, white is a symbol of purity. In Eastern cultures, such as Japan or India, white is a symbol of death or mourning.

Other symbols have no strong meaning for a specific culture. Think of how you feel about the flag of another country. You might recognize the flag of England when you see it. However, it does not fill you with the same sense of patriotism as does the flag of your country. In the United States, the American flag (or the colors red, white, and blue) symbolizes this country.

The meaning of a symbol depends on the context. It also depends on the time and place in which it is used. For instance, the swastika was originally a religious sign in ancient India. It was also used by Mayans and American Indians. Its meaning changed when Hitler adopted it as a symbol. It became one of the most hated symbols in history because it stood for the evil associated with Nazi Germany.

Symbols can be used alone or as parts of other figurative language. The symbol lends its meaning to the overall image. For example, a green-eyed monster refers to someone who is jealous. A broken heart describes a failed romance.

Table: Symbols and Meanings

Color

yellow (fear)

green (jealousy, money, growth)

purple (royalty)

red (anger, danger)

blue (sadness)

white (innocence, purity, death)

black (death)

Animals

owl (wisdom)

fox (cunning, trickery)

lion (strength, bravery)

hawk (war)

dove (peace)

stork (babies)

elephant (memory, Republican party)

donkey (Democratic party)

crow/buzzard/vulture (death)

Objects

heart (love, soul)

rose (love)

cross (Christianity)

red cross (first aid)

skull and crossbones (danger, poison, piracy)

four-leaf clover (good luck)

horseshoe (good luck)

Uncle Sam (United States)

white hats (good guys)

black hats (bad guys)

flag (country)

tree (life)

rainbow (promise)

cloud (trouble)

olive branch (peace)

laurel wreath (victory)

winter (old age, death)

spring (youth)

Figurative Language 4.A

Identify the symbols in each of the following quotations. Then indicate what they represent.

1. "Ah. Fortune smiles. Another day of wine and roses. Or, in your case, beer and pizza!"—Two-Face, *Batman Forever,* 1995

   Symbol(s) _____

   Represent(s) _____

   _____

   _____

2. "The heart is an organ of fire."—Count Laszlo de Almasy, *The English Patient,* 1996

   Symbol(s) _____

   Represent(s) _____

   _____

   _____

3. "I drive a Volvo. A beige one."—Goodspeed, *The Rock,* 1996

   Symbol(s) _____

   Represent(s) _____

   _____

   _____

4. "Well, if it ain't Howard Hughes come to take me home."—Tracy Lapchick, *White Squall,* 1996

   Symbol(s) _____

   Represent(s) _____

   _____

   _____

5. "They say you're the world's only living heart donor."—Sabrina, *Sabrina,* 1995

   Symbol(s) _____

   Represent(s) _____

   _____

   _____

6. Peter: "Religion is nonsense."
   Ben Rosen: "It's also a gold mine if you know where to dig."—*Shine,* 1996

   Symbol(s) _____

   Represent(s) _____

   _____

   _____

Figurative Language 4.B

Read the following poem and then, on a separate sheet of paper or in your journal, answer the questions that accompany it.

AFRO-AMERICAN FRAGMENT

So long,
So far away
Is Africa.
Not even memories alive
Save those that history books create,
Save those that songs
Beat back into the blood—
Beat out of blood with words sad—Sung
In strange un-Negro tongue—
So long,
So far away
Is Africa.

Subdued and time-lost
Are the drums—and yet
Through some vast mist of race
There comes this song
I do not understand,
This song of atavistic land,
Of bitter yearnings lost
Without a place—
So long,
So far away
Is Africa's
Dark face

—Langston Hughes

1. What does Africa symbolize? Does this change from one stanza to the other? If so, how does it change?

2. What do the songs in the first stanza symbolize? How do you know this?

3. Are these symbols personal (specific only to Langston Hughes) or public (specific to no one particular person)? Defend your answer.

Figurative Language 4.C

On a separate sheet of paper or in your journal, identify three symbols that you associate with holidays, sports teams, or businesses. Then, describe why you think each one exemplifies the concept of the holiday, team or business.

SUMMARY

Test preparation is an exercise in critical thinking that requires an understanding of general study strategies as well as the ability to use specific study plans. General study strategies focus on the use of prime study time, the organization of information with analysis and synthesis, the use of association techniques to cue recall, and familiarity with a variety of rehearsal strategies. Specific study plans such as PORPE and POSSE help you prepare effectively for objective and subjective exams.

CHAPTER REVIEW

1. When is your prime study time? How do you know? Do you protect this time? If not, why not? How could or do you protect prime study time?

   _____

   _____

   _____

   _____

2. Suppose by using the assessment in Exercise 4.1, you discover you are a lark. This term, you are taking two night classes. How will you effectively cope with this schedule?

   _____

   _____

   _____

   _____

3. Where do you usually study? Is this location conducive to study? Why or why not? If it is conducive to study, specify what makes it a good study site. If not, locate a better study site, and specify it below. Why is it a better place for you to study?

   _____

   _____

   _____

   _____

4. Do you use idea maps or charts? Why or why not? In your corresponding subject-area notebooks, develop a chart or map for each chapter you are currently studying.

   _____

   _____

   _____

   _____

5. Develop a mnemonic to remember one set of information contained in each chapter you are currently studying. List and describe each mnemonic.

    _____

    _____

    _____

    _____

6. Develop a study schedule for next week that provides opportunities for spaced study. Include any scheduled study group sessions. Indicate the reward system you have established for yourself.

    _____

    _____

    _____

    _____

7. List below each course in which you are now enrolled. Beside each course title, explain how you usually study for exams in that class. Which aspects of the general study strategies discussed in this chapter do you use? Which ones do you need to incorporate?

    _____

    _____

    _____

    _____

8. Use either PORPE or POSSE to create a practice exam for Sample Chapter 6, "The Study of Humanity."

    _____

    _____

    _____

    _____

9. Consider your easiest and most difficult classes. How does your test preparation for each one differ? How are your preparations alike?

    _____

    _____

    _____

    _____

10. Consider the title of this chapter. How can you make test preparation a synthesis of content rather than an accumulation of details about a subject?

    _____

    _____

    _____

    _____

ACTION PLAN

Review the information this chapter contains and respond to the following:

MOVING ON

You're ready. You went to class and took notes. You read the course materials. You prepared for the test by analyzing and synthesizing course content.

How would you judge your test-taking and stress-management skills? Circle the response that best describes the quality of your test-preparation strategies.

EXCELLENT   GOOD   AVERAGE   FAIR   POOR

Students often find it takes more than studying to do well on exams. They need special test-taking strategies and methods for dealing with stress before, during, and after exams to maximize their performances. On the following list, check the test-taking skills you need to improve.

- ☐ Writing responses on subjective exams
- ☐ Taking objective exams
- ☐ Using self-talk to manage stress during an exam
- ☐ Evaluating performance on old exams as a guide for future efforts
- ☐ Taking care of yourself physically before an exam
- ☐ Performing well on open-book and take-home exams
- ☐ Understanding the relationship between finals and other exams
- ☐ Coping with mental stress before an exam

What's next? The moment you've been waiting for—a test and your opportunity to show what you've learned. Chapter 5 provides you with test-taking suggestions and strategies. So, move on to the challenge of test taking.

OBJECTIVES

After you finish this chapter, you will be able to do the following:

1. Apply test-taking tips and test-wise strategies to general (subjective and objective) and specialized (take-home, open-book, and final) testing situations.

2. Identify ways to avoid and manage stress before, during, and after all exams as well as in specific content areas.

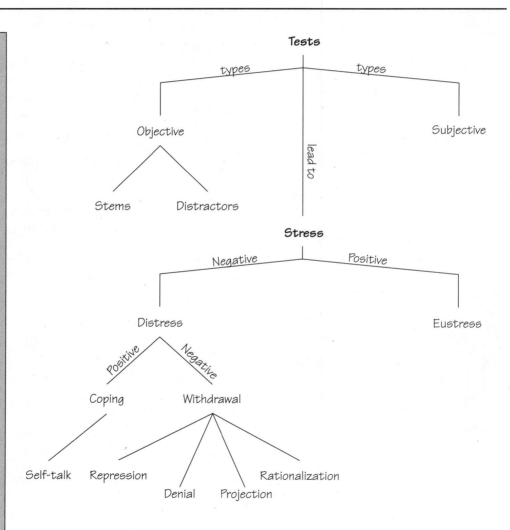

CHAPTER OUTLINE

I. Test-wise strategies
   A. Taking objective and subjective tests
   B. Open-book and take-home tests
   C. A final note about final exams

II. Avoiding the strain: Stress management
   A. Coping before an exam
      1. Wellness
      2. The power of positive thinking
      3. Visualization
      4. Relaxation
      5. Predicting test content
      6. DPTA: Who's on first?
   B. Coping during an exam
   C. Coping after an exam
      1. Examining returned tests
      2. Adjusting to stress
      3. Makeup exams
   D. Coping with specific content areas
      1. Overcoming math anxiety
      2. Writing anxiety: Too wired to write
      3. Stressed over science?
   E. Failure to cope: Withdrawal

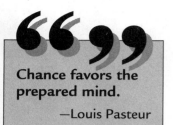

When you don't make the grade you think you deserve on an exam, you probably fault either your study skills or your memory. However, no matter how you sharpen your study and memory techniques, your grade also depends on how well you take tests and manage stress. This chapter shows you how to do both.

TEST-WISE STRATEGIES

Test-taking requires that you prepare your mind with information and then take your chances with the exam. Your chances, however, can be increased if you have at your disposal strategies for taking different types of exams. Coupled with test preparation, these test-wise tips help you make the best grade you can. Table 5.1 lists general test-taking tips. These apply to any type of test.

Taking Objective and Subjective Tests

On objective tests, you are given answers from which you choose the correct one. One part of the question, the **stem,** gives basic information. You pick your answer from among **distractors,** or possible answers. Test-wise principles help you make educated guesses among distractors when you are not sure of the right answer. Table 5.2 contains such tips for objective exams. Exercise 5.1 gives you practice in estimating time allowances for objective and subjective test questions.

Table 5.1   General Test-Wise Strategies

1. *Bring the materials you need for the test.* This includes such items as pencil, paper, blue books, and calculator.

2. *Arrive on time.*

   a. If you arrive early, do not talk about the test with other students. The way they studied could confuse you. The concerns of others tend to increase any worries you have.

   b. If you arrive late, you may miss important verbal directions. Arriving late also makes you feel rushed. If you do come late, take a minute to relax and get organized. Ask your instructor to repeat exam instructions if you feel confused.

3. *Write down formulas or processes you need as soon as you get your test paper.* This clears your mind for thinking rather than simply for storing information. It also eases the stress of worrying about forgetting important facts.

4. *Preview the test.* Note the total number of items. Identify differences in point values between different sections. Judge the amount of time you should spend on each item. Base your estimates on the subject matter and your knowledge of it. Also consider your skill at answering different types of questions. Spend the most time on questions that receive the most credit.

(continues)

Table 5.1   *Continued*

5. *Read all directions slowly and carefully.* Many students make the mistake of ignoring test directions. Directions often state information that will help you get full credit. They also provide information about the way you need to mark answers. Some instructors refuse to give credit for right answers that are not correctly marked.

6. *Underline key terms and steps in the directions and in each question.*

7. *Use appropriate test-wise strategies (see Tables 5.2 and 5.3).*

8. *Answer the easiest questions first.* This builds your confidence. It also triggers your memory for other information. Likewise, if you run out of time before you complete the test, you will have answered the questions you knew.

9. *Expect memory blocks.* Mark difficult questions, then skip them and go on. Return to these questions when time permits, if only to guess.

10. *Attempt every question.*

11. *Make your responses neat and legible.*

12. *Unless you are using a special form that will be scanned for scoring, cross out incorrect information instead of taking time to erase.*

13. *Work at your own pace.* Do not worry if others leave before you.

14. *Review the questions and your answers.* Be sure you understood each question. Also check that you marked the correct response. Some students think it is always better to stay with their first answer, whereas others benefit from thinking about the answer and changing it. You can find out what's best for you by looking at one of your old tests. Count the number of questions you changed to correct answers. Compare that total with the number you changed to incorrect answers.

Table 5.2   **Test-Wise Strategies for Objective Exams**

1. *If you don't know an answer skip it and go on.* Cross out obviously wrong distractors. This saves you time later. Don't waste time mulling over an answer. Answer the questions you know first. This builds confidence and maximizes the use of test time.

2. *When you return to questions you skipped, try to figure out which answers are clearly wrong.* If you can eliminate one or two distractors, you increase your chances of guessing the correct answer.

3. *Eliminate grammatically incorrect distractors.*

4. *Read all choices before answering a multiple-choice question.* All responses might be good answers, but sometimes an instructor asks for the best answer in the directions of an exam or in the stem of a question.

5. *Responses that look like the word to be defined are usually incorrect. Allusion, elusive,* and *illustration* all resemble the word *illusion*. These are called "attractive distractors" because they look appealing. Attractive distractors are almost always poor choices.

6. *Watch for distractors that mean the same thing.* Careful reading occasionally shows that some distractors say the same thing. None of these, then, could be correct.

7. *Use what you know to analyze and make decisions about information.* See if you can relate information and eliminate several of the choices.

8. *If the test contains a true-false section, read each question thoroughly.* Watch for key words such as *always, never, seldom,* and *frequently.* Statements with words like *always* and *never* are often false.

(continues)

Table 5.2   Continued

These words are called absolutes. That means they leave no room for other possibilities. This is why they are frequently false. Statements with *seldom* and *frequently* allow for exceptions. These statements are almost but not quite true. Thus, you need to make sure a statement is completely true before answering true.

9. *Watch your time closely* . Don't spend so much time on harder problems or questions that you cannot finish the test. When you're stumped, move to the next question.

10. *Watch for double negatives.* Just as -2×-2 equals $+4$, negative times negative equals positive in writing. For example, consider the phrase *not unimportant*. Something that is *not unimportant* is *important*.

11. *The longest choice is often the right one.* An instructor often includes a lot of information to make the correct answer clear.

12. *A middle choice (b or c) is often the correct one.* Instructors sometimes feel that putting a right answer either first or last makes it too obvious. Thus, they tend to place distractors before and after the correct answer. When unable to determine the answer any other way, pick a middle answer.

13. *Read carefully and look for clues.* Sometimes instructors provide information about one question when asking another.

14. *Watch for trick questions.* Test-makers are creatures of habit. If you find one trick question, there's a good chance you will find others.

15. *If a multiple-choice question confuses you, consider the stem and each distractor as a true-false question.* This helps you think about each piece of information separately.

16. *Use the side with the longest responses as the stem on matching tests.* Because you normally read from left to right, you might automatically use the left column as the stem questions. Thus, you spend time rereading the longer responses as you look for answers.

17. *Try to determine the relationships between the columns on matching exams.* Sometimes a matching exam is a hodgepodge of terms and information. Other times, a matching exam focuses more on matching certain categories of information—dates, locations, events, people, causes, effects, and so forth. Identifying the relationships between the two columns helps you focus your thoughts in an organized manner.

18. *When all else fails, guess.* When you have answered all the questions you know, return to those you skipped. Reread them carefully. Try to devise an answer in your own words. Then look for a matching response. If none exists, make an educated guess based on test-wise principles. If you cannot make an educated guess, pick an answer. Decide now what your "lucky" letter is going to be. In the future, when you need to guess, pick it. Since few instructor-made exams penalize for guessing, never leave answers blank.

19. *Review your exam before turning it in.* Did you consistently mark the letter of the selection you intended?

Exercise 5.1   For each of the following testing situations, estimate the amount of time you might spend on each question and your rationale for your time allocations. The first one is done for you.

Example

Course: Computer Science

Time Allowed: 90 minutes

Question Types:

    2 programming assignments; point value: 25 points each

Time Needed per Section: _40 minutes_

    5 short-answer questions; point value: 3 points each

Time Needed per Section: _10 minutes_

    35 multiple-choice questions; point value: 1 point each

Time Needed per Section: _30 minutes_

Rationale for Time Allocations: _Need more time for programming assignments and short-answer_ _questions—takes longer and worth more points; less time given to multiple-choice—easier to do_ _and less point value; 10 minutes for previewing test and checking answers before turning it in._

1. *Course:* Chemistry

    Time Allowed: 45 minutes

    Question Types:

        5 gas law problems; point value: 10 points each

    Time Needed per Section: _____

        10 identification of compounds; point value: 2 points each

    Time Needed per Section: _____

        2 analyses of experiments: point value: 15 points each

    Time Needed per Section: _____

    Rationale for Time Allocations: _____

    _____

2. *Course:* Psychology

    Time Allowed: 75 minutes

    Question Types:

        2 essay questions; point value: 5 points each

    Time Needed per Section: _____

        5 short-answer; point value: 4 points each

    Time Needed per Section: _____

Exercise 5.1   *Continued*

---

20 multiple-choice; point value: 2 points each

Time Needed per Section: _____

15 matching; point value: 2 points each

Time Needed per Section: _____

Rationale for Time Allocations: _____

_____

3. *Course:* English Literature

   Time Allowed: 60 minutes

   Question Types:

   3 essay questions; point value: 25 points each

   Time Needed Per Section:

   5 short-answer; point value: 5 points each

   Time Needed per Section: _____

   Rationale for Time Allocations: _____

   _____

4. *Course:* American History

   Time Allowed: 50 minutes

   Question Types:

   2 essay questions to be selected from 3 alternatives; point value: 10 points each

   Time Needed per Section: _____

   10 matching; point value: 3 points each

   Time Needed per Section: _____

   25 multiple-choice; point value: 2 points each

   Time Needed per Section: _____

   Rationale for Time Allocations: _____

   _____

Subjective exams ask you to write out answers rather than choose from a set of possible answers. Thus, answering them is much like writing short papers on assigned topics. Table 5.3 provides information about the words that instructors use in essay questions. It also provides guides for answering essay questions. Essay exams require more labor from you. The steps in Table 5.4 aid your efforts. Practice preparing to answer essay questions in Exercise 5.2.

Table 5.3   **Essay Questioning Words and Guides for Writing Answers**

If You Are Asked to . . .	Then . . .	By Using Transitional Words Such as . . .
Compare or match	Identify similarities	similarly, in addition, also, too, as well as, both, in comparison, comparatively
Contrast or distinguish	Identify differences	however, but, unless, nevertheless, on one hand, on the other hand, on the contrary, in contrast, although, yet, even though
Discuss or describe	Provide details or features	to begin with, then, first, second, third
Enumerate, name, list, outline	Identify major points	first, second, third, next, finally, more, another
Sequence, arrange, trace, or rank	List information in order	furthermore, later, before, after, during
Demonstrate or show	Provide examples	for example, for instance, in other words, in addition to, as an illustration, to illustrate, also
Relate or associate	Show associations	as a result, because, this leads to, if . . . then, in order that, unless, since, so that, thus, therefore, accordingly, so, yet, consequently
Summarize, paraphrase, or compile	Provide a short synopsis	any of the previous transition words
Apply	Show use for	any of the previous transition words
Construct, develop, or devise	Create	any of the previous transition words
Explain, defend, or document	Give reasons for support	any of the previous transition words
Criticize or analyze	Review or evaluate features or components	any of the previous transition words

Table 5.4   **Taking Essay Exams**

1. *Examine the question.* Its wording indicates how you should organize and write your answer. Some questions might require a combination of organizational patterns (see Chapter 2) rather than a single type.

2. *Choose a title.* Even though you won't necessarily title your paper, a title helps you focus your thoughts and narrow your subject.

3. *Outline or map your response before you write.* Listing main points keeps you from omitting details.

4. *Have a beginning, a middle, and an end.* Topic and summary sentences make your answer seem organized and complete.

5. *Use transitional words.* The key words in each question help you identify the transitions you need for clarity (see Table 5.3).

6. *If you run out of time, outline the remaining questions.* This shows your knowledge of the content, if not your writing style. Partial responses often result in partial credit.

7. *Proofread your answers.* Check spelling, grammar, and content.

8. *If a question confuses you, write any thoughts you have about the topic on the back of your paper.* This helps you focus attention and increases your recall.

Exercise 5.2   For each of the following essay questions, create a reasonable title for your essay and, referring to Table 5.2, identify the type of response you are asked to give. The first is answered as an example for you.

Example

1. List and explain three ways microcomputers are used in health-related fields.

    Title: <u>Uses of Microcomputers in Health Fields</u>

    Type(s) of Response: <u>Application, Cause and Effect, Enumeration</u>

2. Trace the sequence of events responsible for the origin of the Furnace Creek and the San Andreas Faults.

    Title: _____

    Type(s) of Response: _____

3. Proponents of bilingual education suggest that it facilitates linguistic transition, while opponents claim it slows integration into American culture. Contrast these viewpoints, then choose one perspective and defend it.

    Title: _____

    Type(s) of Response: _____

4. Define and describe the theoretical approach that best explains the existence of social classes in the United States.

    Title: _____

    Type(s) of Response: _____

5. Based on the chapter discussion, prepare a list of five questions an interviewer might ask a prospective employee.

    Title: _____

    Type(s) of Response: _____

Open-Book and Take-Home Tests

Open-book and take-home tests . . . what could be easier? Your first and fatal inclination might be to think these tests require no study at all. In fact, they require as much studying as any other exam. Why? They ask you to go beyond the knowledge level of mere facts and write answers at much higher levels of understanding. (For information on levels of knowledge, see Bloom's taxonomy in Chapter 1.) Like other tests, they require appropriate strategies (see Table 5.5).

An open-book exam tests your ability to find, organize, and relate information quickly. Thus, the open-book test may be biased toward well-prepared students. Too little studying causes you to waste time while you ponder what a question means or where to find its answer.

Table 5.5   Steps in Taking Open-Book and Take-Home Exams

1. *Know your text.* Mark sections of the text that concern major topics or important formulas or definitions.

2. *Organize your notes.* Mark them the same way you marked your text.

3. *Highlight and label important details in both your text and notes.*

4. *Know how to use your text's table of contents and index to locate information quickly.*

5. *Paraphrase information.* Unless you quote a specific source, do not copy word for word from your text.

6. *Use other applicable test-taking strategies (see Tables 5.1, 5.2, 5.3, and 5.4).*

Take-home exams also evaluate your ability to find, organize, and relate information. They measure your knowledge without the time restraints of in-class tests. Spelling and neatness count more for (or against) you. In most cases, a take-home test allows you to avoid the stress associated with in-class exams. On the other hand, setting your own pace has drawbacks, particularly if you tend to procrastinate. Waiting until the last minute to begin working on such a test makes you as stressed as taking an in-class test. Some kinds of procrastination also decrease the quality of your work. Thus, you need to set a test date for yourself and take the test at that time. This date should be a few days before your test paper is due. This way, you have time to judge your answers and make any corrections or additions.

A Final Note about Final Exams

Read the poem found in Figure 5.1. It parodies a famous Christmas poem. The original accurately portrayed the feelings felt before Santa's arrival. This version correctly characterizes how many students feel about final exams. Such concerns may be overblown, however, because final exams are much like any other test. However, they usually differ in length. They're longer than regular exams. In a way, this works to your advantage. Longer exams cover more information. You get a better chance to find more questions that you can answer. The same suggestions for taking other tests apply to finals as well (see Table 5.1).

Finals are often given in places and at times that differ from your regular class sites and times. Check campus newspapers for final exam schedules. Departments post them as well. Instructors also provide information about finals. If more than two of your exams occur on the same day, you can sometimes ask to reschedule one of them. Procedures for such requests vary from department to department and from school to school. Seeing your advisor well before the exam date is the first step in this process.

Figure 5.1   'Twas the Night Before Finals

'Twas the Night Before Finals
    And all through the college,
The students were all praying,
    For that last minute knowledge.

Most were quite sleepy,
    But none touched their beds.
While visions of essays,
    Danced in their heads.

Out in the Taverns,
    A few were still drinking.
And hoping that liquor
    Would loosen their thinking.

In my own apartment,
    I had been pacing.
And dreading exams
    That I would be facing.

My roommate was speechless,
    His nose in the books.
And my comments to him,
    Drew unfriendly looks.

I drained all the coffee,
    And brewed a new pot.
No longer caring,
    That my nerves were all shot.

I stared at my notes,
    But my thoughts were all muddy.
My eyes were a blur,
    And I just couldn't study.

"Some pizza might help,"
    I said with a shiver.
But each place I called,
    Refused to deliver.

I'd nearly concluded
    That life was too cruel
With futures depending
    On grades had in school.

When all of a sudden,
    Our door opened wide.
And Patron Saint Put Off
    Ambled inside.

His spirit was careless,
    His manner was mellow.
He flopped on the couch
    And started to bellow:

"What kind of student
    Would make such a fuss,
To toss back at teachers
    What they tossed at us?"

"On Cliff Notes! On Crib Notes!
    On Last Year's Exams!
On Wingit and Slingit
    And Last Minute Crams!"

His message delivered
    He vanished from sight,
But we still heard him laughing
    Outside in the night.

Your teachers have pegged you,
    So just do your best.
Happy Finals to ALL,
    And to all a good test.

SOURCE: Janis C. Booth, Ed.D., College Counselor, Millsaps College, boothjc@okra. millsaps.edu, P. O. Box 150435, (601) 974–1200, Jackson, MS 39210

Smart Review 5.1

Check your understanding of the preceding section by answering the following on a separate sheet of paper or in your journal:

1. Which five of the fourteen generic test-wise principles do you consider most important? Why?

2. Create an analogy that compares or contrasts subjective and objective tests.

3. Which of the test-wise tips for objective exams do you consider most important? Why?

4. How is taking an essay exam like writing an in-class paper?

5. Create a chart listing the advantages and disadvantages of open-book and take-home tests.

6. It's been said that final exams are fairer and more accurate than tests given at other times, such as chapter tests or quizzes. Why might this be so?

Avoiding the Strain: Stress Management

A maiden at college, Ms. Breeze,
Weighted down by B.A.s and Ph.D.s,
Collapsed from the strain.
Said her doctor, "It's plain.
You are killing yourself—by degrees!"

If, like Ms. Breeze, you feel the **stress** of life as a postsecondary student, you're not alone. The strain of getting a postsecondary degree affects all students at one time or another. "Just a test" and "only one research paper" don't seem like major stressors. However, they become so when placed in the context of your daily life. Changes in your life, as well as ongoing events and activities, affect how you manage stress. The strain of getting a postsecondary degree affects all students at one time or another. Two Australian researchers (Sarros and Densten, 1989) identified the causes of stress felt by most college students (see Table 5.6).

Table 5.6   Top Ten Stressors of College Students

1. Number of assignments
2. Taking course exams
3. Size of assignments
4. Low grade on the exam
5. Assignment due dates
6. Class presentations
7. Course workload
8. Own expectations
9. Spacing of exams
10. Class assignments

SOURCE: Reprinted with permission from J. C. Sarros, I. L. Densten, *Higher Education Research and Development,* Undergraduate student stress and coping strategies 8(1) © 1989.

You know stress by many names—pressure, worry, concern, anxiety, and nervousness, to list just a few. The connotations of these words are negative. That's because stress hurts more often than it helps you. Such stress is termed **distress.** It results from many causes (see Table 5.7), and it takes many forms (see Table 5.8). Nevertheless, some stress is positive. Positive stress is termed **eustress.** This describes the energy you need to be your best. This happens on the playing field, in a performance, or in the classroom. Here, stress motivates and helps you to think clearly and decisively. For example, health-care professionals face stressful emergency situations as part of their jobs. These professionals use stress to help them perform faster and better. You can harness stress's power to help you make better grades. You do so by avoiding **withdrawal.** Instead, you find ways to **cope,** or manage stress. Coping is more difficult, but it is a longer-lasting and more effective solution to stress than withdrawal. It requires you to prepare for stress before, during, and after all tests, as well as for the stress emanating from specific subjects.

Table 5.7   **Common Sources of Stress**

Classification	Explanation
1. Intrapersonal conflict	The turmoil within you over which paths to take in life. Your questions revolve around goals, values, priorities, and decisions.
2. Interpersonal relationships	Stress resulting from interaction with others. Friends or peers are common sources of stress as you deal with differences amongst yourselves and learn to communicate and compromise.
3. Family	Although a major source of support, family is also a source of stress because of strong emotional ties among the people involved. Also, interaction among family members is more frequently judgmental.
4. Work and school settings	These involve personal performance satisfaction and meeting standards expected of you.
5. Money concerns	These are always with you. Especially for postsecondary students, money problems are usually not a matter of having enough to survive (although it may seem like that at times) but of how to set priorities for spending their income.
6. Global instability	In the United States we are more isolated from the regional wars that occur in many other parts of the world, but conflict in another part of the globe can have immediate, deleterious effects here. In addition, awareness of the destructive presence of nuclear arms can produce "passive" stress.
7. Environmental abuses	These can come in the form of pollution, crowding, crime, overstimulation (especially by the media), and ecological damage.
8. Technology	Advances such as nuclear energy, the automobile, and the computer, are stressful because they require adaptations and speed up the pace of life. Most technological advances are associated with increased risk, such as the toxic waste that accompanies nuclear power plants or the more than fifty thousand accidental deaths per year in the United States involving automobiles.
9. Change	Any sort of change is a source of stress, although certain changes are clearly more stressful than others. The more changes are present in your life and the faster these changes come about, the greater the stress you will encounter.
10. Time pressure	Time deadlines can cause stress. Many people are not instinctively effective at managing their time.
11. Spiritual issues	Coming to terms with codes of ethical and moral behavior can be stressful, especially if it involves rejecting previously held beliefs. Failing to recognize the spiritual or moral dimension of issues can affect how you cope with stress because you may lack direction in your life.
12. Health patterns	Illness, injury, nutritional imbalances, exposure to toxic substances, and the like are fairly obvious forms of stress. The physiological stress response is often more clearly seen in these instances than in situations involving social and psychological stress.

Table 5.8   Signs of Stress

Physical Signs

- Pounding of the heart, rapid heart rate
- Rapid, shallow breathing
- Dryness of the throat and mouth
- Raised body temperature
- Decreased sexual appetite or activity
- Feelings of weakness, light-headedness, dizziness, or faintness
- Trembling, nervous tics, twitches, shaking hands and fingers
- High-pitched, nervous laughter
- Stuttering and other speech difficulties
- Insomnia—that is, difficulty in getting to sleep or a tendency to wake up during the night
- Grinding of teeth during sleep
- Restlessness, an inability to keep still
- Sweating (not necessarily noticeably), clammy hands, cold hands and feet, chills
- Blushing, hot face
- The need to urinate frequently
- Diarrhea, indigestion, upset stomach, nausea
- Migraine or other headaches
- Frequent unexplained earaches or toothaches
- Premenstrual tension or missed menstrual periods
- More body aches and pains than usual, especially pain in the neck or lower back, any localized muscle tension
- Loss of appetite, unintentional weight loss, increased appetite, sudden weight gain
- Sudden change in appearance
- Increased use of mood-altering substances (tobacco, legally prescribed drugs such as tranquilizers or amphetamines, alcohol, or illegal drugs)
- Accident proneness
- Frequent illness

Psychological Signs

- Irritability, tension, or depression
- Impulsive behavior and emotional instability, the overpowering urge to run and hide
- Lowered self-esteem, thoughts of failure
- Excessive worry, insecurity, unexplained dissatisfaction with job or other normal conditions
- Reduced ability to communicate with others
- Increased awkwardness in social situations
- Excessive boredom, unexplained dissatisfaction with job or other everyday conditions
- Increased procrastination
- Feelings of isolation
- Avoidance of specific situations
- Irrational fears (phobias) about specific things
- Irrational thoughts, forgetting things more often than usual, mental blocks, missing planned events
- Guilt about neglecting family and friends, inner confusion about duties and roles
- Excessive work, omission of play
- Unresponsiveness and preoccupation
- Inability to organize, tendency to get distraught over minor matters
- Inability to make decisions, erratic, unpredictable judgment
- Decreased ability to perform different tasks
- Inability to concentrate
- General ("floating") anxiety, feelings of unreality
- Tendency to become fatigued, loss of energy, loss of spontaneous joy
- Feelings of powerlessness, mistrust of others
- Neurotic behavior, psychosis

SOURCE: Reprinted with permission from E. Whitney, and F. Sizer, *Essential Life Choices* ©1989 by West Publishing Company. All rights reserved.

> ### THINKING CRITICALLY
> Examine the physical and psychological signs of stress in Table 5.8. On a separate sheet of paper or in your journal, respond to the following: Which do you experience? How could you cope with these in the future? Which have you observed in others? What would be your advice to people experiencing these symptoms?

Coping Before an Exam

There is no miracle cure for stress—only one that comes through much effort. Such effort requires you to discover your personal stressors and ways of managing them (see Table 5.9). In addition, your physical wellness affects your ability to send positive verbal statements and mental images to your brain. These images, in turn, affect your coping mechanisms.

Table 5.9   Coping with Personal Stressors

Stressor	Solution
Information overload (number and size of class assignments, spacing of exams, and assignment due dates)	1. Reevaluate time management plan. 2. Consider reducing course load. 3. Form a study group for support and assistance.
Mismatch of instructor and student learning styles.	1. Review coping strategies in Table 3.3 (Chapter 3). 2. Form a study group.
Stress carriers (peers who are also overstressed).	1. Find more supportive and positive friends. 2. Seek out counseling services.
Self-doubts (own high expectations, family pressures, concerns about career choices, class presentations, low exam grades, academic competition)	1. Practice taking tests. 2. Avoid cramming. 3. Take stress management course. 4. Practice relaxation exercises. 5. Seek counseling services.
Interpersonal relationships (family conflicts, love decisions, social pressures, family responsibilities, sexual pressures and fears, religious conflicts, job conflicts)	1. Seek counseling services. 2. Talk to family and friends. 3. Examine values and priorities.
Social conflicts (social anonymity, loneliness, depression, anxiety)	1. Seek counseling services. 2. Participation in campus activities. 3. Join postsecondary organizations. 4. Volunteer your services.
Financial concerns	1. Investigate school loans, grants, and scholarships. 2. Share expenses. 3. Cut expenses. 4. Seek additional employment.

> **An apple a day keeps the doctor away.**
>
> —American proverb

Wellness

The "apple" adage holds true for coping with stress before an exam. That's because one of the most important and least considered aspects of stress management is your physical well-being. Maslow's hierarchy of needs (see Figure 5.2) theorizes that physical needs must be satisfied before other needs can be met. Thus, life-style factors such as nutrition, rest, and exercise affect how well you cope with stress. They also have bearing on whether you reach self-actualization. Exercise 5.3 provides an inventory for determining how well your life-style protects you from stress.

Figure 5.2   Maslow's Hierarchy of Needs

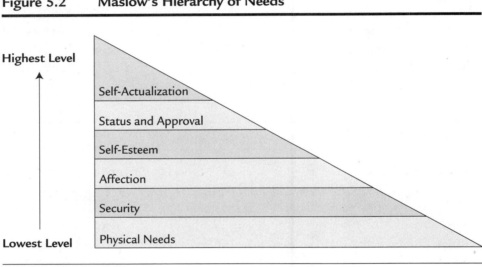

Exercise 5.3   Life-Style and Stress Tolerance

Directions: Answer each of the following questions on a scale of 1 (almost always) to 5 (never), according to how much of the time each statement is true of you.

POINTS

1. I eat one hot, balanced meal a day.   _____
2. I get seven to eight hours sleep at least four nights a week.   _____
3. I give and receive affection regularly.   _____
4. I have at least one relative within fifty miles on whom I can rely.   _____
5. I exercise to the point of perspiring at least twice a week.   _____
6. I smoke less than half a pack of cigarettes a day.   _____
7. I take fewer than five alcoholic drinks a week.   _____

(continues)

Exercise 5.3   *Continued*

8. I am the appropriate weight for my height. _____

9. I have an income adequate to meet basic expenses. _____

10. I get strength from my religious beliefs. _____

11. I regularly attend club or social activities. _____

12. I have a network of friends and acquaintances. _____

13. I have one or more friends to confide in about personal matters. _____

14. I am in good health (including eyesight, hearing, teeth). _____

15. I am able to speak openly about my feelings when angry or worried. _____

16. I have regular conversations with the people I live with about domestic problems (chores, money, and daily living issues). _____

17. I do something for fun at least once a week. _____

18. I am able to organize my time effectively. _____

19. I drink fewer than three cups of coffee (or tea or cola) a day. _____

20. I take quiet time for myself during the day. _____

Total Points _____

Subtract 20 _____

Final Score _____

You obtain your total "stress audit" score by adding your individual scores and subtracting 20. Your life-style is not having a negative effect on your stress tolerance if your score is below 30. If it is between 50 and 75, you are not doing all you can to help reduce your vulnerability to stress, and you may want to consider some fine tuning. If your score is greater than 75, you might want to consider some substantial changes. The behaviors on this questionnaire help increase stress tolerance through basic physical and emotional health and fitness.

SOURCE: "Vulnerability Scale" from the *Stress Audit,* developed by Lyle H. Miller and Alma Dell Smith. Copyright 1983, Biobehavioral Associates, Brookline, MA 02146.

"Are you getting enough to eat, dear?" your family probably asks when they call. "Did you eat lunch today?" a friend might ask when you seem irritable in the evening. Almost everyone seems concerned about your eating habits. It's a worn-out subject, and you're tired of hearing about it. Nonetheless, because nutrition affects your physical well-being, it also impacts your study habits and grades. What you eat affects your stamina and behavior. It's a subject that cannot be avoided, even if you've heard it before.

A balanced diet (see Figure 5.3) supplies the nutrients you need. It serves as the basis of good health. It helps you store energy. Unfortunately, when

Figure 5.3 **The Food Pyramid**

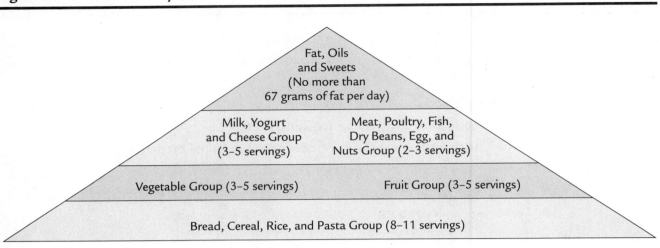

you're a postsecondary student, what and when you eat is not always in your control. Classes, work, and study time play havoc with regular mealtimes. Thus, you need a plan for getting nutrition even when you miss meals. Suppose a class extends past the hours the cafeteria serves lunch. Eating a later breakfast or an earlier dinner helps you cope. Or your school cafeteria might prepare a sack lunch for you. You could also carry some fruit or cheese in your backpack for a between-class snack.

In addition to nutritious food, you need adequate rest. What's adequate? It depends on two factors: your physical condition and the tasks you undertake. High degrees of fitness, interest, or skill help you achieve more with less fatigue. Methods of avoiding fatigue vary in quality and effectiveness. Sleep is the most obvious way to become rested. It is, however, not your only choice. Changing activities—for example, studying different subjects—also rests your mind. Recreational activities help you relax. These might include listening to music, talking to friends, or reading a book.

Study time is the only price you pay for these activities. This price, however, often seems too steep to some students. Such students bypass natural methods of avoiding fatigue. They rely on tranquilizers to relax. They use amphetamines to increase productivity. Other students use alcohol or tobacco to cope with stressful situations. These artificial means are quick, costly, and only temporarily effective (if at all). They create dependencies. They serve as study crutches, not study supports.

Exercise also plays a role in reducing stress. It helps you work off excess adrenaline and energy. You rid your body of these before they make you tired or sick. Paradoxically, exercise also increases your energy level. When this

THINKING CRITICALLY

On a separate sheet of paper or in your journal, keep a record of what you eat and drink for seven days. Categorize what you eat according to the food pyramid in Figure 5.3. What eating patterns do you notice? Identify three ways you can improve your diet.

happens, you cope with stress better because you no longer feel exhausted or overwhelmed. It's not surprising, then, that exercise also decreases fatigue. This is particularly true when you use it as an alternative to challenging mental processes. For example, jogging for thirty minutes breaks the intensity of a long study session. Another benefit of exercise is that it tends to have a positive effect on your life-style. That is, if you exercise regularly, you'll probably find yourself drinking, smoking, and/or overeating less often. This, in turn, causes you to feel and look better. If you often worry about your appearance, as do many people, exercise eliminates this potential stressor as well. Finally, exercise affects your long-term health. It increases strength and flexibility while it decreases your chances of cardiovascular or skeletal-muscular problems. Finally, exercise tends to slow the natural aging process.

The Power of Positive Thinking

For some reason, humans most often remember and believe the worst rather than the best about themselves. You, too, might find yourself dwelling on past embarrassments, problems, and failures. In similar situations, you think that the same disasters will recur. Your anxiety mounts, you lose confidence, and the cycle repeats itself.

Test anxiety is one of these cyclical processes. When this anxiety is prompted, you feel pressure from within and without. You lack the confidence to succeed. Voices echo in your mind. "I must pass, or I'll never get into medical school." "What if I freeze up?" "I must, I must, I must." "I can't, I can't, I can't."

The secret to combating test anxiety is twofold. First, you figure out what stresses you and why. Is the voice you hear that of your own feelings? Is it a ghost from your past? Can you believe what is being said? Is it true? Have you *never* performed well under pressure? Have you *never* been able to recall dates? What is reality? What is not?

Second, you replace negative messages with positive ones. Consider the coach of a team sport. The coach doesn't say, "Well, our opponent is tough. I don't see any way we can win." No, the coach acknowledges the opponent's worth and says, "Well, our opponent is tough. But we've practiced hard all week. I know we're prepared. Do your best. That's all I ask and all we'll need."

"Good thing I'm graduating . . . my success messages are getting out of control!"

The coach's talk before a game motivates players to excel even in stressful situations. Sample success messages appear in Table 5.10. However, the best messages are those you create for yourself. Such statements are personal and, thus, more meaningful. They help you prepare for visualizing success. To be effective, you need to repeat all of them once a day, every day. Exercises 5.4 through 5.6 provide practice with self-talk.

Table 5.10   Sample Success Messages

I am prepared and ready to succeed.

I like the courses I'm taking.

I am working toward a goal I want to achieve.

I like myself.

I like the way I study.

I feel confident about my abilities.

My instructor values my contributions.

My instructor enjoys having me in class.

Exercise 5.4   Think about the ways you view your academic self. What negative messages do you hear? What are their sources? Complete each of the following sentence fragments and mark the source of each. Then in the last two blanks provide examples of messages you tell yourself. Mark their sources.

1. I can't _____

_____

Source: Message comes from me? _____ from others? _____

2. I always _____

_____

Source: Message comes from me? _____ from others? _____

3. I never _____

_____

Source: Message comes from me? _____ from others? _____

4. I don't _____

_____

Source: Message comes from me? _____ from others? _____

5. My friends think I _____

_____

Source: Message comes from me? _____ from others? _____

6. My instructor thinks I _____

_____

Source: Message comes from me? _____ from others? _____

7. My classes are _____

_____

Source: Message comes from me? _____ from others? _____

8. Everyone else _____

_____

Source: Message comes from me? _____ from others? _____

9. _____

_____

Source: Message comes from me? _____ from others? _____

10. _____

_____

Source: Message comes from me? _____ from others? _____

Exercise 5.5   Create three positive messages for each of the following general situations.

1. Writing a paper
    a. _____
    _____
    b. _____
    _____
    c. _____
    _____

2. Solving a problem
    a. _____
    _____
    b. _____
    _____
    c. _____
    _____

3. Taking a final exam
    a. _____
    _____
    b. _____
    _____
    c. _____
    _____

4. Taking an unannounced quiz
    a. _____
    _____
    b. _____
    _____
    c. _____
    _____

5. Reading a chapter
    a. _____
    _____
    b. _____
    _____
    c. _____
    _____

(continues)

Exercise 5.5   *Continued*

6. Taking notes

a. _____

_____

b. _____

_____

c. _____

_____

7. Being called on in class

a. _____

_____

b. _____

_____

c. _____

_____

8. Managing time

a. _____

_____

b. _____

_____

c. _____

_____

9. Choosing a major

a. _____

_____

b. _____

_____

c. _____

_____

10. Getting back a test with a poor grade

a. _____

_____

b. _____

_____

c. _____

_____

Exercise 5.6   Create a positive message for each of the following scenarios. Then in numbers 7–10 provide examples of stressful situations you have faced or will face this term. Create a positive message for coping with these.

1. You enter a class in a subject you know little about. The other students appear much older (or younger) than you.
    Message _____
    _____

2. You have an excellent grade point average and plan to go to law school. Now the time has come to take the law school admissions test.
    Message _____
    _____

3. You are a learning disabled student. You fear explaining to your instructor that you need special accommodations.
    Message _____
    _____

4. You are in a speech class. Your first speech in front of the large class is tomorrow. You are well prepared but afraid.
    Message _____
    _____

5. You have done well on all math homework assignments, but a surprise quiz has just been distributed to the class.
    Message _____
    _____

6. You just got back an English paper. There is no grade on it, but the instructor has written a note. The note asks you to make an appointment to discuss the paper.
    Message _____
    _____

7. Situation _____
    Message _____
    _____

8. Situation _____
    Message _____
    _____

9. Situation _____
    Message _____
    _____

10. Situation _____
    Message _____
    _____

Visualization

Our imaginations either free or bind us. **Visualization** takes positive messages one step further. It uses imagination to put positive messages into action. Thus, instead of imagining the worst and seeing yourself fail, you imagine success. Just as you sometimes embellish the worst with all the gory details, you now imagine the best in all its splendor.

Begin your visualization of academic success by closing your eyes. Imagine yourself in class. Picture yourself as a confident student who understands the lectures and participates actively in class. Watch yourself study for the course. See yourself actively reading and understanding text information. Imagine yourself preparing for a test. You do not feel anxious or tired. See yourself learning and feeling confident about what you learn. The sensation intensifies. You feel prepared for a test. Imagine yourself closing your books and gathering your notes. Picture yourself falling asleep. Then imagine yourself waking up refreshed and ready. Watch yourself review the information. You are calm and prepared. See yourself going to the class in which you have an exam. See yourself walking into the class and sitting down. Visualize yourself being calm and collected. Watch your instructor give you your test. Imagine yourself carefully listening to the verbal instructions and estimating the time needed to complete each section. Watch yourself take the test. You are calm and confident. You think logically. You remember accurately. Watch yourself complete the test and turn it in. Visualize yourself leaving the room. You are pleased with yourself and your performance.

Relaxation

"Relax, you won't feel a thing," say many doctors right before they give you an injection. And while you're sure to feel the needle going in, it really does hurt less if you can ease the tension in your body. Similarly, relaxation eases stress. Even in the throes of a stressful situation, relaxation often occurs. How long it takes for you to relax depends on the time you have available and the way you relax.

Early humans responded to threats by either fighting or fleeing. Contemporary life is not that simple, but people still have this fight-or-flight instinct. As a result, our muscles often respond to stress even when neither option is available. Steps for progressively relaxing your mind and muscles appear in Table 5.11. You can also relax your muscles by doing a physical body check. Whenever you feel tense, stop and see if any muscles are involved that really don't need to be. For example, suppose you feel your shoulders tense as you read. Shoulder muscles play little part in reading, so you need to make a conscious effort to relax them. Finally, conscious deep breathing also relaxes the body.

[Americans] suffer primarily not from our vices or our weaknesses, but from our illusions. We are haunted, not by reality, but by those images we have put in place of reality.

—Daniel J. Boorstin
Twentieth century American historian

Table 5.11   Steps for Muscular Relaxation

1. Sit or lie in a comfortable position with your eyes closed.

2. Picture yourself in a quiet place in which you have felt relaxed in the past (the beach, the forest, a park, your backyard, your room, or elsewhere). Imagine that you're there once more.

3. Breathe in deeply, hold for one count, and exhale. Repeat the word *calm* each time you inhale. Repeat the word *down* each time you exhale.

4. Beginning with your toes, flex then relax your muscles. Progress to the foot, ankle, leg, and so on.

5. Let your thoughts drift. Allow them to come and go of their own accord.

6. Remain calm and quiet. If possible, stay in this state for at least twenty minutes.

7. Open your eyes and remain quiet. Enjoy the feeling of relaxation.

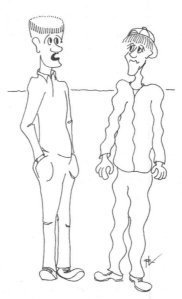

"Either you've been practicing your relaxation techniques again, or you've run out of starch for your ironing."

THINKING CRITICALLY

Using any one of the scenarios in Exercise 5.6, create a visualization to help you imagine success. Record your response to the visualization on a separate sheet of paper or in your journal.

Taking a vacation is also relaxing. Of course, if you're enrolled in school and studying for an exam, you can't go to Nassau for the weekend. A mental vacation, however, serves the same purpose as a real one. It's just not as much fun! Mental vacations are fast and inexpensive. To take one, you simply close your eyes. You visualize your favorite vacation spot; you see a place where you wish to vacation. You don't have to always picture quiet, relaxing places. You can imagine yourself shopping, sightseeing, playing sports, or doing whatever you like to do. Another type of vacation also serves to relax you. Simply changing the way you do things is a kind of vacation. For example, try going to class by a different route, eating in a different location, or shopping at a different grocery. These simple changes of pace refresh you.

Laughter releases tension, too. It often allows you to put things into perspective. If you have time, you can watch a favorite comedy. If not, listening to a radio station that tells jokes and plays upbeat songs yields the same effect. Print cartoons and funny stories also entertain and relieve stress. Browsing through humorous greeting cards at a store is also relaxing.

Predicting Test Content

How many times have you thought, "Who makes up these exams? I wish *I* only had to worry about asking questions and not answering them!" Here's your chance. One way to prepare for tests is to critically examine the information that will be on the test and construct test questions for yourself. How do instructors know what kinds of questions to ask? Table 5.12 contains guidelines that were written to help faculty prepare more effective test questions. Knowing them can help you prepare, too . . . for taking the test!

Source: Copyright © 1997 Lynn Johnston/Distributed by Universal Feature Syndicate. Reprinted by permission.

Table 5.12   Guidelines for test construction

General guidelines

a. The item as a whole should present a problem of significance in the subject-matter field rather than a minor detail.

b. The item as a whole should deal with an important aspect of the subject-matter field, not with a minor element that is of significance only to an expert.

c. The item as a whole should be phrased in language appropriate to the subject-matter field.

d. Items that attempt to measure understanding should include an element of novelty, but too much novelty is likely to make the problem too hard. Trick questions should be avoided.

Rules for stating the problem

a. There must be a single central problem.

b. The problem should be stated briefly but completely; the problem should not test the student's ability to understand complex sentence structure except when the teacher is deliberately measuring ability.

c. The problem should be stated in a positive, not a negative form. Somehow, even intelligent adults often fail to see a "not" in reading a sentence.

d. It should be possible to understand the problem without reading the alternatives.

e. Generally speaking, the test is more interesting if the questions are worded in concrete rather than abstract terms. Such items are particularly worthwhile if you wish to measure ability of the student to apply concepts to concrete situations.

Rules for developing the suggested solutions

a. The suggested wrong answers should represent errors commonly made by the students being tested, not popular misconceptions among the public at large.

b. The right answer should be unquestionably right, checked by two or three independent experts.

c. The suggested answers should be as brief as possible.

d. The position of the right answers should be scattered.

e. Numerical answers should be placed in numerical order.

f. Even wrong alternatives should contain words familiar to students.

g. Use "All of the above" and "None of the above" rarely. Usually they are tossed in when you can't think of another good distractor.

h. The right answer should not be given away by irrelevant clues. A few examples of commonly occurring irrelevant clues are 1) alternatives that include absolute terms, such as *always* and *never* (rarely right answers,), 2) alternatives that are longer and more elaborate than the others (frequently right answers), and 3) alternatives that do not complete a lead statement grammatically (these are obviously wrong).

SOURCE: Reprinted with permission from *Teaching Tips: A Guidebook for the Beginning College Teacher* 8/e by Wilbert J. McKeachie. Copyright © 1986 by D. C. Heath Publishers. All rights reserved.

DTPA: Who's on First? What's on Second?

Assessing what you know and what you need to learn comprises an essential step in preparing for an exam. One way to detail where you are and where you need to go in terms of test preparation is by using a **directed test preparation activity (DTPA).**

Based on a directed reading thinking activity (Stauffer, 1969), the DTPA provides a way for you to critically evaluate knowledge by classifying it as completely known, partially known, or unknown. You can then identify study strategies for converting unknown data to completely known information. The DTPA uses charts to organize study materials and yields a format by which you can predict test questions.

To use the DTPA, you first examine your reading and lecture notes and then place information into the most appropriate of the first three columns (see Figure 5.4). Once you have classified this information, you need to decide which mnemonic method (see Chapter 4) would best fit the information. For example, you might decide to use an acronym or acrostic for a list of steps in a sequence. Writing this mnemonic in your notes or on the chart itself compels you to actively think about the information and begin the study process. Finally, you play *Jeopardy*. That is, you place the information in the form of a

> You've got to be very careful if you don't know where you are going, because you might not get there.
>
> —Yogi Berra
> *Twentieth century American baseball legend*

Figure 5.4   Example of DTPA Chart

What do you really know?	What do you somewhat know?	What don't you know?	What do you need to learn this information?	What question might elicit this information?

question. This helps you predict the questions your instructor might ask. These questions, when written on note cards, form a powerful and active test-preparation tool within themselves.

Coping During an Exam

During an exam, you manage stress by pausing for about fifteen seconds and taking a few deep breaths. You need to force your breathing to flow smoothly and slowly. Breathe as described in step 3 of Table 5.1. This calms your nerves and steadies your mind. A second way to manage stress while taking a test is to use test-wise strategies. For example, remember that answering questions you know first and making notes of information you're afraid you might forget eases stress. Sometimes the way a test is constructed or a question is worded causes stress. You reduce this stress during an exam by asking your instructor for help. Fourth, the positive self-talk that helped you control stress before the exam works equally well during the test.

Basically, four stress situations foster your self-doubt during an exam. Worry about your grade, indecision over answers, concern with the physical symptoms of stress, and anxiety about the consequences of failing the test cause harmful self-talk. To fight a negative mindset during an exam, you follow the steps outlined in Table 5.13. Doing this helps free your mind from worry. It allows you to concentrate on the test.

Coping After an Exam

No matter which type of test-taker you are, once the test is over, it's over. Waiting for your grade, receiving it, and living with it are the next problems you face. How you manage these affects your future performance.

Examining Returned Tests

What do you do when a test is returned to you? Do you throw it away? Do you file it away, never to look at it again? Or do you examine it carefully? A review of your test provides information about both your study and test-taking skills. It helps you decide which of your study and test-taking strategies work and which do not. You use this information to improve future

THINKING CRITICALLY

Your best friend fears flying. You think positive self-talk can help him overcome this fear. On a separate sheet of paper or in your journal, explain self-talk to him. Then provide examples of statements he might use to combat his fear.

Table 5.13   Self-Talk for Use During an Exam

1. *Prepare for an exam question:*

   What is the question I have to answer?

   I know information about it.

   Don't worry. Worry won't help.

2. *Confront and handle the question:*

   I can answer this question.

   One question at a time, I can handle this exam.

   I won't think about fear—just about what I have to do.

3. *Avoid feeling overwhelmed:*

   Keep focused. What is the question I need to answer?

   This exam will soon be over. Life will continue.

4. *Reinforce your coping strategy:*

   It worked! I was able to attempt every question.

   It wasn't as bad as I feared!

   Me and my imagination! When I control it, I control my stress.

SOURCE: Meichenbaum, D. H., & Cameron, R. (1974). The Clinical Potential of Modifying What Clients Say to Themselves. In M. J. Mahoney & C. E. Thorensen (eds.), *Self-Control: Power to the Person*. Adapted by permission of Brooks/Cole Publ. Co., Pacific Grove, CA 93950.

test performance and to reduce the stress of taking another exam in the same course.

Figure 5.5 provides a form for examining your test paper. To complete this worksheet, you list each item you missed in the first column. Then you mark an X under the description that best explains why you missed a question. Sometimes you will mark more than one reason for a question. Next, you add the number of X's under each reason. The results show which test-taking strategies are working for you and which you need to change.

After you obtain as much information as you can about your study and test-taking habits from the exam, you look for information about how your instructor constructs exams. You look for patterns in the types of questions asked. You see whether your instructor emphasized text or lecture information. You determine grading patterns. This information helps you prepare for the next exam. Thus, being prepared reduces stress.

Another way to acquire information after the exam involves asking your instructor for it. You need to make an appointment with your instructor and ask him or her to analyze your exam with you. This helps you determine why some answers received credit and others did not.

Figure 5.5   Worksheet for Examining Returned Tests

Test Item Missed	Insufficient Information						Test Anxiety					Lack of Test-Wisdom						Test Skills					Other		
	I did not read the text thoroughly.	The information was not in my notes.	I studied the information but could not remember it.	I knew main ideas but needed details.	I knew the information but could not apply it.	I studied the wrong information.	I experienced mental block.	I spent too much time daydreaming.	I was so tired I could not concentrate.	I was so hungry I could not concentrate.	I panicked.	I carelessly marked a wrong choice.	I did not eliminate grammatically incorrect choices.	I did not choose the *best* choice.	I did not notice limiting words.	I did not notice a double negative.	I changed a correct answer to a wrong one.	I misread the directions.	I misread the questions.	I made poor use of the time provided.	I wrote poorly organized responses.	I wrote incomplete responses.			
Number of Items Missed																									

"I'm going to set the curve . . . on any nerd that turns in their exam early!"

Adjusting to Stress

Once you've examined your test and learned all you can from it, you need to adjust your thinking. This helps you to prepare for future exams in that same course. Four possibilities exist for this preparation. First, you might see your instructor and ask for suggestions. He or she can make recommendations that will aid you in future study. Second, you might change your appraisal of the situation. All too often the pressure you put on yourself results in the most tension. You can decide that a *B* or *C* is the best you can do in a course and that your best is the most you can demand of yourself. Removing the self-imposed goal of *A*-level work lessens stress. Third, you can change your response to the situation. This means you avoid stress by replacing anxiety with activity. For example, instead of staying awake and worrying about a grade you made, spend the evening either working out or preparing for the next class. Either way, you gain. Finally, you can change the situation. This means you can drop a course if it gives you too many problems. A strategic retreat is just that—a logical and temporary step back. Such a maneuver gives you time to reflect on yourself, your goals, and academic realities. This does not mean you won't ever pass the course. It simply means you will take it again at a better time.

Makeup Exams

As a student, you may feel that instructors do not care about your success in class. Such a misconception often discourages you from seeking the help you need. This is particularly true when it comes to asking for makeup exams.

It is true that instructors hear all too often "I was too ill to take the exam" or "My Great-aunt Wilma is sick, and I have to leave campus immediately." On the other hand, sometimes illness, family, or job pressures do cause you to miss an exam. Perhaps your first idea is to simply skip class and confront the instructor later. Contacting the instructor as soon as possible, preferably before the exam, is a better alternative. Making this special effort shows your concern for your grade. It also indicates your respect for the instructor. Arranging for makeup work at this time decreases stress. That's because you'll know if and when you'll be able to make up the work. If you are ill for a period of time, you need to talk with your instructor about receiving an incomplete or I grade. This enables you to complete the work when you recover. Postsecondary instructors care. Give them an opportunity to do so.

Coping with Specific Content Areas

C. E. Crimmins writes that good (if strange) advice came from her father. He told her the way to cope with life was written on the top of a mayonnaise jar. She wondered for days what "Refrigerate after opening" had to do with life. Then her father told her that when he was young, mayonnaise jars were labeled differently. They said, "Keep cool; don't freeze."

Like most people, you probably manage to keep cool in normal times. It's when you face abnormal or difficult situations that you freeze. One key to coping with stress is realizing that what's hard for you may be easier for others.

This is especially true in school. The subjects that make your stress levels rise energize others. The subjects in which you excel send others up the wall. If you make use of the skill of others, you cope better with difficult subjects. How do you do this? Easy. Find out what good students in those subjects do. Then imitate them!

Overcoming Math Anxiety

Many people think that they simply cannot do math. These beliefs come from past events and voices. Perhaps math anxiety arises from a parent who said you were just like Cousin Jimbo who couldn't do math. Maybe a poor performance on a math test still haunts you. Possibly a third-grade teacher said you were a math failure. Identifying what you believe about yourself and your attitudes toward math forms the first step in coping with math anxiety. Table 5.14 contains a scale for judging your math anxiety.

Table 5.14   Composite Math Anxiety Scale

For each statement, give a number 1 through 4 to indicate whether you strongly agree (1), agree (2), disagree (3), or strongly disagree (4).

1. _____ I see mathematics as a subject that I will rarely use.

2. _____ I usually have been at ease in math classes.

3. _____ I'm no good in math.

4. _____ Generally, I have felt secure about attempting mathematics.

5. _____ People would think I was some kind of a grind if I got A's in math.

6. _____ I'll need mathematics for my future work.

7. _____ I don't think I could do advanced mathematics.

8. _____ I'd be happy to get good grades in math.

9. _____ For some reason, even though I study, math seems unusually hard for me.

10. _____ It wouldn't bother me at all to take more math courses.

11. _____ It would make people like me less if I were a really good math student.

12. _____ I will use mathematics in many ways in the future.

13. _____ My mind goes blank and I am unable to think clearly when working in mathematics.

14. _____ Knowing mathematics will help me earn a living.

15. _____ If I got the highest grade in math, I'd prefer no one knew.

16. _____ I think I could handle more difficult mathematics.

17. _____ Math has been my worst subject.

18. _____ I'm the type to do well in math.

19. _____ Winning a prize in mathematics would make me feel unpleasantly conspicuous.

20. _____ Math doesn't scare me at all.

Scoring:

Total even-numbered responses. Total odd-numbered responses. Subtract the sum of the odds from the sum of the evens. If your score is between –30 and –15, then your anxiety level is high. If your score ranges from –15 to 0, anxiety may pose a problem for you. If your score is positive, your math anxiety is low. The higher your score, the lower your math anxiety.

SOURCE: Adapted from Tobias, S. (1978). *Overcoming Math Anxiety.* New York: W. W. Norton & Company, Inc.

What if you find you have math anxiety? You can do several things to cope. First, analyze your self-talk and the messages you're sending yourself. Determine where the messages originate and check them for accuracy. Were they statements of fact or just someone's opinion? Then, develop new positive messages to replace the negative ones you've held. This form of self-talk and imaging helps you see yourself as a capable math student. Visualization and relaxation exercises reinforce this image. Next, get a good start in your math class. Complete all assigned work during the first few weeks of the course. This initial groundwork gives you a strong foundation on which to build future learning. If you experience difficulty or haven't taken math in several years, reinforce your background knowledge by auditing a lower course. Or you might acquire a lower-level text and work its problems. If worse comes to worst, isolate the math course. This means you take math in the summer as your only course. Then you devote all your time and energy to math.

There are other options for confronting math anxiety. You could take advantage of your school's resources. Find tutors, computer-assisted instruction, videotapes, workshops, and as many other learning aids as you can. At the same time, you can create a network of support. Confide in your campus counselor, trusted friends, and study group. Ask them for their encouragement and support. Ask your math instructor for specific suggestions for learning the content of the course. Finally, consider Bloom's taxonomy (see Chapter 1). Just as the study of history or English requires time to reach higher levels of thinking, the study of math requires time to work through and apply concepts.

Writing Anxiety: Too Wired to Write

Writing anxiety, or an in-over-your-head feeling, is a common problem, even for professional writers. Consider the following, taken from the autobiography of a professional writer.

> The deadline would strike in exactly twenty-one days. I had to start writing. The next morning, a beauteous one in June, I woke up, washed my face and brushed my teeth in a hurry, made a pot of coffee, tightened the sash on my bathrobe, snapped my typewriter out of its case, carefully placed it on the kitchen table, unwrapped the pack of bond paper I had purchased the day before, retrieved my notes from the floor where they were stacked tidily in manila folders . . . opened the first folder, put the top sheet of paper in the typewriter, looked at it, put my head on the keys, wrapped my arms around its base, and cried.
>
> If I had known then how many times, during the next fifteen years, I would have the same feeling—the I'm-over-my-head-and-this-time-they're-going-to-catch-me feeling—I might have become a receptionist in a carpeted law office and married the first partner in a three-piece suit who asked me. But I didn't know. I thought, if I get through this, it'll be over.

SOURCE: Rollin, Betty. (1982). *Am I Getting Paid for This?* Boston: Little, Brown and Company. © by Betty Rollin and Ida Rollin. Reprinted by permission of William Morris Agency, Inc. on behalf of the author.

It's not surprising that writing-anxious students have difficulty recognizing their stress is not something out of the ordinary. Often they think their problem results from a lack of either intellectual ability or writing skill. Oddly, most writing-anxious students are just the opposite. They are good writers who are overcritical of themselves and their writing. Are you a writing-anxious student? The writing anxiety checklist in Table 5.15 could help you decide. If you have a problem, follow the suggestions outlined in Table 5.16. They mirror what expert writers do.

Table 5.15   Writing Anxiety Checklist

Determine if the following statements apply: Never (N), Occasionally (O), Frequently (F), or Always (A).

1. I never know what to write about.	N	O	F	A
2. I wait until the last minute to start a paper.	N	O	F	A
3. I find myself staring at a blank sheet of paper.	N	O	F	A
4. Writing in class makes me feel nervous.	N	O	F	A
5. I never have enough time to complete in-class writing assignments, even when I'm familiar with the material.	N	O	F	A
6. My oral skills are much better than my written skills.	N	O	F	A
7. I prefer objective tests to subjective ones.	N	O	F	A
8. I find it hard to concentrate when I have to write a paragraph or paper.	N	O	F	A
9. I don't like the way I write.	N	O	F	A
10. I usually turn in papers late.	N	O	F	A
11. I fail to turn in assigned papers.	N	O	F	A
12. I dislike writing papers.	N	O	F	A
13. I get much better scores on objective tests than on subjective tests.	N	O	F	A
14. My papers often are shorter in length than everyone else's.	N	O	F	A
15. Writing makes me feel nervous.	N	O	F	A
16. Writing makes me feel depressed.	N	O	F	A
17. Writing makes me feel frustrated.	N	O	F	A
18. I avoid courses in which I would have to write papers or that have subjective tests.	N	O	F	A
19. I get just as nervous writing out-of-class papers as I do in-class papers.	N	O	F	A
20. I make much better grades in math-related courses or courses in which no writing is required.	N	O	F	A

If you answered *F* or *A* to ten or more of these statements, you are probably a writing-anxious student.

Table 5.16   Suggestions for Coping with Writing Anxiety

1. If possible, select a topic that interests you or is about something you know. If your instructor selects the topic, be sure you understand it. If not, ask for clarification.

2. Narrow the scope of your topic. This means limiting the topic to a manageable size.

3. Set realistic goals and deadlines for completing each stage of the paper (selecting a topic, narrowing its scope, collecting information, organizing ideas, writing a rough draft, correcting the rough draft, and writing a final draft).

4. Seek assistance. For example, you might organize a writing study group. Inform group members of your deadlines, and ask them to meet and evaluate your work as each deadline passes. This provides you with an impetus for work (someone is expecting you to accomplish a specific task) and a critique of your writing before an instructor sees it.

5. Force yourself to meet your deadlines. Almost all writing-anxious students tend to procrastinate to avoid the stress of writing. Avoid this trap.

6. Don't be afraid to brainstorm before you write. Writing doesn't just take place with a pen moving across paper. Often the ideas you generate as a result of sitting and thinking increase the value of your paper. Incorporating your own experiences and thoughts also improves the content of your writing.

7. Make an informal outline to guide your writing. This provides a lifeline when you feel yourself drowning and have no idea in which direction the shore lies.

8. Consider investing in a word processor. Some writing-anxious students find that it's easier to write and revise using a computer.

9. Discuss your problem with your instructor. Ask for suggestions for improving your writing and overcoming writing anxiety.

10. See a counselor. If you tend to be anxious about most situations, personal counseling or stress management will benefit you. If you are normally cool, calm, and collected, situational stress best characterizes your writing anxiety, and counseling aids that as well.

SMART SITES

Using the Web to Learn Stress Management or Test-Taking Strategies

A wealth of information related to the topics in this chapter is available on the World Wide Web. For this exercise, access one of the following sites (for the most up-to-date URLs, go to http://www.csuccess.wadsworth.com):

http://www.manhattan.edu/stntlife/ccenter/articles/stress/stre1.html

http://www.manhattan.edu/stntlife/ccenter/articles/academic/acad1.html

Click on any topic related to stress or test taking and use the information within that topic to respond to the following on a separate sheet of paper or in your journal:

1. What topic did you choose?

2. Why did you choose that topic?

3. In what ways does the topic support the content of this chapter? What new information does it provide?

4. What do you think is the most important point in the article? Why?

5. How can you apply the content of the article to your ability to manage stress or take tests?

COOPERATIVE LEARNING ACTIVITY   WALK A MILE IN MY SHOES

Seeing professors about makeup work comprises a stressful situation for many students. Additionally, they often given little thought to the feelings of the instructor with whom they're meeting. To help you and your group members overcome this anxiety, complete the following activity:

1. Write each of the following on separate, unlined pieces of paper:

   a. You are a student who has been seriously ill for several weeks. You have a doctor's note and your hospital bill. You meet with your professor to schedule makeup work.

   b. You are a student who consistently skips class. It's near final exam time, and you have become worried about your grade. You meet with your instructor to schedule makeup work and exams.

   c. You are a student who has missed only one class the entire semester. Your clock battery died in the night, and you overslept. Unfortunately, your instructor assigned a major homework assignment for the next class. You meet with your instructor to get the assignment.

2. Write each of the following on separate, lined pieces of paper:

   a. You are a professor who always attempts to be fair. However, it's been a bad semester, and you've given more makeup work than anything else. You are tired of grading late work and hope you never see another student asking for makeup work.

   b. You are a professor who never allows students to make-up work unless they have documentation from a doctor or a police officer.

   c. You are a professor who has no clear-cut makeup policies. As such, it is difficult for students to pin you down as to what work you will let them make up.

3. Fold the pieces of lined and unlined paper in fourths and place them in a container.

4. Divide the group into sets of partners.

5. Have each partner select a different kind of paper. (One partner gets lined paper; the other gets unlined paper.) Partners do not tell anyone the role they've drawn.

6. Allow each partner a few minutes to think about his or her role.

7. Have each set of partners act out a meeting between the two characters they've drawn.

8. After five minutes of role-playing, have other group members try to guess what kind of student and instructor they just observed.

9. Continue with the next set of partners role-playing their characters.

Stressed over Science?

Have you ever had a friend confess, "I hate science, and I'm not taking it until I have to!" Have you ever said this yourself? Many students fear science because they believe one or more of the myths found in Table 5.17. Consider the word *myth*. By its very definition, a myth is fiction. Myths about learning science can be harmful because they shape your attitude. Your attitude, in turn, affects performance. If your attitude is negative, your performance will be also. Good science students avoid the fiction of myths and seek the facts of scientific exploration. The truths about learning science also appear in Table 5.17.

Table 5.17   Myths (and Truths) about Learning Science

Examine the following statements. Have you ever said (or thought) something like them?

Myth	True
I'm not smart enough to learn science.	People of normal intelligence can learn scientific information. Yes, science is complex and sometimes you need to know math to work problems. However, what's more important is that you need certain learning skills to be able to process, recall, and apply information. Genius or not, you can learn these skills. That's what this book is all about.
I just can't think like a scientist.	Do you think scientists think differently from the rest of us? If some students appear to learn science more easily than you, it's because they already know how to identify and synthesize essential information. They know how to solve problems and reason analytically. What they know, you can learn.
There's too much to learn in science.	Do you fear you won't have time to learn all that's required in your science course? If so, ask yourself if you've overextended yourself. What are your current commitments? Which are essential? Which aren't? You might also consider your preparation for taking a science course. Are your math skills adequate? What kind of background do you have in this subject? Finally, you need to consider your study skills. How well do you take notes? Can you learn information effectively? You need answers to all these questions to determine if your schedule will bring success in science.
I'm afraid I'll fail science.	Do you fear you'll fail no matter how hard you try? In other words, why should you try very hard if you're going to fail anyway? Doing your best requires taking a risk. If you fail after trying your hardest, you can't say, "I could have passed if I'd tried." To succeed in science, you need confidence to risk trying hard.
I don't like science, and I don't want to study it.	What's your motivation for studying science if you don't like the subject? Your goal may be short-term (you want to pass tomorrow's exam) or long-term (you want to graduate and become an engineer). Your motivation might be intrinsic (internal, personal) or extrinsic (external, from others). Intrinsic motivation produces the best results. That is, you need to be willing to study science because it is in your best interest. In short, your motivation must come from yourself, and you must continue to work even when rewards are not immediate.
My memory isn't good enough to handle all the information.	Do all those scientific terms sound alike to you? Does what you've learned seem to slip outside your head? Well, that's normal. Success in science depends on your ability to learn and retain information efficiently. Once you master the basics (certain facts and terms), you'll build on this information as the course continues. Thus, getting started on the right foot determines your destination (the dean's list or elsewhere).

SOURCE: Adapted from Kean & Middlecamp (1986). *A General Approach to Learning Chemistry.*

Failure to Cope: Withdrawal

Withdrawal tends to block behaviors needed for facing and overcoming stress. You withdraw from situations in one of two ways. You either physically or psychologically withdraw. You physically withdraw by dropping a class or dropping out of school. Since you can't physically withdraw every time you face stress, you might also withdraw mentally or emotionally from academic stress.

This psychological withdrawal constitutes a normal, and to some degree unconscious, reaction to stress. It is your psyche's attempt to soften the blow of a stressor. Such withdrawal takes place in one of several ways (see Table 5.18). **Repression**—blocking the cause of stress from your memory—is one way you withdraw from anxiety. This method involves your doing nothing to solve the problem. You think about more pleasant things instead of whatever bothers you. **Denial** also provides a way to withdraw. Again, you fail to prepare. By denying the test's existence or its importance to you, you withdraw from the stress it creates within you. Another way to avoid stress is **projection.** Here, you blame someone or something else for your failure. You refuse to accept responsibility for your actions and project that responsibility onto someone else. Finally, as a fourth way to withdraw from stress, you can **rationalize** being unprepared or not making the best grade possible. Here, you identify a reasonable and acceptable excuse for failure and exchange it for the more distasteful truth. Withdrawal techniques work—at best—as only a temporary check on stress.

Table 5.18   Examples of Withdrawing from Exam Stress

Method of Withdrawal	Typical Withdrawal Statements
Repression	"Oh, that test is next week. I'll study after my date Saturday. Where can we go? I know! We'll go see that new movie. Then, we'll eat dinner at. . . ."
Denial	"I'm not worried about my grade in that course—it's only an elective."
Projection	"Sure, I made a 55%! What did you expect? You know she gives the hardest exams in the entire math department—well, she grades the hardest anyway."
Rationalization	"I didn't have time to study for my history exam because I was so busy volunteering at the hospital. My work with sick children is so much more rewarding than a good grade in one history course."

Withdrawing from stress rather than coping positively with it is essentially a habit. You do it without thought. Like other habits, you can break it. Your first step in doing so is knowing the withdrawal technique you use most often. Once you identify it, you need to consciously stop yourself when you start to withdraw. You replace the withdrawal technique with another coping behavior. That might be self-talk, exercise, visualization, or some other positive method discussed in this chapter. Ending withdrawal, and coping positively with stress, increase your chances of success in school.

Smart Review 5.2

Check your understanding of the preceding section by answering the following on a separate sheet of paper or in your journal:

1. Create an analogy that contrasts distress and eustress.

2. Examine Tables 5.6 and 5.7. Classify the top ten stressors of Table 5.6 under the categories of Table 5.7.

3. Create a mnemonic to help you remember Maslow's hierarchy of needs in Figure 5.1.

4. What role do nutrition, exercise, and rest play in coping with stress?

5. Compare visualization and relaxation as coping techniques.

6. How can you cope with stress during an exam?

7. How does examining a returned test reduce future stress in the same class?

8. Examine Table 4.1 in Chapter 4. Create assertive statements for asking a teacher to allow you to make up an exam.

9. Examine Table 5.19. Rewrite these myths so that they pertain to either math or writing. Then refute them.

10. Create a mnemonic for remembering the types of withdrawal. How can you break the habit of withdrawal?

SMART Information 5.1

Using your password for this course, access InfoTrac College Edition on the World Wide Web.

1. Using the notecards, map, or outline you created for the article in Question 1 of **SMART Information 4.1,** create three multiple choice questions and two essay questions that you think might come from the article.

   _____

   _____

   _____

   _____

   _____

   _____

2. Using the map or outline you created for Question 2 of **SMART Information 4.1,** create three short answer questions and four true-false questions.

   _____

   _____

   _____

   _____

   _____

   _____

3. You recall that your instructor told you that factors of anthropological study (religion, political, society, technology, and economy) will be used in an essay question (see Question 3 of **SMART Information 4.1**). Review the articles you found in your search of one of the topics. Describe three ways that the authors in those articles used the concept of an anthropological perspective. How do these examples help you predict possible essay questions?

   _____

   _____

   _____

   _____

   _____

Speaking Figuratively, of Course...

Grasping Allusions

Allusions are somewhat like symbols (see Chapter 4). Both express ideas in a shortened form. Both require background knowledge for understanding. Both, however, rely on commonly-known information. Symbols draw from similes and metaphors that have become well known over time. Allusions, however, refer to works of literature, history, and the arts. Thus, allusions are aptly named. They *allude* (refer) to some character, writing, event, piece of music, etc.

Consider a **cross-reference** in a dictionary or an encyclopedia. It tells you where to get more information about a word or topic. Allusions comprise a kind of cross-reference that does not tell you where to go for more facts. Instead, when authors use allusions they ask you to connect the allusion to its source from memory. Grasping allusions, then, requires background knowledge.

Authors, as well as speakers, often allude to characters, phrases, terms, or places. These come from mythology (*Pandora's* box, *Herculean* strength, a *Siren* song) and history (honest as *George Washington,* as beautiful as *Helen of Troy,* as traitorous as *Benedict Arnold*). The Bible (*Garden of Eden,* patience of *Job,* wise as *Solomon*) and other works of literature (grinning like a *Cheshire Cat, "I'll think about that tomorrow,"* a *Scrooge*) also provide allusions. Finally, allusions come from media sources like television (*"Beam me up, Scotty"*) and movies (*"Show me the money"; "Play it again, Sam"; "Houston, we have a problem"; "My heart will go on"*).

If you do not recognize an allusion at once, look carefully at the context. This provides clues to the allusion's meaning. Then search your memory for possible links with other information. If nothing comes to mind, you can attempt to look it up. Dictionaries and books of quotations provide the sources of some allusions.

Figurative Language 5.A

1. "Every great man nowadays has his disciples, and it is always *Judas* who writes the biography."—Oscar Wilde

Source: _____

Meaning: _____

_____

2. "*Aunt Jemima and Uncle Tom* are dead, their places taken by a group of amazingly well-adjusted young men and women, almost as dark, but ferociously literate, well-dressed and scrubbed, who are never laughed at."—James Baldwin

   Source: _____

   Meaning: _____

   _____

3. "I don't believe in God because I don't believe in *Mother Goose.*"—Clarence Darrow

   Source: _____

   Meaning: _____

   _____

4. "Every man meets his *Waterloo* at last."—Wendell Phillips

   Source: _____

   Meaning: _____

   _____

5. "I would rather sleep in the southern corner in a little country churchyard, than in the tombs of the *Capulets.*"—Burke

   Source: _____

   Meaning: _____

   _____

Figurative Language 5.B

Read the following essay. Use the steps for reading literary text found in Chapter 2 to create a code for this selection. Code symbols, similes, metaphors, irony, and allusions. Then, on a separate sheet of paper, answer the questions which accompany the selection.

Dying To Lie Down

Wendy Goldberg became the first woman to win the Jack Daniel's Faux Faulkner contest with a parody of the Boston Marathon.

"father says victory is an illusion he would say that wouldn't he that had never won so much as a cross-eyed kewpie doll at a two bit raree show or a dimestore trophy in a third-rate turkey-shoot let alone a crown of laurel halo of honeysuckle in a first class feat of first class feet—the fourteenth Boston Marathon thinks Sprintin' wheeling and careering through sprawling city streets whose sentient cement synapses register the tumult of talcumed toes (ten of 'em) that had heretofore trod (but would never more trudge) the humble hamlets and earthy enclaves of Yoknerpatoffy County but now find themselves pounding pavement prodigiously pockmarked with potholes that had probably come over with the Pilgrims along with the Sox and the pox . . . that what they larned you up at Havahd father winks and shakes his head that tarnished temple of too-much-talk where sour-faced summa cum lately dispense earfuls of errant nonsense to packs of precocious young pups . . . i say O how the mighty have fallen london bridge and my aching arches . . . but the South shall rise again

they came out of nowhere and without warning like an onslaught of acne on a homecoming queen, shades of Sherman shellacking Atlanta: a phalanx of foot soldiers forging fearlessly forward, legions of the lean, the best of the buff; a host of heroes, a galaxy of gods they were!; any number of nimble Nikes, assorted Atalantas, and a myriad middle-aged Mercuries meting out punishment to the muscles merely mortal; sweeping me up in a tide of toe-flexing Titans (trailing glory and Little Sister Time), a vortex of vibrating vertebrae, an army of appendages assiduously advancing whose collective capacity for maximum motion makes the Indy 500 look like a tinker-toy tourney, bringing something of the glory that was Greece to the ballyhooed bastion of Yankee ingenuity—built on equal parts brains and "blustah" (as the locals say)—that is Boston: bona fide birthplace of baked beans

and all that I have ever known or felt remembered or believed or jest plain read about in that feller Faulknah's fast-paced fiction, and all whom I have ever loved or pittied (or parodied), every burden I have borne (along with these six-pound flat-irons), everybody I have bored (especially St. Shreve), all keep pace with me today, stride for stride—breath for breath . . . Why, there's shoeless Joe Kickmiss!—a speed-demon in spandex—with the Right Reverend Highjump drawing nigh; Thomas Shotput shoots by shouting chasin' ragin' Charlie Bonsai—the better to bid him get lost!; which he (Bon) is and will remain, since Miss Rosie Ruiz-Coldfeet—our Lady of the Trolley—shamelessly shanghaied Charlie on the MTA (did he ever return) . . . As I wipe my brow, take my bow, and ease my toes, Addie Bunion looks at me funny . . . so I axes her right-kind (but with a groan): Did you ever have a blistah? Did you? Did you!"

SOURCE: *Sunday Advocate*, 7/27/97. Reprinted by permission of Associated Press.

1. Identify one example of each of the following literary devices: simile, metaphor, irony. Explain each.
2. Identify five allusions and their significance to the essay.
3. The caption identifies this essay as a *parody*. What does this mean? In what manner is this essay a parody? Are parodies ironic? Defend your answer.
4. How does figurative language add or detract from this parody?

Figurative Language 5.C

Re-read the poem found in Figure 5.1. Now examine your answer to the third question in 5.B. On a separate sheet of paper, explain the irony in " 'Twas the Night before Finals."

SUMMARY

Test-taking strategies aid you during the exam. These include special suggestions for taking subjective and objective exams, test-wise strategies, and information about open-book, take-home tests, and final exams. Stress management involves coping before an exam (through physical wellness, mental preparation, visualization, and relaxation), during an exam, and after an exam (by examining returned tests, adjusting to stress, and using appropriate mechanisms to schedule make up exams).

CHAPTER REVIEW

1. Reexamine the test-wise principles in Table 5.1. Which of these use content or format features to ensure test-wisdom? Which depend more on your own logic, motivation, and stress control?

    _____

    _____

    _____

    _____

    _____

2. How do you cope with stress before, during, or after an exam? Explain one method you will add to your coping repertoire for handling stress before, during, and after tests.

    _____

    _____

    _____

    _____

    _____

3. Reexamine the steps in taking objective tests found in Table 5.2. Which items should be done prior to answering any questions? Which steps should be used while you answer questions?

    _____

    _____

    _____

    _____

    _____

4. List five specific situations about which you are concerned. Develop three positive messages for each one.

_____

_____

_____

_____

_____

5. Describe in three to five sentences the quiet place you go to relax. Then describe ten specific features you plan to use in creating a vivid relaxation visualization of that location.

_____

_____

_____

_____

_____

6. Perform an after-exam survey of your last test in each of your classes. What is your most common mistake? How can you solve this problem?

_____

_____

_____

_____

_____

7. A student applies for a job but fails to get it. Create three positive and three negative forms of self-talk that the student might use in this situation.

_____

_____

_____

_____

_____

8. What effect would adjusting to stress after an exam have on future self-talk? Give three examples to illustrate this effect.

_____

_____

_____

_____

_____

9. What makes students think that finals are more difficult than any other exam? Is this an accurate assessment? Why or why not? What makes

students think that take-home tests are easier than other exams? Is this an accurate assessment? Why or why not?

_____

_____

_____

_____

_____

10. How does previewing your test help you increase your test score? How does examining your test after it is returned help you increase your test score?

_____

_____

_____

_____

_____

ACTION PLAN

Review the information this chapter contains and respond to the following:

MOVING ON

You're finished! You've now undertaken all the aspects of learning one at a time. The rest of this text provides you with an opportunity to practice and refine your strategies for learning. Your course now becomes focused on particular academic subjects—those likely to arise in your other courses. You'll be asked to read chapters about economics, health, and history; take notes from videotaped lectures on these subjects; create mnemonic and study aids to learn the information in these areas; and take exam covering the content you've lerned. So, move on to success as a postsecondary student!

Sample Chapter 6

The Study of Humanity

Reprinted by permission of *Humanity: An Introduction to Cultural Anthropology* by Peoples & Bailey. Copyright 1997 by Wadsworth. All rights reserved.

The following application table of contents and chapter will be used to demonstrate the learning tasks involved in the first five chapters of *SMART*. Once you complete this chapter, you will have worked through the tasks involved in learning information for a college course. Subsequent sample chapters will be used for course simulations. The sample chapters used for the course simulations will provide you with additional opportunities to practice the learning tasks without risking a course grade in a real course.

This chapter, "Humanity: An Introduction to Cultural Anthropology," is a social science. Social science subjects also include history, political science, economics, sociology, psychology, and geography. Such subjects focus on the science of societies (individuals or groups)—their lives and the effects of those lives, as well as the facts, situations, problems, and customs that surround them. The goal of such courses is to give you a better understanding of yourself and the world around you and to help you contribute to the world in a meaningful way. This helps you explain and predict how people of various cultures think, act, and behave.

Social science courses often reflect much of the same information but from a variety of perspectives. Individuals (psychology) form groups (sociology) at particular times (history) and in particular places (geography and anthropology). They are governed (political science) and survive by trading among themselves and with other groups (economics). Thus, one key to maximizing your understanding of social science courses is to identify concepts both within a course and across courses rather than isolate concepts from one another. A second key is to look for the organization of ideas in social science.

Use the following checklist to manage your time for completing the activities required in learning the content of this chapter.

Date Assigned	Due Date	Date Completed	Assignment
			Record assignments on term planner (Chapter 1)
			Complete weekly schedule (Chapter 1)
			Complete prioritized TO DO list (Chapter 1)
			Preview chapter: Create chapter outline or map (Chapter 2)
			Read, mark, and label chapter (Chapter 2)
			Record lecture notes (Chapter 3)
			Schedule study and rehearsal time (Chapter 4)
			Prepare for test by predicting test questions and creating charts, maps, or other study aids (Chapter 4)
			Rehearse and practice information (Chapter 4)
			Take test (Chapter 5)
			Evaluate returned exam results (Chapter 5)

CONTENTS

SAMPLE CHAPTER 6   THE STUDY OF HUMANITY

CHAPTER 16

Personality Formation and the Life Cycle   303

PART IV

ANTHROPOLOGY IN THE MODERN WORLD   322

CHAPTER 17

The Changing Human World   324

CHAPTER 18

Ethnicity in the Modern World   350

CHAPTER 19

Applied Anthropology and World Problems   377

Boxes in Humanity

CHAPTER

1

THE STUDY OF HUMANITY

CONTENTS

Where and how did the human species originate? How have humans changed over time, both biologically and culturally? Is there a common human nature, and, if so, what is it like? In what ways do people who live in different times and places differ? And how can we explain why there is so much variation among human societies, even though humanity is a single species? Such questions are the concern of anthropology, the study of humanity.

❖ SCOPE OF ANTHROPOLOGY

Anthropologists are interested in almost everything about people. We want to know when, where, and how the human species began, why we evolved into what we are, and the ways our biological nature affects our lives today. Anthropologists try to explain why people in some cultures believe that sickness is caused by dead ancestors, whereas others claim that tarantulas throw magical darts into their bodies, and still others tell you that the spirits of evil humans leave their bodies at night and devour the internal organs of their victims. We want to know why most Christians eat beef but devout Hindus do not, and why some New Guinea people periodically gorge themselves with pork but some religions teach that pig flesh is unclean. We want to know why so many Balinese are fascinated by cockfights, so many Japanese by sumo wrestling, so many Spaniards by bullfights, and so many Americans by football. In short, anthropologists are liable to be curious about practically everything human: our evolution, our genes, our emotions, our behaviors, our languages, and our religions.

If you already have the impression that anthropology is a broad field and that anthropologists have quite diverse interests, you are correct. In fact, it is commonly said that the distinguishing characteristic of anthropology—the thing that makes it different from the many other fields that also include people as their subject matter—is its broad scope. A good way to emphasize this broad scope is to say that anthropologists are interested in *all* human beings—whether living or dead, Asian or African or European—and that they are interested in many different *aspects* of humans, including their skin color, family lives, political systems, tools, personality types, and languages. No place or time is too remote to escape the anthropologist's notice. No dimension of humankind, from genes to art styles, is outside the anthropologist's attention.

❖ SUBFIELDS OF ANTHROPOLOGY

Anthropology, then, is a diverse field. No individual anthropologist can master the whole range of subjects encompassed by the discipline. For practical reasons, almost all modern anthropologists specialize in one of five principal subfields. Physical (or biological) anthropology is concerned mainly with the evolutionary origins and physical diversity of the human species. Archaeology focuses on the technological and cultural development of human societies over long time periods. The subdiscipline known as cultural anthropology describes and analyzes contemporary and historically recent societies, trying to understand how and why the world's cultures are so diverse. Anthropological linguistics deals with human languages and their relation to cultures. Finally, applied anthropology uses anthropological concepts, methods, and theories to try to solve contemporary human problems. Anthropology is even more complicated than this fivefold division implies because each of these subfields is in turn divided into several specializations. Although cultural anthropology is the primary subject of this book, a brief look at the other subfields is essential to understand the whole discipline.

Physical Anthropology

Physical (also called **biological**) **anthropology** is concerned with the biological evolution of the human species, the anatomy and behavior of monkeys and apes, and the physical variations between different human populations. As these subjects indicate, physical anthropology is closely related to the natural sciences in its goals and methods.

An important goal of physical anthropology is to understand how and why the human species evolved from prehuman, ape-like ancestors. Scholars who investigate human biological evolution are known as **paleoanthropologists.** Over decades of searching for fossils and meticulous excavations and laboratory studies, paleoanthropologists have reconstructed the history of how humans evolved anatomically. The outlines of human evolution are becoming clear. Most scholars agree that the evolutionary line leading to modern humans split from those leading to modern African apes (chimpanzees and gorillas) around five million years ago. It also appears that fully modern humans, *Homo sapiens,* evolved surprisingly recently, probably less than 100,000 years ago. Of course, the fossil record is incomplete and can be interpreted in various ways, so new discoveries may alter our current understanding.

Primatologists, another kind of biological anthropologist, specialize in the evolution, anatomy, social behavior, and adaptation of primates, the taxonomic order to which humans belong. By conducting field studies of how living primates forage, mate, move around in their environment, and interact socially, primatologists hope to shed light on the forces that affected early human populations.

Primatological research on the behavior of group-living monkeys and apes has added significantly to the scientific understanding of many aspects of human behavior, including sexuality, parenting, cooperation, tool use, and intergroup conflict and aggression. Field studies of African chimpanzees and gorillas, the two apes genetically most similar to the human species, have been especially fruitful sources of hypotheses and information.

Yet another type of biological anthropologist is interested in how and why human populations vary physically. All humans are members of a single species, and one of the basic tenets of anthropology is that the physical similarities among the world's peoples far outweigh the differences. Nonetheless, the residents of different continents were once more isolated from one another than they are today, and during this separation they evolved differences in overall body and facial form, height, skin color, blood chemistry, and other genetically determined features. Anthropologists who study **human variation** seek to measure and explain the differences and similarities among the world's peoples in these and other physical characteristics.

Most physical anthropologists work in universities or museums, as teachers, researchers, writers, and curators. But many people trained in biological anthropology also work in "practical" jobs, applying their knowledge of human anatomy to find answers to problems. For instance, **forensic anthropologists** work for or consult with law enforcement and other agencies, where they analyze and help identify human skeletal remains. Among their contributions are determining the age, sex, height, and other physical characteristics of crime or accident victims. Forensic anthropologists know how to gather evidence from bones about old injuries or diseases, which then are compared with medical histories to identify victims. In 1984, the democratically elected government of Argentina hired forensic anthropologist Clyde Snow to help identify people killed by death squads in the late 1970s, the years of military rule in Argentina. Snow also has disinterred the bones of some of the northern Iraqi Kurds killed by Saddam Hussein's government in the late 1980s. In 1993, he located a mass grave in eastern Croatia, where Serb forces had gunned down 200 Croatian patients and staff from a medical center. In the 1990s, teams of forensic anthropologists have exhumed remains from graves in Bolivia, Guatemala, El Salvador, and Haiti in efforts to identify victims of political assassination and determine the exact causes of their deaths.

Archaeology

Archaeology is the investigation of the human past by excavating and analyzing material remains. Because it investigates the ways in which human life has changed over the centuries and millennia, archaeology has much in common with history. It differs, however, in its methods and, to some extent, its goals. Modern archaeology usually is divided into two major kinds of studies: prehistoric and historic.

Prehistoric archaeology is the investigation of ancient cultures—those that never kept written records of their activities, customs, and beliefs. Although prehistoric peoples lacked writing, evidence of their way of life exists in the tools, pottery, ornaments, bones, plant pollen, charcoal, and other materials they left behind, in or on the ground. Through excavation and laboratory analysis of these material remains, prehistoric archaeologists reconstruct the way people lived in ancient times and trace how human cultures have changed over the centuries. In fact, research conducted by prehistoric archaeologists provides our only source of information about how people lived before the development of writing.

To learn about the more recent past, historians use written materials such as diaries, letters, land records, newspapers, and tax collection documents. Written records provide useful data, but they typically are fragmentary and provide information only on specific subjects and subgroups within a society. The growing field of **historic archaeology** supplements written materials by excavations of houses, stores, plantations, factories, and other historic structures. Historic archaeologists often uncover hard data on living conditions and other topics lacking in written accounts.

Archaeologist Larry McKee, for example, works for the Hermitage, a reconstructed cotton plantation near Nashville, Tennessee, once owned—along with its enslaved Africans—by President Andrew Jackson. McKee's excavations of living quarters have filled in many details about the everyday lives of enslaved people on the plantation. Materials found in houses reveal that families hunted for meat to supplement their food rations; bartered for plates, pots, dinnerware, and other objects; and continued to practice at least some elements of their ancestral African religions.

Cultural Anthropology

Cultural anthropology (also called **ethnology**) is the study of contemporary and historically recent human societies and cultures. As its name suggests, the main focus of this subfield is culture—the customs and beliefs of some human group. Ethnologists are especially fascinated by the great variety of the world's peoples and cultures. Describing and attempting to understand and explain this cultural diversity is one of their major objectives. Making the public aware and tolerant of the cultural differences that exist within humanity is another mission of ethnology.

To do their research and collect their data, ethnologists conduct **fieldwork**. Fieldwork ordinarily involves moving into the community under study, communicating in the local language, and living in close contact with the people. Intimate interaction with the members of a community provides ethnologists with firsthand experiences that yield insights that could not be gained in any other way. Fieldworkers usually report the findings of their research in books or scholarly journals, where they are available to the general public. A written account of how a single human population lives is called an **ethnography** (which means "writing about a people").

Anthropological Linguistics

Defined as the study of human language, linguistics is a field all its own, existing as a separate discipline from anthropology. Linguists describe and analyze the sound patterns and combinations, words, meanings, and sentence structures of human languages. Language has some amazing properties, and the fact that humans are able to learn and use language at all is truly remarkable.

Language interests anthropologists for several reasons. For one thing, the ability to communicate complex messages with great efficiency may be the most important capability of humans that makes us different from primates and other animals; certainly our ability to speak is a key factor in our evolutionary success. Cultural anthropologists, especially, are interested in language because of how the language and culture of a people affect each other. The subfield of **anthropological linguistics** is concerned with the complex relations between language and other aspects of human behavior and thought. For example, anthropological linguists are interested in how language is used in various social contexts: What style of speech must one use with people of high status? What does the way people attach labels to their natural environment tell us about the way they perceive that environment?

Applied Anthropology

In the past, almost all professional anthropologists spent their careers in some form of educational institution, most commonly in colleges and universities, or in museums. Today, hundreds of anthropologists hold full-time positions that allow them to apply their expertise in governmental agencies, nonprofit groups, private corporations, and international bodies. Many more make their living as consultants to such organizations and institutions. These institutions and organizations employ anthropologists because they believe that people trained in the discipline will help them in problem solving. In recognition of the growth of noneducational employment opportunities, the American Anthropological Association (the professional organization of anthropologists) officially recognizes **applied anthropology** as a separate subfield. In fact, in the 1990s, about half of those with new anthropology Ph.D.s acquire jobs in some federal, state, or local governmental agency or in the private sector.

Many archaeologists are employed not in universities, but in museums, public agencies, and for-profit corporations. Museums offer jobs as curators of artifacts and as researchers. State highway departments employ archaeologists to conduct surveys of proposed new routes in order to locate and excavate archaeological sites that will be destroyed. The U.S. Forest Service and National Park Service hire archaeologists to find sites on public lands so that decisions about the preservation of cultural materials can be made.

Those who work in the growing field of **cultural resource management** locate sites of prehistoric and historic significance, evaluate their importance, and make recommendations about total or partial preservation. Since the passage of the National Historic Preservation Act in 1966, private corporations and government bodies who wish to construct factories, buildings, parking lots, shopping malls, and other structures must file a report on how the construction will affect historical remains and on the steps taken to preserve them. Because of this law, the business of **contract archaeology** has boomed in the United States. Firms engaged in contract archaeology bid competitively for the privilege of locating, excavating, and reporting on sites affected or destroyed by construction. Hundreds of (mostly small) contract archaeology companies exist.

Within the subfield of cultural anthropology, applied anthropologists are ever more numerous and work for a wide range of organizations. We discuss some of the ways applied anthropologists have contributed to the alleviation of human problems in later chapters. For now, a few examples will illustrate some of the work they do.

Medical anthropology is one of the fastest growing specializations. Medical anthropologists are trained to investigate the complex interactions between human health, nutrition, social environment, and cultural beliefs and practices. Because the transmission of viruses and bacteria are greatly affected by people's diets, sanitation, sexual habits, and other behaviors, one role of medical anthropologists is to work with epidemiologists to identify cultural practices that affect the spread of disease. Different cultures have different ideas about the causes and symptoms of disease, how best to treat illnesses, the abilities of traditional healers and doctors, and the importance of community involvement in the healing process. By studying how a human community perceives such things, medical anthropologists can provide information to hospitals and agencies that help them deliver health care services more effectively.

Development anthropology is another area in which anthropologists apply their expertise to the solution of practical human problems, usually in the Third World. Working both as full-time employees and as consultants, development anthropologists provide information on communities that help agencies adapt projects to local conditions and needs. Examples of agencies and institutions that employ development anthropologists include the U.S. Agency for International Development, the Rockefeller and Ford Foundations, the World Bank, and the United Nations Development Program. Perhaps the most important role of the anthropologist in such institutions is to provide policymakers with knowledge of local-level ecological and cultural conditions, so that projects will avoid unanticipated problems and minimize negative impacts.

Educational anthropology also offers jobs in public agencies and private institutions. Some roles of educational anthropologists include advising in bilingual education, conducting detailed observations of classroom interactions, training personnel in multicultural issues, and adapting teaching styles to local customs and needs. An increasingly important role for North American educational anthropologists is to help teachers understand the learning styles and behavior of children from various ethnic, racial, and national backgrounds.

Increasingly, corporations employ cultural anthropologists. Especially since the 1980s, the growth of overseas business opportunities led North American companies to need professionals who can advise executives and sales staff on what to expect and how to speak and act when they conduct business in other countries. Because of their training as acute observers and listeners, anthropologists are employed in the private sector in many other capacities as well.

As these examples show, anthropologists apply their knowledge and skills to the solution of practical human problems in many ways. Speaking very broadly, cultural anthropologists are valuable to agencies, companies, and other organizations because they are trained to do two things very well: first, to observe, record, and analyze human behavior; and, second, to look for and understand the cultural assumptions, values, and beliefs that underlie that behavior.

Cultural anthropology is the largest subfield. Of the doctoral degrees awarded in the United States in 1994—5, 52% were in cultural anthropology, 24% in archaeology, 10% in physical/biological anthropology, 1% in linguistics, and 12% in applied anthropology. However, these figures are misleading in one respect. New Ph.D.s in other specializations—especially in cultural anthropology—often acquire jobs that use their research and analytical skills in solving institutional problems and providing human services; such people may also consider themselves applied anthropologists. Box 1.1 provides some additional interesting facts and figures about some recent changes in anthropology as a whole.

❖ CULTURAL ANTHROPOLOGY TODAY

As the overview of the five subdisciplines confirms, anthropology is indeed a broad field. Even by itself, cultural anthropology—the main subject of this text—is enormously broad, for modern ethnological fieldworkers study human communities from all parts of the world, from the mountains of Tibet to the deserts of the American Southwest, from the streets of Calcutta to the plains of East Africa.

In the popular imagination, cultural anthropological fieldworkers go to far-off places and study exotic peoples, or "natives." Except for the stereotypes about the "natives," this image was reasonably accurate until the 1970s. Until then, ethnology differed from sociology and other disciplines that studied living peoples and cultures mainly by the kinds of cultures studied. Cultural anthropologists mainly focused on small-scale, non-Western, preindustrial, subsistence-oriented cultures, whereas sociological studies mainly dealt with large Euro-American, industrial, money-and-market countries. Cultural anthropologists themselves often sought out pristine, untouched tribal cultures to study because living among the "primitives" brought prestige and enhanced one's reputation in the discipline.

All this has changed. Today's ethnologists have studied modern factory workers, Swedish churches, Chicago motorcycle gangs, Canadian medical clinics, American bodybuilders, British witches' covens, Appalachian towns, and the recent decline of the middle class—to name just a few illustrations of how, more and more, contemporary anthropologists are studying their own societies. There are many reasons for the trend away from the "far away" in favor of "here-at-home" studies. One is the realization that anthropological concepts and fieldwork methods can yield insights about modern societies that other disciplines miss. Another is that increasing numbers of anthropologists are using their knowledge and training to solve real-world problems.

The boundaries between cultural anthropology and other disciplines (especially sociology) are much less firm than they were even a few decades ago. Most ethnological fieldwork, however, still occurs in relatively small communities (on the order of a few hundred to a few thousand) where the researcher can participate firsthand in the lives of the people. More than any other single factor, the fieldwork experience distinguishes cultural anthropology from other disciplines concerned with humankind. Also, cultural anthropology remains far more comparative and global in its scope and interests than the other social sciences and humanities.

In many ways, modern cultural anthropology overlaps with numerous other disciplines that study people. For example, a fieldworker may be especially interested in the agriculture, leadership patterns, legal system, or art of a culture or region. He or she will, therefore, want to be acquainted with the work of economists, agronomists, political scientists, and artists or art historians—disciplines that have made some particular dimensions of human life their specialization. Likewise, an ethnologist who specializes in some geographical region (such as West Africa, China, or Brazil) will read the works of historians, sociologists, novelists, and political

BOX 1.1   A PROFILE OF ANTHROPOLOGY

Most anthropologists in Canada and the United States are members of the American Anthropological Association (AAA, or "Triple A"). The AAA is the professional organization for North American anthropologists—similar to the American Medical Association for physicians and the American Bar Association for attorneys. Each year the AAA publishes a *Guide to Departments,* which contains information about universities and colleges, museums, government agencies, and many private corporations that frequently hire anthropologists. A few basic facts and figures taken from the 1995–6 Guide will help in understanding the field of anthropology and how it has changed over the years.

Number of Anthropology Degrees Granted in U.S. Since 1950

	Bachelor's Degree	Master's Degree	Ph.D. Degree
1950	352	69	22
1960	449	117	55
1970	3,103	553	195
1980	3,623	929	389
1990	4,504	980	375
1994	7,184	1,206	400

Sex of New Anthropology Ph.D.s, Various Years

	Males	Females
1972	68%	32%
1976	62%	38%
1982	59%	41%
1988	56%	44%
1995	41%	59%

- Number of American universities in 1995 that awarded a doctorate in anthropology: 93
- Number of anthropology Ph.D.s in the United States in 1995: 11,000
- Percentage of Americans who hold the Ph.D. in anthropology: 0.004%
- Average age at which anthropology Ph.D.s are received, 1995: 40
- Percentage of American anthropologists identifying themselves as "white," 1995: 84%
- Percentage of new anthropology Ph.D.s who did *not* acquire jobs in colleges and universities or in research in the early 1970s: 13%
- Percentage of new anthropology Ph.D.s who did *not* acquire job in colleges and universities or in research between 1975 and 1990: 41%

Source: American Anthropological Association 1995: 306–317

---

scientists who also have written about the region. Cultural anthropologists regularly study subjects that are the specializations of other disciplines, as is nicely illustrated by anthropological specializations in such areas as ethnomusicology, ethnopoetics, ethnobotany, and ethnolinguistics. (Here's an amusing and at least half-true general principle: Any subject can be made into a subject for ethnological research by prefixing it with "ethno.") Cultural anthropology thus cuts across many disciplines, encompassing many of the subjects that other scholars consider their special province—law, religion, literature, music, and so on.

❖ ANTHROPOLOGICAL PERSPECTIVES

Because cultural anthropologists study many of the same kinds of things studied by other scholars, obviously it is not *what* they study that makes the field distinct. Most ethnologists believe that the main difference between their discipline and other social sciences and humanities lies not so much in the kinds of subjects they investigate as in the approach they take to studying humankind. We believe it is important that cultures and communities be studied holistically, comparatively, and relativistically. Because it is these perspectives as much as anything else that make cultural anthropology distinctive, they need to be introduced.

Holism

To study a subject holistically is to attempt to understand all the factors that influence it and to interpret it in the context of all those factors. With respect to studies of human cultures and societies, the **holistic perspective** means that no single aspect of a community can be understood unless its relations to other aspects of the community's total way of life are explored. Holism requires, for example, that a fieldworker studying the rituals of a people must investigate how those rituals are influenced by the people's family life, economic forces, political leadership, relationships between the sexes, and a host of other factors. The attempt to understand a community's customs, beliefs, values, and so forth holistically is one reason why ethnographic fieldwork takes so much time and involves close contact with people.

Taken literally, a holistic understanding of a people's customs and beliefs is probably not possible because of the complexity of human societies. But cultural anthropologists have learned that ignoring the interrelations between language, religion, art, economy, family, and other dimensions of life results in distortions and misunderstandings. Although more complicated than this, the essence of the holistic perspective may be stated fairly simply: *Look for connections and interrelations between things, and try to understand parts in the context of the whole.*

Comparativism

As we have already seen, in the early decades of its existence ethnological research focused mainly on non-Western peoples, many of whom thought and acted quite differently from the citizens of the anthropologist's own (usually European or North American) nation. Anthropologists soon learned that the ideas and concepts that applied to their own societies often did not apply to those of other peoples, whose cultural traditions were vastly different. They learned, for example, to mistrust the claims put forth by French scholars about human nature when the only humans these scholars had ever encountered lived in Western Europe.

More than most people, anthropologists are aware of the enormous diversity of the world's cultures. This diversity means that any general theories or ideas scholars might have about humans—about human nature, sexuality, warfare, family relationships, and so on—must take into account information from a wide range of societies. In other words, general theoretical ideas about humans or human societies or cultures must be tested from a **comparative perspective.** The ways of life of people in different times and places are far too diverse for any theory to be accepted until it has been tested in a range of human populations. For now, we may state the comparative perspective as: *Generalizations about humans must take the full range of cultural diversity into account.*

Relativism

Fundamentally, the perspective known as **cultural relativism** means that no culture is inherently superior or inferior to any other. The reason anthropologists adopt this perspective is that concepts such as "superiority" require judgments about the relative worthiness of behaviors, beliefs, and other characteristics of a culture. Such judgments are inevitably rooted in one's values, and one's values, by and large, depend on the culture in which one was raised. (You may think, incidentally, that surely there are universally valid standards for judging and evaluating cultures. Perhaps you are right; the trouble is, people don't agree on what they are!)

To see why approaching the study of cultures relativistically is important, we may contrast cultural relativism with **ethnocentrism.** Ethnocentrism is the belief that the moral standards, manners, attitudes, and so forth of one's own culture are superior to those of other cultures. Most people are ethnocentric, and a *certain degree* of ethnocentrism probably is essential if people are to be content with their lives and if their culture is to persist. Mild ethnocentrism—meaning that people hold certain values dear but don't insist that everyone else hold and live by those values—is unobjectionable to ethnologists. But extreme ethnocentrism—meaning that people believe that their values are the only correct ones and that all people everywhere should be judged by how closely they live up to those values—breeds attitudes and behaviors of intolerance that are anathema to cultural anthropology.

Ethnocentric attitudes are detrimental to the objectivity of ethnographic fieldworkers. However difficult in practice, anthropologists should try not to evaluate the behavior of the people being studied according to the standards of the fieldworker's own culture. Like the holistic and comparative perspectives, the essential point of cultural relativism may be stated simply: *In studying another culture, do not evaluate the behavior of its members by the standards and values of your own culture.*

❖ THE VALUE OF ANTHROPOLOGY

What insights does the discipline of anthropology offer about humanity? What is the value of the information anthropologists have gathered about the past and present of humankind? We have already seen that applied anthropologists help in planning and implementing programs, and in future chapters we look further at how anthropological research contributes to the solution of human problems. For now, we want to note some of the more general insights of the field.

First, because of its broad scope, anthropology gives us the information we need to understand the biological, technological, and cultural development of humanity over long time spans. Most of the reliable data now available about human biological evolution, prehistoric cultures, and non-Western peoples were collected by anthropologists. Because much of this knowledge has become part of our cultural heritage, where it is recorded in textbooks and taught in schools, it is easy to forget that someone had to discover and interpret these facts. For example, only in the late nineteenth century did most scientists accept that people are related to apes, and only in the late twentieth century did the closeness of this relation become apparent.

But anthropology has contributed more than just factual material to our understanding of the human condition. Concepts first developed or worked out by anthropologists have been incorporated into the thinking of millions of people. For example, in this chapter we have used the term *culture*—a concept that we assume our readers are aware of and a word that commonly is used in everyday life. You may not know that the scientific meaning of this word, as used in the phrase "Japanese culture," is not very old. Into the nineteenth century, people did not fully understand the importance of the distinction between a people's culture (the learned beliefs and habits that made them distinctive) and their biological makeup (their physical characteristics). Patterns of acting, thinking, and feeling often were thought to be rooted in a group's biological constitution—carried in their genes, as we say today. For example, because there often were readily observable differences in the physical appearances of various races, it was thought that these physical differences accounted for differences in beliefs and habits as well. In other words, differences that we now know are caused largely or entirely by learning and cultural upbringing were confused with differences caused by biological inheritance. Early twentieth-century anthropologists such as Franz Boas, Alfred Kroeber, and Ruth Benedict marshaled empirical evidence showing that race and culture are independent of each other. As this example shows, anthropologists have already contributed to our understanding of the human condition, although most people are not aware of these contributions.

Another value of anthropology (ethnology, especially) is that it teaches us the importance of understanding and appreciating cultural diversity;

that is, it urges us not to be ethnocentric in our attitudes toward other peoples. The orientation known as cultural relativism is not only important to the objectivity of ethnologists but also one of the main lessons anthropology offers to the general public. Mutual toleration and understanding among the world's peoples is increasingly important in this era of world travel, international migration, global business, and ethnic conflicts. To be sure, if everyone in the world became less ethnocentric, the world's problems would not be solved. But a relativistic outlook on cultural differences might help to alleviate some of the prejudices, misunderstandings, interethnic conflicts, and outright racism that continues to victimize so many people in all continents.

A related point is that anthropology can help people to avoid some of the miscommunication and misunderstandings that commonly arise when people from different parts of the world interact with one another. As we shall see in future chapters, our upbringing in a particular culture influences us in subtle ways. For instance, Canadians know how to interpret one another's actions on the basis of speech styles or body language, but these cues do not necessarily mean the same thing to people from different cultures. A Canadian salesperson selling products in Turkey may wonder why her host will not cut the chitchat and get down to business, whereas the Turk can't figure out why the visitor thinks they can do business before they have become better acquainted. A North American trying to exude self-confidence in his dealings with a Latin American may instead come across as arrogant or egotistical. Anthropology teaches people to be aware of and sensitive to cultural differences— people's actions may not mean what we take them to mean, and much misunderstanding can be avoided by taking cultural differences into account in our dealings with other people.

Finally, because of its insistence on studying humanity from a comparative perspective, anthropology helps us to understand both our own individual lives and our societies. By encouraging you to compare and contrast yourself and your ways of thinking, feeling, and acting with those of people living in other times and places, anthropology helps you see new things about yourself. How does your life compare to the lives of other people around the world? What assumptions do you unconsciously make about the world and other people? Do people in other cultures share the same kinds of problems, hopes, motivations, and feelings as you do? Or are individuals raised in other societies completely different? How does the overall quality of your existence—your sense of well-being and happiness, your self-image, your emotional life, your feeling that life is meaningful—compare with people who live elsewhere? Anthropology offers the chance to compare yourself to other peoples who live in different circumstances.

Anthropology also gives new insights about modern life. Many citizens of the wealthy nations of North America, Europe, and East Asia are dissatisfied with their lives in spite of the fact that, compared to most humans living today, they are highly privileged. In North America, widespread unhappiness and dissatisfaction seem common. In the United States, affluent New Agers move to Sedona, Arizona or to Santa Fe, New Mexico in search of enhanced self-awareness, harmonic convergences, shamanic knowledge, Hindu philosophy, and other alternative "lifestyles" they hope will lend meaning to their lives. Baby boomers who have made it into the middle class enter middle age in fear of losing their middle management jobs, all the while doubting that Social Security will be there for them. Their children of Generation X worry that they will never get a chance to live the American Dream no matter how many goods and how much education their frazzled parents buy for them. Are people of the late twentieth century in fact more stressed out than people were in previous centuries? Have people always lived in such fear and uncertainty?

At the national level, too, a multitude of what many people interpret as symptoms of societal breakdown exist. Someone blows up the Federal Building in Oklahoma City, killing 168 people. A young South Carolina woman confesses to drowning her two sons. An Arizona man beheads one of his sons, believing him possessed by the devil. In Tokyo—"the safest city in the world"—members of a religious sect release poison nerve gas into a commuter train, resulting in 12 deaths and over 5,000 injuries. In Bosnia, formerly part of Yugoslavia, Serbs try to rid areas of Muslims and Croats in the name of "ethnic cleansing." In the West African nation of Liberia, chaos results as armed rival political factions and ethnic groups roam the streets of Monrovia. Have comparable problems always afflicted human societies? Will people ever be able to live together in harmony, or is humanity forever destined to live with terrorism, hatred, and warfare? Are large numbers of people doomed to live with sickness, poverty, and hunger? No one truly knows the answers to such questions, but anthropologists do have contributions to make, some of which are discussed in future chapters of this book.

❖ SUMMARY

Defined as the study of humanity, anthropology differs from other disciplines in the social sciences and humanities primarily because of its broad scope. The field as a whole is concerned with all human beings of the past and present, living at all levels of technological development. Anthropology is also interested in all aspects of humanity: biology, language, technology, art, politics, religion, and all other dimensions of human life.

As a practical necessity, however, anthropologists must specialize. Traditionally, the field is divided into five subdisciplines. Physical anthropology studies the biological dimensions of human beings, including our biological evolution, the physical variations between contemporary populations, and the biology and behavior of nonhuman primates. Archaeology uses the material remains of prehistoric and historic cultures to investigate the past, focusing on the long-term technological and social changes that occurred in particular regions of the world. Cultural anthropology, or ethnology, is concerned with the social and cultural life of contemporary and historically recent human societies. By conducting fieldwork in various human communities and describing their findings in ethnographies, cultural anthropologists contribute to the scientific understanding of cultural diversity and to making the general public more aware and tolerant of cultural differences. Anthropological linguistics studies language, concentrating on nonwritten languages and investigating the interrelations between language and other elements of a people's way of life.

Finally, applied anthropology uses the concepts, methods, and theories of the discipline of anthropology to solve real-world problems in such areas as health, development, and education.

Until around 1970 cultural anthropology (the main subject of this text) concentrated on human cultures that are popularly known as "tribal," "premodern," or "preindustrial." This is not as true today, when anthropologists often do their research in the complex urbanized and industrialized nations of the developed world. It is increasingly difficult to distinguish ethnology from the kindred discipline of sociology. However, firsthand, extended fieldwork in villages or relatively small towns or neighborhoods continues to be a hallmark of cultural anthropology.

Cultural anthropologists are different from other scholars who study living people, not so much by what they study as by their approach. There are three main characteristics of this approach. Holism is the attempt to discern and investigate the interrelations between the customs and beliefs of a particular society. The comparative perspective means that any attempt to understand humanity or explain cultures or behaviors must include information from a wide range of human ways of life, for anthropologists have learned that most customs and beliefs are products of cultural tradition and social environment, rather than of a universal human nature. The perspective known as cultural relativism refers to fieldworkers' efforts to understand people's behaviors on their own terms, not those of the anthropologist's own culture. This requires that anthropologists avoid being ethnocentric in their research, for each people have their own history and values.

Anthropology has practical value in the modern world, and it is not as esoteric as many people think. Only anthropology allows us to see the development of human biology and culture over long time spans. Most of the knowledge we have about human evolution, prehistoric populations, and modern tribal societies was discovered by anthropologists. Early anthropologists were instrumental in popularizing the concept of culture and in showing that cultural differences are not caused by racial differences. The value of inculcating understanding and tolerance among citizens of different nations is another practical lesson of anthropology, one that is increasingly important as the economies of the world become more interdependent and as the development of weaponry makes the consequences of international misunderstanding more serious. The information that ethnographers have collected about alternative ways of being human allows us to judge the benefits against the costs of industrialization and progress. The comparative perspective of anthropology helps us see which elements of our societies are amenable to change and what the consequences of these changes might be.

KEY TERMS

physical (biological) anthropology
paleoanthropologists
primatologists
human variation
forensic anthropologists
archaeology
prehistoric archaeology
historic archaeology
cultural anthropology (ethnology)
fieldwork
ethnography

anthropological linguistics
applied anthropology
cultural resource management
contract archaeology
medical anthropology
development anthropology
educational anthropology
holistic perspective
comparative perspective
cultural relativism
ethnocentrism

SUGGESTED READINGS

Fagan, Brian M. *In the Beginning: An Introduction to Archaeology.* 8th ed. New York: HarperCollins, 1993.

Comprehensive look at archaeological methods and prehistory.

Fagan, Brian M. *The Journey from Eden: The Peopling of Our World.* London: Thames and Hudson, 1990.

A history of the spread of the human species from our African homeland into all the continents of the earth.

Fagan, Brian M. *World Prehistory: A Brief Introduction.* 3rd ed. New York: HarperCollins, 1996.

Covers human prehistory from a global perspective. Prehistory of various continents is presented, with an overview of the development of civilization in different regions.

Farb, Peter. *Word Play: What Happens When People Talk.* New York: Knopf, 1974.

A highly readable introduction to language and how it is used in social life.

Fromkin, Victoria, and Robert Rodman. *An Introduction to Language.* 5th ed. San Diego: Harcourt Brace Jovanovich, 1993.

Witty and thorough introduction to linguistics.

Jurmain, Robert, Harry Nelson, and Lynn Kilgore. *Essentials of Physical Anthropology.* 2nd ed. St. Paul: West Publishing Company, 1995.

Relatively brief introduction to primates, human evolution, physical variation, and other topics in the field.

Renfrew, Colin, and Paul Bahn. *Archaeology: Theories, Methods, and Practice.* London: Thames and Hudson, 1991.

A lengthy and detailed yet very readable introduction to archaeological methods, focusing especially on how prehistorians use artifacts to draw conclusions about the past.

The following ethnographies are excellent for introducing the ways of life of various people around the world. All are highly readable.

Balikci, Asen. *The Netsilik Eskimo.* Prospect Heights, Ill.: Waveland, 1989.

A well-rounded description of an Eskimo people.

Chagnon, Napoleon A. *Yanomamo: The Last Days of Eden.* San Diego, Harcourt Brace Jovanovich, 1992.

A readable ethnography of an Amazonian people who are threatened by the incursions of missionaries, miners, tourists, and other outsiders.

Farrer, Claire R. *Thunder Rides a Black Horse: Mescalero Apaches and the Mythic Present.* 2nd ed. Prospect Heights, Ill.: Waveland, 1996.

Concise account of ethnographer's experience with the modern Apache. Focuses on girls' puberty ceremonies, interweaving Apache culture into the account.

Fernea, Elizabeth. *Guests of the Sheik.* Garden City, N.Y.: Anchor, 1969.

A writer, journalist, and academician's account of her experiences in an Iraqi village with her anthropologist husband.

Kraybill, Donald B. *The Puzzles of Amish Life.* Intercourse, Penn.: Good Books, 1990.

Focuses on how the Amish of Lancaster County, Pennsylvania, have maintained intact communities and their values by selectively using modern technologies.

Service, Elman. *Profiles in Ethnology.* New York: Harper & Row, 1978.

One of the best resources for one who wishes a short comparative overview of the way of life of diverse peoples. Contains short sketches of the life of twenty-three societies found on all continents.

Shostak, Marjorie. *Nisa: The Life and Words of a !Kung Woman.* New York: Vintage, 1983.

> *An outstanding biographical account of a San woman.*

Thomas, Elizabeth Marshall. *The Harmless People.* 2nd ed. New York: Vintage, 1989.

> *A wonderfully written account of the customs and beliefs of the San (formerly called "Bushmen") of southern Africa.*

Turnbull, Colin. *The Forest People.* New York: Simon & Schuster, 1962.

> *A readable and sympathetic ethnography about the traditional culture of the BaMbuti pygmies of the African rain forest.*

Ward, Martha C. *Nest in the Wind.* Prospect Heights, Ill.: Waveland, 1989.

> *A delightful account of a fieldworker's experiences and difficulties on a tropical Pacific island.*

Sample Chapter 7

The Consumer in Our Global Economy

Reprinted by permission of *Economic Issues for Consumers* by Miller and Stafford. Copyright 1997 by Wadsworth. All rights reserved.

The following table of contents and chapter are from *Economic Issues for Consumers.* Like anthropology, economics is a social science. Review the introduction to Sample Chapter 6 for more information about social science courses.

Use the following checklist to manage your time for completing the activities required in learning the content of this chapter.

Date Assigned	Due Date	Date Completed	Assignment
			Record assignments on term planner (Chapter 1)
			Complete weekly schedule (Chapter 1)
			Complete prioritized TO DO list (Chapter 1)
			Preview chapter: Create chapter outline or map (Chapter 2)
			Read, mark, and label chapter (Chapter 2)
			Record lecture notes (Chapter 3)
			Schedule study and rehearsal time (Chapter 4)
			Prepare for test by predicting test questions and creating charts, maps, or other study aids (Chapter 4)
			Rehearse and practice information (Chapter 4)
			Take test (Chapter 5)
			Evaluate returned exam results (Chapter 5)

CONTENTS

CHAPTER 3

RATIONAL CONSUMER DECISION MAKING   **63**

CHAPTER 4
ENVIRONMENTALLY RESPONSIBLE CONSUMER BEHAVIOR   81

CHAPTER 5
A FLOOD OF ADVERTISING   101

CHAPTER 8
YOU HAVE TO LIVE WITH WHAT YOU HAVE   **169**

CHAPTER 11

PURCHASING NONDURABLE GOODS AND CONSUMER SERVICES

CHAPTER 12
BUYING DURABLE GOODS   265

CHAPTER 13

GETTING THERE IS HALF THE WORRY   293

CHAPTER 14

PUTTING A ROOF OVER YOUR HEAD — **319**

UNIT 4: FINANCIAL MANAGEMENT   349

Chapter 15
Banks and the Banking System   351

CHAPTER 16

THE INDEBTED CONSUMER

377

CHAPTER 17

SAVING   **403**

CHAPTER 18

INVESTING   **421**

UNIT 5: RISK MANAGEMENT   447

Chapter 19
The Health-Care Dilemma   449

SAMPLE CHAPTER 7   THE CONSUMER IN OUR GLOBAL ECONOMY

CHAPTER 20

INSURING YOUR HOME AND YOUR AUTOMOBILE   481

UNIT 6: LOOKING TO THE FUTURE 529

CHAPTER 22
YOUR RETIREMENT YEARS 531

CHAPTER 1

The Consumer in Our Global Economy

CONSUMERS
Individuals who purchase (or are given) use, maintain, and dispose of products and services in their final form in an attempt to achieve the highest level of satisfaction possible with their income limitation.

SERVICES
Intangible actions that have the ability to satisfy human wants.

This is a book about consumer economics. That means it has to do both with economics and with you, the consumer. The goal is to help you apply economic principles when making consumer decisions—such as whether to buy a house, how to buy it, what kind of insurance to purchase, whether a new or a used car is a better deal, what type of checkable and savings accounts to use, and so on. The list of such decisions is virtually endless, since we are all **consumers,** and will be all our lives. An understanding of economics helps us to be more rational consumers, abling us to analyze alternatives and base our decision making on facts relevant to us.

Accountants, lawyers, and other professionals who work in specialized fields must acquire the unique knowledge that enables them to provide the **services** of their chosen occupation. Unlike these professionals with special training, American consumers often make buying decisions before they have had any formal instruction in the basic principles that determine economic behavior in the world around them. The task of this chapter is to put the horse back before the cart, so to speak, by presenting some of the fundamental economic concepts that apply to you as a consumer. The finer points of economic theory do not concern us here. We leave that kind of instruction for a course in either microeconomics—the study of individual and business decision-making behavior—or macroeconomics—the study of economy-wide problems such as inflation and unemployment.

SCARCITY AND THE CONSUMER

SCARCITY
The condition in which we are unable to provide enough products to satisfy all people's needs and wants because of our limited resources.

We begin our discussion of economics with the problem of **scarcity** because it is the heart of economic analysis. Would you like to have more time to study and still have time for all the other things you want to do, like going to the student center with your friends? Would you like to have a bigger house or apartment, or a bigger room in your dorm or fraternity or sorority house? Would you like to have more clothes without giving up buying other products you enjoy? Indeed, why can't we all have more of everything? The answer is that individually and collectively we face the problem of scarcity.

Scarcity exists because we have unlimited wants and only a limited supply of resources to produce products that satisfy our wants. Scarcity is a relative term. For someone who has no food, a crust of bread is a scarce product, while others may experience scarcity in their inability to afford steak or lobster every night. As long as we are not able to have everything we want, scarcity exists. This means that scarcity and poverty are not the same thing. Scarcity can exist in an environment of affluence and abundance.

Imagine you were the richest person in the world. You still could not have everything you want. The most obvious example of scarcity in this case would be your scarcity of time. With only one life to lead, you would be unable to enjoy all the things you owned.

Usually people perceive scarcity in terms of having a limited amount of money to spend. Although from their personal point of view they are correct, from the perspective of the entire economy there is a different cause of scarcity. Remember, scarcity is the result of our limited ability to produce **goods** and services to satisfy our wants. If our government printed enough money to give every person $1 million, the food, clothing, houses, swimming pools, yachts, and other products they wanted to buy with that money would not be available in sufficient amounts for everyone; more of these products would not magically come into existence. There would be no more oil in the ground, factories, workers, or other **productive resources** than previously existed, so it would not be possible to create enough products to satisfy everyone's wants. We would all have more money, but we would not have solved the problem of scarcity. Thus, scarcity is an unavoidable fact of everyone's life.

GOODS
Tangible objects that have the ability to satisfy human wants.

PRODUCTIVE RESOURCES
Raw materials, tools, and labor that may be used to produce other goods or services that have the ability to satisfy human wants.

UNIVERSAL SCARCITY

The problem of scarcity is not unique to consumers, it is faced by businesses, the government, and by all nations in the world. Successful businesses in the United States earn a **profit** when they receive more income from sales than the costs they pay to produce and offer products for sale. When a firm uses its profits to buy resources to produce a television set, it cannot use those same resources to produce a VCR or CD player. A business that buys machines to assemble automatically electric mixers cannot use that money to hire more workers. Businesses must make these types of choices because the supply of resources they may use to produce products to offer consumers are scarce regardless of how much profit they earn.

We all receive valuable services from our government. The roads on which we drive, the schools we attend, and fire and police protection are only a few of the many government services we all need but that most individuals could not afford to purchase for themselves. Our government pays for the resources it uses by taxing or borrowing money.

PROFIT
The difference between the total amount of money income received from selling a good or a service and the total cost of providing that good or service.

When our government buys resources to provide services, it faces the problem of scarcity because it cannot use the same money to accomplish more than one objective. Money paid for road repairs, for example, may not go to pay schoolteachers. The government may also be seen as contributing to the problem of scarcity for other parts of society. The resources it uses are not available to people and businesses to buy and use for other purposes. Within our country, consumers, businesses, and the government compete for the scarce resources we have.

Just as Americans must deal with scarcity, all nations in the world face this problem. Resources that go to build automobiles in Japan cannot help to reduce the shortage of affordable housing in that country. Land for growing sugarcane in Cuba may not be used to raise other crops. Oil that is pumped from the ground in Saudi Arabia today will not be available in the future. Although the way in which economic decisions are made will vary from one nation to another, all nations face this problem. Differences in the way resources are distributed in the world and how decisions are made to allocate scarce resources form the basis for international trade that affects all our lives. More will be said about the global nature of our economy later in this chapter.

Every choice you make requires you to give something up.

THE NECESSITY OF CHOICE

Scarcity forces us, as consumers, to make choices all the time. We must choose how we spend our time, how we spend our labor power (that is, what kind of work we do), and how we spend our income (our purchasing power). Life would be simple without scarcity. You and I would not have to bother much about consumer economics. In a world without scarcity, choices would not have to be made because everyone would possess every good or service they want. But we never will achieve such total satisfaction. That is why a knowledge of consumer economics is essential for maximizing the value we can derive from the consumer decisions we make.

For example, in making a budget, you need to decide whether you would receive more satisfaction from the purchase of new clothing or from taking a relaxing vacation. Or you may decide to save your money to buy a new car in the future instead. You can think of consumer decision making as a rational way of determining how to allocate your scarce time and money resources. Later in this chapter we will consider how consumer decisions in our country help determine the way our productive resources are allocated.

CHOICE AND OPPORTUNITY COST

Every choice you make requires you to give something up. When you sit down to read this book, you have chosen not to do at least a thousand other things with your time. You could have read your English text, you could have watched television, you could have slept, you could have gone to the movies, and so on. Thus, scarcity of time has led you to choose to read this book rather than do something else that is presumably of less value. The something else that you chose not to do is the cost associated with spending time reading this book. Economists call it **opportunity cost.**

Let's assume that of all the other things you could have done instead of reading this book, the thing you most wanted to do, but didn't do, was watch television. If that's the case, then the value of the enjoyment you would have received from watching television is your opportunity cost of reading this book. Opportunity cost is defined as the value of a second-best choice that is given up when a first choice is taken. Opportunity cost is an unavoidable part of all decisions consumers make. It helps us place a value on the scarce resources that go into producing products that satisfy our wants.

OPPORTUNITY COST
The value of a second-best choice that is given up when a first choice is taken.

THE TRADEOFFS FACING YOU

Whatever you do, you are "trading off" one use of a resource for one or more alternative uses. The value of a **tradeoff** is represented by the opportunity cost just discussed. Let's go back to the opportunity cost of reading this book. Assume that you have a maximum of ten hours per week to spend studying just two subjects—consumer economics and accounting. The more time you study consumer economics, you believe the higher your grade will be in this subject. The corresponding is true for accounting. There is a tradeoff, then, between spending an hour reading this book and spending that time studying accounting. A better grade in consumer economics must be purchased at the expense of a lower grade in accounting.

Similar tradeoffs occur for every choice you make. If you decide to join your school's basketball team, you must trade the value of other uses of your time for the value of the enjoyment received from participating in that sport. Whenever businesses, the government, or people in other nations make choices, they also make tradeoffs in which an opportunity cost is paid for the choice that is made.

TRADEOFF
A term relating to opportunity cost. To get a desired economic good, it is necessary to trade off some other desired economic good whenever we are in a world of scarcity. A tradeoff involves a sacrifice, then, that must be made to obtain something.

AN IMPLICIT ASSUMPTION

Economic analysis rests on an assumption that we should make clear at this time: Most people generally make choices that are intended to make themselves better off. Making oneself better off can take many forms, depending on each person's individual values. For the purpose of economic analysis, however, we may assume that people attempt to make themselves better off in such things as their opportunity for leisure time and their ability to buy goods and services that satisfy their wants.

MARKETS

MARKET
The sum of all transactions that take place between buyers and sellers of a particular type of product.

In economics, a **market** is the sum of all transactions that take place between buyers and sellers of a particular type of product. Therefore, if we talk about the "used car market," we are referring to the transactions between people who buy and sell used cars. The "labor market" is made up of the agreements between workers and their employers. There is even an "education market" in which students pay tuition to receive instruction and academic guidance.

Markets exist between and among people, businesses, governments, and other nations in the world. To demonstrate the importance of international markets, consider the fact that in 1995 roughly $1 out of every $10 spent in this country went to buy a product that was manufactured in a different nation. At the same time, millions of Americans relied for their employment on our ability to sell American-made products in other nations. Despite its importance, however, the American economy is only a part of the larger world economy. To understand markets in that international economy, as well as local and national markets, we need to learn more about the way transactions are carried out.

VOLUNTARY EXCHANGE IN U.S. ECONOMY

VOLUNTARY EXCHANGE
Transactions completed through the free will of those involved.

In the United States, consumers and producers are generally free to use their resources to buy and sell products as they choose. This means that we enjoy the right of **voluntary exchange** in most situations. You can spend your income collecting stamps, and I can buy an expensive boat. Other people are free to start businesses that offer rare stamps or expensive boats for sale. Although limitations do exist on the types of products, Americans may legally buy or offer for sale (drugs, for example), individuals in the United States are free to make most economic choices.

Whenever a voluntary exchange takes place, it is reasonable to assume that both the buyer and the seller will benefit. Imagine you paid $10 for gasoline for your car. You must have felt that the gasoline had greater value than the $10 you spent. The owner of the filling station, in contrast, must have valued the $10 more than the gasoline. When the transaction was completed, both parties gained, because they valued the money and the gasoline differently. The same must be true of all other voluntary exchanges, because people would not choose to complete a transaction that they did not feel benefited them.

DEMAND AND SUPPLY ANALYSIS— A BRIEF INTRODUCTION

In the U.S. economy the forces of demand and supply most often work together to determine which products will be produced and the quantity of each type of product that will be offered for sale. Later in this text you will discover how these same forces help consumers make many other economic decisions.

LAW OF DEMAND

The term **demand** refers to the quantity of a product consumers are willing and able to buy at each possible price. The **law of demand** states that if nothing else changes, consumers will buy a greater quantity of a product at a lower price than at a higher price. Therefore, if the price of a product falls, the quantity demanded will grow; and if the price increases, the quantity demanded will fall. Imagine that you and several of your friends have made a habit of going to the movies together every Friday night after work. If the price of a movie ticket increased by $2, some of the people in your group might not be able to afford it, while others might prefer to spend their money on some other product. In either case, the quantity of movie tickets demanded would be less because of the increase in price.

The quantity of a product consumers demand at any price depends on many factors other than price. These factors include taste, income, the price of other, related products, and expectations of what may happen in the future. For example, if your friends all chose to wear a particular brand of clothing, your demand for this brand of clothing might increase even if the price remained unchanged. If you were offered a new job that paid you more than you earn now, you could afford to demand a greater quantity of products like new cars or vacations. An increase in the price of gasoline, however, could cause you to drive fewer miles. This would reduce your demand for replacement tires for your car. As a final example, suppose your boss tells you that you will be laid off in two weeks. At the present you still have an income, but you know you won't in just 14 days. Your demand for many products would be less

DEMAND
The quantity of a product that will be purchased at each possible price.

LAW OF DEMAND
A basic economic principle that states that as the price of goods or services rises, the quantity of those goods and services demanded will fall. Conversely, as the price falls, the quantity demanded will rise.

because you expect your income to be smaller in the near future. Each of these examples demonstrates one of many possible reasons why consumers might demand more or less of a product when there is no change in its price.

LAW OF SUPPLY

SUPPLY
The quantity of a product businesses are willing to offer for sale at each possible price.

Supply refers to the quantity of a product businesses are willing to offer for sale at each possible price. Businesses in the United States intend to earn a profit. The more consumers are willing to pay for a product, the more likely firms are to earn a profit by supplying it. Therefore, consumer acceptance of higher prices often causes existing firms to increase their production, as well as encouraging the creation of new firms that produce this type of good.

LAW OF SUPPLY
A basic economic principle that states that as the price of goods or services rises, the quantity of those goods and services supplied will increase. Conversely, as the price falls the quantity supplied will also decline.

The **law of supply** states that if nothing else changes, a greater quantity of a product will be supplied at a higher price than at a lower price. Therefore, if the price of a product increases, the quantity of the product that is supplied should also increase, and if the price falls, the quantity supplied should decline. You may see the law of supply in your own life. Ask yourself how many hours you would be willing to work at $1 an hour? $5 an hour? $100 an hour? Isn't it true that you would be willing to supply more of your labor as the wage (price) you receive grows?

Other factors that affect the profit a firm earns will also change its willingness to supply products. For example, a firm that produced bread might choose to go out of business if a 50-percent increase in the cost of flour eliminated its profit. A firm that found a way to produce carpet with fewer workers would be encouraged to supply more of its product because of its reduced labor costs and increased profits. Generally, an increase in a firm's costs of production will reduce the quantity of products it will supply at each possible price, while a decrease in its costs will cause it to supply greater quantities.

EQUILIBRIUM PRICE

EQUILIBRIUM PRICE
A price at which the quantity of a good or service demanded is exactly equal to the quantity that is supplied.

The price you pay for most goods and services you buy is determined by the forces of demand and supply. There is a price for every product at which the quantity demanded would be exactly equal to the quantity supplied. Natural forces exist within markets that tend to force prices toward this **equilibrium price.**

Suppose that lettuce farmers were selling their products for $3 a head. This high price would encourage many farmers to grow more lettuce. However, it would discourage consumers from buying the product. As a result, there would be a surplus of lettuce, which would force the price down until it reached the equilibrium price (let us say $1.50) where the quantity supplied and the quantity demanded were the same.

In a similar fashion, prices below the equilibrium price tend to be forced up by demand and supply. If farmers can get only $1 for a head of lettuce, they will be discouraged from supplying many units of this product. The low price, however, will cause consumers to demand more lettuce. The result will be a shortage of lettuce that will encourage farmers to increase their price to the equilibrium price ($1.50) where the quantity they are willing to supply is equal to the quantity consumers are willing to buy.

Although prices may be set in our economy that are not equilibrium prices, the forces of demand and supply still tend to push prices to this level. Prices may remain at other levels for extended periods of time only when there is imperfect competition. This condition will be discussed later in this chapter.

To see how economists frequently represent demand, supply, and the equilibrium price, see Exhibit 1–1.

EXHIBIT 1–1
DEMAND, SUPPLY AND EQUILIBRIUM PRICE

Economists often demonstrate demand, supply, and equilibrium price through tables or graphs like those shown here. Suppose Jeff, a high school student, wants to earn spending money by doing yardwork for his neighbors. He discovers that the number of hours he will be hired depends on the hourly price he charges for his labor. As you would expect from the law of demand, the higher the price he charges the fewer hours he works. This is shown in the table in column (1), "Price Charged," and column (2), "Quantity Demanded."

Jeff, like most teenagers, has more things he would like to do than he has time to do them. When he works he can't be meeting with friends, playing sports, watching television, or doing homework. The number of hours he is willing to work depends on the price he is able to charge his customers. As you would expect from the law of supply, the higher the price, the

more hours he is willing to work. This is shown in column (1), "Price Charged," and column (3), "Quantity Supplied."

There is a price for Jeff's labor at which the number of hours he is willing to work is exactly the same as the number of hours that will be demanded by his customers. This equilibrium price is $6 per hour and can be seen in the boldface row C in the table.

The same information can be presented in graphic form. The demand curve on the graph has been plotted from the values in columns (1) and (2) in the table. In a similar way, the supply curve has been plotted from the values in columns (1) and (3). The curves intersect at the equilibrium price of $6, where 10 hours of Jeff's labor is demanded and supplied each week.

(continues)

EXHIBIT 1–1 (continued)
DEMAND, SUPPLY AND EQUILIBRIUM PRICE

DEMAND-AND-SUPPLY SCHEDULE FOR JEFF'S LABOR

	(1) Price Charged	(2) Quantity Demanded	(3) Quantity Supplied
A	$8	6 hours	18 hours
B	$7	8 hours	14 hours
C	$6	**10 hours**	**10 hours**
D	$5	12 hours	6 hours
E	$4	14 hours	2 hours

GRAPH OF DEMAND AND SUPPLY FOR JEFF'S LABOR

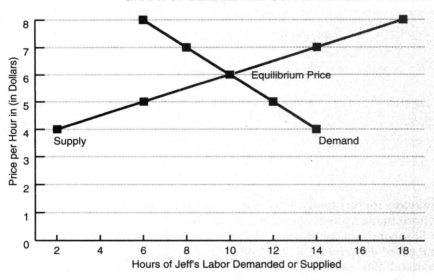

RELATIVE PRICE
The price of a commodity expressed in terms of the price of another commodity or the (weighted) average price of all other commodities.

MONEY PRICE
The price we observe today in terms of today's dollars. Also called the *absolute, nominal,* or *current price.*

RELATIVE PRICE

The **relative price** of any product is its price compared with the prices of other goods in the economy. The price we pay in dollars and cents for a product at any point in time is called its **money price** (also known as *absolute, nominal,* or *current* price). Consumer buying decisions, however, depend on relative, not money prices. Consider the hypothetical example of prices of compact discs (CDs) and cassettes in Exhibit 1–2. Note that the money prices of CDs and

EXHIBIT 1–2
MONEY PRICE VERSUS RELATIVE PRICE

The money price of both compact discs (CDs) and cassettes has risen. But the relative price of CDs has fallen (or conversely, the relative price of cassettes has risen).

	MONEY PRICE		RELATIVE PRICE	
	Price Last Year	Price This Year	Price Last Year	Price This Year
CDs	$12	$14	$\dfrac{\$12}{\$6} = 2$	$\dfrac{\$14}{\$8} = 1.75$
Cassettes	$ 6	$ 8	$\dfrac{\$6}{\$12} = 0.5$	$\dfrac{\$8}{\$14} = 0.57$

To find the relative change in price of two products, you can use the following formulas. If the result of the top equation is larger than that of the bottom equation, product B's price has gone up more rapidly. If the result of the bottom equation is larger, then the price of product A has increased relatively more.

$$\frac{\text{Original price of product A}}{\text{Original price of product B}} = \underline{\qquad}$$

$$\frac{\text{Current price of product A}}{\text{Current price of product B}} = \underline{\qquad}$$

cassettes have risen during the year. That means consumers have to pay more for both of them in today's dollars and cents. If we look at the relative prices, however, we find that last year CDs were twice as expensive as cassettes, whereas this year they are only one and three-fourths as expensive. Conversely, cassettes cost only half as much as CDs last year, whereas today they cost 57 percent as much. In the one-year period, the prices of both products have gone up in money terms, but the price of cassettes has gone up more rapidly. Therefore, the relative price of CDs has fallen while the relative price of cassettes has risen. If the law of demand holds true, then over this one-year period a relatively larger quantity of CDs will have been demanded while a relatively smaller quantity of cassettes will have been sold, other things being equal.

Once the distinction between money prices and relative prices is made, there is less chance of confusion about the effect of price increases on the quantities of different products that are demanded during a period of time when all money prices are increasing. Products whose money prices increase more rapidly than most will be demanded less, while those whose money prices increase less rapidly will be demanded more.

Someone not familiar with this distinction might believe that the increased demand for CDs, despite their higher price, violates the law of demand. But, as we can see, the price of CDs must be considered in relation to the prices of other products, in this case the price of cassettes. Although this example involves only two products, in our economy the prices of all products must be considered. The demand should grow for any product that experiences lower rates of price increase than the average for most goods, while it should fall for goods that experience price increases greater than the average.

MARKET ECONOMY
An economy that is characterized by exchanges in markets that are controlled by the forces of demand and supply.

PERFECT COMPETITION
A market condition in which many businesses offer the same product for sale to many customers at the same price.

CONSUMER SOVEREIGNTY
A situation in which consumers ultimately decide which products and styles will survive in the marketplace; that is, producers do not dictate consumer tastes.

CONSUMER SOVEREIGNTY IN A MARKET ECONOMY

The American economy is a type of **market economy** because it is characterized by transactions that are free exchanges based on the laws of demand and supply. In a market economy, individuals are free to use resources as they see fit to produce goods and services that are then offered for sale to consumers, who are free to buy or not to buy them. In an ideal market economy there would be **perfect competition** and **consumer sovereignty.** In such a world no firm would be large or powerful enough to set prices for its products higher than those charged by other firms that offered similar goods or services for sale. Consumers would buy products they desired at the lowest possible prices. The most successful firms would be those that produced goods and services most efficiently. Their success would allow them to expand their own production and encourage others to open similar businesses. Money and resources would flow to the types of production that consumers demanded. Therefore, consumers would determine how scarce resources would be used to produce goods and services that were best able to satisfy their wants. If perfect competition existed in our economy, consumers would control production through the way they spend their money. They would be sovereign.

IMPERFECT COMPETITION
A market condition in which individual businesses have some power to set the price and quality of their products.

THE REAL WORLD OF IMPERFECT COMPETITION

In the real world, **imperfect competition** prevents consumers from always controlling production decisions and the allocation of scarce resources. There may be a limited number of producers, or other suppliers may be prevented from offering a similar product for sale by various barriers. In this event, a high price and large profits will not necessarily increase the quantity of the product that is supplied in the market or of the resources allocated to that type of production.

Suppose you produce a medical device that doctors have found very useful in surgery. Suppose also that you have patented your device and have not sold the patent rights to any other producer. You have restricted entry into the market for this device because no other firm may legally produce it or offer it for sale while you hold your patent. Although you might charge a high price for your device and earn a large profit, other individuals may not use their resources to produce an alternative product to compete with your product. Even if other firms could make the product more efficiently and offer better quality, they would not be allowed to do so. In this situation you would have a **monopoly.** This is a simplistic example, of course, but it illustrates how the principle of consumer

MONOPOLY
The only producer of a product that has no substitutes.

sovereignty can be invalidated by an economy made up of firms that hold some degree of monopoly-like power.

Businesses that hold monopoly-like powers are sovereign because they do not need to respond to the demands of consumers. Not that many are sovereign, however. Most small firms are quite competitive, and there is a limit to what even the largest firms are able to do with their economic power. Consider the difficult times experienced by American automobile manufacturers that once had significant monopoly-like powers in our economy. Even when large firms use sophisticated marketing techniques, they often lose the battle for sovereignty to consumers. It has been estimated that nine our of every ten new products offered to American consumers fail within one year. Essentially, such failures are due to the unwillingness of consumers to demand these products at a price that would allow the producing firms to earn a profit.

Even where consumer choice exists individuals may be forced by law to buy some products. For example, in many states, it is illegal to drive a car without also purchasing automobile liability insurance. To be sure, some people ignore the law, but if they are apprehended they may pay a heavy penalty.

As shown in Exhibit 1–3, consumers confront a range of purchasing situations. In some cases they have almost total control over production through their purchasing decisions. In others they may be faced with government regulations or with the power of firms that possess monopolylike power. Even advertising may reduce their control over the types of products offered in the market. It is

---

EXHIBIT 1–3
THE RANGE OF CONSUMER CHOICE AND SOVEREIGNTY

At one extreme, no one forces us to buy anything, at the other, we are required to purchase an item whether we like it or not. Generally, depending on the situation, we are somewhere in between.

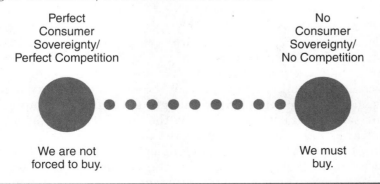

Perfect Consumer Sovereignty/ Perfect Competition	No Consumer Sovereignty/ No Competition
We are not forced to buy.	We must buy.

safe to say that we generally are in the middle of the range of purchasing decisions, somewhere between being forced to purchase and being able to make independent choices.

Given our imperfectly competitive economy, neither complete producer sovereignty nor complete consumer sovereignty can exist. As a result, from an early time in our nation's history the government has imposed regulations on various markets to protect both business and consumer interests.

ROLE OF GOVERNMENT

Everyone in the world is a consumer of goods and services when he or she uses products to fill basic needs for food, shelter, and clothing. The role and economic power of consumers vary from country to country, because each nation has its own unique **economic system.** In some countries resources have been owned, controlled, and allocated by an agency of the government. Individual consumers were given little power to determine what products would be produced or how resources would be used. Many nations with these **socialist economic systems,** after experiencing great economic difficulties and individual hardship, have changed their economic systems to rely more on the forces of demand and supply.

In nations such as the United States, an economic system known as **capitalism** has dominated production. Capitalism is an economic system in which the ownership and control of resources and businesses are held largely by private individuals, and the forces of demand and supply are relied on to control the production of goods and services and the allocation of resources.

A strong theme in the American economic experience has always been "the less government, the better." This view holds that we should not hamper the functioning of the laws of demand and supply in our markets with unnecessary government regulation and intervention. Individuals willing to take the risk of establishing businesses to reap profits or suffer losses should be allowed to do so. During the 1800s and early 1900s, this "hands-off" attitude prevailed. But beginning around the turn of the century, and accelerating during the Great Depression of the 1930s, some economists began to advocate government intervention in the marketplace to aid economic stability and to prevent the catastrophe of recurring recessions. A deepening involvement of government in our economic system was characterized by the New Deal legislation of President Franklin Roosevelt during the Great Depression.

This does not mean that the government had nothing to do with the economic life of the nation before this century. From the beginning of our nation's history the government has been active in many

ECONOMIC SYSTEM
A set of understandings that governs the production and distribution of goods and services that satisfy human wants.

SOCIALIST ECONOMIC SYSTEM
An economic system in which there is group (most often government) ownership of productive resources and control over the distribution of goods and services.

CAPITALISM
An economic system based on private ownership of the means of production and on a demand-and-supply market. This system emphasizes the absence of government restraints on ownership, production, and trade.

economic areas—developing railroads, building canals, establishing tariffs to promote domestic industrial growth, and, to a limited extent, regulating business activities to protect both businesses and consumers. Indeed, although most people think of government involvement in our economic system as a relatively recent development, it actually has a long history. Much more will be said of this involvement in later chapters of this book.

AMERICAN CONSUMERS IN THE GLOBAL ECONOMY

In 1945, the last year of World War II, less than 2 percent of the products sold in the United States were imported from other nations. American consumers had little choice as to where the products they bought had been made. Most other industrialized nations were involved in the war and the productive capacity of many had been largely destroyed. They were in no position to export goods or services to the United States.

Half a century later, in 1995, the situation had changed dramatically. In that year nearly $740 billion worth, or more than 10 percent, of the goods and services purchased in America were produced in foreign countries. This trend toward more purchases of foreign-made products by American consumers is even more apparent when specific products are considered. For example, nearly 20 percent of the automobiles sold in the United States in 1995 were produced in other countries. Almost all of the televisions, VCRs, tennis shoes, and a large share of the microwave ovens we purchased were imported. The list of foreign-made products we buy goes on and on.

In a similar way, many American consumers earn their living by producing products that are exported to other nations. In 1995 foreigners purchased almost $560 billion worth of American-made goods. It was estimated that sales of these goods and services created nearly 16 million jobs in this nation. By examining Exhibit 1–4 you can see the growing importance of international trade in the American economy. There are many indications that this trend will continue into the future.

A recent demonstration of the growing importance of trade can be seen in the 1993 ratification of the North American Free Trade Agreement (NAFTA). This treaty is designed to eliminate trade barriers between the United States, Canada, and Mexico over the 15 years between 1993 and 2009. Although the treaty has not yet been fully implemented, its early results can already be seen in the roughly 33 percent growth of trade among the signatory nations in its first two years of existence. NAFTA is a clear indication that American consumers are faced with a growing need to understand and evaluate the costs and benefits of buying imported goods when they make consumer decisions.

EXHIBIT 1–4
VALUE OF U.S. MERCHANDISE EXPORTS AND IMPORTS, 1986–1995
(IN BILLIONS OF DOLLARS)

*1995 estimated values based on the first six months of that year.
Source: Economic Indicators, *September 1995, p. 36.*

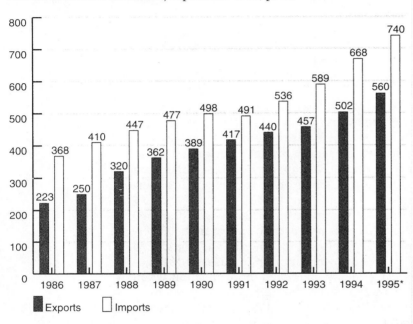

BENEFITS OF TRADE

SPECIALIZATION
The concentration of efforts on one area of production with the aim of having an advantage in the marketplace. Students specialize when they major in a certain subject at college, thus allowing them to have a comparative advantage in the job market later—assuming there is a demand for their specialized knowledge.

Not all nations are equally well suited to produce all types of goods and services. Since countries have different types and qualities of raw materials, climates, workers, transportation systems, and technology, they can be more efficient when they **specialize** in producing certain goods and then trade them for other goods. By specializing and trading this way, countries are able to increase their standard of living.

The United States, for example, is well suited to the efficient production of food and other agricultural products. We have vast areas of fertile land with sufficient rainfall to grow far more food than we need for ourselves in most years. We also have an extensive interstate highway system, many navigable rivers, and railroads that allow bulky agricultural products to be shipped quickly and at relatively low cost. It makes good sense for the United States to specialize in the production of farm products that can be purchased by nations that are less well suited to this type of production. In return we can buy from them products we are not able to produce as efficiently.

American consumers often choose to buy foreign-made products because these goods are less expensive than similar American-made products. In some cases consumers may believe imported goods have higher quality or superior design. And some of the goods Americans want to own are made only in foreign nations. In 1995, for example, no television picture tubes were manufactured in this country. It was therefore impossible for an American consumer to buy a truly American-made television set regardless of the label, or trademark, that it might have been sold under.

We should remember that selling American-made products in other countries provides many benefits to our economy and to American consumers. Products we export provide employment and income for American workers. They generate profits for U.S. firms, and tend to increase growth in the U.S. economy. When Americans are working at making products for export, there is more income for the government to tax. There is also less need for government social programs. Finally, selling products to other countries provides income that allows American consumers to buy the products we need from other nations.

COSTS OF TRADE

Although many individual Americans benefit from international trade, there are clearly some who do not. When American consumers choose to buy imported goods, they provide income for foreign workers and their employers. Although this money may eventually be returned to the United States if foreigners use it to buy our products, it is nevertheless income that is not immediately going to American workers or their employers. Many businesses in this country have been forced to close by competition from imported products. It has been estimated, for example, that more than half of the jobs that existed in the U.S. textile industry in 1960 have been lost to foreign competition. Certainly the individual workers who lost their jobs, and the owners of the firms that were forced out of business, are not better off because of international trade.

When a country imports a greater value of goods than it exports, it has a negative **balance of trade.** Countries that have a negative balance of trade tend to have more unemployment, lower business profits, slower growth, and higher interest rates than they otherwise might expect to have. The United States has had a negative balance in the value of goods it trades in each year since 1975. Study Exhibit 1–5 to see how this balance has changed over the years.

> **Although many individual Americans benefit from international trade, there are clearly some who do not.**

BALANCE OF TRADE
The relationship between the value of a country's imports and exports: if exports have a greater value it has a positive balance of trade; if its imports have a greater value it has a negative balance of trade.

SAMPLE CHAPTER 7   THE CONSUMER IN OUR GLOBAL ECONOMY

EXHIBIT 1–5
U.S. BALANCE OF MERCHANDISE TRADE, 1986–1995
(IN BILLIONS OF DOLLARS)

*1995 estimated values based on the first six months of that year.
Source: Economic Indicators, *September 1995, p. 36.*

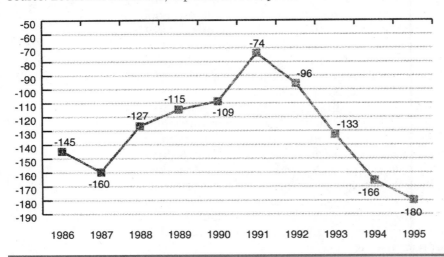

BEING A RESPONSIBLE CONSUMER IN THE GLOBAL ECONOMY

"Buy American" slogans are intended to help create more jobs, production, and income in this country. But although many American consumers recognize a need to achieve these goals, they continue to buy imported goods in large quantities. Some people even argue that buying American-made goods when imports offer lower prices or better quality is not necessarily good for the American economy in the long run.

Foreign competition has helped bring about technological advancements that have benefited many American firms. The U.S. steel industry, for example, is much more efficient today than it was 25 years ago. The number of worker-hours required to produce a ton of steel was cut roughly in half between 1970 and 1990. Some of this improvement was made necessary because of competition from lower-cost foreign steel.

In some cases U.S. firms have surpassed foreign competition in their own markets. In the 1980s the Motorola Corporation undertook investments in research and development that have made it the largest producer of cellular telephones in the world. In the early 1990s it exported millions of dollars worth of this product to Japan and other Asian nations each year.

The prices American consumers pay for many products are lower because of imported goods. It has been estimated that in the decade of the 1980s Americans would have paid as much as $400 billion more for the automobiles they purchased if they had not been able to buy less expensive imported cars. The same argument can be made for imported textiles, shoes, and garments. Although some Americans have lost their jobs because of these imports, most Americans benefited from lower prices and in some cases higher quality. In other words, most Americans have been able to enjoy a higher standard of living because of international trade.

When consumers choose whether or not to buy imported goods and services, they are choosing whether to (1) help save some American jobs by buying products made in this country, or (2) by buying imported goods, possibly encourage greater efficiency and different types of growth in our own economy. The continuing loss of jobs in types of production where this country is not the most efficient probably cannot be stopped. It may make more sense to concentrate our resources in types of production that take advantage of our unique abilities to create growth in the future. Ultimately, the decision to "buy American" is an individual choice that all American consumers must make for themselves. This choice, and the growing importance of our global economy, will be recurring themes throughout this text.

Consumer Issues: An Introduction

Each chapter in this text is divided into two parts. The first presents information about different aspects of consumer economics that is essentially factual in nature, to provide students with a base of knowledge that can help them make better decisions. The second part of each chapter concerns a "Consumer Issue" that shows how consumers may apply knowledge they have gained to situations they are likely to face in their own lives. You might think of these two parts as the "What" and the "How" of consumer economics. Consumer Issue 1, describes how knowledge of our economy you have gained from this chapter may be applied when consumers make ethical choices in their lives.

CONSUMER ISSUE 1

Ethics and the Consumer

When Americans make consumer decisions, they usually consider more than the price and quality of products offered for sale. Other factors that may influence their choices include where and how the items were produced, if they were made by union labor, and whether they were made in an environmentally responsible way. For example, you might choose not to shop at a store you believe discriminates against women or ethnic minorities. Many people are willing to pay higher prices for products manufactured or offered for sale in what they believe are socially responsible ways.

In a similar way consumers often make choices that reflect values they have set for their personal behavior. How often have you seen a store clerk make a mistake that would have caused you to pay less than the actual price for what you were buying? Did you tell the clerk that he or she had made a mistake, or did you take advantage of the situation to pay a lower price? If you broke a dish by accident in a china store would you feel responsible to pay for it? If you were harmed by a defective product you had purchased, would you sue for an amount of money that was greater than the value of your loss? Although some people do these things, many American consumers choose to behave in what they regard as a socially/morally responsible way.

All consumers have duties and responsibilities that can be summarized in one sentence: The consumer has a duty to act honestly and ethically when purchasing products and services. An age-old aphorism holds that "what goes around comes around." In the context of consumer dealings, this means that if enough consumers act dishonestly, prices of consumer products and services will rise, harming all other consumers.

WHAT IS ETHICAL BEHAVIOR?

Ethical behavior essentially means acting in accordance with one's moral and ethical convictions as to what is right and what is wrong. Many commonly held ethical convictions are written into our laws. But ethical behavior sometimes requires us to do more than just comply with laws in order to avoid the penalty of breaking them. In some circumstances, one can break the law and be fairly certain no one will ever find out about it.

Imagine, for example that you purchased a number of items from your local Wal-Mart and discovered when you got home that the cashier had failed to charge you for a $16 CD you had chosen. What is your obligation? Obviously, the CD does not legally belong to you—you have not paid for it. But why should you have to take the time and trouble to return to the store to pay for the item? After all, it wasn't your fault that the cashier did not ring up the purchase price of the item. What would your decision be? Would it make a difference if the item had a much higher or a much smaller price?

Consider another possible situation where you know something is wrong before you actually get a product home. Suppose you regularly buy a particular brand of spaghetti sauce that you know costs $2.19 per jar. One day while shopping at a convenience store (that does not use a barcode scanner to determine product prices at the checkout) you see several jars that have been mispriced at $1.19. What would you do? Would you try to buy all the jars at the lower price, only one or two of them, or would you tell the clerk that a mistake had been made? This time you cannot rationalize your decision by saying "I didn't know." But then it isn't your fault a mistake was made. What do you believe the ethical consumer choice would be?

It's Not Always Easy

These examples illustrate that it's not always easy to do the "right thing"— or even to know what the right thing to do is in a given set of circumstances. You could be pretty certain that in the case of the CD no one would ever know you had obtained the product without paying for it. Wal-Mart officials surely wouldn't report you to the police or come knocking at your door. They have no idea where their merchandise goes to. The case of the mispriced spaghetti sauce is only a little different. If anyone asked you about the price, you could simply say you didn't know what the price should have been. In cases like these, there is a temptation to take the "gift" offered to you by fate. In addition to having more money left over to buy other products, your sterling reputation in the community as an ethical person would not be marred in the slightest, because no one else would ever know what you had done. But you would. And this is what ethics is all about. At the heart of ethical decision making is determining whether you personally feel that a given action is right or wrong, and acting accordingly. After all, you're the one who has to live with your conscience.

Somebody Has to Pay

When trying to determine the rightness or wrongness of a given action, it is helpful to consider the consequences of each alternative. Keep in mind that if you don't pay for benefits you receive, someone else will have to. As economists are prone to emphasize, there is no such thing as a "free lunch." In other words, somebody, somewhere, has to pay for all that is produced and consumed. And that somebody is another consumer—or, rather, other consumers. This is because sellers who absorb these added costs will pass them on eventually to all purchasers in the form of higher prices.

EXAMPLES OF UNETHICAL CONSUMER BEHAVIOR

While most consumers act responsibly in their purchase transactions, they are obviously not saints any more than businesspersons are. And examples are plentiful of consumers who give in to the temptation to evade the letter of the law in order to get "something for nothing." Consider, for example, the following scenario: Jeannie orders by mail a new Nikon camera from Flash Electronics, a discount house in a distant city. The camera arrives by mail, and Jeannie immediately uses it to take photographs to be included in the book she is writing. A few days later, she drops the camera and breaks the casing. She decides to "pass the buck" to the seller and returns the camera to Flash Electronics, claiming that the camera was broken when it arrived and demanding a replacement. Jeannie, who eventually receives the replacement camera, has just saved herself the cost of repairing the broken camera—at the expense of the discount firm, of course, or the manufacturer. But she suffers few pangs of conscience about her dishonesty. After all, she reasons, Flash Electronics and Nikon are huge and profitable businesses. Whereas the repair

bill would be but a drop in the bucket for Flash Electronics or Nikon, it would represent Jeannie's entire food budget for a week.

What Jeannie overlooks in her reasoning is the long-run consequences of her behavior. In the short run, yes, the discount house or the manufacturer will pay for the repairs. But, ultimately, who pays? Other consumers, like Jeannie, who buy cameras or other products from the discount house and Nikon and who have to pay more because of Jeannie's fraud. But Jeannie might still rationalize that the cost of the camera repair—when spread out over thousands of consumers—would represent no real burden to each individual consumer, which is true. But, if all-or even a substantial number of—consumers acted similarly to Jeannie, what then?

It takes little effort to imagine dozens of other ways in which consumers have behaved dishonestly or unethically to gain a personal benefit at the expense or inconvenience of others. We look here at just a few variations of this theme.

So Sue Me

Most consumers periodically receive in the mail invitations to subscribe to certain magazines, or to "sign here" and receive a product to try out for 30 days, and so on. A typical offer is to sign up for membership in a book club. All you have to do is sign and send a card to receive, say, four books for which you will be billed $1 at some future date. Of course, having signed up for membership in the club, you will be obligated to purchase a given number of books per year—or at least notify the club each month if you don't want a particular book or books. You

receive the four books and, after a few months, have received several more. You haven't had time to read the books, don't really want them, and don't really want to be a member of the club. But you're busy and fail to do anything about **it.** Eventually, the book club begins to send stern demands for payment—you owe them $69. You are a struggling student, short of money, and you ignore the bill. It certainly does not take priority in your budget. If they want to sue you for collection, fine. You are not worried about it because you know that the amount is too trivial to justify any legal action against you by the book club. Eventually, to your relief, they stop sending you any bills at all—your account has been written off as a "bad debt"—along with hundreds of others. And you have acquired six "free" books.

Me First, Please

Many consumers have been inconvenienced by delays and other travel complications because of overbooked airline flights. They could not board their designated flight—for which they had reservations—because the plane was full. Airlines overbook flights because they can predict, based on past flight records, that a certain number of passengers will cancel or change their reservations at the last minute or simply not show. Some passengers pay higher fares for the privilege of changing flights at the last minute, if necessary. Other passengers cancel their planned trips owing to unforeseen circumstances that arise. But part of airline overbooking is due to consumers who make multiple reservations. Although airlines, by requiring advance ticketing, have curbed the problems caused by multiple reservations somewhat, it is still estimated that between one-third and one-half of over-booking is done because of multiple reservations made by consumers.

More "Me First"

Toni buys an expensive new dress for a special party she has been invited to attend. She wears the dress to the party, receives many compliments on it, but decides it was really far too expensive a purchase. She returns it to the store for a refund. The sales clerk does not inspect the dress closely and fails to notice the ginger ale stains on the front. Toni gets her refund. The result? Either the next purchaser gets a slightly soiled dress instead of the brand-new garment she paid for, or the store must discount the price of the dress heavily to sell it if the stain is discovered.

Make the Manufacturer Pay

In the past two decades American courts and consumer-protection statutes have increasingly sought to protect the "little person" against the powerful corporate entity or business firm. This has been a boon to consumers who are injured by faulty products they have purchased. It allows them to sue sellers and manu-facturers for compensation, in the form of money damages, for injuries caused by careless-ness in product design or pro-duction. But now and then a consumer will take advantage of these laws and of the court system, to seek damages from the product manufacturer or retailer. Assume, for example, that John, a minibike enthu-siast, purchases minibikes for his two sons, ages 9 and 11. In the instruction manual, and clearly indicated in large let-

ters on the bikes themselves, are instructions not to use the bikes on city streets and al-ways to wear a helmet while riding them. Nonetheless, John allows his sons to ride on the city streets without hel-mets. One day, while racing with another friend on a mini-bike, the oldest son, Chad, carelessly runs three stop signs and then enters a fourth intersection while looking backward toward his friend. Chad is hit by a truck and injured. John sues the manu-facturer of the minibike for damages, claiming that the minibike is a dangerous prod-uct and should not have been placed on the market.

The Nuisance Suit

Sellers are also often faced with so-called nuisance law-suits. A typical one might involve the following series of events: Jerry, in a daze about his latest girlfriend, walks through a hardware store, carelessly trips over a steplad-der being displayed very close to a wall (and definitely not a hazard), falls, and falsely claims that he injured his back. Alleging that the owner was negligent by having the stepladder displayed as it was, he sues the owner for dam-ages. Similarly, Jane sues the owner of a national chain store for $10,000, alleging that a can of paint displayed on a shelf in the owner s store fell on her toe and injured it. And on and on. Such suits are often settled by the store owners out of court, because it would cost them more to defend themselves in court than to settle. Even though most store owners carry liability insur-ance, out of which such claims are paid, the insurance is not free to the store—and the premiums will rise (and they have risen dramatically

in recent years) as more claims have to be paid by insurance firms.

ETHICS IN AN IMPERSONAL MARKETPLACE

In the increasingly impersonal and mechanized marketplace of today it is much easier to lose sight of our responsibili-ties toward others than it once was. This is because in today's consumer world, the "others" are usually abstract entities and not people we know per-sonally. In the past, when stores were smaller and most transactions were conducted face to face, consumers were more motivated to act hon-estly and ethically because they also faced the conse-quences of their actions di-rectly. Imagine, for example, that Jeannie in the camera example had lived in 1900 instead of the 1990s. After breaking her camera, she re-turned it to her local camera store, claiming that it was already broken when she pur-chased it from the seller. Very likely, the seller would re-member the transaction, would know that the camera had been in good condition, and would know that Jeannie was acting dishonestly— re-gardless of whether he could prove it. Jeannie might be deprived of—or at least face a reduced quality in—the ser-vices of that store, and her reputation in the community could be affected. Because of these possible negative conse-quences, it might not even occur to Jeannie to defraud the seller. Moreover, if she knew the merchant quite well, she might have some strong ethical reservations about requiring the merchant to pay for the broken casing for which she alone was responsible.

Now let's return to the present and to a much different marketplace. When Jeannie returned the camera to the discount house, she knew that she was being dishonest, but she would not lose sleep at night over the "victim" of her fraud—who was not a real person but an *X* quantity of "others." Moreover, and perhaps most significantly, Jeannie was quite sure that she would never be "caught." No one would ever know of her dishonesty, and she would face no negative consequences. The worst that could happen is that the discount store would refuse to repair or replace her camera. In short, Jeannie felt little incentive to be ethical.

Because there are fewer *external* constraints to guide us toward ethical consumer behavior, an understanding of one's responsibilities in the marketplace is even more important today than it was in the past. Huge chain-store operations and computerized networks are increasingly hiding the identities—and the behavior—of individual buyers and sellers in the marketplace. And if we are slightly dishonest or violate our own ethical standards occasionally, who will know?

ETHICAL SHOPPING

Although consumers may not be sovereign, there is no doubt that they can and do affect, by their choices, the financial well-being of business firms. This means that, if you have doubts about the ethical behavior of a certain corporation, you can cast your "ethical vote" by not purchas-

---

EXHIBIT 1–6

CORPORATE SOCIAL RESPONSIBILITY—ASSESSMENT CRITERIA USED BY THE COUNCIL ON ECONOMIC PRIORITIES

SOCIAL ISSUE	CRITERIA FOR RANKING SOCIAL RESPONSIBILITY
Charity	Percentage of pretax earnings given to charity
Women's advancement	Number of women on board of directors or at vice presidential (or higher) level
Minority advancement	Number of minority members on board of directors or at vice presidential (or higher) level
Military contracts	Number of contracts with Department of Defense to make weapons, supply fuel, etc., to military
Animal testing	Use of animals in research and testing; extent of contribution, if any, to alternative methods of research
Disclosure of information	Willingness to disclose corporate information to CEP and type of information disclosed
Community outreach	Involvement in community education, housing, and other projects benefiting community
Nuclear power	Involvement in construction and maintenance of nuclear plants or providing consulting services

---

ing that firm's products. The major block to such ethical shopping is, of course, the time it requires to investigate the ethical or not-so-ethical practices of the numerous corporations that produce the products we frequently use.

To assist those consumers who wish to engage in **ethical shopping,** the Council on Economic Priorities (CEP) has created a guide for ethical shopping entitled *Shopping for a Better World.* This 126-page booklet rates the producers of over 1,300 brand-name prod-

ucts on their performance relative to ten current social issues. These issues and the ranking criteria used by the CEP in determining the social responsibility of each corporation are listed in Exhibit 1–6.

If you are interested in purchasing this guide or in membership in the CEP—which is a nonprofit organization formed to promote corporate responsibility—you can write to CEP, 30 Irving Place, New York, NY 10003, or call toll-free (800) 822-6435. In New York, call (212) 420-1133.

EXHIBIT 1–7
"ETHICAL FUNDS" WITH 1994–1995 AND 1992–1995 RETURNS

FUND NAME & TELEPHONE	SALES CHARGE	1994–1995 RETURN*	1992–1995 RETURN*	PORTFOLIO
Pax World 800-737-1729	None	18.9%	5.7%	Avoids liquor, tobacco, gambling industries; Department of Defense contractors
New Alternatives 516-466-0808	4.75%	14.1%	7.4%	Purchases stock in firms involved in conservation and recycling
Calvert Social Equity 800-368-2748	4.75%	6.5%	4.1%	Avoids investments in firms that discriminate against women or minorities
Dreyfus Third Century 800-646-6561	None	19.5%	9.1%	Invests in companies with policies on the environment, employment, and consumer protection
Parnassus 800-999-3505	3.50%	31.4%	23.6%	Invests in companies sensitive to employees, customers, and communities

*Average annual return. SOURCE: *Kiplinger's Personal Financial Magazine,* September 1995, pp. 62–80.

ETHICAL USE OF GOVERNMENT SERVICES

Our government provides services that are intended to benefit specific groups of citizens who are disadvantaged or who have special needs. Some people make unethical use of such benefits. An obvious example is the able-bodied person who parks in a handicapped parking space. Other people take advantage of social programs like welfare, food stamps, or Medicaid by providing false information to government administrators. Some health care providers have been convicted of billing the government for Medicaid or Medicare services that were unnecessary or never performed. These practices add to the cost taxpayers bear.

On a simpler level, people may abuse or purposefully destroy public property—breaking up picnic tables in parks to build fires, stealing road signs to be sold as scrap aluminum, and charging government accounts for private travel. Such behavior adds to the cost of government and may also reduce the quantity of goods and services that government is able to provide to those who truly need them.

ETHICAL INVESTING

Ethical investing consists of making investments only in those companies that engage in socially responsible behavior. In recent years, ethical investment funds have been on the increase, climbing from $40 billion in 1984 to $800 billion in 1995. The money managers of these ethical funds scan the universe of over 8,500 publicly held companies to determine which ones meet their ethical standards. The funds vary widely, however, in what they will or won't invest in, as you can see from Exhibit 1–7. In some cases, the determining factor may be a firm's involvement in defense contracts or in nuclear power plants; in others, it may be the extent to which a firm is concerned with environmental preservation or consumer protection.

The performance of ethical funds varies. A study comparing 1990 returns on ethical investments to the Dow Jones Industrial Average (DJIA) showed that, while some funds gained higher returns than the DJIA, overall the ethical funds lagged behind in rate of return. More recently, however, Ritchie Lowry, who publishes an investment newsletter called *Good Money,* has reported that the ethical funds he monitors had a return of more than four times that of the DJIA. According to Lowry, "The companies that are socially aware tend to be the best managed, too," and thus investments in such firms pay off. Although Lowry is right overall in his assessment some ethical funds have not done well (see Exhibit 1–7).

If you are interested in investing "morally," CO-OP America publishes the *Socially Responsible Financial Planning Guide*, which lists numerous brokers, financial planners, insurers, bankers, and credit unions that engage in ethical investing. For a copy, contact Co-op America, 2100 M St., N.W., Suite 310, Washington, DC 20063.

ONLY YOU CAN DECIDE

Obviously, there is no exact formula for ethical behavior. Every individual has his or her own set of values and moral principles, and every situation is different. But it is important to remember that, although moral and ethical convictions are necessarily very personal qualities, our individual behavior always, in one way or another, affects others around us. This is true in all of our activities—as family members, as citizens, as employers or employees, and as consumers. Ethical decision making involves becoming aware of how our behavior affects others and evaluating whether these consequences are desirable. And this is something only you can decide.

TERMS

Ethical behavior (p. 19) Behavior that is directed by moral principles and values; determining what is "right" in a given situation and acting in accordance with that determination.

Ethical shopping (p. 22) Purchasing products manufactured by socially responsible business firms and refusing to purchase products manufactured by firms whose ethical behavior is perceived to be reprehensible.

Ethical investing (p 23) Investing in corporations that are deemed to be socially responsible according to a given set of ethical criteria.

SUMMARY

1. Consumer economics is the study of how consumers can apply economic principles in their decision making. Some consumers make buying decisions without understanding the basic principles that guide economic behavior in the world around them.

2. Scarcity is a problem faced by consumers, businesses, and the government in all nations. Because of scarcity, choices and tradeoffs must be made. As consumers, we must choose how we spend our time and effort, as well as how we spend our income. A knowledge of consumer economics can help us maximize the satisfaction we obtain from the choices we make.

3. Because time, money, and productive resources are scarce, whenever we use any of these resources we must forego some other option that we could have devoted the resources to. The value of the secondmost-valuable forgone option is the opportunity cost of our first choice. A tradeoff is the process of giving up one alternative for another. Tradeoffs must be made because scarcity exists. An opportunity cost is involved in every tradeoff.

4. A basic assumption in consumer economics is that people try to make themselves better off in their standard of living—that is, in their command over leisure time and their ability to buy goods and services that will satisfy their wants.

5. In economics a market is the sum of all transactions that take place between the buyers and sellers of a particular type of

product. Markets exist between and among people, businesses, governments, and other nations in the world. In the American economy most transactions in markets are voluntary exchanges that benefit both buyers and sellers, although not necessarily in equal proportion.

6. The law of demand states that if nothing else changes, consumers will buy a greater quantity of a product at a lower price than at a higher price. The quantity of a product that consumers will buy at any particular price may change as the result of a change in consumer tastes, income, the price of related products, or in their expectations of the future.

7. The law of supply states that if nothing else changes, a greater quantity of a product will be offered for sale at a higher price than at a lower price. The quantity of a product that is supplied at any particular price may change as the result of a change in the cost of supplying that product.

8. Prices are determined in competitive markets by the forces of demand and supply. The price that we pay for a good or service at any point in time is its money price. The price of an item relative to other items in the marketplace is its relative price. Consumer buying decisions depend on relative, not money, prices.

9. In a world of perfect competition, many businesses would make the same products and offer them for sale to many customers. Consumers would control what is produced through their spending decisions. The result would be complete consumer sovereignty. To earn a profit, businesses would allocate more resources to the production of products that sell well, and fewer to the production of goods or services that are less in demand.

10. In the real world there are many cases of imperfect competition where businesses have more control than consumers over the products they produce and the prices they are able to charge. In such situations the businesses have a degree of sovereignty over production. The most extreme case of imperfect competition is a monopoly, where there is no competition.

11. Our government has often intervened in our economic system in an attempt to make it work better or to protect the rights of consumers or business owners. Although the amount of government intervention has increased in recent years, it has been manifested to some degree since the United States was first created in the 1700s.

12. International trade has become a larger part of the American economic system in recent years. Almost one-tenth of the products purchased in the United States in 1995 were imported. Roughly 16 million Americans depend on trade for their employment.

13. American consumers have benefited and paid costs as a result of the increasingly global nature of our economy. Trade has made it possible for us to buy better-quality products at lower prices. It has encouraged American businesses to become more efficient and to offer a wider selection of goods and services for sale.

14. Competition from imported goods has cost many individual Americans their jobs and has caused some businesses to fail. When American consumers choose to buy, or not to buy, imported products, they may weigh the costs and benefits of their decision both in terms of their own values and in relation to the impact their choice may have on the American economy.

15. Ethical behavior is acting in accordance with one's moral and ethical convictions as to what is right and what is wrong. Whenever a consumer takes advantage of a situation and acts in an unethical way to obtain something to which he or she is not morally entitled, it inevitably results in other consumers receiving less than they are entitled to. There is no such thing as getting a product for "free" by acting unethically.

16. Consumers may shop ethically by choosing to buy and use products they believe were produced and marketed in a socially and environmentally responsible way. They may also use goods or services provided by the government in an ethical way by taking no more than they are entitled to and by causing no unnecessary damage that could reduce the quantity of these products that are available to others or that would add to the cost of providing them.

KEY TERMS

Balance of trade (p. 17)
Capitalism (p. 14)
Consumers (p. 4)
Consumer sovereignty (p. 12)
Demand (p. 8)
Economic system (p. 14)
Equilibrium price (p. 6)
Goods (p. 5)
Imperfect competition (p. 13)
Law of demand (p. 8)
Law of supply (p. 9)
Market (p. 7)
Market economy (p. 12)
Money price (p. 11)

Monopoly (p. 13)
Opportunity cost (p. 6)
Perfect competition (p. 12)
Productive resources (p. 5)
Profit (p. 5)
Relative price (p. 11)
Scarcity (p. 4)
Services (p. 4)
Socialist economic system (p. 14)
Specialization (p. 16)
Supply (p. 9)
Tradeoff (p. 6)
Voluntary exchange (p. 8)

QUESTIONS FOR THOUGHT AND DISCUSSION

1. If you were a millionaire, why would you still be faced with the problem of scarcity?

2. What is your opportunity cost for taking a course in consumer economics?

3. Describe a tradeoff that you have made recently.

4. How do the forces of demand and supply result in an equilibrium price for most products?

5. If the prices charged by all fast-food restaurants increased, but at a lower rate than most other prices, what would happen to the demand for their products? Explain the reasons for your answer.

6. How would consumers control the production of goods and services in a world of perfect competition?

7. How many firms in imperfect competition harm consumers?

8. Why has the need for government involvement in our economic system increased in recent years?

9. Describe several situations in the United States that demonstrate the increasingly global nature of our economy.

10. What benefits and costs to our economy might American consumers consider when they choose whether or not to buy imported goods?

11. Why do unethical decisions made by one consumer always result in greater costs for other consumers?

12. What are several ways in which some consumers rationalize (make excuses for) their unethical decisions?

13. Why do some consumers choose to invest their money in what they regard as ethical ways even if they do not expect to receive the greatest possible return on these investments?

14. Assume you have a part-time job at a local office-supply store. You have noticed that your supervisor frequently takes home various supplies—a ream of paper, a carton of file folders, an electric pencil sharpener, and so on—for her own use. You are quite sure that she is not paying for them. You like your job and the supervisor has been nice to you. What should you do?

THINGS TO DO

1. Analyze a recent consumer decision you have made. Explain how scarcity forced you to make this decision. Identify the opportunity cost of making this choice. Describe how government regulations affected your decision.

2. Describe and contrast the characteristics of two markets you buy products in. One should be essentially competitive and the other should demonstrate a degree of imperfect competition. Which market do you believe serves your consumer interests best? Explain the reasons for your choice.

3. Research the history of a specific type of legislation that has influenced the way American consumers make decisions. Possible topics could include laws that limit the powers of firms with monopoly-like powers or that regulate labeling of consumer products. Include a discussion of the benefits and costs to consumers as a result of these laws.

4. Choose a type of consumer product you use that is both produced in this country and imported from other nations. Investigate the price and quality of these alternative products. Write a report that identifies and explains the benefits and costs American consumers may consider when they choose whether to buy imported or domestically produced brands of this product.

5. Ask several friends or family members what they would do if they found that their bank had made a $50 error in their favor on their checking account statement. Would they report it, or keep the money and hope the bank never found the error? What do personal ethics have to do with their choices?

APPLICATION

In the summer of 1995 a series of hurricanes destroyed large numbers of homes and other structures on the Gulf coast of Florida, Alabama, and Mississippi. Within days the price of lumber and other building supplies in that part of the country jumped by as much as 50 percent. Write an essay that explains how this situation demonstrated the economic concepts of scarcity, tradeoffs, demand, supply, and equilibrium price.

SELECTED READINGS

• Ambry, Margaret. *Consumer Power: How Americans Spend Their Money*. Ithaca, NY: New Strategists Publications, 1991.

• Becker, Gary S. "Working Woman's Staunchest Allies: Supply and Demand." *Business Week*, December 2, 1991, p. 18.

• Griswald, C. L. "Conscience of Capitalism." *The Wilson Quarterly*, Summer 1991, pp. 53–56.

• "How to Avoid Problems with Purchases," *Consumers' Research Magazine*, February 1995, pp. 30–34.

• "How to Use Your Computer to Effect Change," *Compute*, March 1993, pp. S7–S9.

• Jacob, Rahul. "Capturing the Global Consumer," *Fortune*, December 13, 1993, pp. 166–168.

• Miller, Roger LeRoy. *Economics Today*, 8th ed. New York: Harper & Row, 1994.

• Miller, Roger LeRoy, and Gaylord A. Jentz. "Ethics and Social Responsibility." *Business Law Today*, 3rd ed. St. Paul: West, 1994, Ch. 27.

• Miller, T. J. "Can America Compete in the Global Economy?" *Kiplinger's Personal Finance Magazine*, November 1991, pp. 81–84.

• Remington, R. H. "Eastern Europe After the Revolution." *Current History*, November 1991, pp. 379–383.

Sample Chapter 8

Fitness and Stress Management

Reprinted by permission of *The Fitness Triad:
Motivation, Training and Nutrition* by DeBrwyne,
Sizer & Whitney. Copyright 1991 by West
Publishing. All rights reserved.

The following table of contents and chapter are from *The Fitness Triad:
Motivation, Training and Nutrition.* This text would probably be used for a
health course. Health courses are generally classified as technical or specialized courses. Such courses prepare learners for work in professional
areas. Health courses, however, also involve natural science, the study of
the physical universe.

Natural science courses grew from humans' basic need to know—to
understand themselves and the world in which they lived. Natural sciences
are organized into two different divisions: physical sciences which concern
nonliving materials and biological sciences which concern living organisms. More than any other field, science is the study of questions. The information you read in a science book forms the answer to the questions
that scientists posed.

Technical or specialized courses apply knowledge to practical situations. Such courses may provide a broad overview of an area or an in-
depth development of a specific area. They help students develop career
and life skills.

Use the following checklist to manage your time for completing the
activities required in learning the content of this chapter.

Date Assigned	Due Date	Date Completed	Assignment
			Record assignments on term planner (Chapter 1)
			Complete weekly schedule (Chapter 1)
			Complete prioritized TO DO list (Chapter 1)
			Preview chapter: Create chapter outline or map (Chapter 2)
			Read, mark, and label chapter (Chapter 2)
			Record lecture notes (Chapter 3)
			Schedule study and rehearsal time (Chapter 4)
			Prepare for test by predicting test questions and creating charts, maps, or other study aids (Chapter 4)
			Rehearse and practice information (Chapter 4)
			Take test (Chapter 5)
			Evaluate returned exam results (Chapter 5)

Contents

· TEN ·

**Fitness and Stress
Management**

· ELEVEN ·

**Preventing Accidents
and Healing Injuries**

T E N

Contents

Fitness and Stress Management

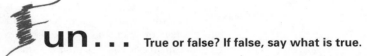

JUST FOR Fun . . .   True or false? If false, say what is true.

1. Some stress is beneficial.
2. Buying a new car and taking a final exam are more similar than different as far as your body is concerned.
3. The fight-or-flight reaction is a tactical military maneuver designed to allow fighter jets to avoid enemy bullets.
4. Whether an event is stressful depends more on the person experiencing it than on the event itself.

5. Being able to talk to close friends about personal matters helps people manage stress.
6. You cannot change the way you react to stress.
7. You know you need to reduce your stress if you find that you are unable to make even the smallest decision.
8. Machines can help you to learn to relax.

stress: the effect of demands on the body that force it to adapt. Stress that provides a welcome challenge is *eustress;* stress that is perceived as negative is *dis-*tress.

1. Some stress is beneficial.
   True.

Chapter 1 defined fitness as the characteristics of the body that enable it to engage in physical activity. A broader definition of fitness includes the body's ability to withstand **stress.** People normally think of stress as harmful and, indeed, it can be harmful when it occurs in excess of the body's ability to cope with it. However, stress can also be beneficial if it occurs in doses small enough to challenge, but not to overwhelm, that ability. Physical activity is itself a form of stress, and like all stresses, it can be harmful in excess, but it is usually beneficial because it is the one form of stress that leads to greater fitness. When the body practices meeting this stress, it becomes able to withstand other stresses as well. This relationship has many implications for your health and provides still another reason in addition to all the others you have already learned for engaging in regular physical activity.

Stress and the Body's Systems

Stress can be positive or negative, depending on your reaction to it. When one person claims to be under stress, he may mean that he is feeling an unwelcome strain. Perhaps he is ill, or his love life has gone awry, or he is under financial pressure. In contrast, another person who says she is under stress may mean that she is excited and happy. She may have just started a new job or be about to buy the car she has always wanted. Stress is *any* change, and fitness derived from physical exertion helps enable you to cope with *any* kind of stress—desirable or undesirable. Therefore, your dedication to personal fitness can make a major contribution to your ability to manage all of the challenges your life presents.

2. Buying a new car and taking a final exam are more similar than different as far as your body is concerned. **True.**

adaptive: with respect to behavior, that which benefits the organism. Behavior that brings about results that are harmful to the organism is termed *maladaptive* behavior.

nervous system: the system of nerves, organized into the brain, spinal cord, and peripheral nerves, that send and receive messages and integrate the body's activities.

hormonal system: the system of glands—organs that send and receive bloodborne chemical messages—that integrate body functions in cooperation with the nervous system.

immune system: the cells, tissues, and organs that protect the body from disease; composed of the white blood cells, bone marrow, thymus gland, spleen, and other parts.

white blood cells: the blood cells responsible for the immune response (as opposed to the red blood cells, which carry oxygen).

antibodies: large protein molecules produced to fight infective or foreign tissue.

immunity: the body's capacity for identifying, destroying, and disposing of disease-causing agents.

homeostasis (HO-me-oh-STAY-sis): the maintenance of relatively constant internal conditions by corrective responses to forces that would otherwise cause life-threatening changes in those conditions. A homeostatic system is not static. It is constantly changing, but within tolerable limits.

First of all, though, what does a stress such as exercising, taking an exam, or buying a new car do to your body? You may say it is "scary" or "exciting" (as opposed to "relaxing"), but what does that mean physically? It means, among other things, that your heart beats faster and that you breathe faster than normal—in other words, that your body gets ready to exert itself physically. All external changes stimulate you this way to some extent, requiring your mind or body to change internally in some physical way—that is, to adapt. All environmental changes—changes in the temperature, the noise level around you, what is touching you, and countless others—require such adaptation. So do all psychological events, both desirable and undesirable (see Table 10–1). The greater the **adaptive** changes you must make internally, the greater the stress.

All of the body's systems are affected by stress, but of particular interest are the **nervous system,** the **hormonal system,** and the **immune system.** Figures 10–1 and 10–2 show the anatomy, and describe the workings of the nervous and hormonal systems. The immune system parts are so widespread in the body that to show them in a figure would require a picture of almost every organ and tissue. Many tissues characterize the system: **White blood cells** made in the bone marrow and incubated in other glands, **antibodies** made by white blood cells, and other tissues all work together to confer **immunity** on the body. These systems connect all the body's parts so that they act as a unit.

Whether a particular stressful event presents a mental challenge, such as an exam, or a physical one, such as a fistfight, the responses are always the same. The efficient functioning that results from the body's adjustment to changing conditions is **homeostasis**.

The stress of cold weather can serve as an example to show how the nervous system in particular works to maintain homeostasis. (Remember, all stresses have similar effects, so even if you never experience cold weather, this applies to you.) When you go outside in cold weather, your skin's temperature receptors send "cold" messages to the spinal cord and brain. Your nervous system reacts to these messages and signals your skin-surface capillaries to shut down so that your blood will circulate deeper in your tissues, where it will conserve heat. The system also signals involuntary contractions of the small muscles just under the skin surface: Goose bumps with their by-product heat. If these measures do not raise your body temperature enough, the nerves signal your large muscle groups to shiver. The contractions of these large muscles produce still more heat. All of this activity adds up to a set of adjustments that maintains your homeostasis (a constant temperature in this case) under conditions of external extremes (cold).

Now let's say you come in and sit by a fire and drink hot cocoa. You are warm, and you no longer need the body's heat-producing activity. At this point, the nervous system signals your skin-surface capillaries to open up again, your goose bumps to subside, and your muscles to relax. Your body is back in homeostasis. It has recovered.

Now imagine that the system is constantly under stress—having to work to stay warm, to repair injuries, and to deal with fears and anxieties. You can see how, without periods of relaxation between times, this would be stressful.

TABLE 10–1 • Physical and Psychological Challenges Experienced as Stressful

Physical Stresses[a]

Light and changes in light	Drugs/medicines/alcohol
Heat/cold and changes in temperature	Foodborne chemicals and contaminants
Sound and changes in sound level	Bacteria/viruses/other infective agents/allergens
Touch/pressure and changes in touch stimuli	Injury, including surgery
Airborne chemical stimuli (odors, smoke, smog, air pollution)	Exertion, work
Waterborne chemical stimuli	X rays/radioactive rays/other forms of radiation

Psychological Stresses[a]

Death of spouse or other loved one	Son or daughter leaving home
Divorce or marital separation (breakup with boyfriend/girlfriend)	Trouble with in-laws or parents
Jail term	Outstanding personal achievement
Marriage or marital reconciliation	Spouse beginning or stopping work
Being fired from a job or expelled from school	School beginning or ending (final exams)
Retirement	Change in living conditions
Change in health of a loved one	Revision of personal habits (self or family)
Pregnancy or sex difficulties	Trouble with boss or professor
Gain of new family member or change of roommate	Change in work or school hours or conditions
Business readjustment or change in financial state	Change in residence (moving to school, moving home)
Change to different line of work or change of major	Change in recreation, church activities, or social activities
Taking on a large mortgage or financial aid	Change in sleeping habits or eating habits
Foreclosure of mortgage or loan	Christmas or other vacation
Change in responsibilities at work or change in course demands	

[a]The items in this table are ranked in order of highest stress to lowest stress.

Source: Adapted from Lifescore: Holmes Scale. *Family Health,* January 1979, p. 32.

stress hormones: epinephrine and norepinephrine, secreted as part of the reaction of the nervous system to stress.

epinephrine (EP-uh-NEFF-rin), **norepinephrine:** two hormones of the adrenal gland; sometimes called the stress hormones, although they are not the only hormones modulating the stress response. (The *adrenal gland* nestles in the surface of the kidney.)

The hormonal system, together with the nervous system, integrates the whole body's functioning so that all parts act smoothly together. And like the nervous system, the hormonal system is very busy during times of stress, frantically sending messages from one body part to another in an attempt to maintain order. Among the hormones important in stress, collectively called the **stress hormones,** are **epinephrine** and **norepinephrine,** which are secreted by the adrenal gland and mediate the stress response. A little practice (such as from the stress of physical activity) helps keep the hormonal system in good shape, but too much stress, unrelieved, is exhausting and debilitating.

The immune system is crucial in defenses against infectious disease agents, which are always present in all environments. It defends not only against colds, flu, measles, tuberculosis, pneumonia,

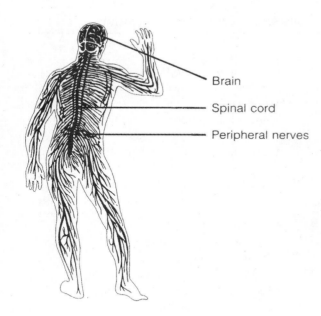

Brain

Spinal cord

Peripheral nerves

FIGURE 10–1 The Organization of the Nervous System The brain, spinal cord, and nerves make up a vast system of wiring that connects every body part. The nerves in the distant parts of the system gather information about the environment, both internal and external, and deliver it to the master control organ, the brain. The brain and spinal cord that make up the **central nervous system** act as a control unit for the body, and the nerves that make up the **peripheral nervous system** provide the wiring between the center and the parts.

A second distinction is between the part of the nervous system that controls the voluntary muscles (**somatic nervous system**) and the part that controls the internal organs (**autonomic nervous system**). Your conscious mind wills the movement of your legs, but your pancreas operates automatically with no conscious demand from you.

central nervous system: the central part of the nervous system, the brain and spinal cord.

peripheral nervous system: the outermost part of the nervous system, the vast complex of wiring that extends from the central nervous system to the body's outermost areas.

somatic nervous system: the division of the nervous system that controls the voluntary muscles, as distinguished from the autonomic nervous system, which controls involuntary functions.

autonomic nervous system: the division of the nervous system that controls the body's automatic responses. One set of nerves within this system helps the body respond to stressors from the outside environment. The other set regulates normal body activities between stressful times.

and hundreds of other diseases, but even against some kinds of cancer. Cancerous tumors grow from the host's body tissues, but the immune system can often recognize them as abnormal tissue in their early stages and fight them off. Anything that impairs the immune system threatens life; anything that strengthens the system—such as improved fitness—supports health.

Like the other systems, the immune system is affected by stress. Small amounts of stress, alternating with times of relief from stress, are not harmful, but prolonged stress can impair immunity and make a person unusually vulnerable to disease.

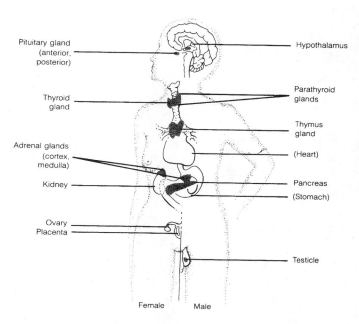

Pituitary gland
(anterior,
posterior)

Thyroid
gland

Adrenal glands
(cortex,
medulla)

Kidney

Ovary
Placenta

Hypothalamus

Parathyroid
glands

Thymus
gland

(Heart)

Pancreas

(Stomach)

Testicle

Female   Male

FIGURE 10–2 The Hormonal System These are the major glands that regulate the body's activities. The hormonal system coordinates body functions by transmitting and receiving messages. A hormonal system message originates in a **gland** and travels as a chemical compound (a **hormone**) in the bloodstream. The hormone flows everywhere in the body, but only its **target organs** respond to it because only they possess the equipment to receive it. Like the muscles at the ends of nerves, the target organs of the stress hormones respond by suppressing digestion, immunity, and circulation.

gland: an organ of the body that secretes one or more hormones.

hormone: a chemical messenger; it is secreted by a gland and travels to a *target organ,* where it brings about a response.

target organ: an organ of the body that responds to a hormone.

The Experience of Stress

When students encounter stress, very often it is psychological and involves the pressure to achieve in school (see Figure 10–3). In addition to the demands of school are the need for parental approval and the need to meet students' own high standards. These are all psychological stressors that cause tension. Meeting these demands can lead to the satisfaction of achievement, but sometimes these demands cause stress that can lead to mental and physical harm. To avoid this harm, the student's physical systems must be able to mobilize their resources against stress. Fitness enhances the body's capacity to meet everyday challenges and can ease the student's task of coping with both the physical and psychological effects of stress.

Consider what stress, whether it is physical, psychological, or both, does to the body. Whatever form of stress you encounter, the **stress response** has three phases—**alarm, resistance,** and **recovery** or **exhaustion** (see Figure 10–4). Alarm occurs when you perceive that you are facing a new challenge. Stress hormone secretion begins, activating all systems. Resistance is a state of speeded-up functioning in which stress hormone secretion continues, favoring muscular activity over other body functions (we'll describe this

stress response or **general adaptation syndrome:** the response to a demand or stressor, brought about by the nervous and hormonal systems. It has three phases. In the *alarm* phase, the person perceives the demand or stressor; in the *resistance* phase, the body's systems are mobilized to deal with the demand. The third phase is either *recovery* (a return to the normal, relatively stress-free state) or *exhaustion* (breakdown of resistance with consequent harmful side effects).

resistance: the body's ability to withstand stress. See *stress response.*

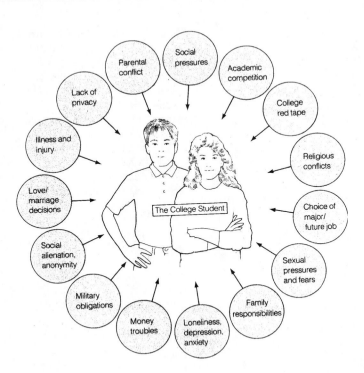

FIGURE 10–3 Psychological Challenges in the Lives of Students

unbalanced state in more detail shortly). During the resistance phase, your resources are mobilized just as an army mobilizes its equipment and supplies to fight a battle. In the case of your body, the resources are your attention, strength, fuels, and others, but the principle is the same. You can use your resources until they run out or wear out; then you need to replace or repair them.

Hopefully, before your resources are exhausted, a recovery period is permitted. You relax and recuperate. Stress hormone secretion ceases, all systems slow down, normal functioning resumes, needed repairs take place, fuel stores are refilled, and you become ready for the next round of excitement. It is because of the need for recovery between times of stress that the military provides "R and R" (rest and relaxation) times for its personnel.

If you have to stay in overdrive for too long, however, your resistance finally breaks down and recovery is delayed or becomes impossible. This is exhaustion.

The stress response evolved eons ago to permit our ancestors to react appropriately to immediate *physical* danger. It is often called the **fight-or-flight reaction** because fighting and fleeing are the two major alternatives when someone is faced with a physical threat. Every organ responds to an alarm and readies itself to take action. The heart rate and respiration rate speed up. The pupils of the eyes widen so that you can see better. The muscles tense up so that you can jump, run, or struggle with maximum strength. Circulation to the skin diminishes (to protect against blood loss from injury); circulation to the digestive system and internal organs (which

fight-or-flight reaction: the response to immediate physical danger; the stress response.

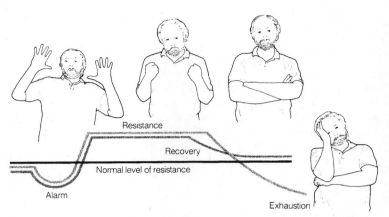

FIGURE 10–4 The Stress Response and Its Ending in Recovery or Exhaustion Alarm briefly lowers resistance but is followed by a high level of resistance. Recovery restores the normal level. If resistance is required for too long, exhaustion sets in, and resistance temporarily falls below the level normally maintained.

3. The fight-or-flight reaction is a tactical military maneuver designed to allow fighter jets to avoid enemy bullets.
False.
The fight-or-flight reaction is the body's stress response that prepares it to cope with danger.

can wait) also diminishes. Circulation to the muscles and brain (which are needed now) increases. The kidneys retain water (in case you should be injured and lose water by bleeding). The immune system temporarily shuts down, including the part of it that produces inflammation at a site of injury (the body can't afford to deal with irritation at a time when it needs to cope with external threats).

While the nerves bring about some of these effects, the hormones go to work, too. The brain initiates a hormone cascade that calls gland after gland into play and affects every organ in the body.

The nerves and hormones of the stress response produce not only the effects you feel—tense muscles, sharp eyesight, speeded-up heartbeat and respiration—but also other deep, internal responses that make you ready for fight-or-flight in other ways. They alter the metabolism—the chemical changes affecting energy—of every cell.

We called the state of stress resistance an *unbalanced state* earlier. The description just given shows how unbalanced it is. It is a state in which muscular activity is favored over other necessary body functions such as digestion and immune defenses. The state of stress resistance represents the body's effort to restore normal times when digestion and normal immune defenses can resume. Both states are important—normal functioning to keep you running smoothly during peaceful times, and stress resistance to get you through emergencies and back to normal functioning during times of change.

The stress response occurs each time you exercise vigorously, and especially when you compete. Think about it: What is the physical difference between running from a man-eating tiger or running a race in the Olympics? The emotion you feel may be fear or joy, but in either case, the hormones you secrete are the same; the reactions of the nerves, muscles, cardiovascular system, immune system, and all other body systems are the same. Afterward, the recovery process is the same: You relax. Either the running away or the athletic event can also progress to exhaustion.

4. Whether an event is stressful depends more on the person experiencing it than on the event itself.
True.

It should be becoming clear that stress can either benefit you or harm you, depending on your response to it. Suppose, for example, that you experience alarm (anxiety, fear), but that you *don't* fight or flee—that is, your body takes no physical action. The body gets *ready* to exercise, mobilizes its resources, but doesn't use them. You have been drained, but you haven't improved your response capability. Alarm without a physical response is harmful. If you experience stress repeatedly and don't have sufficient recovery periods between times, that, too, is harmful, and explains the importance of rest, relaxation, and sleep, which are discussed next.

If a round of stress leads to recovery and to a greater ability to adapt to the next round, then it has benefited you. On the other hand, if it leaves you drained and *less* able to adapt the next time, it has harmed you.

How can you make sure to obtain benefit, rather than harm, from your stressful experiences? By practicing for them—that is, by exercising regularly in appropriate ways and amounts and permitting yourself to recover adequately between times. A round of exercise is a sort of controlled round of stress—you choose when to start it, how intensely to engage in it, and when to stop. During each round, you are practicing for the next one—getting better at it. The wonderful thing about exercise, though, is that it makes you better not only at exercising, but at resisting all other stresses, because (remember?) the stress response is the same, no matter what its trigger. Can you see, then, why fit people withstand all stresses better and recover from them faster than unfit people do?

Fitness contributes to all aspects of health, as Figure 1–2 in Chapter 1 showed. Beyond cultivating fitness, you can also learn specific stress management strategies that will stand you in good stead when stress is unavoidable.

Stress Management Strategies

Managing stress well involves two sets of skills. One set is for sailing along, when moment-to-moment adjustments can keep you on course; the other is for stormy times.

Wise time management can help you to minimize stress. Time is similar to a regular income: You receive 24 hours of it each day. It is like money, too, in that you have three ways in which to spend it. You can save ahead (do tasks now so you won't have to do them later); you can spend as you go; or you can borrow from the future (have fun now and hope you will find the time later to do things you have to do). If you manage time wisely, you can gain the two advantages that wise money management also gives you—security for the future and enjoyment of the present. It takes skill to treat yourself to enough luxuries so that you enjoy your present life, while saving enough so that you will have time available when you need it. When your friends call on a Sunday to invite you out, you don't want to be caught with no money on hand, no clean clothes, and no studying done for the big exam on Monday. That is an avoidable stress, and planning ahead circumvents it. Make a time budget.

I SPENT ALL WEEK STUDYING FOR THIS EXAM! WELL, ACTUALLY I SPENT SIX DAYS WORRYING AND ONE DAY STUDYING.

It only slows you down to worry about things you have to do.

Remember, you have to do it only once, and an hour of time spent organizing buys many hours of time doing what you choose.

Several planning techniques can help you get the most out of your day while keeping tabs on long-term time needs. One such technique is to make two records—one, a list of things to do, and the other, a weekly time schedule. Figure 10–5 shows how to use these tools for everyday tasks. Sometimes you will need to schedule special projects. To schedule a long-term assignment, such as a term paper, first identify every task you must do to complete the project. Then, working backward from the due date, schedule each task. For example, if it will take you six hours to type the paper, schedule those six hours on a grid that you have started for the due-date week. Back up and schedule time before that to write the final draft and time before that for the research. If you have been realistic about the time each step will take, you will not be caught short at the end.

In addition to effective time management, a person can take many other measures to maintain strong resistance to stress. Many of these have been described in earlier chapters. Obtain regular exercise, relaxation, and sleep. Eat nutritious, balanced meals that will maintain your appropriate body weight. Cultivate strong emotional and spiritual health, and stay drug-free. These strategies strengthen your resistance between stressful times. Now, consider the times of stress themselves. You have to cope.

The means of handling pain and stress are behaviors known as **coping devices,** and some are more adaptive than others (see the Box, "Coping Devices"). The less adaptive ones are ways of continuing to avoid the pain as much as possible, whereas the more adaptive ones are ways of dealing with it and working it through. The maladaptive coping behaviors are sometimes known as **defense mechanisms,** and they are listed in a box of their own.

An intermediate type of coping behavior is **displacement,** the application of energy to another area altogether. Displacement is suitable for a time. Healthy people have a hierarchy of displacement behaviors with which they handle life's ups and downs. A truly adaptive coping behavior is **ventilation.** Ventilating means letting off steam, by expressing feelings to another person.

Too many people believe they must wait until the effects of stress are beginning to become severe before they take steps to relieve it. That's not true. At each step along the way, it's possible to intervene and obtain relief. The alarm step is the first step at which you can intervene. Recognize your own alarm reaction. You can then seek to identify the source of the stress and begin to deal with it immediately.

coping devices: behaviors, both adaptive and maladaptive. used to deal with the reality of an unpleasant or painful situation. See the Box, "Coping Devices."

defense mechanisms: automatic and often unconscious forms of emotional avoidance in reaction to emotional injury. See the Box. "Defense Mechanisms."

5. Being able to talk to close friends about personal matters helps people manage stress. **True.**

Coping Devices

displacement: channeling the energy of suffering into something else—for example, using the emotional energy churned up by grief for work or recreation.

ventilation: the act of verbally venting one's feelings; letting off steam by talking, crying, swearing, or laughing.

	Monday	Tuesday
	Today ↓	
6 A.M.	Wake-dress	Ditto
7	Eat-travel	Ditto
8	ENGLISH	ENGLISH TEST
9	↓	↓
10	SOCIOLOGY	CHEMISTRY
11	↓	↓
12	Lunch	Lunch
1 P.M.		SPANISH
2		
3	☐ time	
4	Club meeting	
5	- Exercise -	- Exercise -
6	Supper	Supper
7	TV time	TV time
8		
9		
10		
11	☐ time	
12		

Things to do

Buy new shoes - POSTPONE
Library research for term paper - MUST DO
Study for English test - MUST DO
Call friends to plan party - CAN POSTPONE
Pick up dry cleaning - CAN FIT IN

FIGURE 10–5 Time Management On a grid that lists the days of the week across the top and the hours of the day down the side, fill in your set obligations such as class meetings or work schedule. Allot a space for exercise each day. Prioritize other obligations such as bill paying or grocery shopping on a "things to do list," and find space throughout the week in which to do them. Check tasks off the schedule when you have completed them, and place any that you do not complete on next week's list of things to do. Be sure to plan time for nutrition, for sleep, and for play.

Defense mechanisms: Forms of mental avoidance.

Defense Mechanisms

denial: the refusal to admit that something unpleasant or painful has occurred: "No, I don't believe it."

fantasy: delusion, in the face of a painful or unpleasant situation, that something positive has happened instead: "He hasn't really left me. He's gone to buy me a present."

oral behavior: ingesting substances such as drugs, alcohol, or unneeded food.

projection: the conviction, in the face of an unpleasant or painful situation you have caused, that it is the other person's fault: "The teacher asked the wrong questions on the exam."

rationalization: the justification of an unreasonable action or attitude by manufacturing reasons for it: "I couldn't prevent the accident because I had to pay attention to something else."

regression: the reversion to inappropriate childish ways of dealing with painful realities, such as chronic crying or whining.

repression: the refusal to acknowledge an unpleasant or painful event or piece of news: Not hearing it.

selective forgetting: memory lapse concerning an experience or piece of news too painful to bear: Not remembering it.

withdrawal: disengaging from people and activities to avoid pain. Examples: Engaging in extended periods of fantasy (daydreaming), refusing to talk with anyone, or sleeping excessively.

6. You cannot change the way you react to stress. **False.** People can change the way they react to events so that the events aren't so stressful.

Stress management strategies:

1. Identify tensions when they first arise.

2. Recognize stress and identify its source.

3. Control responses. Identify inappropriate responses and change them.

4. Focus your attention and energy right on the task you are facing.

5. Recognize the warning signals of too much stress.

Symptoms of stress indicate that you are exhausting your ability to cope if:
- You know you are under severe stress.
- The same symptoms, in the past, appeared just before your resistance failed.

7. You know you need to reduce your stress if you find that you are unable to make even the smallest decision. **True.**

6. Identify which stressors you can control. Put the others out of your mind. List priorities and start taking action.

7. Learn to release tension whenever appropriate, by exercising, laughing, or willing yourself to relax.

We said earlier that the person's reaction, not the situation, determines the severity of stress. People can change the way they react to events so that the events aren't so stressful.

An example is public speaking. The stress response can help you get "up for it." Some excitement and anticipation ahead of the event, with the associated rapid heartbeat and breathing, will give you the physical energy to turn out a spectacular performance. You are at your most attractive when you are aroused and alert. But too much stress is debilitating. If you allow yourself to think about what a catastrophe it will be if you do less than a perfect job, you will be trembling visibly, your teeth will be chattering, and your knees will be knocking together. In such a state, you can hardly reach your audience at all, and you will be unduly exhausted afterward. It is to your advantage to learn to *perceive* the event as not so stressful.

This example illustrates another strategy: Use the stress response to your advantage. Direct and control the energy the stress response gives you. It is a magnificent, adaptive response to challenges, after all. It's only when the energy is scattered and wasted that it drains you without giving you anything in return. (In other words, it's OK to have butterflies in your stomach as long as they're all flying in formation.)

It is helpful to monitor your body for the many warning signals of too much stress. If you are alert to their appearance, you can initiate preventive action before exhaustion sets in and does damage. (See Table 10–2).

The length of the lists of signs of stress is impressive. Some people have some of the symptoms all the time. Everyone has some of them some of the time. The presence of a few symptoms is not cause for alarm, but there is a time to take them seriously. You should be concerned about the appearance of these symptoms under conditions that you know are stressful for you and that have, in the past, proved to be the forerunners of serious illness or inability to cope.

The cumulative effects of stress create a situation in which even small details become overwhelming. The person under chronic stress may become unable to handle even small problems. Example: A student who is breaking up with his girlfriend, moving out of his home, and changing schools all at the same time is trying to get his personal effects packed. He picks up a paper clip and can't decide what packing box to put it in. He starts to sob; he can't cope.

At such a time, you need to reduce your stress. Ask yourself which elements of the situation you can control, and pay strict attention to only those. In the case of our friend, he needs to take a deep breath and calm down. Once the crying has relaxed him, he should ask himself what he can control right now and what he can't. The breakup, the move, and the change of schools are beyond his control right now. The packing is not. He can go on with it or stop. He may need to take a break—for food, sleep, or exercise. He may need to tap a friendship—get help moving boxes or just make plans for dinner. These are the tasks he has to handle right now. He can let go of the rest.

Finally, even in the midst of severe stress, you can learn to relax and indulge in moments of recovery.

TABLE 10–2 · Signs of Stress

Physical Signs	Psychological Signs
Pounding of the heart, rapid heart rate.	Irritability, tension, or depression.
Rapid, shallow breathing.	Impulsive behavior and emotional instability; the overpowering urge to cry or to run and hide.
Dryness of the throat and mouth.	
Raised body temperature.	Lowered self-esteem; thoughts related to failure.
Decreased sexual appetite or activity.	
Feelings of weakness, light-headedness, dizziness, or faintness.	Excessive worry; insecurity; concern about other people's opinions; self-deprecation in conversation.
Trembling; nervous tics; twitches; shaking hands and fingers.	Reduced ability to communicate with others.
Tendency to be easily startled (by small sounds and the like).	Increased awkwardness in social situations.
High-pitched, nervous laughter.	Excessive boredom; unexplained dissatisfaction with job or other normal conditions.
Stuttering and other speech difficulties.	Increased procrastination.
Insomnia—that is, difficulty in getting to sleep, or a tendency to wake up during the night.	Feelings of isolation.
Grinding of the teeth during sleep.	Avoidance of specific situations or activities.
Restlessness, an inability to keep still.	Irrational fears (phobias) about specific things.
Sweating (not necessarily noticeably); clammy hands; cold hands and feet; cold chills.	Irrational thoughts; forgetting things more often than usual; mental "blocks"; missing of planned events.
Blushing; hot face.	
The need to urinate frequently.	Guilt about neglecting family or friends; inner confusion about duties and roles.
Diarrhea; indigestion; upset stomach nausea.	Excessive work; omission of play.
Migraine or other headaches; frequent unexplained earaches or toothaches.	Unresponsiveness and preoccupation.
Premenstrual tension or missed menstrual periods.	Inability to organize oneself; tendency to get distraught over minor matters.
More body aches and pains than usual, such as pain in the neck or lower back; or any localized muscle tension.	Inability to reach decisions; erratic; unpredictable judgment making.
	Decreased ability to perform difficult tasks.
Loss of appetite; unintended weight loss; excessive appetite; sudden weight gain.	Inability to concentrate.
Sudden change in appearance.	General ("floating") anxiety; feelings of unreality.
Increased use of substances (tobacco, legally prescribed drugs such as tranquilizers or amphetamines, alcohol, other drugs).	A tendency to become fatigued; loss of energy; loss of spontaneous joy.
Accident proneness.	Nightmares.
Frequent illnesses.	Feelings of powerlessness; mistrust of others.
	Neurotic behavior; psychosis.

Willed Relaxation

relaxation response: the opposite of the stress response; the normal state of the body.

The exact opposite of the stress response is the **relaxation response** (see Table 10–3). Relaxation occurs naturally whenever stressors stop acting on you, and it permits your body to recover from the effects of stress. But you can also will it to happen, even in the midst of a stressful situation.

progressive muscle relaxation: a technique of achieving the relaxation response by systematically relaxing the body's muscle groups.

One way to relax is through **progressive muscle relaxation.** The technique involves lying flat and relaxing the muscles all over the body, beginning with the toes. The goal is to locate and erase tension wherever it is occurring in the body. People who have never tried this are astonished to discover the number of different muscles used in creating tension, especially in the abdomen, the upper back and neck, and the face.

8. Machines can help you to learn to relax.
True.

A way to learn muscle relaxation is to use a machine (the electromyograph, or EMG) that can measure muscle tension. Harmless electronic sensors can be fastened to the forehead, neck, jaw, or anywhere muscles may be tense. A tone feeds back information to the person by changing pitch when the muscle tension changes. The pitch drops lower and lower as the person relaxes, and so the person learns what to do to become fully relaxed. Another biofeedback tool, the pulse monitor, can make the heartbeat audible, so that the subject can learn how to slow it down, thus achieving the same thing—relaxation.

You can practice muscle relaxation whenever you think of it—not only when you have time to lie down for 30 minutes. If your shoulders (for example) are tense while you are reading, what good does that do you? Relax them.

TABLE 10–3 • The Stress Response and the Relaxation Response

Stress Response	Relaxation Response
Stress hormone activity	Normal hormonal activity
Rapid metabolism	Normal metabolism
Fast heart rate	Normal heart rate
Raised blood pressure	Normal blood pressure
Rapid respiration	Normal respiration
Tense muscles	Relaxed muscles
Blood supply to digestive organs and skin diverted to muscles	Normal blood circulation restored
Water retention	Normal water balance restored
Lowered immune resistance	Immune resistance restored

meditation, self-hypnosis:
two methods of relaxing that involve closing the eyes, breathing
deeply, and relaxing the muscles

Two similar relaxation techniques are **meditation** and **self-hypnosis.** Both involve closing the eyes, breathing deeply, and relaxing the muscles. This chapter's Quick Tips section presents steps to relaxation. If you use them once or twice daily, after a while, the response will come with little effort. Practice the relaxation steps before meals; the digestive processes seem to interfere with the response.

To practice relaxation at intervals is to assume control of the body's responses, and it has a benefit beyond the simple pleasure it brings. Just as stress leads to disease, stress management helps to prevent it.

The joy of life is in meeting its challenges, developing new ways of dealing with them, and engaging in experiences that will facilitate new learning. The next chapter offers ways to prevent and deal with the physical stress of injuries and accidents that may occur when the challenges you take on prove to be greater than you anticipate.

Steps to Relaxation

To relax at will:

1. Assume a comfortable sitting position.
2. Close your eyes.
3. Become aware of your breathing. Breathe in deeply, hold it, then breathe out. Each time you breathe out, say the word *one* silently to yourself.
4. Allow each of your muscles to relax deeply, one after another. Imagine that you are floating, drifting, or gliding.
5. Maintain a passive attitude and permit relaxation to occur at its own pace. (Any way that you are proceeding is correct.) Thoughts will pass through your mind; allow them to come and go without resistance.
6. Continue for 20 minutes. You may open your eyes to check the time, but do not use an alarm. When you finish, sit quietly for several minutes, and open your eyes when you are ready.

PERSONAL FOCUS

Your Need for Exercise, and Relaxation

Fitness, derived from physical activity, permits you to deal with stress; relaxation enables you to recover from it. The more stress (other than physical activity) you experience in your life, the more you need physical activity and relaxation. To help you to discover your own needs for these parts of life, do the following two-part exercise.

First, consider how you, personally, respond to stress, for each person is different. Read carefully and answer each of the questions on Part A of this chapter's Lab Report: The Stress Mode Inventory. Check the boxes next to the symptoms that apply to you. Add up your points to determine your score as shown.

Compare your psychological and physical totals. Which is higher? These scores reflect whether you respond to stress with mostly physical symptoms or mostly psychological symptoms. Most people experience a mixture of both types, but often a trend is apparent.

Review the symptoms you checked. Watch for these symptoms to occur; they warn that stress is getting out of control.

An occasional bout of stress is easy to cope with, but when the stress is repeated, it may wear down resistance and threaten health. To discover which daily events are stressful for you, use Part B of the Lab Report, the Daily Stress Log, to keep an hourly log of the events of one day and your reactions to them. Try to pick a typical weekday; do not pick a day that you expect to be unusual in any way. You can also choose one weekend day to log; you may be stressed in some ways on weekdays and other ways on weekends. The example in Table PF-1 shows one way to record daily events and reactions; record your day the same way.

On Part B of the Lab Report, the Daily Stress Log, make a record of every hour of your day. In the first column, make note of the time of day when you begin to record events. In the next column, write down what you do during that time. Just a word or two to help you remember later is sufficient.

Under the heading *Environmental Conditions,* list anything you notice about the conditions around you. Are you too cold? Too hot? Is your chair too hard? Do your shoes pinch? Is the weather adverse? Notice your surroundings, both near and far, and make note of them. Next, note which social interactions or class activities you perceived as stressful or not stressful. Who was there? What was done or said that affected you? (Try to be specific.)

Even your own thoughts are important because your perceptions of events determine your reactions to them. In the column marked *Thoughts,* record how you react to each occurrence on your list. Write what occurs to you. Also list your emotions as they occur, without trying to change them.

Finally, list the physical and psychological signs of stress you experience. Be on the lookout for such subtle signs as frowning, jaw clenching, extra loud laughing, or reacting irritably with others, in addition to the symptoms you checked on Part A. Did you notice any symptoms that you didn't recognize before?

Now on Part C of your Lab Report, assess your stress log. Look over the first and last columns and write a paragraph or two answering the questions on the Lab Report.

Part D of the Lab Report asks you to list some ways you can change some things about your recurring stresses. Just writing down your recurring stresses may have made you aware that you can do something about them. For instance, in the sample form, the student recorded starting off the day with a stress reaction to traffic and fear of lateness. From now on, this student might be able to alter the morning routine to reduce stress. The student might, for

TABLE PF–1 • Example Daily Stress Log

Time	Activity	Environmental Conditions	Social Interactions	Thoughts	Emotions/ Feelings	Stress Symptoms
8:00–9:00	Driving, parking	Loud traffic, parking lot full	—	"Traffic is making me late."	Fear of lateness; anger at traffic	Tight jaw, neck, shoulders
9:10–10:00	Spanish class	Quiet, comfortable	Greeted friends	"I made it on time."	Relief, paying attention	—
10:10–12:00	Study for exam	Chair is hard	Friends going to lunch	"It's too late to study. Go to lunch."	Worry, fear	Bored, can't concentrate
12:10–1:00	Lunch	Loud music, smoke in air	Discuss weight, then friend brags	"Don't order anything fattening."	Feel punished, jealous of others' food	Plan to eat cake later
1:10–2:00	Biology exam	Hot, I'm sweating	—	"Nothing I can do now will help."	Regret, confusion guilt	Feel powerless, anxious
2:10–6:00	*Work on campus	Pleasant	Greeted boss, coworkers	"Now I can relax."	Competency	—
*At about 5:30	Patron came in to complain	irate patron —	Handled "I will not with diplomacy	Pride, get mad— I'll smile."	Sweating, superiority satisfaction	muscles tight
6:10–6:30	Driving to mall	Exciting, colorful	No one here I know	"I can't afford to buy the radio I want."	Unhappy	Bought and ate cake.

example, leave the house at 7:45 instead of 8:00, change the route to school to avoid the traffic, or take public transportation to eliminate parking.

Part E of the Lab Report asks you how you might adjust your attitude to the stress-causing events that cannot be changed. For instance, the student in the example felt fearful and angry, and these feelings triggered the stress response. Next time, the student might choose to accept being late once in awhile and relax about it, as well as to plan not to be late as often in the future.

Still, you are bound to be left with some events and circumstances that are truly stressful for you. These signify a need for more physical activity and relaxation in your life. Part 6 of the Lab Report asks you how you might include these in your day. Better organization and more fun in all forms—activity, spiritual reflection, and socialization—can go a long way toward defusing the stress response.

For Review

1. Define *stress*.
2. Describe the harmful side effects of prolonged stress on the body's systems.
3. Describe an effective time management strategy.
4. Describe some ways of dealing with emotional pain (defense mechanisms and coping devices), together with the limits of their utility.
5. Describe some of the physical and psychological signs of stress.
6. Describe the relaxation response and several different means of achieving it.

Sample Chapter 9

Truman, the Cold War, and the Anticommunist Crusade, 1945–1952

The following table of contents and chapter are from *On the Edge: The U.S. Since 1941*. Some colleges classify history as a social science like economics or anthropology. Review the introduction to Sample Chapter 6 for more information about social science courses.) However, other colleges classify history as a humanities course.

The study of humanities is the student of individuals. Thus, people—human nature as well as the character or qualities of humankind—form the common link. Humanities generally include cultural as opposed to more technical or scientific studies.

Use the following checklist to manage your time for completing the activities required in learning the content of this chapter.

Date Assigned	Due Date	Date Completed	Assignment
			Record assignments on term planner (Chapter 1)
			Complete weekly schedule (Chapter 1)
			Complete prioritized TO DO list (Chapter 1)
			Preview chapter: Create chapter outline or map (Chapter 2)
			Read, mark, and label chapter (Chapter 2)
			Record lecture notes (Chapter 3)
			Schedule study and rehearsal time (Chapter 4)
			Prepare for test by predicting test questions and creating charts, maps, or other study aids (Chapter 4)
			Rehearse and practice information (Chapter 4)
			Take test (Chapter 5)
			Evaluate returned exam results (Chapter 5)

Contents

2

TRUMAN, THE COLD WAR, AND THE ANTICOMMUNIST CRUSADE, 1945–1952

Six days after the atomic bombing of Hiroshima, radio commentator Edward R. Murrow observed, "Seldom, if ever, has a war ended leaving the victors with such a sense of uncertainty and fear, with such a realization that the future is obscure and that survival is not assured." Although the United States emerged from World War II virtually undamaged and prepared to assume leadership in world affairs, divisions within the Grand Alliance left many unsolved problems to threaten the peace. Within two years of victory, President Harry S Truman brought the nation into another global war—the "Cold War"—which altered the scope of government activity and inevitably affected political life on the home front.

PROBLEMS OF RECONVERSION

"The ultimate duty of government," declared Truman in September 1945, was "to prevent prolonged unemployment." Identifying with Roosevelt's New Deal, the president promptly asked Congress for full-employment legislation as well as a package of liberal measures, such as a permanent Fair Employment Practices Commission (FEPC), public housing, higher minimum wages, and urban redevelopment. This ambitious program soon collided with a conservative Congress of southern Democrats and northern Republicans opposed to government intervention in the economy. "It is just a case of out-New Dealing the New Deal," complained one House Republican leader. Fearing "creeping socialism," Congress opted for "maximum" rather than "full" employment. Although the Employment Act of 1946 committed the federal government to maximize employment, neither Truman nor his successors supported the creation of government jobs to ease unemployment. Indeed, the abrupt layoff of women workers after World War II brought no government response. Likewise, when Truman requested an extension of wartime economic controls in 1946, the conservative Congress resisted granting additional economic powers to the president.

Truman's efforts to control the rash of postwar labor strikes nevertheless alarmed liberals more than conservatives. Responding to a national railroad workers strike in May 1946, Truman first seized the railroads, then asked Congress to authorize court injunctions to keep workers on the job, to allow the army to operate the trains, and to permit the drafting of strikers into the military to force them to work. Although the walkout ended before Congress could act, Truman's proposal brought wide criticism. "In his angry determination to get the trains running on time again," protested the liberal *Nation*, "Truman [took] . . . a leaf from the book of another man who made railroad history, Benito Mussolini." Nonetheless, Congress approved the use of court injunctions to stop certain strikes.

Truman soon used government power to end a coal strike by John L. Lewis's United Mine Workers (UMW). Several times during the war, this union had broken labor's "no-strike" pledge. When Lewis called another strike in 1946, Truman seized the mines and ended the walkout by accepting an inflationary settlement. Six months later, the UMW defied the government again by calling a strike. Unlike Roosevelt, who in wartime had met Lewis's demands, Truman obtained an injunction and a $3.5 million judgment against the union (and another $10,000 judgment against Lewis), which forced the UMW to surrender. According to a Gallup poll, the president's antiunion stand increased his popularity.

Although liberals scorned Truman's failure to maintain price controls and his hostility to unions, Republicans criticized him for promoting big government, for administrative ineptness, and for laxity in protecting federal agencies from communist influence. "The choice which confronts Americans this year," advised the Republican national chairman, "is between Communism and Republicanism." New Republican candidates, such as Joseph R. McCarthy of Wisconsin and Richard M. Nixon of California, openly appealed to popular fears of communist subversion. Their allegations gained credibility from two highly publicized scandals: the discovery in 1945 of stolen secret documents in the offices of *Amerasia*, a left-wing diplomatic journal, and the capture of Soviet spies in Canada the following year. Republican red-baiting, as well as public disapproval of strikes, inflation, and bureaucracy, fueled criticism of the White House. With the simple campaign slogan "Had Enough?" Republicans won a landslide in 1946, obtaining a congressional majority in both houses for the first time since 1928. McCarthy and Nixon stood among the victors.

Once in control of the Eightieth Congress, Republicans reestablished a working alliance with southern Democrats to thwart civil rights legislation and to block Truman's other liberal measures, such as public housing, federal aid to education, higher Social Security payments, and certain farm benefits. Conservatives of both parties joined to pass the Taft-Hartley Act of 1947, which limited labor union activities. (For more on Taft-Hartley, see Chapter 3.) Criticizing such "vindictive" legislation, Truman vetoed the bill, but in a show of conservative muscle, Congress easily overrode the veto. The president's opposition, however, helped return organized labor to the Democratic camp.

POSTWAR FOREIGN POLICY

Although the public widely approved of U.S. participation in the United Nations, demands for rapid demobilization and military budget cuts in 1946 showed a limited commitment to global involvement. Public pressure forced Truman to reduce the size of the armed forces from 12 million to 3 million within months of V-J Day. The president's failure to reach postwar agreements with the Soviet Union contributed to his loss of popularity, but public suspicion of the Soviet Union and world communism enabled Truman to develop an increasingly militant and internationalist position. The president's primary postwar goal was to secure the nation from any foreign threat—military or economic. "We must face the fact that peace must be built on power," said Truman in 1945, "as well as upon good will and good deeds." Such power hinged not only on military preparedness but also on a stable world economic environment. The huge expenditure of natural resources during World War II underscored the importance of protecting U.S. access to raw materials.

"Our foreign relations inevitably affect employment in the United States," explained Secretary of State James F. Byrnes in August 1945. "Prosperity and depression in the United States just as inevitably affect our relations with other nations of the world." Such assumptions echoed the Open Door policy first formalized in 1900, which proposed free international trade with China as an alternative to imperialist spheres of influence. To ensure access to markets and resources and to prevent economic stagnation at home, postwar leaders advocated a worldwide system of free trade. "Peace, freedom and world trade are indivisible," Truman later remarked. "We must not go through the thirties again."

This economic approach to foreign affairs partially reflected the social background of many of the nation's policymakers in the postwar period. Leading State Department officials like Dean Acheson and John Foster Dulles often had personal ties to the nation's largest corporations and held powerful positions as corporate lawyers, financiers, or big-business executives. For example, the names of five of the six secretaries of state between 1945 and 1960 and of five of the six secretaries of defense between 1947 and 1960 appeared in the Social Register of the nation's richest families. Such men, appointed by both Democratic and Republican presidents, formulated a foreign policy that expressed and protected the values of the corporate elite. "I am an advocate of business," conceded Secretary of Defense James Forrestal in 1947. "Calvin Coolidge was ridiculed for saying . . . 'The chief business of the United States is business,' but that is a fact."

The International Monetary Fund and the World Bank, both created at the Bretton Woods Conference of 1944, sought to stabilize international currency and trade for postwar economic expansion. Leaders in Washington sought to direct a new economic order that would dissolve prewar economic blocs and assure economic growth. Although foreign trade comprised only 6 percent of the gross national product in 1945, State Department planners hoped to use U.S. economic power to force Great Britain, France, and the Soviet Union to open their trading blocs to U.S. business. When these nations applied for U.S. loans in 1945 to replace the wartime assistance provided under the Lend-Lease Act, negotiators delayed action to win trading concessions. Such pressure forced Britain to open its empire to U.S. trade before receiving a $3.75 billion loan in 1946. Nearly bankrupted by the war, Britain had no choice but to accept U.S. conditions. The French made similar concessions, but the Soviet Union, although devastated by the war, refused to accept U.S. conditions.

Although Soviet leaders continued to advocate the Marxist-Leninist doctrine of worldwide communist revolution, Josef Stalin primarily sought to rebuild his war-ravaged country with German reparations. Stalin also established "friendly governments" in eastern Europe to prevent another invasion of Russia. Given historic conflicts between the Soviet Union and anticommunist nationalists in eastern Europe, Stalin rejected "free and unfettered elections" in some areas occupied by Soviet troops. In Poland, for example, the Red Army repressed political freedom to promote a pro-Soviet regime. During the war, Roosevelt had minimized the problem of Soviet expansion in eastern Europe, largely because he could do nothing about it and wanted to preserve the Grand Alliance against Hitler. Although he remained suspicious of Stalin and refused to share information about the atomic bomb, the president tried to treat the Soviet Union as a "normal" state that was only protecting its national interests.

Roosevelt failed to attract public support for his foreign policy. Fearful of a resurgence of isolationism, he hesitated to move ahead of public opinion. Nor did he challenge the popular view that the United Nations, like the League of Nations, would be based on the Wilsonian principle of equal representation for all nations. Yet Roosevelt believed that the organization could succeed where the League of Nations had failed only if the Big Powers dominated international diplomacy. He assumed that the Big Four (Britain, China, the United States, and the Soviet Union) would use their veto power in the Security Council to protect their national interests. At Yalta, for example, Roosevelt and Churchill acknowledged Soviet dominance in eastern Europe, the British claimed special privileges in the Mediterranean, and the United States sought to maintain power in Latin America. Such spheres of influence contradicted Wilsonian internationalism as well as the Open Door policy, Roosevelt accepted these limitations because he understood the special interests of each Allied nation.

At Roosevelt's death, Truman knew nothing about these foreign policy assumptions. Instead, the new president viewed the Soviet presence in eastern Europe as an infringement of the principle of national self-determination and a violation of the Yalta agreements. Determined to prove his strength in the diplomatic arena, Truman clashed angrily with Soviet Foreign Minister V.M.

Molotov in April 1945 about the undemocratic character of the Polish government and decided to withhold U.S. economic aid until Stalin retreated.

The new administration also shifted U.S. policy toward the British, Dutch, and French empires, most significantly in French Indochina. Opposed to French imperialism, Roosevelt had proposed that Indochina be placed under international trusteeship until the French colony achieved full independence. Although the leader of the Indochinese national liberation movement, Ho Chi Minh, drafted a declaration of independence in 1945, British pressure forced Roosevelt to accept the return of French troops—but with the goal of ultimately granting Indochinese independence. Truman dropped that essential qualification. Pressed by Churchill, who feared that the liberation of French colonies would set a precedent for the British empire, Truman agreed to return Indochina to France. Ho's sympathy toward communism had alarmed State Department officials. Equally important, Truman wished to retain French support in Europe, where France could join Britain as an ally against the Soviet Union. In 1945 the United States provided ships and military assistance to transport French troops back to Indochina. Thereafter, the U.S. State Department ignored Ho Chi Minh's appeals for support.

While restoring French imperialism in Southeast Asia, Truman proceeded with prewar plans to grant independence to the Philippine Islands, first seized from Spain in 1898. Yet, before departing from that strategic region, the United States negotiated long-term treaties providing for military bases and the stationing of U.S. troops in the Philippines. Besides ensuring military security, such treaties protected U.S. economic investments and reinforced the rule of conservative elites. Similar arrangements brought the United States a string of military bases in Iceland, in North Africa, in Okinawa, an island near Japan, and the Azores, a group of islands in the Atlantic Ocean. In Spain, the United States accepted the fascist dictator Francisco Franco as a defender against socialist revolution and Soviet influence.

THE COLD WAR BEGINS

The Big Three met in Potsdam in July 1945 but failed to settle their differences. Stalin, concerned primarily with obtaining German reparations, expressed little interest in reducing Soviet influence in eastern Europe, but Truman, emboldened by the first successful test of the atomic bomb that month, rejected such a Soviet sphere of influence. He also proposed smaller reparations from Germany in hopes of maintaining Soviet dependence on U.S. exports. Failing to reach agreement, the Big Three postponed resolution of these issues until the Foreign Ministers Conference in London in September 1945. Frustrated by Soviet stubbornness, Truman decided to exclude the Soviet Union from participation in the occupation of Japan.

The atomic bombings of Japan in August 1945 reinforced Truman's confidence but aroused Soviet suspicions. At the London conference, the Soviets offered minor concessions on elections in Bulgaria and Hungary, but the Truman administration demanded Western-style political contests. Again, the diplomats

Exhibit 2–1.   Origins of the Cold War, 1945–1949

Year	Event
1945	Yalta Conference
	V-E Day: Germany surrenders
	Potsdam Conference
	Atomic bombings of Japan and Japanese surrender
1946	Kennan telegram
	Churchill's "Iron Curtain" speech
	Soviet occupation of northern Iran
	Acheson-Lilienthal and Baruch Plans for Atomic Energy
	Atomic Energy Act (creates AEC—Atomic Energy Commission)
1947	Truman Doctrine
	Federal Employee Loyalty Program
	National Security Act
1948	Communist coup in Czechoslovakia
	Marshall Plan—European Recovery Program
	Berlin airlift
1949	NATO
	Soviet A-bomb detonated
	Communist victory over Chinese Nationalists

could not reach an agreement. This failure showed the futility of atomic bomb diplomacy. When Molotov asked jokingly whether U.S. Secretary of State Byrnes had an atomic bomb in his pocket, Byrnes replied, "If you don't cut out all this stalling . . . I am going to pull an atomic bomb out of my hip pocket and let you have it!" To the surprise of U.S. negotiators, the Soviet Union would not be coerced into accepting Truman's demands. Secretary of War Stimson, who had once viewed the bomb as a diplomatic lever, now saw an opportunity to ease tensions by sharing atomic secrets with the Soviet Union. "If we fail to approach them now and merely continue to negotiate with them, having this weapon rather ostentatiously on our hip," he warned, "their suspicions and their distrust . . . will increase." Yet after a high-level policy debate, the president chose to maintain the U.S. atomic monopoly.

Despite doubts about further negotiations, Secretary of State Byrnes met with Stalin in Moscow in December 1945, producing tentative agreements about portions of eastern Europe, about Korea, and especially about a United Nations Atomic Energy Commission. Yet pressure from congressional conservatives, who opposed any concessions to Stalin, forced Truman to adopt a more rigid position, and he abruptly disavowed Byrnes's agreements. "Unless Russia is faced with an iron fist and strong language another war is in the making," he declared. "I'm tired of babying the Soviets."

Truman's firmness won support within the State Department from George F. Kennan, a longtime analyst of Soviet affairs. "We have here," Kennan cabled from Moscow in February 1946," a political force committed fanatically to the belief that . . . it is desirable and necessary that the internal harmony of our

Exhibit 2–2.   Iran, 1946

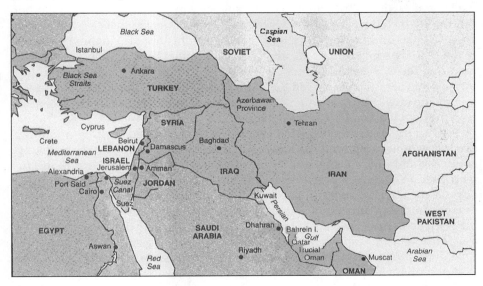

society be disrupted, our traditional way of life destroyed, the international authority of our state be broken if Soviet power is to be secure." Kennan's "long telegram" confirmed the president's belief that there could be no compromise with communist nations. One month later, Truman accompanied Winston Churchill to Fulton, Missouri, where the former prime minister attacked the Soviet Union for drawing an "iron curtain" around eastern Europe. The speech, approved by Truman, brought wide editorial criticism but publicized the change in foreign policy

The United States also challenged the Soviet Union within the United Nations. The first major crisis involved Soviet occupation of northern Iran in 1946. The problem was oil. During the war, the Soviets, the British, and the Americans had occupied Iran jointly, but the Soviets hesitated to leave until they received oil concessions similar to those won by the British. Fearing a Soviet attempt to control vital oil resources, the White House supported Iran in the Security Council, where the United States controlled a preponderance of votes. Such diplomatic pressure forced Iran and the Soviet Union to negotiate oil concessions in exchange for a Soviet withdrawal. Afterward, however, Iran repudiated the agreement. Using U.N. institutions, the United States had thwarted Soviet expansion.

The United Nations also sanctioned the U.S. decision to maintain a monopoly on atomic weapons. In 1946, to ease public fear of atomic war, the Truman administration announced the Acheson-Lilienthal plan, which proposed that atomic energy be made an internationally shared technology. The United States would relinquish control of atomic weapons in stages. During the transition, the United States would maintain an atomic monopoly and other countries would be required to allow international inspection. The United States "should not under any circumstances throw away our gun until we are sure the rest of the world can not arm against us," said Truman. In presenting the program to the United Nations, Truman's advisor, financier Bernard Baruch, added other conditions, including the surrender of the U.N. Security Council veto on atomic energy issues and the imposition of "condign punishments" against violators of the plan by a majority vote (which was controlled by U.S. allies). Although fearful of the U.S. atomic monopoly, the Soviet Union was rushing to build its own atomic bombs and rejected the Baruch plan. Instead, the Soviets suggested immediate nuclear disarmament and sharing of atomic secrets. Truman considered the Soviet alternative unacceptable.

Frustrated by Soviet negotiators, U.S. leaders accused Stalin of violating every wartime agreement. Yet most diplomatic quarrels involved arguments about the ambiguous language of the original agreements. No less than Truman, Stalin sought to protect his nation's best interests. Truman's inability to appreciate Soviet concerns, especially about atomic bombs, reflected the uncompromising anticommunism that dominated Cold War thinking. Defining Soviet communism as "red fascism," U.S. leaders were determined to avoid a repetition of the "appeasement" that had allowed Germany to control Europe in the 1930s. "The language of military power is the only language which disciples of power politics understand," presidential adviser Clark Clifford assured Truman in 1946. Moreover, in identifying the Soviet Union with Nazi Germany, Truman broadened support for his policy. Under the principle of "bipartisanship," Republicans, led by Senator Arthur Vandenberg and foreign policy expert John Foster Dulles, supported Truman administration diplomacy, at least in Europe.

As a Cold War consensus crystallized in Washington, one former New Dealer emerged as a major critic—Henry A. Wallace, secretary of agriculture during the 1930s, Roosevelt's third-term vice president, and now Truman's secretary of commerce. In September 1946, after gaining Truman's approval, Wallace spoke publicly at Madison Square Garden, arguing that the United States had "no more business in the political affairs of Eastern Europe than Russia had in the political affairs of Latin America, Western Europe, and the United States." Yet when other members of the administration protested the speech, Truman abruptly fired Wallace. "The Reds, phonies, and the 'parlor pinks,'" Truman wrote, "seem to be banded together and are becoming a national danger."

Fear of communist influence permeated the nation. Preparing for a Soviet attack, FBI Director J. Edgar Hoover developed a Custodial Detention Program and compiled lists of suspected subversives who would be arrested at the outbreak of war. When the White House tried to minimize the communist threat, Hoover aligned with more militant anticommunists in Congress. "Communism," Hoover told the House Committee on Un-American Activities (HUAC), "is . . . an evil and malignant way of life." Persuaded by such testimony Congress voted to provide more funds for FBI investigations of government workers. These political pressures pushed Truman toward a more militant anticommunist position.

The dismissal of Wallace revealed the administration's growing intolerance of positions that had seemed acceptable only one year before. After conservative Republican victories in the 1946 elections, some liberals deserted Truman and formed a coalition group, Progressive Citizens of America (PCA). Complaining that the Democratic Party had departed from the tradition of Roosevelt, the PCA urged a return to liberal principles or the creation of a third party. Although the PCA did not discriminate against members of the Communist Party, most liberals bitterly opposed communism and especially resented conservative accusations that liberals were tools of Soviet foreign policy. In January 1947 these anticommunist liberals formed Americans for Democratic Action (ADA). Like the PCA, the ADA endorsed expansion of the New Deal, the United Nations, and civil rights, but the ADA explicitly rejected "any association with Communists or sympathizers with communism."

THE TRUMAN DOCTRINE

Early in 1947 U.S. intelligence detected a relaxation of Soviet policy in changes ranging from military demobilization to a willingness to negotiate about Germany. The State Department concluded that such changes were deliberately deceptive. This mistrust was reinforced by growing concern about the slow pace of economic recovery in Europe. The State Department feared that economic unrest both encouraged communist expansion and undermined U.S. exports. The problem climaxed in February 1947 when Great Britain announced it could no longer provide support for Greece, a client state it had supported since World War II in a civil war against communist guerrillas. Truman welcomed the opportunity to replace Britain in the area, but U.S. intervention required congressional approval at a time when conservatives sought to cut government expenses. Moreover, the public appeared uninterested in Greek affairs.

Truman decided, in the words of Vandenberg, to "scare hell out of the American people." In an impassioned speech, the president personally presented the "Truman Doctrine" to a special session of Congress in March 1947, requesting $400 million in economic and military assistance to Greece and Turkey. Condemning a communist system based on "terror and oppression, a controlled press and radio, fixed elections and the suppression of political freedoms," Truman depicted an emergency situation that forced the U.S. to "support free peoples who are resisting attempted subjugation by armed minorities or by outside pressures."

The Truman Doctrine represented a major turning point in foreign policy—the announcement that the United States would initiate unilateral action without consulting the United Nations or the Soviet Union. The Truman Doctrine also abandoned the idea of effecting changes within the Soviet sphere of influence and instead stressed the importance of containing Soviet expansion. This decision divided the globe into areas of "freedom" and zones of "terror and oppression." Such divisions allowed no room for compromise: all communists were evil, and all communist threats became equally critical. Furthermore, the Truman Doctrine expanded the definition of "national security" to encompass regions throughout the entire world. "Wherever aggression, direct or indirect, threatened the peace," Truman later explained, "the security of the United States was involved." George Kennan elaborated on this idea of containment in an influential article, "The Sources of Soviet Conduct," published anonymously in the journal *Foreign Affairs* in 1947.

Truman's belief that communism represented a monolithic threat placed the United States on the side of authoritarian governments in Greece and Turkey Viewing Greek communists as minions of Moscow, Truman supported a conservative monarchy that had little popular support. In Turkey the United States backed a repressive regime that had cooperated with the Germans during World War II and continued to crush internal dissent. The administration justified these alliances by articulating what later became known as the domino theory: "If Greece and then Turkey succumb," one State Department official advised, "the whole Middle East will be lost. France may then capitulate to the communists. As France goes, all Western Europe and North Africa will go." Such logic alarmed conservatives and liberals alike. Republican Senator Robert Taft protested that Truman had made fundamental policy choices without adequately consulting Congress. Meanwhile, the liberal Wallace broadcast a scathing critique: "There is no regime too reactionary" to receive U.S. aid, he said, "provided it stands in Russia's expansionist path."

Truman believed that international politics was too complex for average voters, whom he considered overly idealistic. Rather than risk divisive partisan debates, the president preferred to rely on foreign policy experts and then seek public support. Conservative Republicans such as Taft objected that Congress and the public were left to ratify Cold War policies instead of formulating them. The administration's attempt to influence public opinion proved effective, however, and the announcement of the Truman Doctrine raised the president's approval rating from 49 percent to 60 percent in two months. Yet U.S. aid neither suppressed the Greek rebellion nor made the monarchy less oppressive." There is no use pretending . . . that for $400 million we have bought peace," admitted Vandenberg. "It is merely a down payment."

Although the Truman Doctrine addressed U.S. fears of communist subversion, the slowness of postwar economic recovery in Europe created conditions that encouraged communist criticism of capitalism. Seeking to end economic shortages in Europe, stabilize economic growth, and stimulate U.S. trade, Secretary of State George C. Marshall unveiled the administration's innovative European Recovery Program in a highly publicized speech at the Harvard University commencement in June 1947. Describing severe economic problems in Europe, Marshall called for a massive program of economic aid offering assistance to all European nations, including communist governments. "Our policy is directed not against any country or doctrine," he stated, "but against hunger, poverty desperation, and chaos." However, Marshall's purportedly unselfish offer of aid to the Soviets was deceptive because the plan threatened the independence of the Soviet economy. In addition, the program attempted to return to prewar conditions that left eastern Europe far less industrialized than the West. Instead of receiving reparations, the Soviet Union might have to contribute food to other countries. Finally the plan would rebuild the German economy and hasten German integration with western trade.

The State Department correctly predicted the effect of these proposals: the Soviets rejected participation in what came to be known as the Marshall Plan and forced its client states in eastern Europe to do the same. The Russians also moved to tighten political control in eastern Europe. Meanwhile, sixteen nations drafted a four-year program of economic recovery and gladly accepted

Exhibit 2–3.   Greece, Turkey, and the Mediterranean, 1947

$17 billion in U.S. aid. Wielding this economic power, Washington persuaded political leaders in Italy and France to exclude the Communist Party from participation in their coalition governments.

Despite the anticommunist aspects of the Marshall Plan, the conservative majority in Congress remained suspicious of executive power, foreign aid, and potential benefits to large exporters rather than domestically oriented small firms. Moreover, as late as November 1947, 40 percent of the public had never heard of the Marshall Plan, but as economic conditions in western Europe continued to deteriorate and Communist Parties throughout Europe organized protests, street demonstrations, and strikes, the White House moved quickly to arouse domestic opinion. Mustering big-business executives, organized labor, the ADA, and the Farm Bureau, the administration launched a public relations campaign to lobby Congress.

"We'll either have to provide a program of interim aid relief until the Marshall program gets going," Truman warned a group of congressional leaders, "or the governments of France and Italy will fall, Austria too, and for all practical purposes, Europe will be Communist." Drawing on his personal standing among Republican leaders, Marshall sold Congress on the idea. Pleas that Europe be saved from communism undermined conservative scruples about government spending abroad. Summoning a special session, Truman played down the economic basis of the plan and returned to the militant anticommunist rhetoric of the Truman Doctrine. The strategy worked, and Congress passed an interim aid measure. By 1950 the program had delivered $35 billion in government grants and loans to European countries and was credited with restoring European morale and revitalizing Europe's political centrism.

GEORGE CATLETT MARSHALL, JR.
1880–1959

When Indiana Senator William Jenner opposed George Marshall's nomination as secretary of defense in 1950 by dismissing the general as a "living lie . . . a front man for traitors," it was as if someone had attacked the integrity of George Washington. Described by President Truman as "the greatest living American," Marshall had designed and coordinated the Normandy invasion. Serving as Truman's army chief of staff and principal military advisor, he was the highest-ranking general when World War II ended. A veteran whose distinguished career dated back to service in the Philippines in 1902, Marshall became secretary of state between 1947 and 1949 and headed the Defense Department from 1950 to 1951. The key architect of the European Recovery Program, known as the Marshall Plan, in 1953 he became the first career soldier to win the Nobel Peace Prize.

"We are now concerned with the peace of the world," Marshall declared as World War II concluded. One day after the general resigned from the military, Truman appointed him special presidential emissary to China with orders to seek an accord between warring Nationalists and Maoist communists. U.S. officials worried that a victory by Maoists would strengthen Soviet influence in Asia. Arriving in China in 1946, Marshall used the lever of U.S. aid to compel the Nationalist government of Chiang Kai-shek to cease troop movements and institute democratic reforms. Meanwhile, he tried to convince the communists to agree to a coalition government and unified army under Chiang's leadership.

Aware that domestic political pressures prevented a complete cessation of U.S. aid to an anticommunist ally, Chiang ignored Marshall's pleadings and launched a major military offensive. Perceiving that negotiations had "reached an impasse," Marshall warned Washington that "the Communists have lost cities and towns but they have not lost their armies." After more than 300 meetings with the disputing parties, Marshall returned home in 1947, citing "complete, almost overwhelming" mutual suspicion as "the greatest obstacle to peace" in China.

The failure of the China mission underscored the lessons Marshall had drawn from nearly half a century of military experience. First, power was not limitless and could not be equated with moral purity. Second, armed strategy was to serve policy, not drive it. These principles prompted Truman's most trusted military advisor to recommend the firing of Korean War commander General Douglas MacArthur in 1951. Months later, Senator Joseph McCarthy denounced Marshall as an accessory to the 1949 victory of the Chinese Maoists and a coconspirator in the communist quest for world domination.

"God bless democracy," Marshall once had exclaimed. "I approve of it highly but suffer from it extremely." A tall, erect, and decisive leader, the general embodied the techniques of professional administration in molding postwar military life. Marshall understood how economic, political, social, and psychological conditions provided the context for military effectiveness. Such insight allowed him to popularize the Marshall Plan as a fight against the enemies of "hunger, poverty, desperation, and chaos." Yet the "fall" of China challenged the U.S. plan for global peace, prosperity, and democracy, and the principal architect of the postwar world became the centerpiece of recriminating debates that tore at the Cold War consensus. ■

RED SCARE

Anticommunist foreign policy paralleled an anticommunist crusade at home. Believing that the Soviet Union was a hostile and expansionist foreign power, Washington assumed that the U.S. Communist Party served as Stalin's domestic agent. After the Republican election victories in 1946, Truman had attempted to defuse the explosive issue of communist influence in government by creating a Temporary Commission on Employee Loyalty. Nine days after enunciating the Truman Doctrine, the president created a permanent Federal Employee Loyalty program to eliminate subversives from government. The announcement reflected continuing pressures from congressional conservatives as well as anticommunist feelings within the administration. In 1947 the House Un-American Activities Committee (HUAC) resumed investigation of communist infiltration of government, Hollywood, education, and labor unions. HUAC's inquiry into the movie industry resulted in contempt charges against the "Hollywood Ten," a group of writers and directors who refused on First Amendment grounds to answer questions about their political activities. After the Supreme Court refused to hear their appeals, the Hollywood Ten went to prison.

Attempting to preempt similar investigations of government employees, a presidential Executive Order mandated loyalty investigations of all federal workers and job applicants. The president also ordered dismissal of workers for whom "reasonable grounds" for suspicion of disloyalty existed. Truman instructed Attorney General Tom Clark to publicize a list of "subversive" organizations, and ninety-one groups were so designated in 1947. The Justice Department contended that groups on the attorney general's list were "fronts" for the Communist Party. Federal investigators were to treat membership in such organizations as grounds for further disloyalty inquiries for suspected individuals. "There are many Communists in America," the attorney general declared. "They are everywhere—in factories, offices, butcher shops, on street corners, in private businesses—and each carries with him the germs of death for society." The list stigmatized opponents of government policy encouraging public and private discrimination against members.

"What," asked a HUAC pamphlet, "is the difference in fact between a Communist and a Fascist? Answer: None worth noticing." In 1947 J. Edgar Hoover published a widely circulated article, "Red Fascism in the United States Today," warning of the imminent danger of communist subversion. Seeking judicial sanction for surveillance and detention programs, Hoover pressed the Department of Justice to prosecute leaders of the Communist Party for violating the Smith Act of 1940, which made it a crime to advocate the overthrow of government by force or to belong to a group with such a goal. In 1948 the Justice Department charged twelve leading communists with violations of the Smith Act, winning convictions and stiff prison sentences.

Despite claims of Soviet espionage, Truman's Loyalty Program found no government spies. Domestic communism did not represent a political threat as much as a suspect ideology. Many eastern European ethnic groups hated Soviet communists for invading their homelands and attacking Christian churches. However, the core of anticommunism lay in public perceptions of Stalinist Russia. The popular novels of Mickey Spillane, Hollywood films like

J. EDGAR HOOVER
1895–1972

Without question, J. Edgar Hoover was the most successful bureaucrat in U.S. history. A man whose entire life centered on Washington, D.C., he was the son of a bureaucrat, born and raised a few blocks from the Capitol. After graduation from George Washington University, he took a job with the Department of Justice, beginning a half-century career that ended only with his death in 1972. The young Hoover was assigned to the Enemy Alien Registration Section of the Bureau of Investigation and played an important role in investigating and deporting radicals during the Red Scare of 1919—1920. He also played a part in federal probes of black activist Marcus Garvey, which ultimately led to Garvey's conviction and deportation. During the Harding presidency, the Bureau of Investigation became so corrupt and ineffective that Hoover considered resigning, but after Harding's death, a new attorney general, Harlan F. Stone, offered the twenty-nine-year-old attorney the direc-

torship. Hoover accepted with the stipulation that he be given the authority to professionalize the bureau and to insulate it from politics.

Energetic and capable, Hoover applied modern management techniques to the bureau (it became the Federal Bureau of Investigation in 1935) with remarkable results. He hired agents with backgrounds in law or accounting and schooled them in the application of scientific principles to law enforcement. He supervised the assembling of a huge centralized fingerprint file, the creation of a sophisticated crime laboratory, and the establishment of the National Police Academy to train other law enforcement officers in scientific investigation. Simultaneously, Hoover recognized the enormous value of good public relations and steadily built the image of the G-man through shrewd manipulation of popular culture. The image was enhanced by well-publicized and successful manhunts for such celebrated

---

The Iron Curtain (1948), and a spate of magazine articles all portrayed communism as the epitome of heartless atheism, deadening bureaucracy and ruthless totalitarianism. Hostile to Soviet expansion, many Americans believed that communism jeopardized traditional views of religion, family, individual liberty, and personal initiative. "Communism is secularism on the march," J. Edgar Hoover told a Methodist gathering. "It is a moral foe of Christianity."

Ironically, the growth of government bureaucracy, big corporations, and impersonal, homogenized communities already threatened traditional values. "Our problem is not outside ourselves," admitted Republican presidential candidate Thomas E. Dewey in 1948. "Our problem is within ourselves." Anticommunist spokesmen such as Joseph McCarthy, J. Edgar Hoover, and Richard Nixon saw themselves as defending individualism, religion, and free enterprise. Their wrath focused not so much on actual communists as on the sophisticated, cosmopolitan State Department elites who tolerated communists in government and accommodated the Soviet Union. "I look at that fellow," Senator Hugh Butler of Nebraska remarked about Secretary of State Dean Acheson. "I watch his smart-aleck manner and his British clothes and that New Dealism, everlasting New

gangsters as John Dillinger and "Machine Gun" Kelly. This concern for image also led Hoover to impose on the bureau a code of conduct rooted in the Victorianism of his upbringing in turn-of-the-century Washington. Special agents should wear dark suits and white shirts; women did not smoke; and FBI employees did not take coffee breaks.

After World War II, Hoover's tenure at the FBI became increasingly controversial. Some critics charged that the FBI focused on sensational but episodic criminal activity while ignoring organized crime and white collar crime. In addition, the FBI zealously investigated communist subversives, an activity that broadened considerably as first the civil rights movement and later the antiwar movement stirred the Director's disapproval. In the process of conducting extensive domestic surveillance of political dissidents, the FBI collected a set of files on literally millions of Americans, files which Hoover was willing to use ruthlessly. Most notorious was the bureau's attempt to destroy Martin Luther King, Jr., with a tape recording of sexual activity involving the civil rights leader. Although the effort failed, the King incident illustrates the enormous power Hoover derived from domestic surveillance. As a former aide put it, "I'm afraid of him. I can't imagine what he'd do to me, but I'd rather not mess with him."

Even presidents felt the same way. His relationship with John Kennedy was tense, but his position remained secure, perhaps in part because Hoover had a potentially embarrassing tape of a Kennedy sexual liaison during World War II. His disdain for both Kennedy brothers was plain, however. When Hoover telephoned Robert Kennedy to report that President John F. Kennedy had been killed, Kennedy later remembered that Hoover sounded, "not quite as excited as if he were reporting the fact that he had found a Communist on the faculty at Howard University." Kennedy's successor, Lyndon Johnson, delighted in the bits of scandal that Hoover regularly passed along, and both he and Richard Nixon waived mandatory retirement rules to enable Hoover to remain on the job until his death in May 1972. ■

Dealism in everything he says and does, and I want to shout, 'Get out, Get out. You stand for everything that has been wrong with the United States.'"

Conservative Republicans like Nixon and McCarthy exploited the anticommunist crusade to attack Democrats and the New Deal tradition. Meanwhile, public distrust of elites who were unaccountable to voters—government bureaucrats, intellectuals, scientists, media and entertainment leaders—encouraged loyalty oaths, "naming names" of alleged communist associates, blacklists, and legal persecution. Spillane's detective novel *One Lonely Night* (1951), which sold 7 million copies, advocated another method to eliminate communists: "Don't arrest them, don't treat them with the dignity of the democratic process of courts of law . . . do the same thing that they'd do to you! Treat 'em to the inglorious taste of sudden death."

Backed by public opinion and the courts, law enforcement officials and anticommunist activists faced few obstacles in purging "red" elements from American life. As the FBI budget increased from $35 million in 1947 to $53 million in 1950 to $130 million by 1962, the agency's watchdogs processed nearly 5 million loyalty forms between 1947 and 1954. Under Truman, more than 7,000 federal government employees lost their jobs; thousands more were never hired in the first place. State and municipal governments adopted similar programs barring "subversives" from public employment. Workers and managers in private industry cooperated to harass suspected employees. Teachers, union leaders, even factory workers were forced to sign loyalty oaths; refusal usually meant dismissal. New York City high school students had to sign loyalty oaths to collect their diplomas. Meanwhile, the U.S. Post Office intercepted and opened mail from certain communist countries. "If ignorant people read it," said one censor, "they might begin to believe it."

Such excesses might have been checked by an independent judiciary, but Truman's appointments to the Supreme Court, including Attorney General Clark, consistently voted against civil liberties. In the *Dennis* case (1951) the Court upheld the convictions of eleven Communist Party leaders, ruling that "communist speech" was not protected by constitutional guarantees because communists participated in an international movement. As a result of 141 indictments and other harassment, many Communist Party leaders went "underground," and the party lost half its membership.

THE MILITARY CRISIS

The sense of national emergency stimulated the reorganization of the military services. The National Security Act of 1947 unified command over the armed services within the new Department of Defense, formalized the Joint Chiefs of Staff, and created an independent air force prepared to incorporate the newest advances in technology. The law also established the National Security Council (NSC) and the Central Intelligence Agency (CIA) as secret bureaus responsible only to the president. The NSC would coordinate and refine foreign policy for the White House and act as the president's liaison to the security bureaucracy. The CIA would preside over the gathering of intelligence information. The agency's congressional charter also provided for "such other functions as the Director of Central Intelligence shall, from time to time, deem appropriate." This loophole allowed the agency to develop secret military and political projects overseas. Amendments to the charter in 1949 exempted the CIA from budgetary accounting requirements, thereby releasing the agency from strict congressional oversight.

By rationalizing decision making, the National Security Act consolidated the power of the executive branch. Foreign policy decisions increasingly became insulated from external scrutiny and confined to a narrowing group of advisers. In a critical choice of military strategy, Truman opted in 1948 for an "air-atomic" plan that made strategic bombing, including nuclear weapons, the primary military force. Yet the United States possessed few atomic bombs or technicians capable of assembling more. To the budget-conscious president, however, air-atomic technology seemed an inexpensive way to build an unassailable defense. The plan had the additional advantage of reducing the need for a huge fighting army.

The decision to rebuild U.S. military strength faced opposition from both conservatives and liberals. Wallace, who announced his presidential candidacy

Exhibit 2–4.   Berlin Blockade, 1948

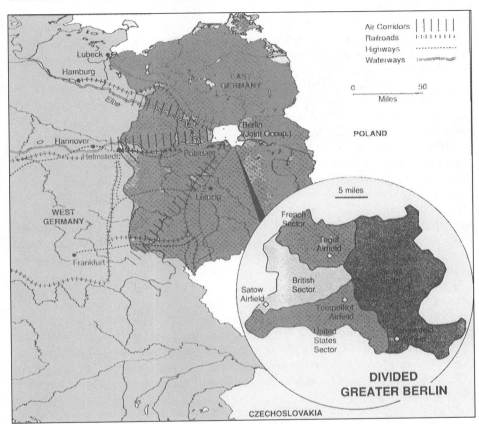

as leader of the new Progressive Party, chastised Truman for ignoring the United Nations and provoking the Soviet Union. More powerful opposition came from Republicans like Taft who denounced the swollen federal budget and argued that the war with communism was ultimately a contest of ideas, not military might. When the president requested funds for the air-atomic plan in January 1948, Congress seemed uninterested. "The outlook for greatly increased aviation budgets is not bright," the trade journal *Aviation Week* lamented early in 1948.

Congress abruptly snapped to attention, however, when communists seized power in Soviet-occupied Czechoslovakia in February 1948. Although the State Department had treated Czechoslovakia as part of the Soviet bloc, news of the communist coup shocked the public, confirming fears of Soviet aggression through internal subversion. Truman resolved not to repeat the Munich sellout of Czechoslovakia of 1938, when British and French "appeasement" had permitted Hitler to occupy Czechoslovakian territory. Looking to the past, Truman responded quickly when U.S. military officers stationed in Germany reported a change in Soviet attitudes.

Speaking to a joint session of Congress in March 1948, the president warned that the United States was on the verge of war. The Soviet Union had "destroyed the independence and democratic character of a whole series of nations," said Truman, and so revealed "the clear design" to conquer "the remaining free nations of Europe." "There is some risk involved in action—there always is," he admitted, "but there is far more risk in failure to act." The somber speech persuaded Congress to approve the Marshall Plan and to reestablish the military draft. Conservatives managed to defeat a proposal for universal military training, but Congress allocated an extra $3.5 billion for military purposes, which was 25 percent more than the White House had requested.

Military confrontation came one step closer when the Soviet Union blockaded Berlin in June 1948. Since the end of the war, the great powers had failed to sign a final peace settlement. While the United States and the Soviet Union argued about German reparations, their former enemy remained divided into occupied zones. As the United States and Britain planned to integrate their occupied zones and initiate currency reform, Stalin realized that the Western allies were hastening German independence to bring Germany into the Western alliance. In response the Soviets blocked access to Berlin through East Germany.

Truman saw war on the horizon. Determined to support Berlin, Truman ordered a massive airlift of food and supplies that lasted eleven months. Unwilling to go to war, Stalin had to accept U.S. plans for West Germany. Yet the crisis escalated the level of conflict. In July 1948 Truman ordered B-29 bombers to England. These were the only planes capable of dropping atomic bombs in Europe, although (unknown to the Soviets) they were not modified for such work until 1949. For the first time, atomic weapons had become an explicit instrument of foreign policy.

The Cold War crisis enabled Congress to reverse administration policy in Asia. The corruption of Chiang Kai-shek's Nationalist regime in China and the success of Mao Zedong's communists had persuaded the president to allow the Chinese Civil War to run its course, but the Truman Doctrine had suggested that any communist expansion threatened U.S. interests. Influenced by a well-funded pressure group known as the China Lobby, congressional conservatives led by Republican Senator William Knowland of California insisted on a literal interpretation of the Truman Doctrine. Contrary to administration intentions, Congress proceeded to appropriate funds to support Chiang's regime, committing the United States to a repressive but noncommunist government and influencing subsequent foreign policy in Asia for three decades. Meanwhile, Truman's decision to abandon Chiang accelerated accommodation with Japan, which now appeared to be a likely noncommunist ally. In 1947 Truman extended economic assistance to Japan and strengthened U.S. military forces there.

Washington also solidified its sphere of influence in Latin America. The Rio Pact of 1947 provided for collective self-defense of the Western Hemisphere. The following year, the Bogota Treaty created the Organization of American States to coordinate policy, and the United States disavowed intervention in the affairs of other states. In creating this alliance, the administration avoided economic commitments, preferring to support private development. Yet in a series of bilateral agreements, Washington offered military assistance, including the training of Latin American armies. Such support stabilized military and landed elites throughout Latin America and increased their dependence on U.S. trade.

THE ELECTION OF 1948

As the nation faced a series of foreign policy crises, political pundits questioned Truman's leadership. A March 1948 Gallup poll showed that the Democrats would lose the presidential election to any one of several Republican challengers: Dewey, Vandenberg, former Minnesota Governor Harold Stassen, or General Douglas MacArthur. Meanwhile, Henry Wallace announced an independent candidacy. "There is no real fight between a Truman and a Republican," said Wallace. "Both stand for a policy which opens the door to war in our lifetime and makes war certain for our children." Yet military mobilization against Soviet communism worked to the president's advantage. By identifying Wallace as procommunist, the president kept most liberals in the Democratic Party. Moreover, Truman's endorsement of African American civil rights, including an executive order to desegregate the military, appealed to northern liberals. Truman also improved his standing among Jews by promptly recognizing the new state of Israel in 1948.

The Wallace insurgency emboldened Republicans. Renominating Dewey for president, Republicans adopted a moderate platform that called for federal

Exhibit 2–5. Election of 1948

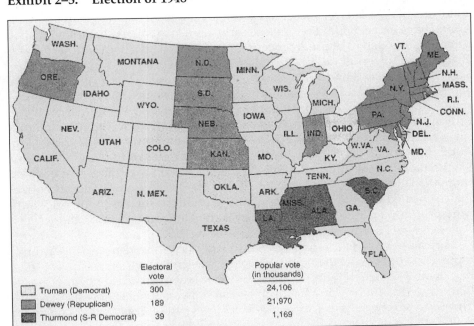

	Electoral vote	Popular vote (in thousands)
Truman (Democrat)	300	24,106
Dewey (Republican)	189	21,970
Thurmond (S-R Democrat)	39	1,169

support of housing, farm payments, abolition of poll taxes, a permanent FEPC, and increases in Social Security benefits. Confident of an election victory, Republicans deliberately excluded foreign policy issues from debate, which freed Truman from having to defend his positions. The president then undermined the Republicans by calling the Eightieth Congress into special session and daring the Republican majority to enact the party platform.

Truman also confronted divisions within the Democratic Party. Liberals, led by Minneapolis Mayor Hubert Humphrey, demanded a commitment to civil rights legislation. "The time has arrived for the Democratic party to get out of the shadow of states rights," Humphrey told the Democratic National Convention, "and walk forthrightly into the bright sunshine of human rights." Democrats responded by backing a strong civil rights plank. Angry southern delegates who opposed this plank promptly bolted from the convention. Three days later, these Dixiecrats met in Birmingham, Alabama, formed the States' Rights Party, and nominated South Carolina's Strom Thurmond for president. Other southern Democrats simply ignored the party platform. Running in Texas for the Senate, Lyndon B. Johnson attacked the FEPC ("because if a man can tell you whom you must hire, he can tell you whom you cannot employ"), antipoll-tax proposals, and federal antilynching laws.

Supporters of Henry Wallace proceeded to organize the Progressive Party and launched another independent campaign. Although communists held important positions in the party, the platform primarily reflected liberal principles. Offering a genuine alternative to Truman's Cold War and Dewey's bipartisanship, the Progressives argued that "ending the tragic prospect of war is a joint responsibility of the Soviet Union and the United States." Yet the Progressives could never overcome their association with communism. "Politicians of both major parties have tried to pin the Communist tag on the followers of . . . Wallace," observed pollster George Gallup. "Apparently their efforts have succeeded." The Wallace campaign encountered harassment, mob violence, and denial of public meeting places, particularly in southern states that refused to permit racially mixed gatherings.

While Dixiecrats and Progressives attacked Truman, the special session of the Eightieth Congress convened. If Republicans enacted their platform, Truman would get credit for goading them to act; if not, they would appear hypocritical. After much discussion, Congress adjourned without passing significant legislation. The decision gave Truman campaign ammunition against "do-nothing" Republicans. While preelection polls forecast a Republican victory, Truman took to the stump, launching a whistle-stop campaign that covered more than 20,000 miles. "Give 'em hell, Harry!" became a rallying cry as Truman appealed to anxious farmers about Republican threats to the price support program and became the first president to campaign for the African American vote in Harlem.

The results brought a surprise Democratic victory in November when Truman topped Dewey by more than 2 million votes. "The publishers' press is a very small part of our population," gloated Truman. "They have debauched [their] responsibility . . . to the country and the people have shown them just how they like it." The electoral college gave Truman 304 votes, Dewey 189, Thurmond 34 (all in the South), and Wallace none. Each third-party candidate attracted slightly more than

1 million votes, but Truman did best among farmers, organized labor, and blacks, all groups that supported Roosevelt's New Deal.

THE FAIR DEAL

"Every segment of our population and every individual," Truman told the Eighty-first Congress, "has a right to expect from our Government a fair deal." Working again with a Democratic majority in Congress, the president called for increased Social Security benefits and minimum wages, civil rights legislation, federal aid to education, national health insurance, and repeal of the Taft-Hartley Act. However, White House proposals soon met resistance from the true majority in Congress—a conservative coalition of southern Democrats and midwestern Republicans. By controlling the congressional committee system, these groups prevented consideration of Truman's program. Although Congress passed the Housing Act of 1949, providing for slum clearance and federally funded low-income housing, insufficient appropriations limited implementation of the program. In addition, civil rights legislation died in committee, and, choosing to avoid a hopeless skirmish, Truman avoided pursuing its passage.

Truman's support of civil rights appeared ambiguous. Despite the president's 1948 order to desegregate the armed services, the military evaded enforcement. In Truman's inauguration parade of 1949, African American soldiers marched with whites, but the army blocked full integration by segregating platoons, a policy that persisted during the Korean War. Truman's Department of Justice supported civil rights suits, but the Federal Housing Authority continued to accept residential segregation, even after the Supreme Court outlawed restrictive covenants. (For the legal issues, see Chapter 3.) As for equal employment opportunity, the president hesitated to reestablish the FEPC, then failed to halt discrimination in war industries. Nonetheless, African Americans praised Truman's moral support. "No occupant of the White House since the nation was born," wrote the NAACP's Walter White in 1952, "has taken so frontal or constant a stand against racial discrimination as has Harry S Truman."

The limitations of Truman's Fair Deal reflected basic changes in liberal thinking. After the defeat of Wallace, liberals repudiated associations with communism and moved away from radical positions. Anticommunist liberals, including theologian Reinhold Niebuhr and historian Arthur M. Schlesinger, Jr., argued that the search for a perfect society such as a communist utopia appeared naive and self-deceptive, and led to totalitarian excesses. At a time

Exhibit 2-6.   Federal Budget Deficits, 1945—1950 (in rounded billions of dollars)

1945	47.6
1950	3.1

Source: *Economic Report of the President* (1988).

when more middle-class citizens were enjoying personal prosperity, supporting the baby boom, and celebrating conformity, U.S. liberalism understandably supported the status quo.

LIMITING BIPARTISANSHIP

Although political disagreement eventually undermined the foreign policy consensus, a bipartisan spirit prevailed on European issues until 1951. In June 1948 the Senate passed the Vandenberg Resolution, which permitted participation in a peacetime military alliance with the nations of western Europe. The next year, the United States signed the North Atlantic Treaty, a pact which provided for a collective defense against the Soviets by forming the North Atlantic Treaty Organization (NATO). At the same time, the administration moved to create a new West German state, and in 1949 the Federal Republic of Germany joined the Western alliance. Although the treaty obligated the United States to send military assistance to European allies, its purposes appeared less military than political. First, NATO served as a diplomatic deterrent to Soviet expansion. Second, the alliance ensured U.S. domination of western Europe by obliging its members to adopt a united, U.S.-influenced approach to the region's security. Third, the pact linked German industrial and military power with the rest of western Europe to avoid renewing old rivalries. Opposed to permanent military commitments, Taft led the fight against the treaty's ratification but could not overcome the president's policy. The House, however, hesitated to allocate funds to implement the treaty's provisions. Then, in September 1949 the president announced that the Soviet Union had exploded an atomic bomb. Within a week, the House gladly provided funding for NATO.

Perceiving the Soviet Union as a relentless enemy that now possessed devastating weapons of destruction, Republicans and Democrats alike felt increasingly vulnerable to attack both at home and abroad. Although Soviet spies accelerated the development of a Soviet atomic bomb (probably by fewer than two years), fears of domestic subversion assumed nightmarish proportions. Allegations that government "traitors" such as former State Department official Alger Hiss passed secret documents to communist agents reinforced the climate of suspicion. Yet Washington recognized that the Soviet Union lacked the military capacity to launch an atomic attack. Even so, Truman opted to strengthen U.S. military power. Despite unanimous objections by scientists and civilians on the Atomic Energy Commission's General Advisory Council, commission head Lewis Strauss, backed by physicist Edward Teller, urged the development of a super bomb—the hydrogen bomb. In January 1950 Truman ended the debate by ordering development of the bomb. By the end of the next year the United States had successfully tested the new weapon; within two years the Soviet Union did the same.

Although he had strengthened the U.S. arsenal, Truman faced Republican criticism for neglecting China's Chiang Kai-shek. Despite appropriations exceeding $1 billion for the Chinese Nationalists, communist armies steadily destroyed Chiang's crumbling forces. By August 1949 the State Department

ARTHUR H. VANDENBERG
1884–1951

"The Old Guard dies but never surrenders," wrote journalist Milton S. Mayer of the last-ditch noninterventionists in 1940; "Vandenberg surrenders, but never dies." Michigan Senator Arthur H. Vandenberg stood for many other conservative Americans when he made the transition from prewar antiinterventionism to postwar internationalism. Although staunch Old Guard Republicans such as Robert Taft of Ohio refused to compromise their "America-first" principles, Vandenberg believed that national security required a new internationalist commitment. Insisting that the Soviet Union constituted a threat to U.S. interests around the world, he worked with the Truman administration to build a national consensus in support of the Cold War.

Born in Grand Rapids, Michigan, Vandenberg embraced the conservative middle-class midwestern values of his surroundings. As editor of the *Grand Rapids Herald*, he backed Woodrow Wilson's decision to seek intervention in World War I but opposed U.S. entry into the League of Nations. Appointed to the Senate in 1928, Vandenberg supported Hoover's efforts to end the Depression and later backed early New Deal programs in the interests of bipartisanship. By 1935, however, he rejected Roosevelt's leadership and became an outspoken critic.

Vandenberg also dissented vigorously against Roosevelt's foreign policy. In 1933, for example, he was one of only two senators to oppose U.S. recognition of the Soviet Union. During the 1930s he favored strict neutrality legislation. With other antiinterventionists, he attacked the Lend-Lease plan, arguing that it would hasten U.S. entry into the European war. The trauma of Pearl Harbor changed Vandenberg's position. Embracing international-ism, he appealed to Roosevelt to establish a joint congressional-executive committee to forge a united foreign policy. (Roosevelt, unwilling to share foreign policy with anyone, ignored the plea.) Then, in January 1945 Vandenberg presented a widely hailed speech, announcing his support of a postwar United Nations organization.

To win Republican backing of the postwar settlement, Truman chose Vandenberg to attend the first United Nations conference in San Francisco in 1945. Vandenberg succeeded in persuading the delegates to adopt Article 51 of the U.N. Charter, providing for regional alliances. Intended to protect U.S. influence in Latin America, this article later provided the basis for NATO and other regional pacts.

Considered the leading internationalist in the Republican Party, Vandenberg demanded a voice in foreign policy in exchange for bipartisan support of the Cold War. Criticizing any sign of "appeasement" of the Soviet Union, he denounced negotiations to internationalize atomic energy in 1946. Yet Vandenberg was personally vain and easily subject to flattery and pressure. Using the principle of bipartisanship, the administration won his support of the Truman Doctrine, Marshall Plan, and NATO. Vandenberg also intervened with Republican leaders to prevent any serious debate of foreign policy in the 1948 presidential election.

Unlike Taft, Vandenberg did not question the high cost of the Cold War or the growth of a national security state. Taft's opposition to the military state prevented him from winning the Republican nomination in 1948 and 1952. Yet Vandenberg, whose foreign policy position seemed more popular, failed to win the respect of his colleagues and never became a party leader. ■

Exhibit 2–7.   The North Atlantic Treaty Organization (NATO)

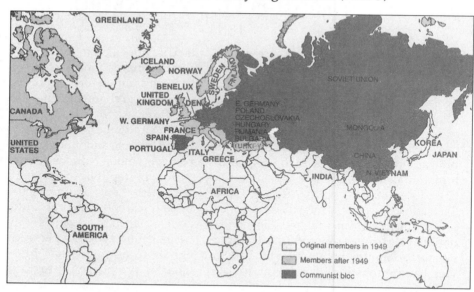

predicted a communist victory and halted further assistance. "The only alternative open to the United States," asserted a State Department "White Paper," "was full-scale intervention in behalf of a government which had lost the confidence of its own troops and its own people." Yet, although it conceded the inevitability of a communist victory, the Truman administration rejected accommodation with the Chinese insurgents. Four months later Mao Zedong's communist forces swept into power, forcing Chiang to abandon the mainland and flee to the island of Taiwan (Formosa).

Given the logic of containment, the communist victory in China could only be seen as a defeat of U.S. policy especially after Mao signed a mutual assistance pact with the Soviet Union in 1950. The China Lobby including such leading Republicans as former president Herbert Hoover, Taft, and Knowland, attacked the administration for failing to support an anticommunist ally. Such criticism reinforced Truman's reluctance to negotiate with Chinese communists. Instead, the United States adopted a policy of nonrecognition that lasted for more than two decades. Meanwhile, the CIA secretly supported anticommunist Chinese in an ineffective effort to disrupt the mainland regime.

FEAR OF SUBVERSION AND THE RISE OF MCCARTHY

Anxieties over the "loss" of China and the Soviet explosion of an atomic bomb escalated in January 1950 when a jury found Alger Hiss guilty of perjury for denying that he had passed classified documents to erstwhile communist Whittaker

Chambers in the 1930s. For anticommunists, the sensational case proved an inseparable link existed between Hiss's New Deal liberalism and communist influence in government. The case particularly embarrassed the Democrats because Truman had labeled HUAC's investigation of Hiss "a red herring" and issued a 1948 executive order barring Congress from access to government loyalty files without presidential approval. Traumatized by the possibility that Hiss may have been "duped" by communist spies, liberals henceforth took pains to disassociate themselves from political activities that might prove embarrassing. The Hiss case and the arrest of other spies in Britain solidified the Cold War truism that association with the U.S. Communist Party was equivalent to service to the Soviet state. Indeed, the Soviets found willing agents among U.S. Communist Party members. However, most U.S. communists attempted to affect policy through more conventional political activities such as participation in labor groups, elections, or public events. Except in the extremely ambiguous Hiss case, investigators never found communist agents in government. Nonetheless, HUAC's Richard Nixon, who had sparked the Hiss investigation, denounced "high officials" for concealing a larger subversive "conspiracy."

One month after the Hiss conviction, Senator Joseph McCarthy captured national attention by claiming to have proof of a communist conspiracy in government. "I have in my hands," he told the Women's Republican Club in Wheeling, West Virginia," a list of 205 [government employees] that were made known to the Secretary of State as being members of the Communist party and who nevertheless are still working and shaping policy in the State Department." In later versions McCarthy changed the number of alleged communists, but he vigorously defended the charge that subversives permeated the federal government.

McCarthy's attacks on communism mirrored the national mood. The arrest of Julius and Ethel Rosenberg in June 1950 on charges of transmitting atomic bomb secrets to the Soviet Union during World War II underscored the domestic threat. New evidence suggests that Julius Rosenberg provided proximity fuses and sketches of an atomic bomb to Soviet agents, although the value of such information to Soviet physicists was slight. Yet, without specific information, Nevada's conservative Democratic Senator Patrick McCarran introduced the Internal Security Act, which authorized the president to declare an "internal security emergency" and to detain suspected dissidents. The law banned communists from employment in defense industries, established a Subversive Activities Control Board, required communists to register with the attorney general, and excluded communists from obtaining passports. Truman vetoed the bill "because any governmental stifling of the free expression of opinion is a long step toward totalitarianism." Congress overrode the veto by an overwhelming margin. Terrified by the prospect of an atomic war with the Soviet Union, the public supported such anticommunist measures.

McCarthy's accusations concerning communists in government attracted the support of conservative Republicans, who, despite occasional misgivings, endorsed these attacks on the Truman administration. In 1950 a Senate investigating committee chaired by Maryland Democrat Millard Tydings found no evidence to support McCarthy's charges and concluded that the allegations were "a fraud and a hoax." Yet the Senate responded to the report along strict party lines. Such party loyalty enabled McCarthy to remain a presence if not a decisive factor in the 1950 congressional elections. In Maryland, McCarthy smeared Tydings as a procommunist and contributed to Tydings's defeat. Meanwhile, in California, Nixon defeated Helen Gahagan Douglas, whom he dubbed the "Pink Lady" to win election to the Senate.

After the 1950 elections, McCarran's Senate Internal Security subcommittee focused on communist influence at the United Nations, and HUAC resumed investigations of Hollywood figures in 1951. Meanwhile, McCarthy's accusations that communists were employed in the State Department gained wide public attention. Truman called McCarthy a liar. Yet the administration reacted to the charges not by defending the civil liberties of the accused but by affirming its own anticommunist credentials. In April 1951 Truman issued an executive order introducing a new standard for ferreting out subversives: a federal employee could be fired not when there were "reasonable grounds" but rather when there was "reasonable doubt" about the person's loyalty. The burden of proof thus shifted from the accuser to the accused.

In 1952 Congress endeavored to protect U.S. borders by establishing new rules for immigration. The McCarran-Walter Immigration Act, passed over Truman's veto, gave the president power to exclude any foreigner deemed "detrimental" to the national interest. Continuing previous immigration policies, the law favored immigrants from northern and western European countries but sharply limited newcomers from colonies of those countries. While slightly increasing Asian immigration quotas and permitting wider immigration from Latin America, these rules reduced immigration from the West Indies and Africa. Consistent with the anticommunist crusade, the McCarran-Walter Act also limited immigration from countries under communist control and facilitated expulsion of undesirable aliens and even naturalized citizens.

THE KOREAN WAR

By 1950 the sense of an impending international crisis led the National Security Council to develop a comprehensive analysis of U.S. foreign policy in a secret document labeled NSC-68. Asserting that "the Soviet Union . . . is animated by a new fanatic faith . . . and seeks to impose its absolute authority over the rest of the world," the report emphasized the possibility of immediate war and recommended that the United States be prepared to halt Soviet expansion throughout the world. Such a goal demanded a global defense system that included hydrogen bombs, expansion of conventional military forces, and a network of international alliances. To finance this policy NSC-68 recommended a quadrupling of the $13 billion national defense budget. This costly plan faced considerable opposition in Congress, particularly because the Soviet Union had avoided any overt action since 1948 that justified U.S. military intervention. Meanwhile, in secret meetings, the administration debated plans to defend Taiwan from invasion by Chinese communists.

The tense peace was shattered on 25 June 1950, when North Korean troops suddenly invaded South Korea. Six months earlier, Acheson had remarked in a speech to the National Press Club that Korea and Taiwan lay beyond the U.S.

Exhibit 2–8.   The Korean War

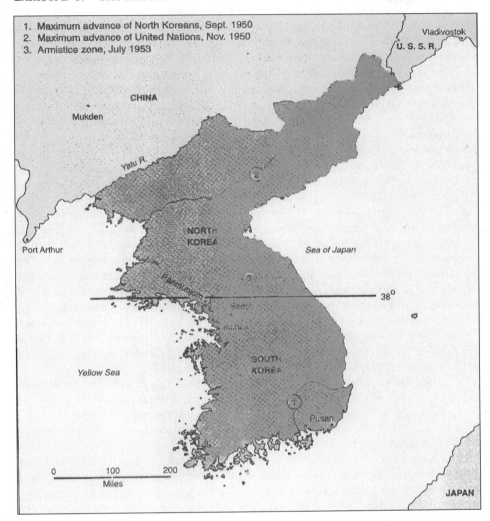

1. Maximum advance of North Koreans, Sept. 1950
2. Maximum advance of United Nations, Nov. 1950
3. Armistice zone, July 1953

CHINA

Mukden

Vladivostok

U. S. S. R.

Yalu R.

Port Arthur

NORTH KOREA

Sea of Japan

Panmunjom

38°

Seoul

Inchon

Yellow Sea

SOUTH KOREA

Pusan

0   100   200
Miles

JAPAN

"defense perimeter" in the Pacific. The statement, challenged by Republican conservatives, justified a reduction of aid to Chiang Kai-shek, but as North Korean armies advanced quickly, Truman ordered military assistance to South Korea and directed the Seventh Fleet to sail between mainland China and Taiwan to prevent an invasion of the Nationalist-held islands. The next day the United States called an emergency session of the U.N. Security Council, which branded North Korea an aggressor. (The Soviet delegation, boycotting the Security Council on another matter, missed the critical vote.) As South Korean armies collapsed, Truman ordered U.S. troops into action. "The attack upon Korea," he declared, "makes it plain beyond all doubt that communism has passed beyond the use of subversion to conquer independent nations." The United Nations later approved Truman's action, giving international sanction to U.S. policy. Sixteen nations eventually participated in the war, but the United States provided most of the resources and leadership.

Intervention in Korea stemmed from the conviction that the United States had to "draw the line" against communist aggression and demonstrate its willingness to fight the Soviets anywhere in the world. As with earlier decisions to challenge the Berlin blockade and develop hydrogen bombs, the president bypassed consultation with congressional leaders, thereby setting important precedents for successors. Although Taft denounced Truman's "complete usurpation . . . of authority to use the armed forces," public opinion supported the president's action. Indeed, Truman's claim to be enforcing U.N. policy won favor among liberals, even though the U.S. military commander, General Douglas MacArthur, took orders directly and exclusively from Washington.

U.S. forces arrived in Korea just in time to stop a complete North Korean victory. After hard fighting near the southern port of Pusan, the U.N. Allies forced the enemy to retreat. At the start of the war, the administration insisted that fighting was "solely for the purpose of restoring the Republic of Korea to its status prior to the invasion." In September 1950, however, Truman authorized a military advance north of the thirty-eighth parallel, the border between North and South Korea, in an effort to liberate North Korea from communism before U.S. congressional elections. General MacArthur promised victory by Christmas. In October Truman conferred with MacArthur at Wake Island and agreed to allow Allied troops to proceed to the Yalu River, which bordered China. Even before these decisions, China had decided to protect North Korea. By November Chinese forces had stopped U.S. advances, driving the U.N. armies into a retreat south of the thirty-eighth parallel.

Confrontation with Chinese troops also raised the possibility of another world war, including the use of nuclear weapons. Truman, however, exercised his power as commander-in-chief to restrain MacArthur and prevent an attack on China. By 1951 battle lines again stabilized around the thirty-eighth parallel, but MacArthur criticized the limits of U.S. involvement. "There is no substitute for victory," he declared. Unfamiliar with the concept of limited war, public opinion appeared ambivalent, showing both strong support for the use of atomic bombs and a desire to withdraw from the war altogether. When Truman announced a stalemated "cease fire," MacArthur, harboring his own presidential ambitions, publicly criticized the president's "no-win" policy.

Exasperated by MacArthur's insubordination, Truman fired the general in April 1951. The decision infuriated conservatives, who spoke of impeaching the president and welcomed MacArthur home with parades and a unique address to a joint session of Congress. The general took the opportunity to condemn the idea of limited war. Yet the removal of MacArthur facilitated the opening of truce negotiations that began in 1951. These talks lasted for two years, while the fighting continued under the command of General Matthew Ridgeway. Truman's refusal to repatriate communist prisoners of war who declined to return to their homelands stalled negotiations. The impasse ended only after the inauguration of the next administration in 1953. The limited war had cost 34,000 U.S. lives.

The Korean War justified the military buildup envisioned in NSC-68. Wartime appropriations expanded the armed forces and nuclear arsenal and increased the number of overseas bases. Funding for aircraft research and development escalated from $1.8 billion to $3.1 billion. Furthermore, the CIA expanded in size and scope of operations and increased its staff from fewer than 5,000 in 1950 to 15,000 by 1955. The war led the president to hold regular meetings with the National Security Council, setting a precedent for Truman's successors. To check inflation, Congress gave Truman authority to establish wage, price, and rent controls. In December 1950 the president declared a "national emergency" and implemented those economic powers, stabilizing the cost of living index for the remainder of the war. The military crisis emboldened Truman to seize operations of the steel industry to end a strike in 1952, but the Supreme Court ruled the act unconstitutional.

The Korean crisis also prompted the Truman administration to proceed with plans to rearm Germany. When France objected, Truman offered to station U.S. troops in Europe permanently to ensure stability. Congressional conservatives protested these unprecedented peacetime military commitments. In the "Great Debate" of 1951, Republicans leaders ended the bipartisan foreign policy that had characterized Cold War politics since 1947. Attacking the poorly executed land war in Korea and expressing frustration that Chiang Kai-shek had not been permitted to enter the fray, Republicans focused on the unilateral nature of Truman's military decisions and insisted that Congress have a role in the formation of foreign policy. Dramatizing these concerns, Republicans sponsored a Senate resolution that blocked U.S. troops from being sent to Europe without approval from Congress. Although testimony from NATO's supreme commander, General Dwight D. Eisenhower, blunted some of the Republicans' criticism, Congress passed a compromise version of the resolution that limited troop deployments to four divisions.

The Korean War also stimulated a more aggressive policy in Asia. Although the Truman administration had been prepared to accept a communist Chinese invasion of Taiwan in early 1950, the Korean conflict provided an excuse to send the Seventh Fleet to protect the besieged island. Truman also deepened U.S. involvement in Indochina. When Ho Chi Minh, leader of the anti-French liberation movement, accepted support from China and the Soviet Union in 1949, the United States increased aid to France. After the Korean War began, Truman permitted U.S. military personnel to assist French forces. "If Indochina went," explained a State Department official in 1951, "the fall of Burma and the fall of Thailand would be absolutely inevitable." These would be followed by communist victories in Malaysia and India. Such assumptions led to increasing commitments in Southeast Asia that culminated in the Vietnam War.

Investment in the French empire contrasted with lack of support for colonized peoples. In his 1949 inauguration address, Truman introduced the "Point Four" program, asserting that the United States had a responsibility to spread "the benefits of our scientific advances and industrial progress" to the "underdeveloped areas" of the world. Yet Point Four foreign aid offered no alternatives to existing economic relations: "underdeveloped areas" were seen only as suppliers of raw materials and consumers of industrial goods. Rather than a humanitarian program, Point Four funded economic studies to facilitate private business investment. Even so, the administration could not persuade Congress to appropriate more than a token $27 million in 1950.

Such priorities reflected the overwhelming emphasis on using procapitalist countries as allies in the Cold War. Japan's U.S-dictated Constitution of 1947 sought to uproot traditional militarism and ultranationalism by disavowing war. The United States also brought Japan's rebuilt economy into an Asian anticommunist network, including South Korea, Taiwan, and Indochina, to stabilize relations in the Pacific. A new treaty of 1951 then restored Japanese control of their home islands but allowed U.S. occupation of Okinawa and the stationing of troops on Japanese territory. To overcome objections from Japan's former enemies in the Pacific, the United States promised to protect Australia and New Zealand from attack, an agreement formalized in the ANZUS treaty of 1951. With such alliances, Washington established an anticommunist barrier against Chinese and Soviet expansion in the Pacific.

Alliances with former enemies also promoted support of Italy and Spain. In 1951 the Western allies lifted military restrictions imposed on Italy at the end of World War II. At the same time, Truman entered negotiations with Franco's Spain, which culminated in a 1953 treaty that allowed U.S. military bases in Spain in exchange for economic and military assistance. (Meanwhile, on the home front, the attorney general placed Veterans of the Abraham Lincoln Brigade, whose members had fought against Franco in the Spanish Civil War, on a list of subversive organizations.) In supporting Spain, Italy, Germany and Japan against China and the Soviet Union, Truman had ironically reversed the Grand Alliance of World War II.

By 1952 the Truman administration had lost control of foreign and domestic policy. Truman's commitment to Soviet containment had wrecked earlier State Department hopes for an international extension of the Open Door policy; U.S. trade with eastern Europe and China remained minimal. Even worse, containment had bogged down in the "limited" Korean War, which promised neither victory nor an early end. In domestic affairs, the Fair Deal lacked a political base to overcome the opposition of congressional conservatives. Seeking support for his foreign policy, Truman allowed his liberal domestic programs to founder. Meanwhile, McCarthy continued a campaign to expose alleged communists in government. Revelations of corruption by administration officials compounded Truman's difficulties. Republican leaders expected to change government policy by capturing the White House in 1952.

SUGGESTED READINGS

The major issues of the Truman years are explored in Alonzo L. Hamby, *Beyond the New Deal: Harry S Truman and American Liberalism* (1973). A conventional and sympathetic account of the Truman presidency is Robert J. Donovan's two-volume study, *Conflict and Crisis* (1977) and *Tumultuous Years* (1982). Two good biographies are Robert H. Ferrell, *Harry S Truman: A Life* (1994), and Alonzo L. Hamby, *Man of the People: A Life of Harry S Truman* (1995). Also useful as an introduction to the period is an anthology, Barton J. Bernstein, ed., *Politics and Policies of the Truman Administration* (1970). A convenient collection of primary sources is Barton J. Bernstein and Allen Matusow, eds., *The Truman Administra-*

tion (1966). See also Gary W. Reichard, *Politics as Usual: The Age of Truman and Eisenhower* (1988).

For Truman's farm policies, see Allen Matusow, *Farm Policies and Politics in the Truman Years* (1967); for labor, see R. Alton Lee, *Truman and Taft-Hartley* (1966). Analysis of a landmark case involving the relation between government and business appears in Maeva Marcus, *Truman and the Steel Seizure Case* (1977). The Wallace candidacy is described in Richard J. Walton, *Henry Wallace, Harry Truman, and the Cold War* (1976), which contains many primary sources, and in Norman D. Markowitz, *The Rise and Fall of the People's Century: Henry A. Wallace and American Liberalism* (1973). James T. Patterson's *Mr. Republican: A Biography of Robert A. Taft* (1972) examines the career of the leading conservative. For the early career of Lyndon B. Johnson, see the second volume of Robert Caro's *The Years of Lyndon Johnson: Means of Ascent* (1990).

The domestic anticommunist crusade is described by Richard M. Fried, *Nightmare in Red: The McCarthy Era in Perspective* (1990). The political consequences of anticommunism are explored in Francis H. Thompson, *The Frustration of Politics: Truman, Congress, and the Loyalty Drive, 1945–1953 (1979);* in Athan Theoharis, *Seeds of Repression: Harry S Truman and the Origins of McCarthyism* (1971); and in Alan D. Harper, *The Politics of Loyalty* (1969). The impact of the Red Scare is thoroughly documented in David Caute, *The Great Fear: The AntiCommunist Purge Under Truman and Eisenhower* (1978). Also illuminating is Les Adler, *The Red Image: American Attitudes Toward Communism in the Cold War Era* (1991). The investigations of Hollywood are detailed in Larry Ceplair and Steven Englund, *The Inquisition in Hollywood: Politics in the Film Community, 1930–1960* (1980), and in Victor Navasky, *Naming Names* (1980). An oral history exploring these issues is Griffin Fariello, *Red Scare: Memories of the American Inquisition* (1995).

There are numerous books about the dramatic political trials of the era: Allan Weinstein, *Perjury: The Hiss-Chambers Case* (1978), contends that Hiss was guilty, whereas John Chabot Smith, *Alger Hiss: The True Story* (1977), avers his innocence; Ronald Radosh and Joyce Milton, *The Rosenberg File* (1987), asserts the guilt of Julius Rosenberg (not Ethel Rosenberg), whereas the Rosenbergs' innocence is defended by Walter and Miriam Schneir, *Invitation to an Inquest* (1983). For the harassment of U.S. Spanish Civil War veterans, see Peter N. Carroll, *The Odyssey of the Abraham Lincoln Brigade: Americans in the Spanish Civil War* (1994). McCarthy's attack on one State Department official is told in Robert P. Newman, *Owen Lattimore and the "Loss" of China* (1992). A good background to such trials is Stanley Kutler, *The American Inquisition: Justice and Injustice in the Cold War* (1982). More sympathetic to the anticommunist crusade is Richard Gid Powers, *Not Without Honor: The History of American Anticommunism* (1995). The role of the FBI is detailed in Richard Gid Powers, *Secrecy and Power: The Life of J. Edgar Hoover* (1987), and in Athan G. Theoharis and John Stuart Cox, *The Boss: J. Edgar Hoover and the Great American Inquisition* (1988).

For Joseph McCarthy the best starting point is David M. Oshinsky, *A Conspiracy So Immense: The World of Joe McCarthy* (1983), but also see the titles listed at the end of Chapter 10. The close relation between domestic anticommunism and foreign policy is presented in Richard M. Freeland, *The Truman Doctrine and the Origins of McCarthyism* (1972). For the split between liberals and radicals, see

William O'Neill, *A Better World: The Great Schism: Stalinism and the American Intellectuals* (1983), and Mary Sperling McAuliffe, *Crisis on the Left* (1978).

The literature on the Cold War is vast. A sensible and readable introduction is Walter Lafeber, *America, Russia, and the Cold War* (1985), as is Bernard Weisberger, *Cold War, Cold Peace* (1984). More detailed on the origins of postwar foreign policy is Melvyn P. Leffler, *A Preponderance of Power: National Security, the Truman Administration, and the Cold War* (1992), which can be supplemented with Daniel Yergin, *Shattered Peace: The Origins of the Cold War and the National Security State* (1977). A valuable analysis of foreign policy issues is John Lewis Gaddis, *Strategies of Containment: A Critical Appraisal of Postwar American National Security Policy* (1982). The importance of the atomic bomb in foreign policy and military planning is analyzed carefully in Gregg Harken, *The Winning Weapon: The Atomic Bomb in the Cold War, 1945–1950* (1980). The role of key personalities in policy-making emerges in Robert L. Messer, *The End of an Alliance: James F. Byrnes, Roosevelt, Truman, and the Origins of the Cold War* (1982). See also Michael J. Hogan, *The Marshall Plan: America, Britain, and the Reconstruction of Western Europe* (1987). The persistence of isolationism is the subject of Justus D. Doenecke, *Not to the Swift: The Old Isolationists in the Cold War* (1979). A useful anthology on the dissenters from Truman's policies is Thomas G. Paterson, ed., *Cold War Critics* (1971).

The Cold War in Asia is described in Robert M. Blum, *Drawing the Line: The Origin of the American Containment Policy in East Asia* (1982); in William Whitney Stueck, Jr., *The Road to Confrontation: American Policy Toward China and Korea, 1947–1950* (1981); and in Nancy Tucker, *Patterns in the Dust: Chinese American Relations and the Recognition Controversy, 1949–1950* (1983). A good analysis of postwar Asian policy is Gordon H. Chang, *Friends and Enemies: The United States, China, and the Soviet Union, 1948–1972* (1990). The background of the Korean War is best studied in James Irving Matray *The Reluctant Crusade: American Foreign Policy in Korea, 1941–1950* (1985), in Jian Chen, *China's Road to the Korean War: The Making of the Sino-American Confrontation* (1994), and in William Whitney Stueck, Jr., *The Korean War: An International History* (1995), which may be supplemented by Bruce Cumings's two-volume study *The Origins of the Korean War* (1981–1990), and Rosemary Foot, *The Wrong War: American Policy and the Dimensions of the Korean Conflict, 1950–1953* (1985). Still valuable is Ronald Caridi, *The Korean War and American Politics* (1968). For U.S. policy in Indochina, see the relevant chapters of Lloyd C. Gardner, *Approaching Vietnam: From World War II Through Dienbienphu, 1941–1954* (1988).

U.S. policy in the Middle East is presented in Aaron David Miller, *The Search for Security: Saudi Arabian Oil and American Foreign Policy, 1939–1949* (1980); in Barry Rubin, *Paved with Good Intentions: American Experience in Iran* (1980); and in Zvi Ganin, *Truman, American Jewry, and Israel, 1945–1948* (1979). For international economic affairs, see Fred L. Block, *The Origins of International Economic Disorder* (1977). Also insightful is Ernest R. May *"Lessons" of the Past: The Use and Misuse of History in American Foreign Policy* (1973).

Glossary

A

acronyms   Chapter Four: a word formed from the first letter or the first few letters of several words; used as a memory technique

acrostics   Chapter Four: a phrase or sentence created by using the first letter or letters of items on a list

active listening   Chapter Three: conscious control of the listening process

adult self-talk   Chapter One: one of three inner dialogue voices, the one who thinks analytically and solves problems rationally

affixes   Chapter Two: a word part attached to the beginning or end of a word; alters the meaning and/or the part of speech of the word

analysis   Chapter One: the fifth level of thinking or understanding on Bloom's Taxonomy; requires being able to break apart complex ideas and examine the various components

application   Chapter One: the fourth level of thinking or understand-ing on Bloom's Taxonomy; requires being able to use information

appositives   Chapter Two: words that define the words that follow

assertive   Chapter Four: a type of language or behavior in which a student states what he/she needs without being blunt or accusatory

association   Chapter Four: a type of memory technique that links information known with information to be learned

audio-visual   Chapter Three: supplemental teaching aids that include films, overhead transparencies, video-tapes, interactive video, computer software etc.

B

background-based context   Chapter Two: knowledge of language and the world that helps an individual figure out the meaning of an unknown word

background knowledge   Chapter One: the information that a student has been exposed to prior to study-ing a topic; helps build a foundation for learning the topic

behavior modification   Chapter Four: changing behav-ior that is not conducive to learning into behavior that is conducive to learning

Bloom's Taxonomy   Chapter One: a sequential list of levels of thinking and learning

broken record   Chapter Four: a type of assertive lan-guage in which the student continues to repeat a message over and over in a calm voice; discourages other students from robbing study time

burnout   Chapter One: the feeling that results when no breaks in tasks have been taken

C

cause/effect   Chapter Three: information from reading or a lecture that shows why something happens or the result of an action

charts   Chapter Four: an organizational method that arranges information by rows and columns

child self-talk   Chapter One: one of three inner dialogue voices, the part of you that wants to have fun and have it now

closure   Chapter One: the positive feeling that occurs in an individual when a task is completed

comparison/contrast   Chapter Three: information from a lecture or reading that shows similarities or differ-ences between two or more items

comprehension   Chapter One: understanding the message heard or read

compromise   Chapter Four: a type of assertive language in which a student agrees to a request but on his/her terms; protects study time

connotation   Chapter Two: the emotional response to a word; depends on individual background knowledge or world knowledge

context   Chapter Two: the surrounding words that suggest the meaning of an unknown word

cope   Chapter Five: manage

Cornell System of Notetaking   Chapter Three: a notetaking system developed by Walter Pauk at Cornell University; involves recording, reducing, reciting, reflecting and reviewing information

cramming   Chapter Four: frantic, last minute memorization of information prior to a test; not an effective study technique

critical thinking   Chapter One: thinking logically about information, people, and choices so you can make reasonable, informed decisions about learning, relationshps, and life

critic self-talk   Chapter One: one of three inner dialogue voices, the one who thinks analytically and solves problems rationally

curve of forgetting   Chapter Three: a graph that illustrates how long it takes to forget information after reading or hearing it

D

denial   Chapter Five: a type of withdrawal in which a student fails to acknowledge that a stressful situation such as a test exists

denotation   Chapter Two: the dictionary definition of a word

distractions   Chapter Three: physical occurrences or mental thoughts that draw a student's attention from reading or listening

distress   Chapter Five: a type of stress that hurts more than it helps

distributed practice   Chapter Four: a type of rehearsal that alternates short study sessions with breaks; usually involves setting goals and rewards; spaced study

E

enumeration/sequence   Chapter Three: information from reading or a lecture that is arranged as a list or in chronological order

eustress   Chapter Five: a positive stress that gives an individual additional energy

evaluation   Chapter One: the seventh level of thinking or understanding on Bloom's Taxonomy; requires an individual to judge the relative worth of information

external distractions   Chapter Three: a type of distraction that comes from outside factors

F

figurative language   Chapter One: written or spoken words that use sensory images to create pictures in the mind's eye

fogging   Chapter Four: a type of assertive language in which the student agrees in principle to a request that threatens study time but still refuses to quit studying

formal outline   Chapter Two: an outline that uses Roman numerals, letters, and numbers to indicate points and subpoints

G

general vocabulary   Chapter Two: common words

H

headings   Chapter Two: titles of sections of reading that are usually in boldfaced or italicized print

I

idea maps   Chapter Four: an organizational method that arranges information spatially

implied main idea   Chapter Three: the central point of a lecture or passage that is not explicitly stated; identified by using the given information and determining what the information means

informal outline   Chapter Two: an outline that uses dashes or bullets instead of Roman numerals etc.

internal distraction   Chapter Three: a type of distraction that comes from within an individual

interpretation   Chapter One: the third level of thinking or understanding on Bloom's Taxonomy; requires explaining what information means

intrachapter guides   Chapter Two: text signals within a chapter that provide direction as students read; includes highlighted words, headings, and subheadings

introduction/summary   Chapter Three: beginning/end of a passage or lecture; indicated by transitional words such as "Today's lecture begins . . ." or "In conclusion . . ."

J

jingles   Chapter Four: a rhyme that can be used as a memory technique

K

kinesthetic perception   Chapter Four: one of the methods of taking in information; involves doing a physical task such as writing to enhance learning

knowledge   Chapter One: another name for the recall level of thinking and learning of Bloom's Taxonomy

L

learning style   Chapter One: the intake and output preference that a student has; can refer to sensory preference, hemisphere preference or other conditions for learning

lecture patterns   Chapter Three: the organizational structure of a lecture; can be identified by listening for signal or transitional words

left-brained   Chapter One: a preference for intake and output of information; includes a preference for logical, sequential organization, analytical tasks, mathematical reasoning etc.

location   Chapter Four: a memory technique that associates information with specific places

long-term memory   Chapter Three: a storage area in the brain for information that has been learned

M

main idea   Chapters Two and Three: the central thought or meaning of a paragraph, passage, or lecture; what the author or speaker wants the reader or listener to know about a topic

mapping   Chapter Two: an organizational structure for information; uses pictures to show relationships among concepts

marginal notes   Chapter Two: notes found in the margin of a text or lecture notes that summarize information

mnemonics   Chapter Three: a memory technique that improves the ability to associate information

mnemonigraph   Chapter Four: a memory aid that makes a mental image a concrete one; involves drawing a mental image on paper

mental imagery   Chapter Four: a type of mnemonic in which a student visualizes a picture associated with a word

multi-sensory   Chapter One: a reference to learning that includes learning from many different sensory channels and through as many avenues as possible

N

nontraditional text format   Chapter Two: supplemental readings that do not usually include headings, subheadings, boldface type and other types of aids for students

O

objectives   Chapter Two: a list of learning goals that students are expected to gain after reading a chapter

objective test   Chapter Four: a true-false, matching, multiple choice, or fill-in-the-blank test that requires students to recognize or reason information from the options given

outlining   Chapter Two: an organizational format for the main points of information; arranged vertically using indentations to show sub-points

overlearning   Chapter Four: the continuous reinforcement of information that must be learned exactly; uses overlapping study

P

parodies   Chapter Four: humorous imitation of common words, poems, stories and songs by the use of satire or burlesque; can be used as a memory technique

physical imagery   Chapter Four: the transferring of a mental association by writing it down; also called mnemonigraph

PORPE   Chapter Four: a study plan for subjective tests that has five steps: predict, organize, rehearse, practice, and evaluate

POSSE   Chapter Four: a study plan for objective tests that has five steps: plan, organize, schedule, study, and evaluate

postchapter guides   Chapter Two: information at the end of the chapter that summarizes important concepts; includes summary, questions, chapter reviews, suggested readings, etc.

postlecture reading   Chapter Three: information read after a lecture

prechapter guides   Chapter Two: introductory chapter information; may include objectives, terms, titles, case studies, quotations, questions, etc., to help students access background knowledge

prefixes   Chapter Two: an affix or word part that is added to the beginning of a word and alters the meaning of that word

previewing   Chapter Two: the first step in SQ3R; includes looking at what is included in chapter or text to get an overview of the information to be learned

prime study time   Chapter Four: the time of day that a student thinks and learns best

procrastination   Chapter One: delaying or putting off actions

projection   Chapter Five: a type of withdrawal in which a student blames someone or something else for failure

puns   Chapter Four: humorous use of words or phrases in which more than one meaning is implied; can be used as a memory technique

R

rationalization   Chapter Five: a type of withdrawal in which a student attempts to identify a reasonable and acceptable excuse for failure rather than acknowledging lack of preparation

recall   Chapter One: the lowest level on Bloom's Taxonomy; also known as the knowledge level; requires recitation of information only

recitation   Chapter Four: silent, oral, or written repetition of information to answer study questions

recite   Chapter Three: the third step in the Cornell note-taking system; requires students to use recall column for clues and cover the information from memory; the fourth step in SQ3R

record   Chapter Three: the first step in the Cornell note-taking system; involves writing information in paragraph or outline form on a sectioned part of note paper

reduce   Chapter Three: the second step in the Cornell notetaking system; involves condensing notes taken in step one and transferring the information as labels into the narrow left hand column of sectioned paper

reflect   Chapter Three: the fourth step in Cornell note-taking system; requires students to think about information in notes and to make clarifications after thinking and additional reading

rehearsal   Chapter Four: in learning, practice to transfer information from short-term to long-term memory; can take many forms such as spaced study, recitation, etc.

repression   Chapter Five: a type of withdrawal in which the problem is blocked

review   Chapter Three: the last step in the Cornell note-taking system; requires constant short periods of review of information in notes to transfer information from short-term to long-term memory; the last step in SQ3R

rhymes   Chapter Four: a memory technique that uses words which have the same sound in them to increase recall

right-brained   Chapter One: a preference for intake and output of information; includes the preference for artistic, creative endeavors, mapping of information, and "big picture" learning

root   Chapter Two: word part that contains the essential meaning; the base of the word

S

self-talk   Chapter Three: the internal communication that an individual has with himself/herself; can be positive or negative; affects self-confidence

short-term memory   Chapter Three: a temporary storage place in the brain for information that is heard or read; information not transferred from this memory to long-term memory is not learned.

spaced study   Chapter Four: a type of rehearsal that alternates short study sessions with breaks; usually involves setting goals and rewards; distributed practice

specialized vocabulary   Chapter Two: common terms that have a specialized meaning in a particular subject

SQ3R   Chapter Two: a structured study system that includes previewing or surveying information, asking purpose-setting questions, reading, reciting, and reviewing

stem   Chapter Five: a part of a question in a multiple choice question on a test; contains the basic information

stress   Chapter Five: a physical or emotional factor that causes tension or anxiety

structural analysis   Chapter Two: splitting words into roots, prefixes, and or suffixes to identify the meaning of the word

study site   Chapter Four: where a student studies

subheadings   Chapter Two: subtitles for sections of reading; written in smaller type or different type from headings

subject development   Chapter Three: a type of paragraph development in which all the information relates to the subject but not necessarily to each other

subjective tests   Chapter Four: also called essay tests; requires students to recall, recreate, and use information learned

suffixes   Chapter Two: an affix or word part that is added to the end of a word; changes the meaning or part of speech of that word

summary   Chapter Two: a concluding statement or paragraph of a passage or lecture; covers the main idea of the passage or lecture

synthesis   Chapter One: the sixth level of Bloom's Taxonomy; requires the combining of information from several sources to create something new or unique

T

technical vocabulary   Chapter Two: terms specific to a particular subject

terms   Chapter Three: vocabulary of a course

term calendar   Chapter One: a calendar that includes information pertinent to a term, such as classes, holidays, work commitments, test schedules, etc.

text-based context   Chapter Two: punctuation or other clues in a sentence that signal meanings of an unknown word

text dependent lectures   Chapter Three: a lecture that follows the information and format of the text used in that class

text independent lectures   Chapter Three: a lecture that supplements information in the text or that brings in outside information and relates it to text information

text marking   Chapter Two: also called highlighting; a way to identify the most important information in a section of text

time-management plan   Chapter One: the use of calendars to indicate fixed time requirements and variables in order to maximize study time

transitional words   Chapter Three: also called signal words; words which indicate the direction or organizational pattern of a paragraph, passage, or lecture

translation   Chapter One: the second level of understanding or thinking on Bloom's Taxonomy; requires restating information in different words

typographical aids   Chapter Two: boldface or italics that are used to make words stand out in a text

V

visualization   Chapter Five: using the imagination to put positive messages into action; picturing success

withdrawal   Chapter Five: a negative way of tackling stress; an escape w

word cards   Chapter Four: index cards used to learn course terms and concepts; usually contains at least the word on one side and the definition on the other; additional information may be present

word file   Chapter Four: consists of word cards that contain concepts for further study

word maps   Chapter Four: a word card that includes general headings and picture associations for the term in addition to the meaning

References

Adams, M., & Bruce, B. (January 1980). *Background knowledge and reading comprehension* (Reading Education Report No. 13). Urbana: University of Illinois, Center for the Study of Reading.

Balint, Stephen W. (September 1989). Campus comedy. *Reader's Digest.*

Benson, H. (1975). *The relaxation response.* New York: Morrow.

Berne, E. (1966). *Principles of group treatment.* New York: Oxford University Press.

Bloom, B. (1956). *Taxonomy of educational objectives, handbook 1: Cognitive domain.* New York: David McKay.

Bower, G. H. (1970). Analysis of a mnemonic device. *American Scientist, 59*: 496.

Brown, S. A. (1985). Expectancies versus background in the prediction of college drinking patterns. *Journal of Consulting and Clinical Psychology, 53*: 123–130.

Bryson, Bill (1990). *The mother tongue: English & how it got that way.* New York: Morrow.

Carman, R. A., & Adams, W. R. (1985). *Study skills: A student guide for survival.* New York: Wiley.

Carr, E. (1985). The vocabulary overview guide: A metacognitive strategy to improve vocabulary comprehension & retention. *Journal of Reading, 28*: 684–689.

Cowan, G., & Cowan, E. (1980). *Writing.* New York: Wiley.

Dale, E. (1958). How to know more wonderful words. *Good Housekeeping, 17.*

Eeds, M. & Cockrum, W. A. (1985). Teaching word meaning by expanding schemata vs. dictionary work vs. reading in context. *Journal of Reading. 23*: 492–497.

Grasha, A. E. (1984). Learning styles: The journey from Greenwich Observatory (1796) to the college classroom (1984). *Improving College and University Teaching, 32*: 46–53.

Howe, M. J. (1970). Notetaking strategy, review and long-term relationships between notetaking variables and achievement measures. *Journal of Educational Research, 63*: 285.

Kiewra, K. A. (1985). Investigating notetaking and review: A depth of processing alternative. *Educational Psychologist, 20*(1): 23–32.

Lapp, D., Flood, J., & Farnan, N. (1989). *Content area reading and learning: Instructional strategies.* Englewood Cliffs, NJ: Prentice-Hall.

Larson, C. O., and Dansereau, D. F. (1986). Cooperative learning in dyads. *Journal of Reading 29*: 516–520.

Light, R. J. (1990). The Harvard assessment seminars: First Report. Harvard University Graduate School of Education and Kennedy School of Government: Cambridge, MA.

Light, R. J. (1992). *The Harvard assessment seminars: Second report.* Harvard University Graduate School of Education and Kennedy School of Government: Cambridge, MA.

McWilliams, Peter, and John-Roger. (1991). *Life 101.* Los Angeles: Prelude.

Palkovitz, R. J., & Lore, R. K. (1980). Note taking and note review: Why students fail questions based on lecture material. *Teaching of Psychology, 7*: 159–160.

Pauk, W. (1984). *How to study in college.* Boston: Houghton-Mifflin.

Sarros, J. C., & Densten, Ian L. (1989). Undergraduate student stress and coping strategies. *Higher Education Research and Development,* 8(1).

Shanker, A. (1988). Strength in number. *Academic Connections,* Fall: 12.

Simpson, M. L. (1986). PORPE: A writing strategy for studying and learning in the content areas, *Journal of Reading,* 29: 407–414.

Tenney, J. (March 1986). *Keyword notetaking system.* Paper presented at the Nineteenth Annual Meeting of the Western College Reading Association, Los Angeles.

Thielens, W. Jr. (1987, April). *The disciplines and undergraduate lecturing.* Paper presented at the American Educational Research Association, Washington, D.C.

Tomlinson, Louise M. (1997). A coding system for notemaking in literature. *Journal of Adolescent & Adult Learning,* 40: 6.

Index